Nijinsky (1971)

Diaghilev (1979)

Buckle at the Ballet (1980)

The Most Upsetting Woman (1981)

In the Wake of Diaghilev (1982)

GEORGE BALANCHINE

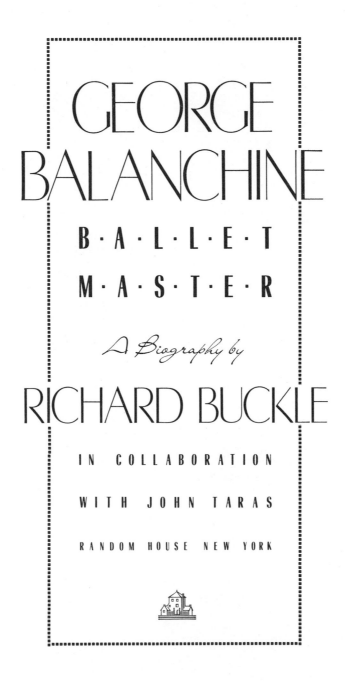

GEORGE BALANCHINE

B·A·L·L·E·T
M·A·S·T·E·R

A Biography by

RICHARD BUCKLE

IN COLLABORATION

WITH JOHN TARAS

RANDOM HOUSE NEW YORK

Library of Congress Cataloging-in-Publication Data
Buckle, Richard.
George Balanchine, ballet master.
Bibliography: p.
Includes index.
1. Balanchine, George. 2. Choreographers—
United States—Biography. I. Taras, John. II. Title.
GV1785.B32B83 1988 792.8'2'0924 [B] 87-42667
ISBN 0-394-53906-0

Manufactured in the United States of America
98765432
First Edition

Typography and book design by J. K. Lambert

ACKNOWLEDGMENTS

JOHN TARAS knew Balanchine better and for much longer than I did, besides knowing most of his ballets thoroughly, so when we began to plan this book, shortly before Balanchine's death, we agreed that he would do the majority of the interviews. He obtained valuable information from, among others, Lew Christensen, who has since died, Alicia Markova, Tamara Toumanova and Diana Adams. A few interviews we did together. After Taras became associate director of American Ballet Theatre in 1985 and could no longer give so much time to our collaboration, I did most of the interviews. William Lawson taped seven, and Tom Lacy, one.

On pages 333–335 is a list of all those who were kind enough to spare the time to be interviewed or who answered questions. With Betty Cage, a friend for over thirty years, and Natalie Molostwoff, a friend for over twenty, I spent long hours of talk. Betty Cage also made available correspondence between herself, Balanchine and Lincoln Kirstein. Rosemary Dunleavy gave up several Saturday mornings to help me. Karin von Aroldingen and Barbara Horgan were wonderfully generous with their time and information.

My own intermittent conversations with Balanchine began in 1948, though my admiration for his work dates from the 1930s. In 1950 we became friends. In 1977, when I was writing the life of Diaghilev, he spared two mornings to talk to me about the 1920s, and, to my surprise, seemed to enjoy looking back.

Lincoln Kirstein made an invaluable contribution by allowing me to read and quote from his diary for 1933–34. Edward M. M. Warburg was generous in sharing his reminiscences of Balanchine's early days in America. Eugene R. Gaddis of the Wadsworth Atheneum Museum archives was helpful in describing the performances at Hartford. Alexandra Danilova not only talked to me for hours, but wrote detailed letters. I have quoted at length from her autobiography, as well as from those of Tamara Geva and Vera Zorina. Kyril Fitzlyon, the distinguished Russian translator, traveled with me to Russia to act as interpreter in my taped conversations with Balanchine's brother Andrei, who, with his whole family, gave us a warm welcome and provided much information on the choreographer's early days in St. Petersburg and on his first visit to Georgia in 1962. Boris Kochno produced fascinating early letters. The Dmitriev contracts and the cables between Kirstein and Balanchine are from the files at the School of American Ballet. A few letters from Balanchine to Diaghilev come from the Dance Collection, Library and Museum of the Performing Arts at Lincoln Center, New York; these were translated by Nathalie Gleboff. I have also drawn on the remarkable archive at Parmenia Ekstrom's Stravinsky-Diaghilev Foundation.

Musicians who helped me were Desmond Shawe-Taylor, Robert Irving and especially Gordon Boelzner. William Lawson worked out the evolution of *Agon* and gave me the benefit of his researches into Balanchine. At the New York State Theater, Edward Bigelow and Deni Lamont played videotapes of various ballets to refresh my memory; so did the helpful staff of the Dance Collection.

Nancy Lassalle and Jane Emerson of Ballet Society and Shields Remine of *Ballet Review* were tireless in assisting me with research on facts and photographs. Patricia Neary wrote and telephoned frequently in reply to questions and lent me a tape of Balanchine she had made in Zurich. Balanchine's two previous biographers, Bernard Taper and Solomon Volkov, were generous and helpful in answering questions. William Lawson did research for me in New York University Library, Sarah Woodcock and Philip Dyer in the

Theatre Museum, London, Jane Pritchard in the archives of London Festival Ballet and Elsa Lowry at Lincoln Center.

I would also like to acknowledge the assistance given by Robert Cornfield, Dr. David Brown, Tom Schoff, Nancy Goldner, Beryl Grey, Michael Somes, Kensington Davison, Natasha Spender, Charles Mackerras, Richard Rapp, Karl Reuling, Charles France, Morton Gewirtz, George Dorris, Robert Craft, Randall Bourscheidt, George and Patricia Harewood, Peter Heyworth, Denisa Beach, David Dougill, David Leonard, Molly Daubeny, Thilo von Watzdorf, Delia Peters, Tina Campt, Virginia Donaldson, Leslie Bailey and Maitland McDonagh. Jane Harriss typed several versions of each chapter as the book evolved and our descriptions of certain ballets were condensed by thousands of words.

Martha Swope and her staff were infinitely patient in helping me find the photographs I needed from their archive. At the Library and Museum of the Performing Arts, Nancy Shaweroff arranged for George Platt Lynes's pictures to be printed. The photographers of Tass in Tbilisi copied Andrei Balanchivadze's precious old pictures in the course of an afternoon.

Jonathan Galassi originally signed up the book, but later left Random House. Anne Freedgood, who took over from him, pruned the manuscript, suggested what was missing and oiled the wheels of narrative: her admiration for Balanchine gave her the strength to overcome every obstacle. Jean-Isabel McNutt worked on the text and notes with sympathy and understanding. It was with pleasure that I found the ideas of James K. Lambert, the designer, coincided closely with my own.

RICHARD BUCKLE
Wiltshire, July 1987

CONTENTS

GEORGE BALANCHINE

Chapter 1

··

A GEORGIAN IN

ST. PETERSBURG:

1904 - 1924

GEORGE BALANCHINE liked to say that he was Georgian. Although this was only half true—and he completely lacked the Georgian swagger—there is much in the Georgian character that may have shaped his own.

Georgia lies in the Caucasus, the mountain barrier extending from the Black Sea to the Caspian. The ancient Greeks believed it was on Georgia's Mount Kazbek that Zeus chained Prometheus as punishment for stealing fire from heaven; and it was to the western coast of Georgia that Jason sailed with his Argonauts in search of the Golden Fleece. Xenophon traveled to the region in 400 B.C., and it later came under the sway of Alexander the Great. Pompey established a Roman hegemony there in 66 B.C. Christianity was introduced in A.D. 303 by Nina, a slave girl from Cappadocia in Asia Minor, who was later canonized. The ancients called Georgia the end of the world, but its inhabitants have always considered it the center.

Present-day Georgians, many of whom remain devout Christians and who clearly have an Oriental strain, nevertheless regard themselves as the heirs of the ancient Greeks. "Georgians are Mediterranean people," Balanchine said late in life, having perhaps come to this conclusion on his first visit, at the age of fifty-eight, to the country of his ancestors. It struck me, when I was there, that they must indeed believe that they are descended from the gods, goddesses and heroes of Hellas: a chambermaid at my hotel in Tbilisi was called Persephone. The choreographer's grandfather was named Amiran—Georgian for Prometheus. Balanchine's father, Meliton ("sweet as honey") Balanchivadze, named the children of his first marriage Nina, after the saint, and Apolon, after the god Apollo. Those of his second marriage were Tamara, after a medieval queen of Georgia famed for her beauty; Georgi, after the saint; and Andrei, after the apostle.

The Balanchivadze family came from the village of Banodzha in western Georgia, five kilometers from the mountain town of Kutaisi—whose coat of arms is the Golden Fleece—where distant cousins of Balanchine still live. In the Middle Ages, a *balanchi* was a court jester; *balanchivadze* means "jester's son." These jesters were also bards or wandering minstrels, their function being not only to make princes laugh but to compose music and recite poetry. When, in 1962, the choreographer, by then an American citizen, came to Tbilisi and learned that the historian Arkady Shanidze had traced the origin of the *balanchini,* he was delighted because the plural sounded "so Italian." "The fools had to be ugly," explained Andrei Balanchivadze recently, twisting his amiable features sideways. He claimed to have detected a slight deformity of the jaw that was shared by his two sons and his elder brother, Georgi: one side was higher than the other. His Uncle Vassili, an actor as well as a painter, had, he said, a completely crooked face.

Amiran Balanchivadze, Balanchine's grandfather, was a priest. Priests of the Russian Orthodox Church are required to be married, and Amiran had three sons and a daughter. Some time after the birth of his daughter in 1873, his wife died, and he was entitled to become a monk. Only monks can attain the rank of bishop; Amiran changed his pagan-sounding name to Anton, and became bishop of Kutaisi.

The bishop's eldest son, Meliton Antonovich, born in 1862, sang from childhood in church choirs and from the age of eighteen in the chorus of the Tiflis (now Tbilisi) Opera, where he later became a soloist. His first wife, also a Georgian, bore him a daughter and a son. By this time he was already collecting the Georgian folk songs and sacred chants to which he was later to devote his life. In 1899, when he was sent to the St. Petersburg Conservatory to study singing, his marriage broke up, and he was divorced. He spent two years learning composition under Rimsky-Korsakov and wrote the first Georgian opera, *Perfidious Tamara,* parts of which were performed in St. Petersburg in 1897. His second wife, a pretty blonde with dark eyes, was twelve years younger than himself. Maria, the daughter of a Baron Nicholaus von Almedingen who abandoned his wife and child and returned to Germany, was given her mother's name of Vasiliev. The three children of Meliton's second marriage were therefore half Georgian, one quarter Russian and one quarter German.

Georgi Melitonovich Balanchivadze, two years younger than his sister, Tamara, two years older than his brother, Andrei, was born on January 22, 1904, in Kirochnaya Street, St. Petersburg, a long street running west–east from the fashionable heart of the city toward the Smolny Convent. (It is now Ulitsa Saltykov-Shchedrin.) On its north side lay the gardens of the Tavrichevsky Palace, built by Catherine the Great for her favorite, Grigori Potemkin. In 1905, this mansion was to house the Exhibition of Historical Portraits that Sergei Pavlovich Diaghilev, with whom Balanchine was so closely associated later, organized before he set off to introduce Russian painting, music, opera and ballet to the West. The show was in preparation at the time of Georgi's birth and was opened by the emperor a year after it.

Before her marriage, Maria Balanchivadze had paid a hundred rubles for a ticket in the state lottery; several years later, her number came up. She won 200,000 rubles (about $30,000). Meliton, who had no head for practical matters, set about enjoying this windfall. The family moved to a larger apartment in Bolshoya Moskovskaya, a charming street with a double row of trees bordering a strip of garden down the middle. One of Maria's first cousins, always called "Aunt Nadia," came to live with them and had her own separate corner in the apartment. Georgi was her special pet.

The newly affluent Meliton gave presents to his friends, financed Georgian restaurants—where very few customers were pressed to pay their bills—and bought a *dacha* in Finland. He also paid for the publication in 1907 of the composer Glinka's letters. But when a factory in which he had invested failed, he was put under house arrest as a debtor—according to Andrei, he was given a set of rooms and forbidden to leave them for four months. He did not go to prison, as has been stated—this was one of Balanchine's romantic exaggerations—and he was allowed to keep his house in Finland.

The apartment in Bolshoya Moskovskaya was near the church of St. Vladimir, an eighteenth-century building in the typical St. Petersburg style, painted pink and white and with a baroque-looking bell tower. (It is now a hospital.) Even though Georgi found the services at St. Vladimir's too long—at Easter the family stood on the stone floor for four hours—he later told Solomon Volkov that the liturgy made a wonderful impression on him; he thought the priests, with their gorgeous miters, looked just like saints, and he envied the choirboys, who sang with angel-like delicacy.

The Balanchivadzes' *dacha* was an isolated house in the woods near Lounatiokki, a village not far from Vyborg. It was here that Georgi first experienced the pleasures of country life and learned from his mother, who was a wonderful cook, the delight in good food that remained with him all his life. It was at Lounatiokki, while he was stumbling through a Beethoven piano sonata, that he suddenly recognized the power of music; as he told Bernard Taper fifty years afterward, it was a revelation. The awareness that something miraculous existed beyond the tedium of piano practice brought tears to his eyes.

Because Meliton was often away, traveling with his choir, the children saw less of him than of their mother. Maria Balanchivadze played the piano, but the children's regular piano teacher was a German lady, Elena Künze. The children also had a German nanny, and grew up speaking the language fairly well. When Meliton was at home, he taught his children Georgian three-part songs, which they performed when he entertained his friends. At Christmas, little Andrei was always delighted to dance for his father's guests, but Georgi stood in a corner and kicked at people because he hated anything to do with dancing. The two brothers were close, and Georgi was always kind to Andrei, but he was very reserved—an un-Georgian characteristic—and never showed his feelings. When he was punished, he used to hide, afraid that someone would see him crying.

Although the children of Meliton's first family were about twenty years older, they were on good terms with his second. Nina, married to Prince Shalva Kordzaya, had a son, Melkhizedek, three years senior to Georgi; Apolon had a daughter, Elizaveta. Because Apolon was a colonel in the police force, he suggested that Georgi, with his straight back and dignified bearing, should become a soldier. Tamara was intended for the Ballet School, Georgi for the Military Academy and Andrei for Technical School. As it turned out, Tamara became an artist, Georgi a choreographer and Andrei a composer.

The brothers' first visit to the theater, when they were about nine and seven, was to hear Rimsky-Korsakov's opera *Tsar Saltan* at the Maryinsky. Did this make a big impression? I asked Andrei. "Overwhelming!" The two boys spent hours afterward playing passages from the opera on the piano.

Their sister Tamara failed her first audition at the Ballet School, and when her mother took her for a second attempt in August 1913, Georgi went with them. One of the school officials who knew Maria asked, "Why is that youngster sitting there doing nothing? Why can't he take the examination, too?" Both sister and brother were accepted, but Tamara, it seems, had little talent for dancing, and she was later dismissed.

The Imperial Theater Ballet School was housed in one of the two long buildings the Italian architect Rossi built in the 1830s to form Teatralnaya Ulitsa (Theater Street), which led out into an open square opposite a bridge over the Fontanka Canal. Its magnificent exterior arcading and white columns stood out against the rosy ocher paint; within, austerity reigned. The boys' huge, bare dormitories were on the top floor, above the girls'. The boarders were allowed to go home only on Sundays, and Georgi became so homesick that he ran away after a week. Knowing his mother would send him straight back, he went to his Aunt Nadia, who managed to hide him in her corner of the apartment for several days before he was discovered.

The students learned the grammar of their art at the school every morning. Traditional exercises at the barre were followed by center practice, in which they performed turns, leaps and short combinations of steps improvised by their teacher; lessons in national and character dancing followed, so that the students could acquire the correct deportment for the stately polonaise, the controlled passion of the Polish mazurka and the alternating languor and frenzy of the Hungarian csárdás. Lessons in adagio—movements performed slowly, so that the dancers could learn control and balance—would come later. When the boys went downstairs to work with the girls, turning, lifting and supporting them, learning how to present them with the noble subservience of ballet cavaliers, conversation between the sexes was discouraged. In the afternoons, there were lessons in music, history, French and mathematics. To Georgi, this daily round was as dull as his piano practice had been until the moment of revelation. At the end of his first year, however, when less promising pupils were weeded out, he passed his tests.

He was sad and lonely if his mother or aunt was unable to bring him home on Sundays, because the school was almost deserted at weekends. "You'd go to the church and stand there for some time. . . . You had to kill time before dinner," he recalled. "I would go to the reception hall and play the piano." Georgi was good at mathematics and preferred theology to history and literature. As he told Solomon Volkov many years later:

I liked reading Jules Verne—*Twenty Thousand Leagues Under the Sea.* . . . I still remember the captions under the pictures. . . . We were also enthralled by the adventures of Sherlock Holmes, Nick Carter, and Pinkerton.

The children were sometimes asked to walk on—or even to dance small parts—in ballets at the Maryinsky Theater, a mile or so away, to which they were driven in closed carriages, six boys in each. One evening, ten of these carriages set off for the Maryinsky, where the children were herded into a dressing room, costumed and made up. The ballet was *The Sleeping Beauty.* This was probably not Georgi's first appearance onstage, but in later years he spoke as if it were that performance that had opened his eyes to the wonders of classical ballet. As he stood in the wings listening to the magical Tchaikovsky music, he perhaps saw part of the variations for the six Fairies before preparing to scuttle on as a little monster in the train of the wicked fairy Carabosse—to find himself facing the blue and silver auditorium, flashing with diamonds. Since he was also in the Garland Dance, he had a chance to watch the evening's Aurora perform her breathtaking Rose Adagio. He marveled at the enchanted forest as it grew to surround the castle, with trees ascending, branches weaving in and out, and at the fairy boat as it moved past the unfolding panorama to the harp arpeggios and pizzicato strings of Tchaikovsky's music. In the last act he may also have danced one of the seven brothers of Hop o' My Thumb. That evening he came to understand the goal beyond the sweat and monotony of ballet school. His vocation was determined.

.   .   .

MARIUS PETIPA, the choreographer of *The Sleeping Beauty,* was a Frenchman, born in Marseilles in 1818. Both his father, Jean, and his elder brother, Lucien, were dancers and choreographers, but Lucien achieved his greatest fame as a performer at the Paris Opéra, where he created the role of Albrecht in *Giselle* and part-nered not only Carlotta Grisi but most of the other principal ballerinas of his day. Jean Petipa's career was largely spent as ballet master of the Théâtre de la Monnaie in Brussels, but he was invited to America in 1839 and took Marius with him. The twenty-year-old Marius, suffering from the aftereffects of a broken leg, had little success in *La Tarentule* at the National Theater on Broadway. It is interesting, however, that Balanchine, who was often called "the heir of Petipa," should have been preceded by him in New York ninety-five years earlier. Had Marius Petipa met with success and remained in America, the history of both Russian and Ameri-can ballet might have been very different.

As it was, the two Petipas sailed back to Europe the same winter. After three more years at La Monnaie, Jean Petipa joined the Imperial Academy of Dancing in St. Petersburg as a professor, and Marius followed him. Perhaps something more than family feeling prompted Marius to go to Russia in 1847. Taglioni retired from the stage that year, and there was a general feeling that the golden age of what we now call the "Romantic ballet" was coming to an end. Apart from Marius Petipa's doubts about making a name or a fortune in France, he may also have felt political apprehension. Eighteen forty-eight was to be the year of revolutions throughout Europe, the year of Louis-Philippe's abdication.

During his early years in Russia, Petipa was eclipsed first by Jules Perrot and later by Arthur Saint-Léon. In 1881, however, Ivan Vsevolojsky was appointed director of the Imperial Theaters, and in 1889 his patronage of Petipa led to their triumphant collaboration with Tchaikovsky on *The Sleeping Beauty.*

Tchaikovsky had previously composed *Swan Lake*; and his last ballet, *Casse-Noisette* (*The Nutcracker*), in which Petipa collaborated with Lev Ivanov, was produced at the Maryinsky in December 1892, shortly before his death.

. . .

DANCING in *The Sleeping Beauty* gave young Georgi a new incentive to work. He liked Samuel Andrianov, his teacher, whom he remembered as a brilliant one, and a "marvelous Siegfried in *Swan Lake*" besides, but who died young, of consumption. Georgi also admired the elderly Pavel Gerdt, who, he later explained, was "the very first [Prince] Désiré in the ballet *Sleeping Beauty* and the very first Prince Coqueluche in *The Nutcracker.*" Another link with Tchaikovsky was the old Italian composer/conductor Riccardo Drigo, a man "just the opposite [of Gerdt], small and friendly, easygoing, with a gray mustache. . . . He spoke a very funny Russian. Drigo had conducted the premieres of both *The Nutcracker* and *Sleeping Beauty.* He had discussed the music and tempi with Tchaikovsky himself! Even in our day he conducted ballet performances in the Maryinsky."

When dancers from the Imperial Ballet came to take classes at the school, Georgi watched them carefully. Felia Doubrovska, a young soloist, always remembered his silent scrutiny and thought to herself, "There's a little boy who doesn't miss a thing." Another dancer, only one year ahead of him in school, was struck by his singularity, by the way he kept to himself and by his charm. This was Alexandra Danilova.

When war broke out in 1914, shortly after his admission to the Ballet School, several artists who had worked with Diaghilev in Western Europe came back to Russia. Mikhail Fokine returned to stage his ballets at the Maryinsky. Georgi loved *Les Sylphides,* called in Russia *Chopiniana,* but was critical of others. He also said later that "Fokine didn't come out too well when he took Rimsky-

Korsakov's *Schéhérazade* and Liszt's *Préludes.* " The former, when
staged by Diaghilev in a setting by Bakst, with Nijinsky dancing
the Golden Slave, had been the sensation of Paris in 1910, but
Diaghilev himself soon began to find it ridiculous, and the young
Balanchivadze knew that the surging music of the last movement,
which in the ballet accompanied the massacre of the Sultan's
unfaithful wives, had been intended by the composer to depict a
storm at sea. Another of Fokine's ballets mounted at this time was
Eros, for which the choreographer used Tchaikovsky's Serenade
in C for strings—music that would accompany the first ballet
Balanchine choreographed in America.

Tamara Karsavina, who had also returned to Petrograd, as it was
now called, at the outbreak of war, was one ballerina Georgi
admired; another was Elizaveta Gerdt, the daughter of Pavel Gerdt
and the wife of Georgi's teacher Andrianov.

Georgi was for the most part unaware of the political situation—
politics meant little to the enclosed community of Theater Street.
Neither Russia's defeats in the West nor the sufferings of her
ill-equipped army affected the students. They had probably heard
that Nicolas II had himself taken over the supreme command of
the armed forces, but they could not have realized that as a result
political power had passed to the empress's ineffectual favorites,
and the country was disintegrating. They must, however, surely
have heard of Rasputin's murder in December 1916 and the czar's
abdication the following March. On April 16, 1917, Lenin arrived
in Petrograd. Bolshevik extremists soon overthrew Kerensky's
moderate socialist government. Revolutionary troops searched the
Ballet School for czarist agents and subsequently closed it. It was
then occupied by the army.

The Balanchivadze family remained together in Petrograd for a
while, but later in 1917 Meliton was appointed Minister of Culture
to the Georgian republic. The following year, he founded the
Balanchivadze School of Music in Kutaisi. The rest of the family
stayed in Petrograd.

In a letter to their father written during the first winter of separation, Georgi and Andrei told him that they had learned how to repair their own galoshes, which was "much cheaper." They then proceeded to scotch a rumor that had caused them—Georgi probably more than Andrei—a little anxiety. The brothers wrote alternate words:

November 27 1917

Dear Daddy,

. . . Who has been saying in the Caucasus that Georgi is a composer and has written many pieces of music and is an excellent musician? But this is not true. When we go to the Caucasus everyone will ask us to play, but we can't play anything special, so you, Daddy, tell everyone that we play only for ourselves.

In the meanwhile all best wishes,
Your loving Georgi and Andrei

Food was more plentiful in Georgia, so in 1918 Andrei was sent to join his father. Maria stayed in the capital to take care of the older children. The husband of their half-sister, Prince Shalva Kordzaya, "disappeared" soon after the Revolution. Uncle Apolon was persecuted and banished because of his former high rank in the czarist police. He later became an accountant and finally a priest. Georgi, aged fourteen, had to take what jobs he could find. He worked as a saddler's assistant and played the piano accompaniment in a movie house in return for bread, soap or matches. He and another former student went on foraging raids, stealing from Red Army barges moored on the Neva. They also rounded up stray cats, took them to an attic, strangled and skinned them, then gave them to Maria to cook. The dispossessed ballet students used to meet outside the school in Theater Street to exchange news and keep in touch. One day in 1918 they found a notice fixed to the door: the school was to open again. Anatole Lunacharsky, the Bolshevik Commissar for Education, had persuaded Lenin that opera and ballet were not counterrevolutionary.

The school was cold, and the food was much worse than in the old days. At the unheated Maryinsky, which had lost its aristocratic audience, the pipes froze and burst. The corps de ballet wore long-sleeved undershirts beneath their costumes. But, as Balanchine described it, "What could the poor prima dancers do? They got pneumonia, one after the other." There was talk of closing down the theater, but once again Lunacharsky came to the rescue. Salaries, however, remained very low.

The breaking down of traditional hierarchies and barriers meant that the Ballet School now had to share its premises with the recently organized School of Russian Drama. This led to Georgi's making a new acquaintance, Yuri Slonimsky from Warsaw, who became a ballet historian.

A reminiscence of Georgi at this time comes from Vera Kostrovitskaya, who later became a senior instructor at the school:

He never teased us little ones . . . but acted as if we were equals, and of the same age, though in those early years a difference of three classes was enormous. . . . He could never pass with indifference any musical instrument. The minute he came down to our floor of the school the sounds of a piano would be heard. . . . Sometimes, in the evening, we would secretly climb the stairs to listen to Balanchivadze playing Liszt, Chopin or Beethoven in the boys' quarters. . . .

For the school performance of 1919 Georgi danced the pas de deux from *Paquita* with two girls who were a year ahead of him, Lidia Ivanova and Alexandra Danilova. Danilova thought that the school authorities must have had high hopes for their future, since they chose them for this important number. She considered Georgi "not yet handsome, but . . . interesting looking, with piercing eyes . . . somehow special . . . very serious for his years."

Most women were to find Balanchine handsome in later life, but his looks were unusual. He had a high forehead, from which his dark-brown hair was brushed back; his nose was Roman. The high cheekbones were Oriental, but his slightly projecting teeth made the upper lip curve outward, so that his chin appeared more receding than it actually was. His wide mouth, with its full lower lip, tended to turn down slightly at the corners. He held himself very straight, as he had done in childhood, but his habit of tilting his head back and looking down his nose may have come from youthful resentment at his failure to grow any taller than five feet seven inches. His eyes, large and dark brown like his mother's, were charming, and his normal expression was one of benign amusement. He had a tic that caused him to twitch his nose and sniff as he talked (at school he had been nicknamed "the rat"), but he spoke softly in a rather high, nasal and reedy voice.

One of the boys' schoolmasters, Grigori Grigorievich Grigoriev, took a particular interest in Balanchivadze. He invited him to stay in his apartment, gave him lunch on Sundays, talked to him about music and lent him books. He was probably in love with him. The world owes something to this jealous old intellectual; according to Danilova, it was he who suggested that Georgi study music at the Conservatory.

In 1920, the sixteen-year-old Balanchivadze made his first attempt at choreography. He asked permission, which was granted, to arrange a dance for the annual school performance (Baryshnikov says the ballet is still danced today in Russia). Danilova recalls the incident in her memoirs:

To a piece of music by Anton Rubinstein [the Romance in E flat], he made a pas de deux called *La Nuit,* which he danced with Olga Mungalova. It was what would today be called "a sexy number." The boy conquered the girl: he lifted her in arabesque and held her with a straight arm overhead, then carried her off into the wings—so, she was *his*! This was the first time we had ever seen a one-arm lift in arabesque, which is now almost commonplace. But the effect that pas de deux had on me was more than the surprise at seeing new steps. It awakened something in me as a woman. Until then, all my boyfriends at the school had been just friends—I had never felt the need for anything more. And then suddenly I thought, there is something else. . . .

Alexandra Danilova graduated that spring, along with Ivanova and three other girls in her class. The departing graduates asked all their schoolmates to write in their yearbooks. Georgi wrote some bars of music in hers. "When I went to the piano and played the notes, I discovered it was Lensky's aria from *Eugene Onegin*: 'I love you, I love you.' I thought it was a joke, just a nice thing to write. I didn't take it seriously."

In the summer of 1919, Balanchivadze applied for admission to the Conservatory of Music, of which Alexander Glazunov was director. He had already met Glazunov, who had once come to the school theater to play his *Raymonda* on the piano—and "played beautifully, fluidly, clearly . . . just right for ballet rehearsal." Although Georgi was accepted, it was almost impossible for an undernourished dancer to work simultaneously at the school and the Conservatory, and he never completed his music course. Georgi's brother, looking back, judged that, from the point of view of a professional musician, he played pleasantly, although his hands were not "set."

On April 4, 1921, most of Balanchivadze's entire class of eight girls and four boys was graduated with honors from the school and joined the company of the State Theater of Opera and Ballet (formerly the Maryinsky). At the graduation performance, Georgi danced the role of Jean in *Javotte,* a ballet to the music of Saint-Saëns.

There can be little doubt that his concentration on both dance and music—the foundation of his later excellence in choreography—coming as it did at a time of dire food shortage, damaged his health for life. By this time he had already begun to show symptoms of tuberculosis and to spit blood, but he never spared himself. His friend Mikhail Mikhailov, a student one class behind him in the school, remembers that during the first or second summer recess after his entry into the corps de ballet of the State Theater, Georgi was chosen by Elizaveta Gerdt, whose usual partner was suddenly indisposed, to support her in an afternoon performance at the outdoor theater at Pavlovsk, the country palace, sixteen miles south of Leningrad, built by Catherine the Great for her son Paul. They were to dance a pas de deux from *Swan Lake.* The flattering summons arrived on the morning of the matinee itself, and Georgi went off in search of a costume. The first half of the performance was over and the bells for the second had rung, and there was still no sign of him. At the very last moment the reassembling audience parted to let through a frantic cyclist, and Georgi arrived at the stage door clasping a parcel. He apologized to his partner. "I am late. Please forgive me. It took a long time to find a costume, and when I got to the railroad station I could see only the end of the train vanishing into the distance. There was nothing for it but to borrow a bicycle from some people I know." After his sixteen-mile bicycle ride, he partnered Gerdt in the *Swan Lake* pas de deux.

■   ■   ■

DANILOVA, among others, remembers that Balanchivadze's most sensational number was the Buffoon's dance in *The Nutcracker* (called Candy Cane in America), in which he jumped through a hoop. The Buffoon is a character role. A character dancer, who is often strong and thickset, is one skilled in national dances such as the mazurka or trepak, or in comic, grotesque roles. He is the opposite of the *danseur noble,* who is usually taller and must have a more elegant line, the better to support and show off the ballerina. A demi-caractère dancer is a good classical dancer who excels in allegro and has a gift for comedy. Danilova rated Georgi as an excellent demi-caractère performer. It is clear from a few surviving photographs that the choreographer destined to extend the vocabulary of classical dance had neither the legs nor the feet of a *danseur noble.* According to Danilova, however, his Candy Cane variation always brought down the house. "His distinguishing features . . . were speed, musicality, a big jump, and a sharp attack." He was assured of a good career in the State Ballet, but the authorities did not approve of his essays in choreographic innovation. Danilova realized that his musical training at the Conservatory had extended his horizons.

More choreographic experiments followed the Rubinstein pas de deux. Georgi was impressed by the odd, acrobatic choreography of Kasyan Goleizovsky, a dancer from Moscow whose erotic ballets shocked the die-hard classicists. The authorities at the State Theater disapproved of Goleizovsky; an original in life as well as in art, he fancied long hair, velvet gowns and earrings. Balanchine was later to describe his choreography as "plastic." By this he presumably meant that the Moscow innovator used sculptural poses that bore no relation to the geometry of classical ballet; that he tied groups of dancers into knots, then led them in and out of mazes formed by their linked hands and arms. Balanchine, who was to become celebrated for his own knots and mazes, also adopted Goleizovsky's so-called sixth position, a stance with toes as well as heels touching: this was a contradiction of the first position of classical ballet, in which the heels are placed together and the toes turned out at an angle of 180 degrees.

Fyodor Lopoukhov, a principal choreographer of the State Theater and one of the few who rebelled against tradition and encouraged experiment, also influenced the young Balanchivadze. Lopoukhov's sister, Lydia (whose name Diaghilev changed to Lopokova on English tours), had defected. In 1922, Balanchivadze and some of his friends gave up their summer holiday to work with Lopoukhov on a ballet to Beethoven's Fourth Symphony, a bold attempt to express the inexpressible in terms of dance. A feature of the choreography was the formation of chains of linked dancers, some standing, others kneeling or recumbent. The small group of eighteen must have been kept busy. When *Dance Symphony: The Creation of the World* (also known as *The Grandeur of the Universe*) was presented—without the approval of the Theater Council—at the State Theater as part of a benefit performance on March 7,

1923, "a mixture of hissing and applause" greeted it. The ballet was never repeated. The acerbic old critic Akim Volinsky, who had opposed Fokine in the past and who had recently opened a school, attacked the experiment. Balanchivadze wrote an article in Lopoukhov's defense, deriding Volinsky's school and sounding the call for reform.

The revolutionary spirit of the poets Mayakovsky and Esenin, of the painters Tatlin, Malevich and Kandinsky, penetrated the world of dance; anything new was irresistible. The awareness of dawning possibilities was akin to that which had inflamed young romantics in the Paris of 1830. Balanchivadze cultivated a cadaverous pallor and wore his hair long. Danilova attributed this to a passion for Chopin and a wish to resemble him. She remembers that he wore nail polish, a cameo bracelet and a black shirt. A photograph dating from this period shows him seated cross-legged in the center of a group of his favorite colleagues, three women and three men. He is wearing white trousers and appears to be their acknowledged leader. It is not easy to cut a romantic, dashing figure when both money and materials are in short supply, but an eager young rebel can be a dandy in rags.

Fired by the experiments of Goleizovsky and Lopoukhov, Balanchivadze decided to form a group of his own. "Group" is perhaps the wrong word, for dancers came and went. Danilova recalled that one of these, Piotr Gusev, was Balanchivadze's closest friend at the time; and later he tried to persuade Mungalova, who became Gusev's wife, to leave Russia and join the Diaghilev Ballet. In the 1970s, by which time Gusev was an Honored Artist of the USSR, he recalled how much he had enjoyed being the raw material for Balanchivadze's choreographic attempts, even to working out parts that were later given to others.

It was Gusev who conducted the first meeting of dancers to discuss the foundation of the new group. When, sternly, he asked them what their credo was, the assembled friends chorused that they would do anything Balanchivadze wanted.

Some time during the first half of 1922, Georgi introduced an outsider into the rebel camp of State Theater dancers. This slight, pretty, ash-blond girl of fifteen named Tamara Zheverzheyeva, who had received her early training elsewhere, had been admitted to the State School for evening classes. (Her name was subsequently westernized as Gevergeyeva, then abbreviated to Geva.) She first caught sight of Georgi at a ballroom-dancing lesson. He had come in with Grigoriev, who told the teacher, "George has a dancing itch." Soon it was the young choreographer, not the teacher, who was "inventing combinations, correcting, shifting partners. . . . His whole presence projected the confidence of a leader. With his aquiline features and Byronic hair, he seemed a combination of poet and general."

Shortly afterward, he invited Tamara to dance with him in *La Nuit.* They were attracted to each other from the start, and quickly became friends.

To Grigoriev's annoyance, Georgi moved into the Zheverzheyev apartment. Realizing how delicate his health was, the Zheverzheyev family looked after him when he was ill. The deserted Grigoriev spitefully made a point of being rude about Tamara's dancing, even in the presence of Balanchivadze. But, Tamara recalled, "George would continue with the conversation as if nothing hurtful had been said"; he never stood up for her.

As soon as Maria Balanchivadze saw that her son was settled with Tamara, she realized that he would no longer be alone in the city and went to join her husband and Andrei in the Caucasus. Georgi never saw her again.

At the first performance of the Young Ballet, or Ballet of Youth, as it was to be called, Georgi staged Chopin's *Marche funèbre.* This took place on June 1, 1923, in the Alexandrovsky Hall, formerly the seat of the City Council. Subsequent performances of the Young Ballet were given in any.club, arena or institute where space could be rented.

. . .

JUDGING from the brief surviving descriptions of Balanchivadze's youthful works, one or two of them seem to be more significant than others. In *Poème,* to the music of the Czech composer Fibich, Balanchivadze "lifted Danilova in classic arabesque and lowered her softly on pointe." At the end, "[He] carried Danilova off, lifting her high in an arabesque with his arms extended. . . ." The gentle lowering onto pointe and the soaring supported exit would occur again in later more famous works.

The *Marche funèbre* was planned to be seen in the round; the dancers entered through the audience. Slonimsky considered that in "the passage of dancers followed by light through the audience" and "the modeling of sculptural groups as if to generalize individual experience," Balanchivadze showed the influence of the experimental theater director Vsevolod Meyerhold. And indeed, in the first performance of Fokine's *Carnaval,* which was given in a St. Petersburg club before it was ever presented by Diaghilev at the Paris Opéra, dancers entered through the auditorium—and Pierrot was played by Meyerhold.

In *Enigma,* to the Arensky music used for the exit of Cleopatra from Fokine's ballet *Une Nuit d'Egypte,* which Diaghilev made the choreographer transform with the addition of music by other composers into the sensational *Cléopâtre,* Balanchivadze at one point turned the ballerina into a bridge, a movement he would repeat some years later in *Le Fils prodigue (The Prodigal Son),* his last ballet for Diaghilev.

Another example of Balanchivadze's "expressionism" was a duet for Ivanova and the choreographer himself called *Valse triste* and set to the piece of that name by Sibelius.

By the age of eighteen, Balanchivadze, trained in the classical discipline of Petipa and in the more poetic classicism of Ivanov, had been exposed to the influence of the sensuous, iconoclastic Goleizovsky, to Lopoukhov, who used to say that dance could express everything with the help of music alone and who had dared to turn a Beethoven symphony into a ballet. and to Meyer-hold.

. . .

DURING a trip to dance in Moscow, as a result of jealousy and the fear of losing Tamara, Georgi suddenly realized he was in love with her. His rival, tall, flamboyant, famous and irresistible—everything, in fact, that Georgi knew himself not to be—was the poet Mayakovsky. He was a friend of Georgi's father, had been brought up in Georgia, and coincidentally had been a pupil of Georgi's uncle, Vassili Balanchivadze, the crooked-faced painter from Kutaisi. Tamara described the episode. Only one room had been provided, with a bed which Georgi and another dancer, Nicolas Efimov, were meant to share, and a couch. When Mayakovsky insisted on taking Tamara out to supper, she was haunted by the unhappy look on Georgi's face. Everybody made a fuss about the poet in the restaurant, but he realized something was wrong and took Tamara home. She found Efimov asleep on the couch and Balanchivadze seated on the bed, waiting for her. He held out his arms.

In his old age, Balanchine was to say, "I heard a story going around that it was Zheverzheyev's idea that Tamara and I get married. Nothing of the kind. . . . [He] paid no attention to Tamara and me . . . Tamara and I got married on our own."

They were married in the chapel of the Theater School. The bridegroom had borrowed a set of tails from the theater wardrobe, and he wore black eyeshadow. The marriage came as a great surprise and shock to Georgi's colleagues at the theater and the school. "All girls were rather upset," Alexandra Danilova told me. "I was."

Tamara considered that her husband had "an impregnable face." She was therefore surprised to observe one day when he returned from rehearsal that he was "visibly annoyed."

"That Semenov is really a bastard," he said.

"Why?" . . .

"He came up to me . . . and in front of all the other people he said, 'Why did you marry that trollop?' "

. . . "And you? What did you do?"

"Nothing. . . . What could I do? I turned my back on him and walked away." . . .

"You didn't defend me—your wife?"

Balanchivadze "looked on helplessly" as Tamara wept. Next day, he came home from the State Theater "sickly pale," accompanied by his friend Mikhailov.

"What is the matter?" asked Tamara.

"I've been suspended for two weeks," he replied.

"Why?"

"I hit him."

"You hit who?"

Since Georgi remained silent, it was Mikhailov who explained. "He hit Semenov. . . . Right in the face. . . . He asked him to apologize for yesterday's remark, and when Semenov refused, he hit him so hard that he almost fell backward."

Tamara threw her arms around her husband's neck, but he stood "completely impassive."

The young couple moved into an unfurnished apartment on the Moika Canal. Tamara's mother allowed her to take away very little furniture apart from a bed, an armchair, a table and a chest of drawers, so it was rather bare and comfortless; but Georgi was impervious to his surroundings. "Even with me," wrote Tamara, "he took me as he found me, and though I'm sure he loved me, he never showed any curiosity about my life before we met, and consequently never knew much about it."

.   .   .

IN 1923, Balanchivadze was appointed ballet master of the Mikhailovsky Opera Theater. That September, he created a dance for the Queen of Shemakhan in Rimsky-Korsakov's opera *Le Coq d'or*, and arranged the elaborate processional march in the last act, as well as providing the choreography for Bernard Shaw's *Caesar and*

Cleopatra, performed by the Petrograd Drama Theater. In December, he staged a dramatically appealing scene in *Hinkemann* (*Eugene the Unfortunate*), Ernst Toller's expressionist tragedy. In Act III, Scene 1, the silhouettes of dancers foxtrotting behind the illuminated windows of a café were contrasted with the prostitutes and crippled war veterans in the street outside, who stretched out their arms in direct appeal to the audience.

Balanchine was renowned in later years for his ability to work at high speed and to carry on several jobs for different companies simultaneously. When he was nineteen, he already showed signs of the same talent.

News of the Diaghilev Ballet's productions in Western Europe had reached Georgi and his colleagues through Tamara Karsavina, who had escaped to the West and was in correspondence with the teacher Agrippina Vaganova. The latter read Tamara's letters aloud at the Theater School, and one of the things she wrote about was Igor Stravinsky's *Pulcinella.* As early as 1918, Balanchivadze had played a small part in Stravinsky's opera *Le Rossignol;* later he had got to know *The Firebird* and *Petrushka.* Still later, a piano score of *Pulcinella* somehow reached Petrograd. In January 1924, Balanchivadze asked Lopoukhov's permission to arrange a ballet to it, but was told this was impossible on the ground that they did not have the hard currency needed to purchase the score. The orchestral parts would have to be bought in Western Europe.

In 1921, when Lenin's New Economic Policy opened the Russian ports for commerce, Lunacharsky persuaded Lenin to send certain groups of artists abroad, especially those whose work was being hampered by the effects of malnutrition. Under this policy, Olga Spessivtseva, whose health was poor, had obtained leave and been engaged by Diaghilev to dance in *The Sleeping Princess*—as he called his production of *The Sleeping Beauty*—in London.

In 1922 or earlier, Balanchivadze had met Vladimir Pavlovich Dmitriev, a former singer who had become a croupier in a government-licensed gambling house. He was a solid man of about forty, handsome in a rugged way but with alarming "sawn-off fingers." As croupier, he was entitled to a percentage of the take, and he had accumulated a considerable sum of money. He somehow managed to obtain permission from the authorities to spend his earnings on presenting a small troupe of artists abroad, ostensibly with the intention of displaying the latest achievements of Soviet culture to the Far East or to Western Europe. On April 4, 1924, an agreement was drawn up and signed by V. A. Dranyshnikov, a conductor at the State Theater, who would act as pianist; the singer O. F. Mshanskaya, who was his girl friend; the dancers Danilova, Zheverzheyeva, Ivanova, Efimov and Balanchivadze; and the "management": Dmitriev, G. D. Neliubim and E. G. Olkovsky:

We agree to participate in a concert tour to the Far East and abroad, the itinerary to be decided in the future. . . . The tour is organized on the basis of comradely relationship, the net profits to be divided in ten equal shares. . . . Should the collective suffer a deficit the members will not be held responsible. . . . The beginning of the tour is projected to start on the day following the end of the season of the State Academic Theater of Opera and Ballet, unless there is an opportunity to leave earlier. . . . The tour will end on [?] September, 1924.

The document bore the official stamp of the State Theater, but Balanchivadze's signature, with many grandiloquent flourishes, looks like a cartoon by Saul Steinberg, as if he were making fun of the pompous nature of the agreement.

Within the next few weeks, the Far East was forgotten, the singer and pianist dispensed with, Neliubim and Olkovsky dropped out and it was agreed that the dancers' tour should be confined to Germany.

Before they left, they were faced with a tragedy. Lidia Ivanova had friends who were high party officials, and somebody apparently decided that she knew too much about a certain political matter. As Balanchine told the story:

One of Lida's admirers talked her into going for a motorboat ride on the Gulf of Finland. He was a big shot in the Cheka, the Bolshevik secret police, and he always . . . wined and dined us. . . . He used to kiss Lida's shoulders. . . . There were five of them in the boat. A big ship crashed into it. The motorboat split up and Lida drowned. I think it was all a set-up. . . . The ship had time to turn. And then, Lida was a marvelous swimmer . . . There wasn't an investigation. I had heard that Lida knew some big secret, and they didn't want to let her out to the West. They . . . decided to fake an accident.

Geva described how she, Balanchine and Efimov were in an open-air theater, waiting for Ivanova and Danilova to dance "their inevitable *Moment Musical*" in the second half of a performance; how Ivanova never turned up; how a sinister-looking man came to tell Danilova that there had been an accident and she need not wait; how the manager of the park theater drove them to Vassilievsky Island; how they split into pairs and searched the shore-line toward Kronstadt; how they found the smashed motorboat and questioned the captain of the double-decker Kronstadt ferry that had rammed her. Danilova confirmed to me that everything happened "exactly as Tamara described." In her memoirs, she provided the additional information that the man who had brought the news of Ivanova's death was the adjutant to the commissar of the State Theater.

Depressed as they were, the little group did not delay their departure. One or two may have thought they were lucky to escape from Russia alive, but Danilova at least expected to return for the fall season. She had been promised the leading role of Kitri in *Don Quixote*. They all sailed for Stettin sometime in the second half of June.

Chapter 2

···

IN   WESTERN   EUROPE:

SUMMER   1924 - WINTER   1933

T HE undernourished Russians gloated incredulously over the
baskets of white bread and abundance of butter on the dinner table of their German ship, and Tamara was amazed
when a stewardess brought tea to her cabin on a tray; she thought
this happened only in Pola Negri movies. They landed at Stettin
and the next day went on to Berlin, which was full of White
Russians. A Russian-language newspaper dutifully reported their
arrival. Dmitriev spoke only halting German, but Tamara's was
fluent, so she took the lead in hiring a hall and organizing a recital.
Although it was the height of summer and audiences were small
and unappreciative, Dmitriev somehow managed to arrange a
Rhineland tour.

It was probably in Wiesbaden that they all agreed to defect—an idea that had doubtless been in Dmitriev's mind all along—for it was there that on September 6 he drew up a contract extending their agreement until November 1. They traveled to Vienna to hear Rachmaninoff play his own works, but when, backstage, Georgi suggested to the composer that he might make a ballet to his concerto, Rachmaninoff exclaimed, "A ballet! To my music! Are you crazy?" and threw them all out. Danilova later recalled that for the rest of his life, whenever the composer was mentioned, Balanchine would say, "Lousy music."

Although they had an undistinguished series of engagements in Germany, they received an invitation to appear in October at London's Empire music hall; they stayed for four weeks, in lodgings near the British Museum. Lydia Lopoukhova, who was not yet married to John Maynard Keynes, visited them at the theater to ask about her brother, Fyodor Lopoukhov. On November 3, Dmitriev drew up yet another contract, binding the dancers to him until April 3, 1925.

When their English work permits expired, they decided to try their luck in Paris. After a few days in a cheap hotel in the rue du Pont-Neuf, near Les Halles, when their money and hopes were running low, a telephone call came from Diaghilev. His company had been in Germany in September and October, and somehow or other he had heard of them. He was always anxious for new blood from Russia, and he had been trying to track them down.

He was in search of a choreographer as well as dancers. It had been Fokine's choreography more than anything else that had made the Russian ballets Diaghilev presented for the first time in Paris such a triumphant success. These ballets were of a new kind, quite unlike the traditional entertainments provided for the czars and their courts, although Diaghilev had hired dancers from the Imperial Theaters to perform them. Stimulated by the American Isadora Duncan's new free style of barefoot dancing, Fokine had initiated a "return to nature" involving dramatic realism, local color, the abolition of virtuosity for its own sake and the use of more symphonic music than was customary at the Maryinsky.

Nijinsky succeeded Fokine as Diaghilev's choreographer; his experiments in Debussy's *L'Après-midi d'un faune* (1912) and Igor Stravinsky's *Le Sacre du printemps* (1913) were even more radical than his predecessor's. Soon after Nijinsky's marriage to Romola de Pulszky in 1913 separated him from Diaghilev, the impresario adopted the young Léonide Massine as his protégé and made him into a choreographer by sheer willpower. Massine's ballets were "character" dances as opposed to classical—comedies of manners in a Russian, Italian or Spanish style. In 1921 he, too, parted from Diaghilev, who was finding it increasingly hard, after the war and the Russian Revolution, to enlist good dancers, although the music he commissioned from advanced composers, together with his dazzling décors—often by painters of the School of Paris—helped to camouflage the deficiencies of his troupe. At the time he contacted Balanchivadze and his colleagues, he was being assisted in devising new ballets by Boris Kochno, a young Russian who remained his closest friend and right-hand man to the end of his life.

The group of defectors was summoned to the Left Bank, to the studio of José-María Sert, whose wife, Misia, was Diaghilev's greatest woman friend. Here for the first time they met Diaghilev and Kochno. Georgi, partnering Zheverzheyeva, showed them his Scriabin pas de deux, and Danilova danced a few steps of *The Firebird,* which Lopoukhov had taught her. Since one of Diaghilev's commitments with the Opéra de Monte-Carlo was to supply dancers for its opera season between January and April, he asked Georgi, "Can you make ballets for operas?" "Yes," the tyro replied at once, not knowing whether he could or not. "Can you do them quickly?" "Yes."

Diaghilev was told that he must take all of the group or none. He replied that they would hear from him. This was in mid-November. Diaghilev returned to London on November 20, by which time the little group had run out of money and Georgi sold his best suit to provide funds for all of them. When Diaghilev telegraphed, Dmitriev evidently suggested certain stipulations, for on November 23, Diaghilev received the reply: *"Acceptons engage-*

ment. Attendez detailles [sic] *par lettre. Balantchivadze.* " (Accept the engagement. Letter follows with details.)

Since Diaghilev had no place for Dmitriev, the others agreed that each would give a fifth of his or her salary to their "manager," who had made it possible for them to leave Russia. The four set off for London a few days later. Telegrams from Russia were ignored. Georgi had made his choice; his vocation was in the West.

· · ·

THE DIAGHILEV BALLET of 1924 was not the large, well-trained company of dancers that had dazzled Paris and London between 1909 and 1914. With courage and determination—and out of love for Massine—Diaghilev had held together a scratch troupe throughout the difficult wartime years, when most European countries were closed to him; he had embarked reluctantly on extensive tours of the United States and had faced starvation in Spain. But after creating several highly successful ballets, Massine had left the company to get married.

In 1921, Diaghilev had staged his grandiose revival of *The Sleeping Princess* at the Alhambra music hall in London. The moderate success of this with English balletomanes—too few at that time to fill a large theater for a long run—left him deeply in debt to the theater's owner, Sir Oswald Stoll, who had rescued him from Spain in 1918. Once more he faced bankruptcy and the dispersal of his company. Once more he was saved, this time by an arrangement that would allow him to give regular ballet seasons at the Opéra de Monte-Carlo and to provide dancers for its operas. Nijinsky's sister, Bronislava, who had fled from Russia in 1921, became his new choreographer, and to her fell the honor of staging Stravinsky's *Renard* and *Les Noces.* When Georgi and his friends joined the Diaghilev Ballet in London, the company was on its first visit to England since the calamitous *Sleeping Princess.* Diaghilev had been paying off his debt to Stoll, but his troupe was still not allowed a proper season: they were appearing as a single act on the bill of Stoll's other music hall, the Coliseum, dancing one ballet every afternoon, one every evening.

Georgi thought the company very poor: "I was *so* disappointed," he remembered later. He admired only the Englishman Anton Dolin and one or two soloists, former members of the Maryinsky company, such as Ludmilla Schollar and Felia Doubrovska, who were well trained. The Massine repertory had consisted entirely of character or demi-caractère dances, and Georgi was at first used solely in character roles. He danced one of the warriors in Fokine's *Polovtsian Dances* from *Prince Igor,* the King of Spades in Massine's *Boutique fantasque* and the polonaise for twelve couples in a selection of numbers from *The Sleeping Princess,* which Diaghilev called *Aurora's Wedding.* Shortly afterward he was a Buffoon in *The Midnight Sun* (*Soleil de nuit*) and a folk dancer in *Children's Tales* (*Contes russes*).

Anton Dolin had been a pupil of Serafina Astafieva, one of Diaghilev's former dancers, who had a school in an old house in the King's Road, Chelsea. On December 1 he persuaded Diaghilev to go with Nijinska and Grigoriev, the *régisseur,* to audition another of Astafieva's pupils, fourteen-year-old Alicia Marks, whose technique was prodigious. Nijinska put her through her paces, and Alicia astonished the Russians with her high jumps, light landings and multiple pirouettes. It was arranged that she should join the company and lodge in Monte Carlo with Nijinska, who had a daughter aged ten.

Diaghilev needed to see a more sustained example of Balanchivadze's choreography than he had in Sert's studio. One Sunday morning, about ten days after the new group's arrival, Georgi demonstrated his Chopin *Marche funèbre* to Diaghilev. The Anglo-Irish dancer Ninette Devalois (as Diaghilev at that time spelled her assumed name) recorded the occasion:

I was summoned to Astafieva's studio with about six other artists. Balanchine was there, young and anxious-looking. He had an engaging charm and a great sense of humor, which made him popular with us. . . . His dancing had proved rather less than indifferent, but we suspected in him some other form of distinctive talent. For two solid hours we learnt a choreographic conception of his. . . . I worked with a will, for I was as acutely aware as others of his gifts. Just about midday Diaghilev, Kochno and Grigoriev arrived, and we went through our choreographic patterns. On such occasions Diaghilev was an enigma. Face impassive, manner aloof . . . and there was no means of fathoming the impression made on our director. I knew that a rumor was circulating . . . that Nijinska was leaving us quite soon, and that the young Balanchine might become our new choreographer . . .

Nijinska was indignant at the idea that there should be a second choreographer in the company. Conscious of her exceptional position as the sister of a god, she had no intention of sharing her honors with a stripling of twenty. She announced her departure. This was a blow to Diaghilev, who needed a choreographer for two new ballets he had commissioned. He even gave his beloved new favorite Serge Lifar—a young dancer from Kiev with a beautiful figure, limited technique and unlimited ambition—a tryout, but this was a disaster. Since Balanchivadze was still a comparatively unknown quantity, Diaghilev made up his quarrel with Massine, who happened to be in London.

Nevertheless, over the weekend of December 21, "the unknown quantity" underwent an historic transformation. Diaghilev, who usually Russianized his English dancers' names, liked to simplify any Russian ones that Westerners might have trouble pronouncing—particularly when they were names he hoped would be on everyone's lips. Nizhinsky had become Nijinsky, Miassin had become Massine, Spessivtseva had become Spessiva. Before the programs were printed for the week beginning Monday, December 22, Georgi Balanchivadze had become George Balanchin. (An "e" would soon be appended for the benefit of the French.)

The Ballet arrived in Monte Carlo on January 12, 1925, and Balanchine and his fellow "freshmen" set eyes on the Mediterranean for the first time. Before the ballet season opened in April, Balanchine had made dances for nine operas. Devalois, who took part in them, had a very high opinion of his resources. "He charged these dreary experiences with a new life and interest, and no demands on him could curb his imaginative facility. . . ." She particularly admired the ballet in Massenet's *Hérodiade,* which Balanchine led himself.

Yet by far the most interesting work that came Balanchine's way in those early months of 1925 was to provide choreography for the world premiere of Maurice Ravel's opera—or "lyric fantasy" as he called it—*L'Enfant et les sortilèges (The Spellbound Child),* to a text by Colette. Danilova recalled later that the composer himself played the piano for the rehearsals.

When Massine arrived, he took no notice of Balanchine and gave orders that he should not be allowed to watch his rehearsals. Balanchine, however, played small parts in ballets by both Massine and Nijinska. He also appeared in Fokine's ballets.

· · ·

ALTHOUGH only a few months earlier Balanchine had been the acknowledged leader of the Young Ballet in Russia, he had yet to find his feet in the strange world of the Diaghilev company. For the time being he was content to do whatever he was told and to remain in the background. The handsome Boris Kochno, librettist for many Diaghilev ballets in the 1920s, and almost exactly the same age as Balanchine, had acquired such sophistication since he left Russia four years earlier that he at first regarded the new arrival as a character so unremarkable as to be almost nonexistent. Kochno also noticed that Balanchine had a childish side and was amused by trifles. However, it was to Balanchine that Diaghilev had entrusted the new staging of *Le Chant du rossignol,* a ballet to music extracted from Stravinsky's opera *Le Rossignol* of 1914.

In London in December, Diaghilev had said to Balanchine, "I have an old ballet that has been arranged before. It is by Stravinsky. Could you manage it?"

"Yes."

Diaghilev looked at him. "You are very sure of yourself!"

Perhaps Diaghilev had already considered young Alicia Marks for the role of the Nightingale. In any case, he had taken Balanchine to Astafieva's studio in London and Alicia had demonstrated what she could do. After the audition with Balanchine, she remembered later, she felt she had been working for three-and-a-half hours. At a New Year's Eve party for the whole company that year she danced Rubinstein's *Valse Caprice,* while Balanchine strummed the piano; she ended the evening seated on the stool beside him. He spoke no English, and she spoke nothing else, but they were already friends; he never talked down to children. Diaghilev had then changed Alicia's name from Marks to Markova.

Diaghilev wanted to be able to use the costumes Henri Matisse had originally designed for *Le Chant du rossignol,* so he persuaded himself that Balanchine might be able to pull Massine's only partly successful work together. But Balanchine, who had played a small role in the complete opera in St. Petersburg, knew the music slightly and thought the flute in the ballet version was no substitute for the soprano voice.

The former teacher of Pavlova and Nijinsky, Maestro Enrico Cecchetti, had been lured from Milan to give classes for the company. This was Balanchine's first sight of the Italian style, which he called "small" in comparison with the "big" St. Petersburg style—speaking of it in later years, he held his hands in front of his chest like a rabbit—but it was in Cecchetti's classes that he observed the further potentialities of Markova. He planned that she should make her entrance as the Nightingale with two men holding her aloft by one leg. She then had to dive and be caught by two other men very close to the floor. Alicia thought that working with Balanchine was like a lesson in arithmetic. "Give me this leg, give me this hand"—and then suddenly the whole sum would come out right. According to Danilova, it was also in this ballet that "Balanchine introduced châiné turns with the arms open, then closed, then open again—no one had ever seen that before."

Kochno observed how Balanchine arrived at rehearsals with the air of someone who had just dropped in to say hello and casually improvised the dance as he went along. After he had invented a passage and stood back to see the dancer perform it, he seemed as surprised as if it had nothing to do with him.

Anton Dolin, who was partnering her, complained that Danilova needed a piano mover to lift her, and she asked Balanchine to watch her from out front. He told her, "You look terrible—you've gotten so fat. What's happened to you?" She bought diet pills from a pharmacy, took five and fainted. Balanchine threw the bottle out the window and gave her a lecture. She was to eat no chocolates and no desserts and to wear a high-necked sweater and woollen leggings in class. She lost weight and blossomed into a beauty. Her charming heart-shaped face, distinguished profile, big green eyes and Cupid's-bow mouth were to become world-famous, as were her perfect legs.

Diaghilev watched rehearsals closely and would sometimes correct tempi wrongly. Stravinsky, who was living with his family at Nice, half an hour's train journey along the coast, often stopped in at rehearsals. Before he arrived, Balanchine had always changed the tempi back again.

Diaghilev had given Stravinsky his first commission, *The Firebird*, in 1908. He had presented his *Petrushka*, *Rite of Spring*, *Nightingale*, *Renard*, *Noces*; now he had brought him together with Balanchine, with whom his destiny was to be so happily linked during the next half century.

The first night of *Rossignol* was attended not only by Georges Braque, who had designed the scenery and costumes for Massine's *Zéphyr et Flore*, but by Pablo Picasso and his wife, Olga, a former Diaghilev dancer, who came from Paris for the occasion. Balanchine was not particularly impressed to find himself among these great painters—or, for that matter, to be creating a ballet with décor by Matisse—because he had hardly heard of them. Of Vladimir Dukelsky's music for *Zéphyr,* which contained a pastiche of eighteenth-century compositions, he later said, "It had some nice music, but Dukelsky never really understood orchestration."

The company left for a two-week season in Barcelona on May 1. This was to be followed by more performances in the music-hall program at the London Coliseum, with a week in Paris sandwiched in between. In Barcelona, a Spanish marquis fell in love with Tamara Gevergeyeva (as Diaghilev spelled her name).

In London, Balanchine took over Vilzak's role as Nemchinova's partner in the grand pas de deux in *Aurora's Wedding.* At the Gaîté-Lyrique, he played the grotesque role of the Mechanical Nightingale in his own ballet. *Le Chant du rossignol* was well received, but the hit of the season was Massine's light-hearted *Les Matelots,* in which Serge Lifar first cast his spell over a Paris audience. Diaghilev's former favorite, Anton Dolin, left the company at the end of the Paris season. So did Tamara Gevergeyeva. She had some anxious weeks of unemployment in Paris, but Diaghilev took her back in time for the London winter season.

Balanchine was as eager as Diaghilev to improve the quality of the company by luring dancers from Russia. On September 15 he wrote to Diaghilev:

> 5 rue de Gavarni, Passy 16me

> I invited Barash and asked Herzenberg to come from Riga. She got her own visa and I sent her 1,000 francs of my own money. I wrote to Vadimova asking her to give you her address. . . .

Both Barash and Vadimova joined the Diaghilev Ballet, but no more was heard of Herzenberg, or of other artists Balanchine recommended.

During his summer holiday in Venice, Diaghilev met a young Italian composer, Vittorio Rieti, from whom he commissioned a ballet-*cum*-cantata on a comic theme entitled *Barabau.* The completed score was given to Balanchine after the company had begun yet another of their two-ballets-a-day seasons at the London Coliseum.

If he had been offered the choice, a farce was probably the last kind of ballet with which Balanchine would have wished to establish his reputation; but he was amenable, he did not despise humor and he took what he was given. Rieti's music appealed to him. The most unusual feature of the work was a group of six black-clad singers who popped up several times from behind a wall to sing *a cappella* a melancholy ballad (based on a nursery rhyme): "Barabau, Barabau, why did you die?" Tamara Geva later reported: "It was the first ballet during which the audience laughed aloud and throughout."

In the less than four years left before Diaghilev's death, Balanchine devised dances for twenty-six more operas. He saw the staging of old works by Fokine and of old and new ones by Nijinska and Massine. Above all, he was given new ballets to create with scores by composers as different as Auric, Satie, Berners, Sauguet, Stravinsky, Handel, Rieti and Prokofiev. It was hard work and poorly paid, but it was a wonderful apprenticeship. The obligation to turn out at high speed ballets for opera—a polonaise for *Boris Godunov,* dances for Honegger's *Judith,* a Hindu number for *Lakmé,* a waltz and a pas de deux for *Les Contes d'Hoffmann,* "medieval" dances for Gounod's *Jeanne d'Arc,* to mention only works produced in February and March 1926—undoubtedly extended Balanchine's natural ease of invention and prepared him for the tasks ahead. The precarious stability of the Diaghilev Ballet's existence depended on its yearly winter sojourn of four to five months in Monte Carlo. Without Balanchine to make the opera ballets, these annual periods of creation and consolidation in an agreeable climate would not have been possible: he was the company's principal breadwinner. If Diaghilev was secretly grateful for the young choreographer's willingness and adaptability, we may be sure he was careful not to express his gratitude in words. He did not like anyone to feel indispensable.

Even with the partial security afforded by the patronage of the prince of Monaco, channeled through the Société des Bains de Mer (i.e., the Casino), the company was run on a shoestring. At last, however, Diaghilev paid off his debt to Stoll and could have proper seasons in London where and when he wished. Thinking of England as a source of steady income, he paid court in Monte Carlo to Lord Rothermere, proprietor of the *Daily Mail,* who he had decided was the most likely backer. As a result, 1926 was a somewhat "English" year.

The first sign of Englishness was the ballet *Romeo and Juliet* by the twenty-year-old Constant Lambert, which Bronislava Nijinska was to arrange and the Surrealists Max Ernst and Joan Miró to design. Tamara Karsavina, whom Balanchine had revered in his youth, but who was now over forty, appeared as a guest artist, and Lifar had to be taught how to support her properly. Balanchine liked Lambert's music, but later observed that "Miró and Ernst were everything"—in other words, the décor was more interesting than the choreography. Massine's *Pulcinella* he described as "a long, boring ballet," adding that "Stravinsky and Picasso were everything."

For *La Pastorale,* Balanchine's own new ballet to a score by Georges Auric, Kochno provided what the choreographer considered a "messy" libretto about a Telegraph Boy (Lifar) who falls asleep beside his bicycle and wakes to find a film company at work on location. He flirts with the Star (Doubrovska) but finally returns to his Young Lady (Gevergeyeva). There was a remarkable pas de deux, in the course of which Lifar, kneeling, had to turn Doubrovska in arabesque by holding her supporting leg by the knee. (Balanchine used this again in later ballets, including *Serenade.*)

Diaghilev liked *La Pastorale* enough to persevere in continual adjustments to it; and although the British, from Sir Thomas Beecham to the music critic Ernest Newman, disliked it intensely, he kept it in the repertory until 1929. Balanchine was unable to read English at the time, so he could not be too depressed by the critics' reactions. "I was living in a [fool's] paradise," he told me once. "If I had known at the time language I should have committed suicide. But I can judge for myself. If I don't like what I do, I throw it away."

Diaghilev celebrated the opening of his first real London season since *The Sleeping Princess* by giving Stravinsky's *Les Noces* on the first night at His Majesty's Theatre. Balanchine heard for the first time the amazing cantata that had been begun before the war and was finished a decade later only after various experiments in orchestration. He thought Nijinska's choreography, with its mass movements and pyramidal formations, amounted to little, "the music was so great and complete."

Thanks to the success of the season at His Majesty's, there was to be a second visit to London in the winter of 1926, and Diaghilev spent much of July racking his brains for a subject that would please Rothermere and his compatriots. His chosen accomplice was the writer Sacheverell Sitwell. Diaghilev commissioned Lord Berners to write a score. Sitwell's story for the ballet would be part Victorian pantomime, with fairies and transformation scenes; part harlequinade; and part science fiction in the style of Jules Verne. The décor was to be copied literally from the printed sheets of scenery used in toy theaters. It was called *The Triumph of Neptune.*

Since Sitwell's father had a castle near Florence and Berners had a flat in Rome, Balanchine was summoned by Diaghilev to spend the latter part of his holiday working on the ballet in Italy. Kochno thought there was also another reason for the invitation: Diaghilev loved to educate his choreographers and leading dancers. How could they exist without drawing energy from the masterpieces of Italian art? Balanchine arrived in Florence with Dukelsky on September 14, and had long discussions with Diaghilev, Sitwell and Berners. Then they moved on to Rome, where Diaghilev left Berners to struggle with his composition while he took Balanchine, Kochno and Lifar to Naples. He showed them Pompeii and Herculaneum, as he had shown Picasso and Massine in 1917. Balanchine returned to Rome when the others went to Capri.

The second London season took place at the Lyceum. Balanchine was Kastchei, the evil enchanter, in a revival of *The Firebird* with new designs by Gontcharova. *The Triumph of Neptune* was given on December 3. Cyril Beaumont, the bookseller and ballet historian, a warm adherent of Diaghilev's since 1911, had thought *Barabau* "vulgar and rather tedious"; and *La Pastorale*—"feeble in action, slight in dance invention"—had not dispelled his misgivings at the appointment of Balanchine. *Neptune* won him over. He praised Balanchine's own solo in the role of the Negro, Snowball, as "a dance full of subtly contrasted rhythms, strutting walks, mincing steps, and surging backward bendings of the body borrowed from the cake-walk . . . a paradoxical blend of pretended nervous apprehension and blustering confidence." This was Balanchine's first creation to show American influence. It was also his last display of virtuoso dancing, for he developed trouble with his knee, had a piece of cartilage removed and was never so agile again.

Danilova had noticed that Balanchine was "somber, pensive." One day, when she had a bad foot, he massaged it—then kissed it. When she asked him a few days later what was wrong, he replied, "Don't you know? I love you."

"What about Tamara?"

"Well, I don't love her."

She was shocked, and even considered going back to Russia to avoid breaking up a marriage, but Balanchine was persistent. He could not get a divorce because his marriage papers had been left in Russia; however, Danilova decided that she loved him enough to forgo marriage. She wrote, "I moved in with him, happy to be with him but crying because I had always dreamed of being a bride and walking down the aisle in a long white dress. . . ."

Diaghilev was not pleased. While the company was at Le Touquet in July 1926, he summoned Balanchine to his hotel and they had a two-hour talk. Danilova asked Balanchine several times what had been said, but he would not tell her.

. . .

AT MONTE CARLO, Balanchine and Danilova stayed at the Hôtel de la Réserve, right on the beach; so did Vladimir Horowitz, whom Balanchine was always to uphold as one of the greatest—if not the greatest—of living pianists. He and Danilova were often awakened by Horowitz playing Liszt's "Valse oubliée" through the wall. When Danilova yearned to go to a nightclub and dance the tango and Balanchine said, "Why do you want to sit in a noisy room full of smoke?" it was Horowitz who took her.

In those days, Balanchine's "worldly" side was shown in his interest in Danilova's hats. "That's awful," he would exclaim. "Go and change it." Or, "How nice! It suits you."

Balanchine was free with the little money he had, and inveterate gamblers among his friends, notably the dancer Léon Woizikovsky, took advantage of him. Faced with a hotel bill for four hundred francs, Balanchine said to Danilova, "Let's go to the Casino." He won six hundred francs. She snatched five hundred, left him to play and went straight back to settle with the hotel.

. . .

THE year 1927 began with performances in Turin and at La Scala in Milan. Diaghilev had succeeded in re-engaging Olga Spessivtseva (whom, of course, he had renamed Spessiva), and she danced *Swan Lake.* The long mime "monologue" in Act II, during which Odette explains to the Prince how she fell under the power of Rothbart and was changed into a swan, was replaced by Balanchine with a passage of dancing, which is still extant in the repertory of several companies. Danilova later described Balanchine as giving Odette "droopy hands and sloping shoulders, to show that she was unhappy."

Apart from such revisions, there was the usual miscellany of opera ballets to be produced in Monte Carlo. *La Traviata* was the first Verdi opera Balanchine worked on (in 1929 he would arrange court dances for *Rigoletto*). In an interview years later he made an interesting disclosure: "From Verdi's way of dealing with the chorus I learned how to handle the corps de ballet, the ensemble, the soloists—how to make the soloists stand out against the corps de ballet and when to give them time to rest."

Balanchine's only new ballet in 1927 was *La Chatte*, with a score by Henri Sauguet. The marvelous Spessiva had failed in ballets by Fokine and Nijinska, so Diaghilev was determined to show her in a new work. Kochno's point of departure was an Aesop fable about a cat who was turned into a woman. Knowing how difficult and unreliable Spessiva was, Diaghilev warned Balanchine that if she liked his ballet, it would probably be no good. During rehearsals she evidently showed that she did not, for Diaghilev said to Balanchine, "Congratulations!" Spessiva danced *La Chatte* only in Monte Carlo, having developed a real or imagined leg injury before the Paris opening on May 26, and Balanchine thought her "wonderful," although she was unmusical and "didn't turn very well."

In her pas de deux, supported by Lifar, Balanchine had her pirouette slowly down to the ground, and Massine complained to Diaghilev that he had always wanted to use this movement. "If it is so easy to steal your thoughts," Diaghilev said, "please don't think."

Spessiva's was the only female role. Lifar, wearing a minimum of celluloid armor, was carried on by six companions, a hero among heroes. Although Alice Nikitina (who replaced Spessiva for the final Monte Carlo performances) paired with him perfectly, Lifar stole the show. What had been a desperate attempt to display Diaghilev's preferred ballerina turned out to be a milestone—a triumphal arch—on Lifar's road to stardom. Danilova, to whom Balanchine had wanted to give Spessiva's part on the morning of the Paris premiere—he had made the role on her, and she already knew it—commented that since Lifar was not a strong dancer, George had created a neoclassical style for him and made him into a star above the ballerinas, including herself. More than anyone—

perhaps even more than Lifar himself, though he worked hard—
Balanchine helped Diaghilev keep the promise he had made to the
young dancer in 1924.

In a letter to Diaghilev dated September 28, Balanchine announced, "Gevergeyeva will not be working this year. Because of
her stupid methods of losing weight she has reached a point where
her doctor has forbidden her to dance. She has joined [Nikita]
Balieff [the presenter of small-scale "artistic" revues] and will sing
in a gypsy chorus and clap her hands."

This was not exactly true. Before Gevergeyeva left with Balieff's
troupe, Les Chauve-Souris, for New York, Balanchine arranged
two solos for her, a dance called *Grotesque espagnole,* to the *Córdoba* of Albéniz, and *Sarcasm,* to Prokofiev's Op. 17. These numbers, in which the renamed Geva enjoyed a considerable success,
were the first Balanchine works to be seen in America.

In another (undated) letter to Diaghilev, Balanchine wrote, "My
leg is unfortunately recovering very slowly. I think I shall have to
take it easy at first."

. . .

BALANCHINE'S knowledge of the music of Stravinsky was increasing
all the time. During the Paris summer season of 1927, Diaghilev
had given three performances of *Oedipus Rex,* presented as an
oratorio without scenery or costumes. Two weeks later, in London,
there was a Stravinsky evening, with *Petrushka, Pulcinella* and *The
Firebird.* On September 30, when Diaghilev was in Monte Carlo
renewing his contract, Stravinsky summoned him to Nice to hear
a new ballet. It had just been commissioned for performance at the
Library of Congress in Washington, D.C., but Diaghilev was to be
allowed to stage the first European production. It was called *Apollon Musagète,* later shortened to *Apollo.*

On January 23, 1928, Balanchine went with Diaghilev to hear
the score for the first time and began rehearsing it immediately,
working out movements on Danilova. In a short Belgian tour in

May, Massine's version of Stravinsky's *Rite of Spring* (*Sacre du printemps*) was revived. Balanchine thought Massine's *Sacre*—at least when given by only forty dancers—"almost a joke." There was one gesture endlessly repeated: the dancers reached down with both hands to the floor on their right, then extended their arms upward to their left. It was as if they were picking books off a pile to place on a shelf, and Balanchine called it "working in a library." His dislike of Massine's version may have been partly what put him off staging the historic score in later life, but in fact he often said the music was "undanceable." Its Dionysian character was not of a kind to attract him.

. . .

BALANCHINE'S circle of acquaintances was being steadily enlarged; he met not only Sergei Prokofiev, but also the young composer Nicolas Nabokov and the painter Pavel Tchelishchev (always thenceforth simplified as "Tchelitchev"), who were collaborating on *Ode*. Despite these encounters, and although Balanchine sometimes dined alone with Diaghilev to discuss projects, he played little part in the social life of his employer's intimate circle; his face was comparatively unknown to the *beau monde*.

. . .

Apollon Musagète was a landmark in Balanchine's career. Its first performance by the Diaghilev Ballet, with a simple décor by the naïve painter André Bauchant, was given at the Théâtre Sarah-Bernhardt on June 12, 1928. The composer conducted. A version with choreography by Adolph Bolm had been performed at the Library of Congress on April 27.

For the sake of theatrical lucidity Stravinsky reduced Apollo's nine Muses to three, and because his composition was a ballet, he gave the favored ballerina role to Terpsichore, Muse of Dance. *Apollon* was written for string orchestra. While Stravinsky's division of the ballet into numbers was traditional, his music, whatever echoes of the past there may be in it, was utterly personal, new and of the twentieth century, so Balanchine had to find an appropriate way of dancing it. His re-use of Goleizovsky's "sixth position," in which the toes and heels of the feet are touching, although "modern," held a suggestion of archaic Greek sculpture; there were syncopated movements and whole passages without a single classical ballet step. The thin thread of story running through the ten numbers tells how Apollo was born, then educated by the Muses; how he took command of them, chose among them, and, conscious of his growing powers, was summoned to lead them to Parnassus.

Each Muse, to whom the god has given an appropriate symbol, performs a solo, watched by the seated Apollo. Stravinsky had the fanciful notion of making Calliope, the Muse of Heroic Poetry, dance partly in alexandrines. During the caesuras, she scribbles on her scroll, then, after she has put it down, clutches her side to convey the pangs of inspiration and extends a hand from her open mouth toward the audience. Polyhymnia, the Muse of Mime, dances a brilliant nonstop allegro, one finger to her lips. Terpsichore's variation is playful, provocative and jazzy, and it is she who seduces Apollo with little runs and kicks, fluttering hands and a backbend.

In Apollo's second variation, Balanchine hit on a startling image to convey that the god is conscious of his divinity. Twice Apollo stands in fourth position, forward left leg bent, left arm behind his back with clenched fist visible to his right, and with the right arm extended upward, the fingers of the right hand splayed like rays of light. Then, as the right fist clenches, the fingers of the left splay out. On—off; on—off; on—off; on—off. Balanchine said this idea came to him from watching an electric sign in Piccadilly Circus. At the end, Apollo sinks to the ground, facing offstage but extending an arm with pointing forefinger behind him. Terpsichore advances to press his finger with her own. This echo of Michelangelo's Sistine ceiling could be regarded as another "electric" image. In the following pas de deux, a sublime adagio, Terpsichore is at one moment supported, reclining, on Apollo's shoulder, facing skyward. She is also lowered to the floor in a deep split and dragged on pointe in arabesque.

The mounting excitement of the Coda, preceding the calm of the Apotheosis, is like the chase in the last sequence of a film, which holds the spectator in suspense before the happy ending. As Apollo stands behind the line of Muses, they grasp his wrists, extending their free arms as they take an arabesque; to an urgent, cantering music, he drives them as of they were pulling a chariot around the stage. Finally the Muses walk away from Apollo, turn about, prance toward him on their heels, clap their hands on a pizzicato chord and extend their open palms, conjoined. On the final pianissimo chord, Apollo abruptly lays his head in their hands.

Of the opening chords of the Apotheosis, Balanchine said, "He hears his father calling." When the principal theme, first heard before the rise of the curtain, sounds again, there is a maze of revolving rings. Then the Muses appear to hang from Apollo, each on one leg, extending the other, so that the extended legs fan out at varying heights to form a sunburst behind him. The theme has been repeating and will continue to the end. Balanchine ignores it. A persistent tremolo is heard on the second violins and violas. As this intensifies, a steady stepping on the second cellos and basses begins. The choreographer disregards the former atmospheric effect, but sets his dancers pacing to the latter music. While the repetition of the theme gives the number its Olympian peace, the mysterious tremolo envelops it in a golden haze, and the stepping contributes solemnity. Led by Apollo, the Muses walk, hands to sides, to climb the slope of Parnassus.

Balanchine's new ballet was well received, but there is no evidence that anyone (except Gordon Craig, who thought it so beautiful that he left the theater immediately after it) recognized a new kind of musical and choreographic masterpiece. Since his early "Russian" period, Stravinsky's music had been regularly derided by French critics. When *Apollon* was given in London on June 25, the critic of the *Times* was to write: "It used to be said that the

Russian Ballet would not be much without Stravinsky: his latest production makes us fear that soon it will not be much with him."

Yet Balanchine's choreography for *Apollon* had extended the language of the classical dance. It related in a novel way—several ways—to a heavenly score. It held in it the seeds of many later works. The ballet looks forward to the new, the "neo"-classicism, which would be the choreographer's gift to America.

Balanchine had trouble with Terpsichore's variation, and after the first night Diaghilev wanted to cut it. "He told me that the choreography for Terpsichore was no good. I said 'The choreography's fine. It's the dancer who is no good.' " This was Nikitina, and from then on Danilova was to alternate with her in the role. According to Danilova, Balanchine made some changes, adding "some soft, light, quick sissonnes," and all turned out for the best.

Earlier in the year, as a compliment to Sir Thomas Beecham, who was a lover of Handel's music (and possibly to avoid staging a ballet by Delius, whom Beecham never ceased to promote), Diaghilev had invited the conductor to send a bundle of scores to Monte Carlo. A choice was made, Kochno devised a slight story "based on eighteenth-century pastoral allegories," and in the course of the London season Balanchine put together a ballet in no time at all. This makeshift work had a totally unexpected success. *The Gods Go A-Begging*, known outside England as *Les Dieux mendiants*, proved so popular that Danilova was prompted to say, "It became our bread and butter."

That summer Balanchine found himself a small apartment in Paris, just north of the Arc de Triomphe, and when he spent a few days in Venice with Diaghilev and Kochno he asked the former to lend him some money for the necessary down payment. But Diaghilev went off with Kochno to Poland in search of rare Russian books. Kochno was always a helpful intermediary in dealings with Diaghilev, and he and Balanchine had by this time become friends. Balanchine's letter asking Kochno to remind Diaghilev that the matter was urgent arrived in Berlin on October 12.

5 Passage Doisy
Paris 17e
11 October 1928

Dear Boris,

I expect you know about my request to Sergei Pavlovich for 4,000 francs by October 15. I'm afraid he may have forgotten about this; but I absolutely must have the money on the 15th for the renting of my apartment. Please remind him and keep him up to the mark. I promise to repay the money in England at the latest, perhaps some of it before. I thank you in advance and kiss you . . .

If you think I have forgotten you you are mistaken.

Yours,

Georges

The news is that Spessiva has just divorced Kniaseff.

On the day Kochno received this letter, Diaghilev cabled his *régisseur* Grigoriev, "Send Balanchine 4,000 [francs]."

Dmitriev moved in with Balanchine and Danilova, who still gave him part of their salaries. Balanchine, wanting to buy some furniture, tried to persuade Woizikovsky and the other gamblers to return the money he had lent them. In this he was unsuccessful. He was, however, steadily gaining the respect of his employer. When there was a question of what should appear on the posters for a British tour at the end of the year, Diaghilev telegraphed to Grigoriev, "*Maître de ballet* Balanchine. Don't put any other artists' names on poster."

■   ■   ■

BALANCHINE'S two new ballets for 1929, both with libretti by Kochno, were as different from each other as it is possible to imagine. Prokofiev's *The Prodigal Son* was to be another vehicle for Lifar, while both Diaghilev and Kochno agreed that Anton Dolin, who had been asking to be taken back into the company, would be an ideal partner for Danilova in Rieti's *Le Bal*.

Lifar already felt apprehensive about his future, because Diaghilev had fallen in love with Igor Markevitch, a sixteen-year-old music student. In 1939, describing his talks with Diaghilev at the end of February 1929, Lifar wrote that Diaghilev did not wish to entrust any more ballets to Balanchine, saying, "I'll soon be sending him packing." When he wrote these words, Lifar had his reasons for disparaging Balanchine's talents. It may safely be assumed that these "talks" were fictitious. In 1977, when I asked Balanchine whether Diaghilev could possibly have been planning to fire him and replace him with Lifar, he replied calmly, "He wasn't such a fool."

For *Le Bal,* Diaghilev had ordered a set and costumes from Giorgio de Chirico; these greatly enhanced the mysterious masked ball, which Kochno had borrowed from a Russian story of the Romantic period. Balanchine devised angular poses, with bent elbows and knees, and Danilova recalls the steps being "very syncopated." The choreographer himself danced a Spanish pas de trois with Doubrovska and Woizikovsky. First given in Monte Carlo on May 7, *Le Bal* was performed in Paris and Berlin before being acclaimed in London as "the most successful novelty of the last few years." Yet this "most successful" work would never be revived.

An element appeared in *The Prodigal Son* that had been absent from Diaghilev's ballets since the days of Fokine and Nijinsky—drama. Lifar could not believe his ears when he heard Diaghilev, who had always been opposed to any hint of intensity in mime, urging him to put more feeling into his role, to dramatize it. For Balanchine, too, it was something new to handle a subject that, despite Kochno's editorial adjustments, was traceable to St. Luke's Gospel. Diaghilev had invited Georges Rouault, the only religious painter of the School of Paris, to design the ballet, and although his sketches for the two sets—the first a harbor with a tower and sailing ships, the second a tent—appear almost perfunctory, they also strike us, after more than half a century, as just right.

Prokofiev was disappointed with Diaghilev's production of his *Prodigal Son.* Toward the end of his life, Balanchine told Solomon Volkov that Prokofiev had hoped for "bearded men sitting and drinking real wine out of real goblets, the dancers dressed with '. . . historical accuracy.' In a word, somewhat like *Rigoletto*. . . . He was horrified by my staging. . . . And Diaghilev, naturally, yelled at Prokofiev that he didn't understand a thing about ballet. . . ." In Kochno's simple libretto, the Prodigal's self-righteous elder brother is replaced by two affectionate servants or sisters; the fatted calf is omitted; and as much as possible is made of the Prodigal's "wasting his substance in riotous living." When the libretto was complete, Prokofiev wrote his score. Then Balanchine was presented with a *fait accompli*.

Of the ten numbers, some are composed as storytelling, some as dancing, some are mixed. In the departure from home of the Prodigal, who is impatient with his reproachful Father and pleading Sisters (or Servants), there is dramatic conflict; and his abject return at the end is pure drama. The Prodigal's meeting with a gang of "boon companions" in a far country and his seduction by the Siren, though dramatic, are celebrated in dance. The scene in which he is robbed while drunk is mime; the dividing of the spoils is part mime, part dance; and the Prodigal's awakening and repentance is again entirely mime.

Prokofiev's music for the Siren is almost ecclesiastical, with an Old Testament solemnity. The composer obviously saw her as a kind of priestess who initiates men in the ritual of love. Balanchine went further and made her terrifying. The tall, long-legged Doubrovska, walking on pointe, wore a towering headdress. Many years later the choreographer stated that the idea of making the Prodigal's boon companions bald, like certain figures with shaven heads in Egyptian reliefs or like creatures from outer space, was his. He was thus obliged to show them from their first appearance as sinister and abnormal, instead of happy-go-lucky confidence men, charming on the surface, who would later be revealed as thieves. It seems possible that he took his cue from the eighth number, called "Pillage" or "The Despoiling," which is indeed alarming; the scampering scales of its clarinets suggest rats or spiders. Yet there was nothing particularly evil about Prokofiev's boastful, stamping march for the entry of the boon companions, so a discrepancy arose. Later in the ballet, Balanchine would have them link arms, back to back in twos, then scud crablike across the stage.

John Taras has described the pas de deux of the Prodigal and the Siren as "a manual of erotic combinations." At one point she wraps herself around his waist like a belt, her hands clasping her ankles. The man, turning as he carries her thus, lets her slide slowly down his widespread legs till she touches the floor: he then steps out of her as if undressing.

Among the production's ingenuities are the several uses to which a single piece of furniture is put. Beginning as the stockade fencing the Prodigal's home, it is turned upside down and becomes a banqueting table in the orgy scenes. Stood on end, it is transformed into a pillar against which the Prodigal is flung to be frisked. Then the gang reverses it to use as a boat in which they play at rowing off, with the Siren as figurehead, her train held aloft as a sail; and it is in position once more as a fence for the homecoming.

Balanchine had been worried about how to deal with the episode of the Prodigal's return, the big emotional scene. Danilova remembers him sitting on their hotel terrace on the beach at Monte Carlo: "I don't know what to do when the son comes home, crawling on his knees—there are six pages of music. . . . I thought maybe he could have a staff, the way shepherds have, and he can hang onto that." So he does, but when he sees his father, he drops the staff.

Then, folding his arms behind his back in penance, the Prodigal advances on his knees, to collapse at his father's feet. The flute sings sweetly of contrition and forgiveness. Slowly the son clutches his way up his father's body, to hang from his neck and nestle like a baby on his breast. The Father, head held high, covers him with his cloak in a protective embrace.

According to Lifar, who never minimized his triumphs, "Pandemonium broke loose. . . . People were crying." "It was Lifar, on his knees, that made the ballet," commented the generous Balanchine.

Royalties on *The Prodigal Son* were to be divided between Prokofiev as composer and Kochno as author. Kochno had to go to court to claim his share, and won his case. Balanchine, whom Diaghilev paid a very meager wage, and who was often hungry, asked the composer, "Couldn't I be included?" Prokofiev screamed at him, "Are you mad? Who are *you?* You are nobody! You are nothing! Leave me alone! Get out!" Balanchine said, "I'm sorry," and went away.

·   ·   ·

THE LONDON season of 1929 was heralded by a long letter from Diaghilev to the *Times,* in which he teased the critics for continually misunderstanding his experiments and praised Balanchine.

Our century interests itself in *Mouvements mécaniques,* but whenever new *Mouvements artistiques* occur people seem to be more frightened of being run over by them than by a motor-car in the street. For 25 years I have endeavoured to find a new *Mouvement* in the theatre. . . . The new definitions of choreography are "Athletics" and "Acrobatics" . . . In the plastic efforts of Balanchine in *The Prodigal Son* there are far less acrobatics than in the final classical *pas de deux* in *Aurora's Wedding.* . . .

Prospects looked good for the future of the Ballet, for, as Diaghilev told the company when he said good-bye to them shortly before the end of the London season, they had bookings in Barcelona and the possibility of a North American and South American tour. Following *La Chatte,* which was a hit, and *Apollon,* which was a masterpiece, Balanchine had brought off two more ballets that were successful in very different ways. Many years later, considering that summer of 1929, I asked Balanchine if he had then felt on top of the world. "No, I never felt that way," he said. He meant never in his life.

While Diaghilev, against his doctor's orders, took the young Markevitch to the music festival in Baden-Baden, then to hear Wagner and Mozart in Munich and Bayreuth, the Ballet went on to dance for a week in Vichy before dispersing for the holidays. The last performance there on August 4—which was also to be the last performance of the Diaghilev Ballet—was an all-Massine program. Balanchine mimed the role of the Corregidor in *Le Tricorne*. He then traveled to London, where he was to arrange a Tatar ballet, *Jealousy*, to music from Mussorgsky's *Khovanshchina*, for the first full-length talking picture made in England, *Dark Red Roses*. This was a kind of Apache number for Lydia Lopoukhova, Anton Dolin and himself. The three dancers were in the garden of the film studio at Isleworth, waiting to be called, when Dolin bought an evening paper and saw a photograph of Diaghilev on the front page. He had died that morning in Venice. It was August 19, 1929.

In later years Balanchine used to express gratitude for what Diaghilev had done for him and the possibilities he had opened up. This was courteous and also what writers and journalists expected to hear. "The first time I realized how beautiful painting was, it was Italian. When Diaghilev took me to Florence . . ." and so on. Yet, it was *not* "because of Diaghilev" that Balanchine came to make his finest ballets in the way he made them, or that he made them acceptable without décor and with a minimum of costume. It was music, not painting, that filled his mind, guiding his brain and hands. Balanchine acknowledged his debt to the impresario, and acknowledged it with grace; but when asked by McNeil Lowry in 1979 what artists in any field had helped to shape his life, he reacted with a doubtful "Ummm."

■   ■   ■

FOR TWENTY years "ballet" had meant the Diaghilev Ballet. When everyone realized that the company was not to continue, it was a case of every man for himself. Outside Russia, what was there except the famous old Paris Opéra Ballet, which had become a joke, and the Royal Danish Ballet, which nobody knew anything about? It is true that Ida Rubinstein, who could not dance, had a troupe for which she commissioned ballets by Bronislava Nijinska, with scores by Ravel and Stravinsky. It was because Stravinsky had composed *Le Baiser de la fée* for her that he and the jealous Diaghilev were barely on speaking terms during the final months of Diaghilev's life.

The hope that Diaghilev's company might continue under Kochno was dashed by Lifar's insistence on being co-director. Lifar had been built up into a star, but although amiable and enthusiastic, he was vain, had little talent for choreography and few ideas beyond a passion for publicity. Without the curb of Diaghilev's criticism, his "personality" was soon out of control. The company refused to serve under him. On the other hand, Kochno's name was comparatively unknown to the general public. The two young men, former rivals for first place in Diaghilev's friendship and almost the same age—as was Balanchine—did not like each other. It looked as if the company, which could not continue under Lifar, was impossible without him.

At this point, in October 1929, Balanchine was asked by Jacques Rouché, director of the Paris Opéra, to make a new version of Beethoven's *Les Créatures de Prométhée.* Balanchine would almost certainly have remained there as ballet master had he not developed tuberculosis. He left the partly completed ballet in Lifar's hands. Danilova took him to a sanitarium in the Haute-Savoie, then returned to Paris.

The next months were a time of isolation and crisis for him. He was fighting for his life and steadfastly refused to have a lung removed, since he regretted having allowed surgery on his leg. He had cut himself off from his family; and his adopted family, the Ballets Russes, had ceased to exist. Who was left except Danilova, Kochno, Lifar and perhaps the former conductor of the Diaghilev Ballet, Roger Desormière? He wrote to his mother for the first time in years; and he hoped that some of his friends would visit him. To Kochno he wrote:

Grand Hôtel de Mont Blanc
Passy
Haute-Savoie
[*undated, but probably late*
November or early December
1930]

Dear Boris,

This is what I have to tell you. My life here is not gay and the only good thing about it is my hope—that is my hope of seeing my old friends around the 6th, when they come here for a rest. Obviously they are not going to find much gaiety waiting for them, but rest they can. We sleep a lot, and the food comes out of our ears. The view is very picturesque. It's pure Picasso. [At the foot of the first page the writing-paper is printed with a view of the hotel. Balanchine has drawn an arrow pointing to one of the arches in the arcaded terrace surrounding the ground floor, and written: "Here lies the body of Balanchine."]

I have had certain thoughts about future GIRLS. [The English word is transcribed in Cyrillic characters.] I'll tell you all about this around the 6th. Please bring with you the white ointment for my lips. It was in the drawer of my night table. My lips are cracked, and I am obliged to put butter on them.

Give my greetings to the kid [Lifar]. [Here Balanchine wrote five bars of music.]

I kiss you,
G. B.

In fact, neither Kochno nor Lifar visited Balanchine in the Haute-Savoie. The first night of the Beethoven ballet took place on December 30, and Lifar was busy establishing himself as *maître de ballet* at the Paris Opéra in Balanchine's place. When the latter returned to Paris with his health improved, he found himself barred from the office, the most prestigious in the world of ballet. He and Danilova were turned away at the stagedoor by orders of "the kid." Danilova later remarked to me that she could forgive Lifar for this perfidy, but she could never forget it.

Meanwhile, Balanchine was invited to London to choreograph numbers for C. B. Cochran's *Cochran Revue* of 1930. Lady Cunard invited him to supper, and he met the Prince of Wales and "his brother George" (the Duke of Kent). He might have decided to remain in England, but even Maynard Keynes, the husband of Lopoukhova and the by-then-famous author of *The Economic Consequences of the Peace,* whom he visited, could not get his visa extended.

After a stay in France, Balanchine accepted an invitation to be guest ballet master at the Royal Theatre, Copenhagen. The work there was uncongenial to him; he was asked to fake new versions of Massine's *Le Tricorne* and *La Boutique fantasque,* and of Fokine's *Schéhérazade* and *Prince Igor.* He could not have enjoyed dancing Fokine's (presumably edited) *Le Spectre de la rose,* with Ulla Poulsen, for a Christmas charity performance, but there was another Balanchine Evening on January 18, 1931, and this time the choreography was genuine Balanchine. In *Apollon Musagète,* Leif Ørnberg (an uncle of Peter Martins) was the second man ever to dance the principal role. Harald Lander interpreted the comic lead in *Barabau,* which had originally been Woizikovsky's. The choreography of Richard Strauss's *Josefs Legende* (*La Légende de Joseph*) must also have been Balanchine's own invention, as he had never seen the Fokine version of 1914. He wrote to Kochno in Paris:

> [*undated, but, since* Joseph *was produced on January 18, 1931, presumably written at the end of that month*]

Dear Boris,

Greetings for the New Year, and I wish you every kind of happiness. Forgive me for not answering your last letter at once—I have been very busy. The people here are shit. [The Russian phrase used is obscene.] Nobody understands anything. Their heads are empty unless they see something resembling a sandwich. All this is a new and unexpected experience for me. So as not to feel lonely I have bought myself a Willis Knight. It's delightful and has a marvelous engine. . . .

I wish you were here with me. We could have done a splendid *Joseph* together. What came out of me is not bad, it would be something to put on for Lifar at the Opéra. Then we might have worked on it together.

I wish you all the best, I kiss you. And I send you every good wish for future happiness.

Yours,
Georges

Best wishes to Bébé [Bérard].

Balanchine returned to Paris with his car and some earrings for Danilova. They were made of lapis lazuli. "In Russia," she wrote, "we didn't consider [that stone] precious—there it was a building material, like marble. . . . I had been expecting diamonds, so I threw the earrings in his face. 'But they are so pretty,' he said. . . . Mr. Dmitriev took me aside and said, 'You see. . . . He will never, never give you the security you are looking for.' And I thought, He doesn't love me. . . . "

By February, Balanchine was back in London, turning out numbers for Sir Oswald Stoll's variety shows at the Coliseum. He also worked on the *Cochran Revue* of 1931, which, like its predecessor, was tried out in Manchester. Stoll owned the Alhambra as well as the Coliseum, and after Balanchine had devised some little Mendelssohn, Chopin and Johann Strauss ballets for that theater, he wrote again to Kochno.

Elisabeth House
Devonshire Street
Portland Place
W.1
[*undated, but probably
April or May 1931*]

Dear Boris,

I'm writing to you from hospital. I'm laid up with a boil on my backside. Giordano [Diaghilev's former doctor] operated on me, and he comes back every day to change the dressings. Thank God, it's much better now, but it was very painful. Thank you for your note. It was very sweet, and I don't think many people are lucky enough to get letters like that. We shall meet in Paris, that's certain. The Alhambra is closing down in May forever. Fate has probably decided all this to help me, for I can't think how I could go on like this, and the closing of the Alhambra will let me out of a lot of [uncongenial] work.

But the one thing that cheers me up is the thought of that game of tennis with you. Give my affectionate greetings to sweet, pretty Bébé.

Looking forward to seeing you again.

Yours,
G. B.

Danilova had taken a job in a musical, *Waltzes from Vienna.* She wrote to Balanchine that she thought it would be better if they went their own ways, because "life was separating us." After a long delay a letter came saying that if she wanted to leave him, she should do exactly as she pleased.

·   ·   ·

IT WAS on his return to Paris that Balanchine discovered the three young dancers whom he was to make famous as the "baby ballerinas": Tatiana Riabouchinska, a pupil of Kchessinskaya, and Tamara Toumanova and Irina Baronova, two precocious fourteen-year-olds whom he found in the school of Olga Preobrajenska. That winter, René Blum invited him to work for the newly formed Ballets de Monte-Carlo. Thus the year 1932 began, as other years had begun in the days of Diaghilev, with Balanchine grinding out dances for the Monte Carlo opera productions. He worked on eighteen before the end of March—and Toumanova was in *Turandot*. April brought the ballet season, and Balanchine created, on libretti by Kochno, *Cotillon*, *La Concurrence* and *Le Bourgeois Gentilhomme*.

Unfortunately, the Blum company was gradually being taken over by the scheming Cossack Vassili Vosskrezensky, who called himself Colonel de Basil. Balanchine's contract expired on May 4, but his new ballets were so successful there was every reason to count on its being picked up. It was not, however. The following letter from Balanchine to Kochno, written from Monte Carlo during the summer holidays of 1932, throws some light on the situation:

> [*undated, but probably*
> *August or September 1932*]

Dear — you-who-hang-about-the-streets-of-Toulon-at-night-and-go-to-bullfights-instead-of-getting-to-work-creating-new-ballets-of-genius — Boris,

Firstly, secondly and thirdly, I proclaim to you as follows. According to rumors coming from Branitskaya [a member of the Ballets de Monte-Carlo] at Juan-les-Pins, which are confirmed by the total silence of Basil, there will be no choreographer [in the Ballets de Monte-Carlo] this year. This is what Vladimir Pavlovich [Dmitriev] and I had decided was certainly the case on the day before we had the news from Juan-les-Pins. Then Hilda Sokolova told me that Woizikovsky [her boyfriend] had signed a contract with Basil as *répétiteur*. That makes it clear that they won't need either you or me [because Woizikovsky was famous for his detailed memory of the old Diaghilev repertory, and it was obviously de

Basil's policy to revive old ballets]. In my opinion now is the moment to start work in earnest. Return to Paris as soon as possible, and I will follow you soon. I do not want to be in Paris right now, as it might look as if I were there hoping to be signed up by them. I have decided to arrive in Paris about the 5th. Then we'll start looking for work together.

Meanwhile, I kiss you,

Yours,

G. Balanchivadze

De Basil engaged not only Woizikovsky but Léonide Massine, who was more famous than Balanchine both as dancer and as choreographer.

Nevertheless, as soon as he was back in Paris, Balanchine began to work with Kochno to create a new repertory, ignoring the fact that they had no backer, company or theater. Their faith was rewarded. The Vicomtesse de Noailles produced a rich young Englishman, Edward James, and he hired the Théâtre des Champs-Elysées for the season. The "work in earnest" that Balanchine had urged in his letter to Kochno turned into a company called Les Ballets 1933. A condition of James's patronage was the inclusion in the company of his Viennese wife, Tilly Losch, the exponent of a fluid style of dance, who often appeared in trailing draperies to mask her limited technique. Balanchine took this in his stride. Besides, he had brought Tamara Toumanova with him from the Monte Carlo company and she was a sufficient source of inspiration to carry him forward.

Chapter 3

···

HOW KIRSTEIN BROUGHT

BALANCHINE TO AMERICA:

JUNE – DECEMBER 1933

O N June 2, 1933, a twenty-six-year-old American arrived in Paris on a curious quest. At a time when the United States was struggling to emerge from the Great Depression, Lincoln Kirstein had the incredible idea that his country could be regenerated by classical ballet. A democrat might well consider it the most effete—if not depraved—of all the arts, but Kirstein's prophetic soul discerned in ballet's order and ritual an ennobling discipline for his troubled republic. This self-appointed ambassador, six feet three inches tall, with a short-cropped bullet head, piercing eyes and jutting nose, hoped to import from the French capital a choreographer who would enlarge the scope of life in a continent where civilization was still, in some ways, immature.

Kirstein's German grandfather, a lens grinder in Jena, had fled with his wife to America after the Revolution of 1848. They were nonpracticing Jews and pre-Marxian atheists. Their son Louis became a traveling salesman who sold spectacles and married a rich girl, Rose Stein, whose family made its fortune mass-producing uniforms for the Union Army during the Civil War. The second child and first son of this couple, Lincoln Edward Kirstein, was born in Rochester on May 4, 1907. About five years later the Kirsteins moved to Boston, where Louis joined the Filene brothers and eventually became a partner in their department store, today the most famous in the city.

Starting in 1922, young Lincoln Kirstein visited London and Europe with his mother every summer. In 1927, after entering Harvard, he and several friends founded a quarterly journal, *The Hound & Horn;* and in the following year, with his classmates John Walker III and Edward Warburg, he started the Harvard Society for Contemporary Art, putting on exhibitions of not only Picasso, Braque, Matisse and Derain, but also the Americans Alexander Calder, Buckminster Fuller and Gaston Lachaise.

The three young men had already had endless discussions on whether there was any way to be a constructive art patron, since all three received constant requests for financial help from artist friends. Kirstein, who had become enamored of the Diaghilev company's performances on his annual trips to Europe, suggested that the answer might lie in ballet, where the dancer, the musician, the painter and the poet could create a coordinated artistic effort and share in the box-office receipts. Overlooking the obvious pitfalls—the cost of new productions and the complicated labor-union rules, which varied from state to state—they agreed that this was a promising solution to the patronage problem, and various undertakings were begun.

In the four years before his mission to Paris in 1933, Kirstein had contributed dance reviews to *The Hound & Horn.* The "modern" dance recitalist Mary Wigman called forth his derision, but, he wrote, "there is actually in this country a potential audience for dancers"; "Americans appreciate good dancing"; and "perhaps it is not too much to hope that next year [i.e., 1932] the League of Composers [who had presented, under Leopold Stokowski, an amateurish production of Prokofiev's ballet *Le Pas d'acier* with the Philadelphia Orchestra Association] will give us Stravinsky's 'Apollo, Leader of the Muses' in the wonderful choreography of Balanchine—a masterpiece of classical dancing brought up to date. . . ."

After graduating from Harvard in 1930, Kirstein and Warburg had continued with their plans to found an American ballet. They concluded that the first necessities were to establish a school and to persuade the best available Russian choreographer to come over and be its director. To broaden his understanding of the field, Kirstein got in touch with Michel Fokine, who, embittered but not impoverished, was living on Riverside Drive in New York City, and took ballet lessons from him. "I know Fokine thinks I'm ridiculous," he wrote in his diary. "I only want to learn the structure of his teaching, but he thinks I'm a sort of mad millionaire (like Ida Rubinstein) who dreams of dancing. Do I want to start an 'American ballet'? I do, but of course this sounds crazy."

Another acquaintance on whom Kirstein counted for an introduction to the mysterious world of ballet was Romola Nijinsky, who came to New York to raise funds for her husband's care in an insane asylum, or, she dared to hope, for his cure. Even before Kirstein entered Harvard, she had agreed to collaborate with him on a life of Nijinsky, and Kirstein tried (with his father's help) to keep her in a semblance of luxury. She was fascinating, unscrupulous and ungrateful.

When he arrived in Paris in 1933, Kirstein half expected to find Romola there, and hoped to continue work with her on their book; but she was in Holland, burying a dead girl friend. Her absence made it harder for him to "insert himself" into the ballet scene.

At that time, the demigods of Paris society were Jean Cocteau and Serge Lifar. Kirstein noticed that shop-window mannequins were modeled in their likenesses. *Le Tout-Paris* went to the ballet. As Dolly Wilde, the niece of Oscar, remarked to him, "It was where one most wanted to be."

Lifar was at the Opéra; the Ballets Russes de Monte-Carlo under Colonel de Basil and Massine was about to open at the Châtelet; Edward James's Ballets 1933 under Balanchine and Kochno would soon be playing at the Champs-Elysées. Like Paris, the Trojan prince, the young American would have the opportunity to sit in judgment and award his apple. His education progressed at lightning pace, his discernment growing sharper from day to day.

On June 2, at the Opéra, Kirstein watched Lifar in his own ballet *Jeunesse,* and although he found the work poor and "post-Balanchine," Lifar's dancing was "a great pleasure." On the seventh, "in a fever of excitement," he saw Les Ballets 1933 at the Champs-Elysées: "First *Mozartiana* with dull decor but nice costumes and very lovely choreography, witty and Mozartian, by Balanchine. . . . *The Seven Deadly Sins* by Kurt Weill to his familiar haunting delayed music. . . . *Songes* of Milhaud and Derain very dull and boring. . . . Too much choreography by one man for Balanchine to do perfectly. He's no Fokine. . . ."

On the ninth, Kirstein attended a morning rehearsal of *Errante* and *Fastes* at the Champs-Elysées. In the former, he thought Toumanova fine but disliked Tilly Losch's music-hall style of movement and found the work nothing more than an animated Tchelitchev painting (which was doubtless what the designer intended) with some "nice passages." He reflected on Balanchine's tragic ideas of the relation between men and women—"always broken up by someone jumping in between"—and watched the twenty-nine-year-old choreographer holding the arms of a little girl, teaching her a passage of mime and placing her correctly.

That evening Kirstein went to the Châtelet. He thought Massine's *Les Matelots* "nearly as charming as ever, except for the part once danced by Lifar, who sat in the front row." He next saw Massine's new *Présages* for the first time. This was the choreographer's daring attempt to arrange a ballet to a well-known symphony, Tchaikovsky's Fifth. The third ballet of the evening, *Le Beau Danube,* had been revived not only because Strauss waltzes were always popular, but because it provided Massine and Danilova with striking roles as the Hussar and the Street Dancer. "*Beau Danube,*" wrote Kirstein, "a continued enchantment. Massine's sly, steady grace, his lovely style . . . We all went up to Fouquet's on the Champs-Elysées . . . [and] drank to [Diaghilev's] immortal memory."

On June 14, at the Opéra, Kirstein watched Lifar in Nijinsky's great role in *Le Spectre de la rose.* Back at the Châtelet for another program by the Monte-Carlo Ballet on June 16, he saw Fokine's *Les Sylphides,* which he enjoyed "beyond anything." *Scuola di ballo,* a new Massine comedy of manners, had "moments of great charm." As for the year-old *Jeux d'enfants,* which Kochno had devised to Bizet's score, then invited Massine to arrange and Miró to design, Kirstein thought it one of the best ballets he had ever seen, with "wonderful turns" by Baronova.

These entries in his diary reveal that even after three weeks in Paris he had not made up his mind which choreographer or performer could best preach and teach the classical ballet to Americans. By the end of his first week, he had written of Balanchine: "He's no Fokine." Yet even if Fokine had created a perfect work in *Les Sylphides,* Kirstein must have known that he had done very little of interest for twenty years. If Kirstein had had unlimited means, which he did not—he was always worried about running short of cash in Paris—he might well have decided that Massine was the right man. But Massine was thirty-eight and apparently settled as the artistic director of a successful company. Balanchine's position seemed less secure, since Edward James was unaccountable.

Just as Kirstein's Paris ballet going drew to a close, and he decided that his only hope lay with Romola Nijinsky, who was still in Holland, he managed to talk to some of the characters in the ballet world. On June 21 he was taken to see Tchelitchev. On June 24 he called on Lifar, "and soon found he would be no use to me at all." Later that morning, he tracked down Boris Kochno. Kochno was leaving for London the next day, but wrote a letter of introduction to Diaghilev's old colleague Walter Nouvel, who warned Kirstein against Romola Nijinsky and gave him the address of Alexandre Benois. He went again to call on Tchelitchev, who made him wince by saying "toe-dancing was over," but who confirmed that Balanchine was a great man.

Kirstein stayed three nights in Holland. Romola Nijinsky was preoccupied with the tomb of her girl friend, but she had done some work on the biography of Nijinsky. Kirstein went on to England with the understanding that she would follow shortly. The oddest thing about his stay in Holland—to judge from his diary— is that he agreed with a "tall, attractive Russian boy, Igor Schwezoff," whom he met in a dance school, that "Balanchine was much less serious than Massine."

In London, the balletomane and critic Arnold Haskell entertained Tamara Toumanova, her mother and Kirstein at a Soho restaurant. Tamara adored Balanchine, and perhaps it was something she said that finally convinced Kirstein of Balanchine's exceptional qualities as a choreographer and as a man.

After telegraphing twice for money, Romola Nijinsky arrived in London on July 7. When, on the following day, Kirstein took her to see Les Ballets 1933 perform *Mozartiana, Songes* and *Errante,* he was on tenterhooks that she might not enjoy Balanchine's ballets as much as he did. That night, because Roman Jasinsky had a splinter in his knee, Balanchine danced *Songes* in his place. According to Jasinsky, he jumped high, turned in the air and landed like a cat. After the ballet, Romola sent a note to the choreographer, and he came out to speak to her. At the Savoy Theatre, Lincoln Kirstein was introduced to George Balanchine at last.

Four days later, at the house in Chelsea that Kirk Askew, the New York art dealer, had taken for the summer, he met him again. Kirstein wrote in his diary, "Balanchine was wholly charming, and I had a long and satisfactory talk with him. . . ."

In their first conversation, thanks to Kirstein's probing questions and Balanchine's apparent eagerness to impart his views, they covered a lot of ground. By rearranging the order of Kirstein's notes, it is possible to see Balanchine's survey of the state of ballet over the past century. The Romantic period? "Taglioni would be an inferior technician to any well-trained modern dancer—always on demi-pointes." Technique had not been developed in her day; and "the music then was all tinkly with small intervals." "The conventions of Petipa" would be "intolerable for the present" and "should be restudied." Mime, the old style of gesture language, was antiquated. "Fokine can no longer compose [ballets]. He can teach, sitting down, but no one can compose long after they forget the actual movement . . . in their own bodies."

Of Massine, Balanchine observed that he had been trained, when choreographing *Le Tricorne,* by Felix, a Spanish dancer, and "the Spanish style had left its strong imprint on him." He added, "He is unmusical. The Fifth Symphony of Tchaikovsky explains itself; it needs no accompaniment in dancing. It is, to start with, a masterpiece."

Lifar had once been modest, now "you couldn't tell him a thing"; he hated competition, and even tried to reduce Spessiva's role in *Giselle.*

Were systems of notation useful? Not really. It was all a question of memory. "Nijinsky notated *Le Sacre du printemps,* but couldn't remember it the next week." Balanchine had learned a notation system in school, but he could compose only with flesh and blood before him, like a sculptor with clay, "putting off here, taking on there." Ballets were like butterflies—"a breath, a memory, then gone. One must never revive anything."

A cynical historian, reading Kirstein's report in his diary, might judge that Balanchine saw in the American, three years younger than himself, a possible savior, and that he was at some pains to discredit rival choreographers. Yet Balanchine was neither calculating nor particularly malicious: confident of his own musical and choreographic powers, he was never shy about expressing in private his views on the limitations of others, and he was convinced that the whole history of ballet was a process of evolution of which he was the most advanced specimen. Luckily, Kirstein's instinct told him that this might well be true.

At the end of their conversation, Balanchine said that he wanted to go to America. He told Kirstein that "with twenty girls and five men he could do wonders; particularly in the classical style or his adaptation of it." Kirstein found Balanchine "intense, convinced, not desperate but without hope." That night he dreamed about him.

During the next ten days there were three more conversations with him; these took place against a background of fantastic scandals and intrigues. Balanchine had to cope with the vagaries of Edward James, the temperament of Lifar, the rivalry between Toumanova and Tilly Losch and rows over money, programs and casting. Edward James had undertaken to back Les Ballets 1933 largely in the hope of making his difficult wife, Tilly, love him more. But she snubbed him, took possession of one of his London houses (while he stayed at the Ritz) and went about telling everybody that he was homosexual. Although the company had been a magnet for *Le Tout-Paris,* Les Ballets 1933 enjoyed no such fashionable triumph in London. Then Lifar and James sued each other. Arnold Haskell, who adored Toumanova, thought she should be with de Basil at the Alhambra, but she would work only for Balanchine.

On July 16, Balanchine had luncheon with Kirstein and Romola Nijinsky. His simple, well-cut English clothes, had he but known it, were bound to prejudice Kirstein in his favor.

Balanchine was charming in a fresh grey flannel suit. . . . We talked in detail about the possibility of an American Ballet. . . . He wants to bring Jasinsky and Toumanova with him; and with little Tamara, Maman has to come. We got frightfully excited about it all. . . . Romola and I could give lectures with the dancers demonstrating. Balanchine says it has always been his dream. He would give up everything to come. Madame

Toumanova could cook for them. . . . Romola will give us all the rights to Vaslav's ballets: systems of notation and education . . .

Kirstein's college friend A. Everett Austin, Jr., known as Chick, was the director of the Wadsworth Atheneum, in Hartford, Connecticut, and was just completing a new wing for that museum which included a theater. Kirstein had envisaged this home of the Muses, within a hundred miles of New York City, as a base for his enterprise. There Balanchine could train young Americans and, when they were ready, present them in the theater. That afternoon he wrote a long letter to Austin, beginning, "This will be the most important letter I will ever write to you. . . . My pen burns my hand as I write. . . . We have a real chance to have an American ballet within 3 years time. . . ." He set out his ideas in some detail, and concluded, "I won't be able to hear from you for a week—but I won't sleep till I do. Just say *Proceed* or *Impossible.* . . . We have the future in our hands."

By July 19, Balanchine's situation in London had become worse than ever, but he spent from three in the afternoon till seven with Kirstein and Romola, "talking about the American project." He said he wanted to stage *Apollon* at once, and proposed starting a class for *maîtres de ballet.* He was frank about his state of health, acknowledged that he had suffered from tuberculosis in the thigh, and said that one of his lungs was all right, the other not. Two days later, he left for Paris on his way to take a holiday in southwestern France.

On July 26, Kirstein received an enthusiastic cable from Chick Austin, and on August 6 a second with the promise of $3,000 from Paul Cooley, James Thrall Soby, Philip Johnson, Edward Warburg and himself. On the eighth, Austin cabled again: "Go ahead, iron-clad contract necessary, beginning October 15. What about entry permits? Can you settle as much as possible before leaving? Bring photos, publicity. Museum willing. Can't wait."

On August 9, Kirstein left for Paris and found that Balanchine would be driving back from the south in two days' time. Austin cabled: "Guaranteed living expenses up to $6,ooo." Still Kirstein worried. Perhaps Toumanova and Jasinsky would not want to come. Or Toumanova's mother might object. And what should be done about Balanchine's friend Dmitriev? In the program of Les Ballets 1933, Dmitriev had been credited with the *"Direction Administrative."* Balanchine had arranged that any profits that accrued from the James enterprise should be divided in three parts among Kochno, Dmitriev and himself; but, of course, there were none.

When, on August 11, Kirstein met Balanchine and Dmitriev in Paris, it became clear that the choreographer took Dmitriev's advice on all matters of business, which bored him, and that it was with Dmitriev that agreements must be made. Kirstein recorded in his diary their first conversation:

[Dmitriev] at once began to make stipulations about money and the control of the future company. He rejected the suggestion that Balanchine go alone to New York to sum up the situation, insisting that the choreographer must arrive with his dancers to demonstrate his work. Balanchine had had other offers, but after the Edward James catastrophe he could accept nothing without proper guarantees; and he needed a longer rest.

After the three men had picked up Dmitriev's girl friend, the dancer Kyra Blanc, they continued the conversation at a restaurant in Montparnasse. Balanchine was apprehensive that an American tour of de Basil's Monte Carlo Ballet, if unsuccessful, would ruin their chances. De Basil was suing Balanchine for taking Toumanova away from the Ballets Russes, while still presenting two of his ballets, but Toumanova and Jasinsky, who usually demanded large salaries, would give up anything to be with him. Dmitriev inquired about the cost of living in the United States.

On the next day, Dmitriev laid down a principle that determined the future of ballet in the United States of America: *"The whole project fell into two basic parts: a school and a ballet company."*

Kirstein wrote in his diary:

Dmitriev said not even to talk about ballets produced for three or four months after starting. They need $3,000 to guarantee passage back and forth for five of them, and let Toumanova's taxi-driver father have a little money to live on. They can all live for $1,000 a month in Hartford. I should hope they could. . . . I told them that the tragic style and *le style noble* were unknown in America. Dmitriev said anything was possible in mixing strains, that the pure Kentucky horse crossed with a Russian strain was better than either virgin breed. They agreed that what was needed more than anything was the insistence on a school. . . . [Piotr] Vladimirov, a miraculous technician, could be brought over to teach the perfection class. Preobrajenska to teach women and children. Even to import Baronova and other dancers. . . . We parted amiably, shaking hands, hoping to see each other in America.

Kirstein was told at the American consulate that the granting of emigration passports to the Russians was entirely a question of money to guarantee their livelihood. If he could get $10,000, it would be easy. He wrote to Balanchine, who had gone to Monte Carlo, "asking him as nicely as possible what the hell Dmitriev did, anyway; was he . . . necessary?"

Kirstein's first visits on his return to America were to Hartford and to Edward Warburg. On September 8, the latter promised Kirstein $5,000 a year for the ballet.

A series of cables went back and forth:

Balanchine in Monte Carlo to Kirstein in New York
29 AUGUST 1933
AWAIT YOUR DECISION   PRESENCE DMITRIEW IS NECESSARY

Kirstein in New York to Balanchine in Monte Carlo
29 AUGUST 1933
LANDED ONLY YESTERDAY   SURE COMPLETE SUCCESS   MINOR DIF-
FICULTIES CLEARED BY SEPTEMBER FIFTEENTH   WILL TRY SEND MONEY
LLOYDS BEFORE   HARTFORD SUPERB EQUIPMENT   GREAT ENTHU-
SIASM

Kirstein in New York to Balanchine in Monte Carlo
30 AUGUST 1933
WOULD YOU OBJECT USE NAME FOKINE STOKOWSKI SPONSORING? . . .

Balanchine in Monte Carlo to Kirstein in New York
1 SEPTEMBER 1933
MUST USE NEW NAME   AWAIT MY ARRIVAL   WAITING UNTIL FIF-
TEENTH VISAS AND MONEY   WILL SAIL IMMEDIATELY

Kirstein in New York to Balanchine in Monte Carlo
5 SEPTEMBER 1933
LETTERS MONEY SENT PARIS TODAY ARRIVE THIRTEENTH

Kirstein in New York to Balanchine in Paris
13[?] SEPTEMBER 1933
WORRIED BY NOT HEARING FROM YOU   PLEASE UNDERSTAND YOUR
PRESENCE WITH DMITRIEW IS OUR ONLY INTEREST   ALL OTHER CONSID-
ERATIONS SECONDARY . . .

Balanchine in Paris to Kirstein in New York
14 SEPTEMBER 1933 [*delivered on the 15th*]
LETTER AND THREE THOUSAND DOLLARS RECEIVED   OWING NECESSITY
DISCUSSING ON THE SPOT ALL ARRANGEMENTS TO BE MADE AND PRESENCE
JASINSKY AND TOUMANOVA NOT INDISPENSABLE PRESENTLY [*at present*]
DECIDED SAIL ALONE WITH MY ASSISTANT DMITRIEW   CABLE AGREE-
MENT

Kirstein in New York to Balanchine in Paris
15 SEPTEMBER 1933
TOUMANOVA JASINSKY ABSOLUTELY NECESSARY TO DEMONSTRATE WHAT
YOU HAVE DONE   MONEY RAISED ON THAT UNDERSTANDING   THEY
CAN FOLLOW LATER IF NECESSARY BUT PREFER ARRIVAL TOGETHER WITH
YOU   SAIL AT ONCE BUT PLEASE UNDERSTAND I AM RESPONSIBLE TO
CITY OF HARTFORD FOR PRESENCE OF ALL FIVE WHO ARE EAGERLY
AWAITED

Balanchine in Paris to Kirstein in New York
   15 SEPTEMBER 1933 [*delivered on the 16th*]
[*in French*] CABLE RECEIVED   PRESENCE NOW TOUMANOVA JASINSKY
ABSOLUTELY UNNECESSARY SINCE AMERICAN DANCERS WILL NOT BE
READY FOR THE BALLETS TO BE CREATED IN YOUR SCHOOL   PREFER
SAVE EXPENSE JASINSKY TOUMANOVA AND MOTHER AND REPLACE THEM
BY FIRST CLASS TEACHER LIKE VLADIMIROV   I UNDERSTOOD THERE WAS
A PLACE TO START SCHOOL AND PREPARE AMERICAN DANCERS   I SUG-
GEST VLADIMIROV DMITRIEW AND I LEAVE IMMEDIATELY   IF YOU PRE-
FER SUGGEST YOU COME IMMEDIATELY TO PARIS OR THAT I LEAVE ALONE
FOR NEW YORK TO SORT EVERYTHING OUT   PLEASE REASSURE YOUR
FRIENDS THREE THOUSAND DOLLARS HELD IN TRUST PENDING YOUR
DECISION

Kirstein in New York to Balanchine in Paris
   16 SEPTEMBER 1933
EXTREMELY DIFFICULT TO EXPLAIN BY CABLE   PREFER YOU WOULD
SAIL ALONE AT ONCE   WHEN YOU HAVE TALKED TO ME YOU ARE AT
PERFECT LIBERTY TO SEND FOR VLADIMIROV DMITRIEW   YOUR PRES-
ENCE WHOLLY NECESSARY TO UNDERSTAND AMERICAN SITUATION
HAVE PERFECT CONFIDENCE IN ALL YOU DO

Balanchine in Paris to Kirstein in New York
   18 SEPTEMBER 1933 [*received on the 19th*]
DMITRIEW LEAVING WITH ME   I WILL PAY HIS EXPENSES   PLEASE ASK
AMERICAN CONSUL PARIS PERMANENT VISAS AS WITH TEMPORARY VISAS
WILL EXPERIENCE GREAT INCONVENIENCE   CABLE

Kirstein in New York to Balanchine in Paris
   25 SEPTEMBER 1933
HAVE SENT CONSUL ONE YEAR CONTRACT AS REQUIRED . . . IN CONTRACT
WE STATE YOU AND DMITRIEW ALONE PAID FIVE HUNDRED DOLLARS PER
MONTH BUT WE HAVE ALSO MONEY FOR OTHERS   HOPE YOU UNDER-
STAND THIS DOES NOT PREVENT OBTAINING VLADIMIROV TOUMANOVA
LATER . . .

Kirstein in New York to Balanchine in Paris

27 SEPTEMBER 1933

MONTE CARLO BALLET DEFINITELY IN NEW YORK NOVEMBER FIF-
TEENTH   DO YOU CONSIDER IT DESIRABLE TO OBTAIN TOUMANOVA FOR
YOUR SCHOOL AFTER SHE FULFILS PRESENT ENGAGEMENTS WITH BASIL?

Dmitriev and Balanchine in Paris to Kirstein in New York

10 OCTOBER 1933

SAILING OLYMPIC   WOULD BE VERY MUCH OBLIGED IF COMMUNICATE
TAMARA GEVA OUR ARRIVAL

The most startling of these cables is that of September 14, in
which Balanchine declared that Toumanova and Jasinsky were
"not indispensable." This change of heart threw Kirstein into
despair. He had felt all along that he must have something to *show*
Austin and his confederates in Hartford, not to mention Warburg
and other potential backers. What more perfect exhibit than the
beautiful Toumanova, marvelous technician that she was, executing, with her partner, Balanchine's choreography? She was to
inspire the youth of America and attract them to the new school
and the new company. Kirstein felt he had been let down, and that
he was responsible for $3,000 being sent under false pretenses.
But the situation was more difficult than he realized.

After the disastrous winding-up of Les Ballets 1933 in London,
Tamara Toumanova had gone to Normandy, leaving her parents
in Paris. Balanchine had told her she would be going with him to
America, and Dmitriev, whom neither she nor her mother liked,
instructed her to do nothing without consulting him. She was aware
that Balanchine allowed himself to be led by Dmitriev: "He hated
scandals and said yes to everything." When she returned to Paris,
she took classes with Preobrajenska and waited for something to
happen. All this time—indeed, since July 4—the Ballets Russes
de Monte-Carlo had been playing at the Alhambra in London; their
success was so great that their season was continually being extended (and eventually lasted until November 4). In Paris

Toumanova received a telephone call from de Basil: he said he was just back from Monte Carlo, where he had seen Balanchine, who had sent her a message. The last time Tamara had set eyes on de Basil was in a French courtroom, just before the Paris opening of Les Ballets 1933, when he had sued her for leaving his company along with Balanchine. With the consent of her parents, she called on de Basil, who embraced her as if nothing had happened. He told her that Balanchine wished her to rejoin the Ballets de Monte-Carlo in London. He would see her there, as he was returning to de Basil's company himself. The only true word in all this was that Balanchine was indeed in Monte Carlo. Tamara packed in a hurry. She and her mother crossed the Channel next day. At the Redcourt Hotel, they met Nina Verchinina and her sister, Olga Morosova, and asked, "Has Balanchine arrived?" As Nina exchanged glances with Olga, Tamara realized in a flash that she had been tricked. So Toumanova rejoined de Basil's company "with" as she said in an interview, "a stone in my heart." She danced in Balanchine's ballet *La Concurrence* on September 13.

Balanchine and Dmitriev had heard in Monte Carlo that Toumanova was back in London. No doubt they thought she had betrayed them. For several days they could not decide how to break the news to Kirstein. Without Toumanova, the whole deal might be off! Sometime between the ninth and the fourteenth of September they returned to Paris. When Kirstein cabled that he was worried by their silence, they felt obliged to reply; but they were not frank with him. Instead of saying, "Toumanova has let us down," they cabled that she and Jasinsky were "not indispensable." Poor Jasinsky had placed high hopes on his future in America. In London, Dmitriev had withheld half his weekly salary; when James offered him a year's contract for a new company he hoped to form around Tilly Losch, he refused out of loyalty to Balanchine and faith in Kirstein's project. He had spent all his savings in Monte Carlo, and now he was callously abandoned. Dmitriev said he could spare him only two hundred francs. (Jasinsky was saved from starvation by Lifar two months later.)

. . .

ALTHOUGH many Europeans thought of America as El Dorado, it is surprising that both Balanchine and Dmitriev saw in the inexperienced twenty-six-year-old Kirstein the fulfillment of their hopes. Even if Balanchine had long nursed romantic dreams about America and its possibilities, even if he loved American movies, jazz and the challenge of Western frontiers, Dmitriev might easily have put him off Kirstein's plan. He could well have objected that Kirstein had no company to dance Balanchine's ballets; that although he must have rich friends, he seemed to have little money of his own; that while Balanchine had solid offers from Denmark and from Ida Rubinstein, it was ten-to-one that Kirstein's Hartford project would founder (and in fact *did* founder), so that they would find themselves stranded in a far land where the name of Balanchine carried no weight. Dmitriev might have said all this and more; but he did not. It is clear that both he and Balanchine trusted Kirstein and were convinced that he offered a new beginning. Dmitriev saw himself, rightly, as it turned out, as an essential part of the perilous American venture, an agent and bodyguard to Balanchine, a mentor to Kirstein—quite aside from the fact that he needed to earn a living.

On September 16, the day Balanchine's next telegram arrived, Kirstein reconciled himself to using only American dancers from the very start of his enterprise. It was not till September 27 that he learned from an article in the *New English Weekly* that Toumanova had rejoined de Basil. Perhaps it was to show that he knew Balanchine and Dmitriev had concealed this from him that he fired off the cable asking if they should not take steps to secure Toumanova's services "after she fulfils present engagements."

On October 1, the scaffolding was down in the new theater at Hartford, and Austin had a congressman working on Balanchine's and Dmitriev's visas. On the fourth, Kirstein had lunch with John Martin, dance critic of *The New York Times,* and asked him what he thought were the prospects for the school; Martin prophesied it would be "swamped with applicants." On the thirteenth, he spent an evening with Fokine, who "expressed contempt for Balanchivadze and Miassin, saying it was his innovation that had made them possible, but they themselves were no good."

.　.　.

KIRSTEIN longed for Balanchine to fall in love with New York at first sight. He had booked a suite with two bedrooms at the Barbizon Plaza, overlooking Central Park from the south. On October 17, he wrote:

Lunch with Mrs. Murray [of the *Hartford Times*], who failed to sell any ballet story to A.P. [Associated Press], and the Austins. . . . Afternoon pouring with rain. . . . Called up the White Star Line: *Olympic* docks at 5:30–6. When we got down to the dock, Eddie Warburg was very professional about what a damn bad landing they were making. The tide had swung the boat around. Finally, it was nosed in, and for the longest time I could find no friendly face on that boat. Had they come First Class or Third? I spotted Balanchine in Tourist, with Dmitriev. Amid the roar of unloading he told me they couldn't land; had to go to Ellis Island in the morning; must stay on the boat all night. I told Eddie, who disappeared. . . . Some months [*sic*] later Eddie emerged saying it was O.K. Use of Felix Warburg's magic name. They had only a six-months' visa with a year's contract. Hence the delay, plus a lousy Immigration Officer. When Balanchine was at the top of the gangway he had misplaced his landing-card. Eddie had a dinner date but waited for a picture, and he snapped one of all of us and left. . . . I took Balanchine and Dmitriev to the duplex apartment, $12 a day, at the Barbizon Plaza, 34th floor. They gasped at the view. . . .

Balanchine, not yet thirty, had been a subject of the czar; he had starved and frozen in revolutionary Russia; he had enjoyed the fleshpots of Western Europe. Now he had stepped, as it were, through the silver screen into a world he had known before only in movies—and was delighted to find himself there. None of the big steps of his life had been taken on his own initiative. He had entered the Ballet School at the suggestion of a stranger; Dmitriev had arranged his departure from Russia; Diaghilev had sought him out; Kirstein had lured him to America.

Other Russians had opened schools of classical ballet in the United States before him. Mikhail Mordkin (1881–1944), a one-time partner of Pavlova's, after touring in America before the war, settled in New York for good in 1924. Adolph Bolm (1884–1951), the original Chief Warrior in Fokine's *Polovtsian Dances,* had remained in America after the second tour of the Diaghilev Ballet in 1917 and founded a school in Chicago. Fokine had lived in New York since 1923. Louis Chalif (1876–1948), from Odessa, had the biggest school in New York, founded in 1907. He was the only one Kirstein and John Martin regarded as a possible rival.

During dinner at the hotel, and later at the Askews', where Kirstein had taken them in hopes of whiskey—for Prohibition was still in force—Dmitriev and Balanchine tried to put off talking business while Austin was present. Kirstein walked them down Park Avenue, through the Waldorf-Astoria, around Rockefeller Center, to Broadway. Back at the Barbizon Plaza, the three men talked till 2:00 A.M. As the two Russians gradually revealed that Copenhagen had asked for a Balanchine ballet, that Blum intended separating from de Basil and hoped Balanchine would join him, that Ida Rubinstein wanted Balanchine for two ballets, that he had been offered a teaching job at The Juilliard School and a show at Radio City Music Hall, Kirstein thought that Dmitriev was holding out for more money. Somewhat chilled, he said he knew "Balanchine's works and services were not to be named in mere figures, but if it was money he wanted he wouldn't be here."

Kirstein suggested that it might be a good idea to accept the Music Hall job, for Balanchine to see what it would be like and also to keep his hand in. But Balanchine said he was not interested; he would have to work nine hours a day at the school. They did not want to start in too small a way; they must plan many years ahead. An American dancer in France had told him that if he were working professionally in the United States he should get not less than $1,000 a week. Finally, the three "agreed to agree in principle, and try to find a form that was satisfactory upon which to proceed." It was an anticlimactic evening for the expectant Kirstein.

Next morning, Kirstein found Warburg getting on well with the new arrivals. When Warburg left, Balanchine remarked, "He is one swell guy." Kirstein took the two Russians to Tamara Geva's, then picked up John Martin, who was to interview Balanchine.

Geva and Balanchine had not met or corresponded for six years. She was now married to another expatriate Russian, Kapa Davidov, whose former wife, Lucia, was soon to become a close friend of Balanchine's. But Dmitriev referred to Tamara as his best friend and obviously adored her. Kirstein was struck by the awful thought that she might lure Balanchine to Broadway. Luckily neither Dmitriev nor Balanchine approved of her suggestion that they hire twenty chorus girls at twenty dollars a week, rehearse them for three months and then put on a sample show. That night Warburg and Kirstein took the two Russians to Radio City Music Hall, and Balanchine decided he could do nothing interesting on its stage. Standing on the top of the R.C.A. building, and looking across at the lighted tower of the General Electric building, he exclaimed in French "My God, they have ruins here already!"

On October 19, the three men drove to Hartford, where they found all the local dance teachers protesting against the importation of Russians. Balanchine and Dmitriev were, Kirstein reported, "well satisfied with the space for the practice halls . . . but when we came to the theater it was a big disappointment; there is no height; they couldn't use any scenery in it; the floor is too hard for dancing; the whole place is much too small." Dmitriev said it might do for school performances. Next day, after a meeting of indignant dance teachers had been faced, there was more talk of budgets. The three drove to Kirstein's parents' home in Springfield; and it was there that the realism of Dmitriev and the quick understanding of Kirstein carried the Grand Design a step nearer to its destined form:

Discussed the possibility of opening in New York . . . without the Hartford preliminaries, perhaps under the auspices of the Museum of Modern Art, which we thought Warburg could arrange, as [his family] had just given them $100,000. . . . As we talked it seemed better and better. Hartford faded into the background. Balanchine, silent, interested, played Negro spirituals . . . and Gilbert and Sullivan, never having heard of them before.

The birch trees, the dogs, the Kirsteins' white *dacha* made Dmitriev homesick. After talking to him at length, Mina Curtiss, Lincoln's sister, said she was sure the Russians could never work with Austin. Yet the three had to drive back to Hartford and face the man they were to disappoint. Because of their reluctance to prolong discussions, Austin became suspicious.

Within a week of Balanchine and Dmitriev's arrival in the United States, the whole Hartford project had been scrapped. It still remained to sort out the money question and to make peace with Austin, who was justifiably bitter. Meanwhile, a rumor that Kirstein's plans were "all washed-up" had spread around Manhattan. When Kirstein tried to introduce Balanchine to Philip Johnson at the Museum of Modern Art, Johnson fled: "The smell of failure terrified him." The idea of attaching the new School to the museum lasted no more than two days. Balanchine was filling in time by "freshening up on counterpoint and harmony with Nicolas Nabokov." Kirstein discovered for the first time his childish sense of humor: when he called Nabokov on the telephone Balanchine said, " 'Allo, this is President Roosevelt."

Convinced at last that the three of them would be better on their own, possibly with financial help from Warburg only—luckily Balanchine and Warburg liked each other at once—Kirstein began to draw up a prospectus for the ballet school and to look for premises.

When two dance companies from Europe appeared in New York, there was the danger that, if they were too good, they might diminish the prospects of Kirstein's enterprise, or, if they were terrible, give ballet a bad name. But Kirstein found the Ballet Jooss from Germany "without the slightest interest whatever" except for two or three good ideas in *The Green Table.* A troupe Serge Lifar brought to the Forrest Theater (which included Jasinsky) was a more serious threat because it was presenting Balanchine's *La Chatte,* and presenting it very badly. Balanchine was furious and said that Lifar could never use his ballets again.

The next day, Kirstein and Dmitriev found the right site for the School, at 637 Madison Avenue. They also signed papers to establish The American Ballet Incorporated, for which they hoped the School would one day provide dancers. The School and the company were to be two separate entities: students would pay to work under Balanchine in the former, but they would presumably have contracts and salaries to dance with the latter.

That autumn and winter the United States conditionally recognized Stalin's regime; Prohibition was abolished; and Fiorello La Guardia was elected mayor of New York City.

On November 10, Balanchine returned with a fever from Philadelphia, where he had been looking over Dorothie Littlefield's dance school. Kirstein escorted him to a doctor, then to be X-rayed. Back in their hotel room, Dmitriev took his temperature continually. Next day the fever was higher. Balanchine was ordered to the hospital and refused to go. The doctor said he should rest for six months and could not live more than ten years. Balanchine, looking green, announced he was going to die. On November 21 he was admitted to Presbyterian Hospital. When he was discharged, he went to stay with Mina Curtiss in Massachusetts, to rest and be fattened up, and he remained there for nearly a month. No clear diagnosis of his illness was ever offered, but Lucia Davidova has always been convinced that Mina Curtiss saved Balanchine's life.

During this anxious period, Balanchine was sometimes resentful of Dmitriev, who complained about him constantly to Kirstein. He told Kirstein that nine days after Balanchine had said he was going to live with Danilova, he went off to Italy with Diaghilev and never wrote her a line. He was "Georgian, heartless"; he had treated Geva and Danilova abominably and would think nothing of screwing his best friend's wife. Once, in 1931, he had telegraphed from London that he was ill and would arrive in Paris by car. He was twelve hours late. Danilova became hysterical, and Dmitriev went to the police. Balanchine walked in gaily at one in the morning. It had never occurred to him to send a telegram.

· · ·

Even in Balanchine's absence, plans for the School were moving ahead. Dancers showed up to inquire about it. Pierre Vladimirov, who had come over with Lifar, agreed to stay and teach for six months at least. Balanchine, much restored, returned from the country on December 21. On December 22, the School of American Ballet opened.

The same night de Basil's Ballets Russes de Monte-Carlo, presented by Sol Hurok, opened at the St. James Theater. Toumanova danced in *La Concurrence,* and Balanchine, who had never before watched his ballet from the front of the house, loved Derain's costumes but said he was "through forever with that kind of stuff" and had lots of new ideas.

Dmitriev considered that a state of war existed between the new School and the Ballets Russes de Monte-Carlo. He condemned Kirstein for having lunched with Haskell, and Warburg for having gone to Hurok's party on the previous evening; when Balanchine ran into some Monte Carlo dancers in the street, Dmitriev quickly separated him from them. Some, however, came to the School and were impressed. Meanwhile, more students were registering. By the end of the month, there were about twenty-two enrolled.

There was to be an impromptu party at the School on New Year's Eve. Eddie Warburg sent over a case of champagne and Kirstein borrowed some of his Persian rugs to make the place look "more inhabited." ". . . The boys brought fruit and nuts. Tilly Losch came early, and we all dressed up. There was plenty to drink and Balanchine banging on the piano. . . . Tamara Geva, George

Kirstein [Lincoln's younger brother] . . . and later Danilova and Jasinsky came in from the ballet." Dmitriev grew almost sentimental.

In that loft on Madison Avenue, at which Kirstein had arrived by such painful stages over the past seven months, four out of the five Russians who had left Leningrad for Germany nearly ten years before were present.

Chapter 4

....

THE SCHOOL ESTABLISHED:

FIRST SKETCH FOR A COMPANY,

JANUARY 1934 - APRIL 1937

I N 1934, the School of American Ballet depended for its existence on six people: Balanchine, Dmitriev, Warburg, Vladimirov, Dorothie Littlefield, whom Balanchine had enticed away from Philadelphia, and Lincoln Kirstein. Balanchine was, of course, the raison d'être of the whole enterprise; Dmitriev was the lawgiver, determined to put the School on a businesslike basis; Warburg was almost entirely responsible for finances until the School could pay its way; Vladimirov and Littlefield did most of the teaching; Kirstein concentrated on propaganda and public relations. A discovery of Dmitriev's, Eugenie Ouroussow, a Russian aristocrat in exile, was the secretary.

Nobody liked Dmitriev. He goaded Balanchine, Warburg and Kirstein, complained of each man behind his back to the other two, and staged appalling scenes. He kept meticulous accounts, and he had spy holes made in his office walls so that he could see that classes were being properly conducted. Yet Balanchine continued to tolerate him; and Kirstein, often rebellious, recognized the value—even the necessity—of Dmitriev's contribution. Either Dmitriev's bullying or Kirstein's persistence led Warburg to increase his subsidy; and when Lincoln's father, Louis Kirstein, eventually forked out, it was partly because of the impression Dmitriev had made on him.

Balanchine, with his Oriental patience, worked hard, but he also enjoyed life in his quiet way; Dmitriev brooded and planned; Warburg, who had many demands on his purse, blew hot and cold; Kirstein encouraged and educated the brighter students, lectured on the history of the dance, wrote articles and badgered his richer friends to give scholarships. During the first half of 1934 hope alternated with fear.

The curriculum of the School was rearranged so as to get more out of Vladimirov. After a long and nervous delay, Kirstein brought himself to ask his father for money and obtained $4,000. Dorothie Littlefield had brought with her from Philadelphia five students whose previous training Balanchine appreciated, and gradually others trickled in. In October 1933, Erick Hawkins, the first of the boys, had turned up. Colorado-born and Harvard-educated, he had studied under the expressionist "modern" dancer Harald Kreutzberg. On January 2, 1934, came Leda Anchutina, who was working at Radio City Music Hall. She had astonishing strength and technique, but she was tiny. Even when exercising at the barre, she used to rise on pointe as soon as Balanchine appeared, because of his known preference for tall dancers. Marie-Jeanne Pelus (who soon dropped her surname because no one could pronounce it correctly) enrolled on the following day. She was the only child of Italian and French immigrants, and although she was only fourteen, she had already tap-danced in public. January 4 brought William Dollar, a native of St. Louis, "the prize pupil of Fokine and Mordkin." Balanchine, who was proud of his newly acquired American slang, seemed delighted by his name: "William Dollar, Dollar Bill. Don't you get it? Isn't it perfect?" Gisella Caccialanza, born in San Diego, enrolled on January 14. She was a pupil of the great Italian teacher Enrico Cecchetti. Charles Laskey, Paul Haakon and Annabelle Lyon also registered at the School in January. In February, the two Christensen brothers arrived. Harold and Lewellyn Christensen, born in Brigham City, Utah, were of Danish ancestry and had been performing for years in vaudeville. Brooklyn-born Ruthanna Boris, trained at the Metropolitan Opera School by Rosina Galli, came in May. Elise Reiman, born of German parents in Terre Haute, Indiana, was studying dancing in California when her sister sent her an article about Balanchine by Kirstein that had appeared in *Vogue.* She headed straight for the School of American Ballet. Thus, from its earliest days, the School attracted pupils of various backgrounds, from various states, representative of many of the racial strains that have enriched the American heritage.

Sixteen-year-old Ruthanna Boris, whose father had been brought from the Caucasus as a baby and whose mother was Viennese, always remembered her first sight of Balanchine and Vladimirov. At the Metropolitan Opera School the girls wore pink tunics to below the knee, with little bows tied so their brassiere straps wouldn't show; and that is how she was dressed.

These two men came into the room. I thought one of them was Chinese. That was Mr. Balanchine. He sat down, and the other man, who had blue eyes and a towel over his shoulder, gave me a full barre. After we had done some center work, Balanchine got up and said, "Corner." He gave me a piqué arabesque, quatrième, two pirouettes, finish in quatrième. Now at the Metropolitan you didn't do two pirouettes till they thought you were ready. I could do one beautiful one. I said, "I don't do two." He said, "But you will, you see. You do, and you'll do two." I did piqué, quatrième, and he gave me a little pat on the behind, and I went round twice and fell down. He laughed and said, "You see? Two!" . . . I could pirouette from then on. Balanchine told me later, "You were so old-fashioned, so cute, so Italian, if you could not dance at all I would have taken you. I wanted to bite your knees."

Sooner or later these professionals and students would have to dance Balanchine's ballets in Balanchine's way, so he had begun from the start to teach them works he had done for Les Ballets 1933. The first was *Errante,* which made no severe technical demands. On the January day that Kirstein saw Balanchine actually rehearsing one of his creations in America, he was moved. A week later the more classical *Mozartiana,* to Tchaikovsky's Suite No. 4, had its first rehearsal.

On March 14, Balanchine began sketching out a ballet to Tchaikovsky's Serenade in C for string orchestra, op. 48. Kirstein has described how *Serenade* took shape:

Balanchine commenced by lining up as many girl students as chanced to be in class. . . . On that day there were seventeen. These he placed in military order according to height. One more, a tiny but brilliant dancer, Leda Anchutina, slipped into the studio late. . . . Her tardy entrance was incorporated. . . . At the next rehearsal only nine girls appeared; at another, only three. For them he arranged other portions of action, exactly as if they had been especially summoned and scheduled. The ballet was structured piecemeal, with no time wasted. . . . At the start no boys were available; when five eventually appeared, three were used.

All the same, Balanchine had his difficulties with the undisciplined American girls. Probably because of the delicate state of his lungs, he disliked raising his voice and had trained himself not to. One day, at a rehearsal of *Serenade* the dancers would not stop talking. He stood on a bench, clapped his hands, obtained silence and said, "If you don't care, why should I?" Then he went to the dressing room. An anxious deputation followed him to apologize.

In mid-May, Warburg's impatience to see the curtain go up overcame Balanchine's reluctance to show raw students perform-

ing in front of an audience. It was agreed that a private tryout
should take place outdoors, on the Warburg estate at White Plains.
Edward Warburg later wrote: "I convinced my long-suffering parents that what I wanted most for my twenty-sixth birthday on June
5, 1934 was to have these ballets performed in the garden of our
family place." The program was *Mozartiana, Dreams (Songes)*, in
remade Derain costumes with new music by George Antheil, and
Serenade. Because the noted stage designer Jo Mielziner had made
some designs for this that were unsatisfactory, the new work was
to be danced in an approximation of practice costume: white tarla-
tan skirts for the girls, and for the boys, shirts from a department
store. Instead of an orchestra, there was an upright piano in the
bushes.

On June 8, the day of the dress rehearsal, the dancers left in
a bus at three. According to Kirstein, "It got dark about nine and
Mozartiana looked heavenly. Very brilliant and the kids superb.
Vladimirov was in all of his states. When he saw Marie-Jeanne
Pelus in the [*Mozartiana*] Ave Verum, he said he was reminded of
the debut of Pavlova."

The weather was a problem on the next two evenings. On the
ninth, a drizzle wasted an hour and a half of rehearsal time.
Balanchine drove himself into town. When the sun came out,
Dmitriev looked in vain for him to rehearse *Mozartiana*. It started
to rain again. When Balanchine finally got back, he merely glanced
at the weather and said, "God's will be done." Guests began to
arrive. At 8:40 it was decided to give as much of the performance
as possible. And so, on June 10, the first version of *Serenade*, a
ballet that would become beloved throughout the world, was, somehow or other, performed at last. According to Warburg, the lawn
where Dmitriev's stage had been erected "never recovered from
the shock."

The School closed for the summer on July 6. The immediate
future had been taken care of. Warburg, who had already given
thousands, paid $6,000 more, two quarters' subsidy in advance,
plus $8,000 for costumes and scenery for future ballets. The

arrival of Doubrovska ensured that her husband, Vladimirov, would not run off to France.

Kirstein was still searching for American themes, musicians and painters "that would make the company more 'Buckeye' and less Russian." He explored the possibility of material in the early minstrel shows and even looked at the text of *Uncle Tom's Cabin* and various Western sagas. Not to be outdone, Warburg came up with a proposal for a ballet relating to college football life, "in the wonderful tradition of team photographs with the players posed like river gods on Greek pediments or posturing against the goalposts." The popular cartoonist John Held Jr. agreed to design the costumes and even managed to include Warburg's old hand-me-down raccoon coat. Kay Swift wrote the score. But Warburg always felt that the ballet was not as successful as it should have been because of Balanchine's steadfast refusal to see a real football game. "Look, Eddie," he protested, "I know already what those games are. I don't need to go. The main thing is that Kay Swift's music is excellent. It will be wonderful ballet." When *Alma Mater* finally premiered, it received mixed reviews, and in Warburg's opinion the weak spot was Balanchine's lack of understanding of the material.

So absolutely were Balanchine and Kirstein under the spell of Diaghilev's inspired window-dressing that it had not yet occurred to either of them that ballets might be presented without the aid of painters or stage designers. When Pavel Tchelitchev moved to America in the summer of 1934—Balanchine had already cabled him in Paris that he was looking forward to working with him—the painter announced in his Delphic way that ballet as they had known it was finished: the time had come to invent a new theatrical form. This is exactly what Balanchine would do; but in the ballets of his new era, painters were to play a negligible part.

·   ·   ·

A DOCTOR had told Balanchine that his state of health would permit him to make love, but that he should not kiss girls for fear of passing on tubercular germs. This injunction was presumably soon forgotten. There had been talk earlier in the year of an ash-blond "fiancée" called Miss Elmore. Then there were Heidi Vosseler and Holly Howard, who had come with Dorothie Littlefield from Philadelphia. All the girls in the School adored Balanchine. Ruth-anna Boris could not resist following him around. One day he felt obliged to tell her, "I'm not a god. When I pull the chain in the toilet, I do it for same reason as you."

Balanchine apparently never felt the need for close friendship with another man. He enjoyed company at the dinner table and liked conversation in small doses, but nothing deeper. Diaghilev's former rehearsal pianist, the plump, charming and amusing Nicolas ("Kolya") Kopeikine, was always on call to keep him company, and several other slaves attached themselves to him in the course of time. But both Dmitriev and Kirstein, who saw him daily for years on end, disclaimed the title of intimate friend. If he took a pretty girl out to dinner, it was unusual if he did not try to make love to her. Nevertheless, he had at least one close woman friend, apart from his professional colleagues. Lucia Davidova, the former wife of Tamara Geva's husband, was small and dark, with classical features; she was also extremely intelligent, loved music and flew airplanes. Balanchine confided in Lucia about all his love affairs, and they remained friends until his death. Another woman friend in the early American years was Nicolas Nabokov's first wife, born Princess Natalie (Natasha) Shakhovskoy. Although he confessed to her, too, the hopes and disappointments of his affairs, she later said she "never thought of him as a man."

On July 12, during the School vacation, while Kirstein was driving him to visit friends in Connecticut, Balanchine had something like an epileptic fit. He grew rigid, then violent and had to be restrained and taken to the hospital. Doctors spoke of meningitis or a brain tumor; and Kirstein foresaw the end of all his hopes. But since no one could agree on a diagnosis, no action was taken. Kirstein drove him back to New York, showed him the enlarged school, with which he was delighted, and took him to hear *Faust*.

After a few days in the country he returned, looking well and happy, for the reopening of the School on August 27. The mystery of the seizure was never solved.

.   .   .

THE SCHOOL'S new term began in an atmosphere of bitterness and bickering. Nothing Warburg, Kirstein or Balanchine did seemed right to Dmitriev, although he depended on them for his livelihood. At a dinner given by Kirstein's father, it was decided to form a separate production company, which would constitute no threat to the School's bank account. When this came into being, Warburg, who had put up the capital, was elected president. There was a row because Vladimirov had dismissed an adagio class half an hour early. Dorothie Littlefield decided to stop teaching because, she said, she wanted only to dance; but her pupils thought it was really because Balanchine did not return her love. Kirstein began to worry about who might one day succeed Balanchine, a problem that would occupy him for the next fifty years.

.   .   .

ONCE when Balanchine conducted the beginners' class, which he hated doing, he spent an hour teaching a boy of fourteen, who took only one lesson a week, how to do a glissade. Elise Reiman had been badly taught by Bolm and realized that she had "sickle feet," which Balanchine, who admired her, was determined to correct by improving her whole placement. When, as sometimes happened, he reduced a girl to tears, his insistence looked to Kirstein like sadism. Ruthanna Boris, however, was fascinated by Balanchine's patient, endless explorations of every possible way to do emboîtés or tendu, and she accepted them as a lesson in choreography.

Balanchine thought the Littlefield pupils from Philadelphia had good feet, but no speed. That, he told dancer Georgia Hiden some years later, was why he made *Serenade.* Lew Christensen, who had been a professional for seven years, thought he "really only learned how to dance from Balanchine and Vladimirov." "I did damn good tricks, nothing else. I knew the steps but not how to put them together."

Balanchine began to sketch out a "Valse romantique" for eighteen girls and three boys to the music of Glinka (which he used in a ballet many years later). The question arose of devising a new dramatic work to give variety to the nascent repertory, and Balanchine wanted to do something Hungarian about the lives of great virtuosi like Liszt or Paganini. Kirstein was allowed to think up the story of a ballet, which became *Transcendence*.

Chick Austin had offered to let the company give a performance at the Avery Memorial Theater in Hartford, and on the eve of the opening the situation was chaotic. The costumes for *Serenade* were awful; those for the principal girls had to be scrapped. Kirstein was pleased with John Held Jr.'s costumes for *Alma Mater* and Franklin Watkins's for *Transcendence,* but Tchelitchev, who had just arrived, described the latter as "*merde.*" Two new pianists played so badly that Balanchine was driven to ask desperately, "What is the use of choreography, or costumes, etcetera? The music is the most important thing."

At Hartford, the new company was billed for the first time as "The American Ballet." Unfortunately the Avery Memorial Theater proved unsuitable from every point of view. The stagehands were volunteer Trinity students, and the chief electrician had to keep darting back to the campus to give lectures. On the night of December 5, Kirstein and Austin helped Franklin Watkins paint the scenery.

On the morning of the sixth, there was a dress rehearsal and photo call. The house was not sold out. In the evening, the stage seemed to be on top of the fashionably dressed audience—which included George Gershwin and Salvador Dali; the dancers could be heard breathing, and their shoes squeaked. Because Austin had not unionized the theater, there were two pickets at the door throughout.

At the dress rehearsal of *Serenade* on December 7, the smallness of the stage became more evident than ever. The primitive lighting and the proximity of the stage to the audience cannot have flattered the ballet. In the evening, Warburg stood at the back and started the applause.

Hartford nevertheless gave Warburg the confidence to show the young troupe to a larger public. Through Alexander Merovitch, president of the Musical Art Management Corporation, the American Ballet was given a week's season at the Adelphi Theater in New York City. The orchestra would be conducted by Sandor Harmati, and Tamara Geva would appear as guest artist in *Errante*. But one more "closing ballet" was needed. *Transcendence*, with its hypnotic Monk (the Devil), its Witches and its final mazurkas, was a strong dramatic piece; *Errante* and *Serenade* were romantic in their different ways; *Mozartiana* was classical. The new ballet, *Reminiscence*, to music by Benjamin Godard, was therefore to be a brilliant divertissement, set in a ballroom.

While Warburg and Kirstein were happy to be able to show their young company on Broadway and to prove that their investments of time, trouble and money had produced dividends, Balanchine regarded the Adelphi season less as a triumphant demonstration than as a valuable experience for his dancers. He knew very well that the few polished artists in whom he took an interest were mixed with others less talented.

The opening program was *Serenade, Alma Mater, Errante* and *Reminiscence.* Balanchine had arranged only three movements of Tchaikovsky's Op. 48 for *Serenade*. (The Tema Russo finale would be added in 1941.) New costumes had been ordered from the French painter Jean Lurçat, and in a photograph they look fussy and hideous. Even apart from the missing movement, the ballet was not yet the wonderful work it became later. (There was, for instance, no man in the Waltz.) Perhaps only the opening Sonatina and the final Elegy were almost as we see them today.

Alma Mater went down well with the audience. They recognized that certain stock American characters had been absorbed for the first time into the exotic medium of ballet. *Errante* was, of course, more a painter's than a choreographer's ballet: the realization of one of Tchelitchev's visions, with fantastic lighting effects. *Reminiscence* was explained, or perhaps excused, in a long program note. The Balanchine who did not give a damn for what anyone thought had an alter ego who was expert at providing the public with what it was supposed to want. His occasional showy, childish or cloyingly sweet ballets were often to music of an obvious kind, which he professed to enjoy. Godard was not a composer to alarm a new public. Kirstein, who recognized *Reminiscence* for what it was, a venial sin more appropriate to de Basil's company than his own, felt all the more furious when John Martin of *The New York Times* wrote that while *Serenade* was "serviceable rather than inspired," *Reminiscence* was "the real hit of the evening." Samuel Chotzinoff in the *Post* wrote, "I liked this number best because I did not have to understand anything." *Serenade* was the least popular work. However, the acclaim the company had received persuaded Warburg to extend the week's season through March 15.

·   ·   ·

THE EXCURSION of the young dancers from the School on Madison Avenue into the harsh realities of performance on Broadway had an unexpected result. Edward Johnson, a former tenor and the new general manager of the Metropolitan Opera House, asked Balanchine to renovate the dance passages in their operas.

Lew Christensen, who was taking classes at the School, remembered how he heard the news. "Harold and I were out buying tickets at the Adelphi box office, and Lincoln and Balanchine came by and said, 'Would you like to join the company?' Balanchine said, 'I think I'm going to be ballet master at the Met. When that time happens we'd like to have you in the company.'" Christensen went back to vaudeville for a while "to get enough to eat." Then he, his brother Harold and Ruby Asquith, Harold's wife, decided they were finished with vaudeville forever, and Lew joined Balanchine.

There were changes at the School. Vladimirov had been replaced by Anatole Vilzak and his wife Ludmilla Schollar, both former dancers in the Maryinsky and Diaghilev companies. Marie-Jeanne later described how the students adored "the handsome and dashing" Vilzak, but resented his wife, who was ten years his senior and "jealous of him looking at his girls." Yet Schollar was the better teacher. The faculty had also been increased by Muriel Stuart, a former member of Pavlova's mainly British company, who had run a school in San Francisco and worked with modern dancers. She came to Kirstein with an introduction from Martha Graham, proved invaluable and remained with the School longer than any other teacher, finally retiring in 1984.

The Metropolitan Opera's engagement of the American Ballet was announced in the press on August 8, 1935. The first voice to be raised in opposition was John Martin's: "It is deeply to be regretted that once again American artists have been passed by for a high artistic post for which at least half a dozen of them are eminently fitted." He granted that Balanchine was "unusually inventive" and would "grace his new position," but the American Ballet was "still an apprentice group," and Lincoln Kirstein should "get to work starting an American Ballet [*sic*]."

Since the Metropolitan season did not begin until the autumn, the enthusiastic Merovitch had booked the American Ballet for a tour to be preceded by outdoor appearances at Lewisohn Stadium in New York and Robin Hood Dell in Philadelphia. The tour, which was supposed to cover sixty towns in ninety-eight days, opened on October 14 with two performances at the Greenwich High School, Greenwich, Connecticut, followed by one-night stands at Bridgeport and New Haven in Connecticut, Princeton, New Jersey, and Harrisburg and Scranton, Pennsylvania. At Scranton, Merovitch's road manager vanished. Warburg was summoned from New York. According to Anatole Chujoy, there had been no money to pay the orchestra, which, unlike the dancers at that time, was unionized; so the musicians walked out. Ruthanna Boris recalls that the company was summoned to a meeting in the Jermyn Hotel, Scranton, where Balanchine announced, "Dancers.

We have manager. We gave him sixty thousand dollars. He has gone and sixty thousand dollars with him. And you know that list you have, tour: we don't have. And bus is outside. Will you please go in bus to New York. Come to class tomorrow, and we will think what to do."

It was during this tour that Elise Reiman first noticed Balanchine's extraordinary calm in the face of disaster. "I remember a performance of *Reminiscence* . . . when I was in the wings waiting to go on in my part with Holly Howard, the Pas de Trois with Bill Dollar. The floor was like glass. Two people had already fallen, and a third fell right in front of Balanchine and me. Instead of getting furious, he leaned his elbow on the wall and said, 'They fall like snow.' He never got mad."

. . .

KIRSTEIN was happy to find himself and his company established at the Metropolitan Opera House in November, but Balanchine, who had worked in many European opera houses, was less impressed. Also, he clearly started off on the wrong foot with the opera company, or perhaps vice versa. Looking at the hereditary costumes for his first opera ballets, heavy with dust and history, he demanded that they be cleaned. His request was refused. A slur on the dignity of his dancers was the kind of thing that ruffled his serenity, for he knew that a girl must feel right in order to look right. It was the first hint of the antagonism of the Metropolitan's permanent staff. "They absolutely loathed us," Elise Reiman recalled.

Indeed, as long as the ballet was at the Metropolitan, the dancers' costumes were always the last to be made—and sometimes weren't finished. Edward Warburg remembers that one evening the girl who was to dance in *Carmen* found that she couldn't move in the costume provided for her. "Balanchine said, 'Eddie, go in your car up to the School and get any costume that was made for her and bring it back here. It doesn't make any difference if it is right for the occasion or not.' And so I did, and when I came back,

the stage doorman said, 'Hello, Mr. Warburg. What are you doing
with that dress?' I said, 'It's the costume of the girl who's got to
go on in the ballet twenty minutes from now. They can't use the
one that was made, so I brought this from the School.' And he said,
'O.K., Mr. Warburg, but put it under your coat. You have to have
a union truck to bring that into this place.' "

The opera season opened with *La Traviata* on December 16,
1935, and before it closed in June 1936 Balanchine had made
dances for thirteen operas. Thus began what Reiman has described
as "the three most hilarious years" of her life. She and the other
young people were astounded at what happened on the vast stage
of the opera house. To begin with, there was an overpowering smell
of garlic. Then, the noise was appalling. The prompter and the
chorus master were shouting above the music. The principal singers used to walk to the back of the stage when they were not
singing, clear their throats and spit. Most newspapers relied on
their music critics to cover such dancing as they thought worthy
of comment, and these gentlemen tended to resent Balanchine's
small innovations.

In *Aida* he inserted "genuine" Egyptian belly dances—and also
"genuine" Egyptian suntan, which the dancers had trouble wash-
ing off because their dressing room was on the floor above that of
the chorus, and the water "didn't get up to their tubs." In desperation the boys turned on the fire hose; the water overflowed into the
costume department, and Balanchine had a lot of explaining to do.

His Venusberg dances in *Tannhäuser* were inspired by Isadora
Duncan in her erotic vein. Even when one of his arrangements
scored a success with the public, it did not necessarily please the
authorities at the Met. Ruthanna Boris's solo in *Carmen* was much
applauded, and the dances in *Aida* stopped the show, but both
brought a reproof from Johnson's deputy Edward Ziegler. Opera
was singing, and the ballet should not have drawn attention to
itself. For Lew Christensen, who had to flirt with Rosa Ponselle,
the prima donna, in the tavern of Lillas Pastia, *Carmen* was an
ordeal. According to Kirstein, the great lady "refused to rehearse;

she was saving her voice. She sent her own dancing teacher to arrange her stage business with Lew; she would learn it all, somehow, 'later.' When they met for the first time onstage and commenced their routine, she seized a goblet of wine (grapefruit juice), quaffed a gulp, and tossed the rest in his face. Then she pulled down his head and smacked him full on the mouth. For six seconds they were locked. It seemed sincere. In the intermission he said: 'I thought she was trying to make me in front of God and everybody.' "

Among Balanchine's few supporters was Dorothy Kilgallen, the celebrated columnist of the *New York Evening Journal.* Miss Kilgallen wrote: "Mr. George Balanchine is the daring young man who lifted the Metropolitan Ballet out of its petticoats, gave it snake-hips, a dash of hi-di-hi. . . . He put a reptilian wiggle into the torsos of the 'Aida' chorus until the dowagers couldn't believe their lorgnettes." She quoted him as saying, "The critics don't know anything about dancing. . . . They like prima donnas. . . . They are like prima donnas."

Elise Reiman considered that Balanchine "gave the dancers things beyond their technical ability" so as to extend their powers. These dancers could also be grateful that they were earning a small salary for six months of the year. They were not paid during the recess from June to October.

During the first 1935–36 season at the Met, either *Reminiscence, Serenade, Mozartiana* or *Errante* was occasionally given on the same bill as *Hansel and Gretel* or *Cavalleria Rusticana* and *Pagliacci* or in "mixed concerts" of opera extracts and ballets. Then, because the Metropolitan's orchestra knew the music, Kirstein devised and Balanchine arranged dances to extracts from *Die Fledermaus* for a ballet called *The Bat,* which proved to be popular and was danced as a curtain raiser to operas.

In February 1936, Chick Austin commissioned Balanchine to do a ballet for the Hartford Festival. This was a *Serenata*—called *Magic* in honor of Austin, who was an accomplished magician—to an unidentified Mozart composition for eight instruments, with sets

by Tchelitchev. In it, Felia Doubrovska gave her last public performance. The Festival culminated in the Paper Ball on the last
night, in which, in costumes by Tchelitchev and to music by
Nicolas Nabokov, the three heads of the American Ballet—Balanchine, Kirstein and Warburg—appeared as beggars. The role obviously appealed to Balanchine, since almost forty years later he
again played one, this time with Jerome Robbins, in the Stravinsky
Festival of 1972.

Another interruption to Balanchine's work on operas—*Mignon,
Manon, La Juive* and *La Rondine*—in the early days of the year,
Die Meistersinger in February—was the invention of dances for the
Ziegfeld Follies, which had its premiere on January 30. The music
of the *Follies* was composed by Vernon Duke, who, under his
original name of Vladimir Dukelsky, had written *Zéphyr et Flore*
for Diaghilev in 1925; and the lyrics were by Ira Gershwin.

Even more interesting was the musical comedy *On Your Toes,*
which, after an out-of-town preview at the Shubert Theater in
Boston, opened in New York on April 11, 1936. This was Balanchine's first collaboration with Richard Rodgers and Lorenz Hart,
and with the producer Dwight Deere Wiman. The Eakins Press
Choreography describes it as "the first Broadway musical to credit
staged dances as choreography (a practice already customary in
Europe), as well as being the first musical in which the dances were
integrated into the plot, performed by dancers who were also
dramatic characters." The subject was the life of a Russian ballet
company. Monty Woolley played a caricature Diaghilev, and there
was a scene in which all the girl dancers, after taking class, went
up to kiss him. Balanchine suggested that the boys should kiss
him, too.

There was a spoof Oriental "Princess Zenobia Ballet" in the
style of Fokine's *Schéhérazade,* of which Brooks Atkinson, drama
critic of *The New York Times,* wrote: "Tamara Geva, who plays the
wicked ballerina, is so magnificent a mistress of the dance that she
can burlesque it with the authority of an artist on holiday." Geva
noticed that "the balcony caught on before the orchestra [stalls]."

"Slaughter on Tenth Avenue," a sensational number that occurred in Act II, Scene 4, was epoch-making. William Dollar assisted Balanchine in working it out, and Herbert Harper helped him with the tap dancing. Ray Bolger gave an unforgettable performance. Geva, in an interview with Nancy Reynolds, declared: "You bet it was a pretty good musical, a milestone. . . . 'Slaughter' . . . started off as a takeoff of Gypsy Rose Lee. I did a strip. . . . There was one moment when Ray Bolger and I were discovered at the bar. Then we started this love duet, and we had a bottle with us. The bottle passed from one hand to the other while we were dancing in such a way that [nobody] knew where the bottle was going. . . . George was a master of things like this."

After Geva was shot by the jealous Big Boss, a waiter passed a message to Ray Bolger that he, too, would be shot at the moment his dance finished. Then came Bolger's brilliantly frantic tap dance over tables and chairs, which, just as it seemed to be coming to an end, would be repeated "one more time" until the police arrived.

After the New York premiere, Balanchine was introduced at a Russian Easter party to a strikingly pretty blond nineteen-year-old who was a member of the Ballets Russes and had been given the name of Vera Zorina. She congratulated him, and her recollection of that first meeting was, "*He* was very nice, *I* was very nice, *it* was very nice."

∎ ∎ ∎

That spring, Kirstein, as well as Balanchine, launched out on a new line of his own. He decided to form a group of dancers called Ballet Caravan to tour during the summer recess. This would not only enable members of the American Ballet to earn a small living during the time the Metropolitan was closed; it would also give some of them an opportunity to try their hands at choreography.

The previous December, Tchelitchev had told Kirstein that he was prepared to design a production at the Metropolitan with Balanchine and the American Ballet. The work, on which Balanchine was happy to collaborate, and which the Metropolitan consented to stage as a curtain raiser to *Cavalleria Rusticana,* was Gluck's *Orpheus and Eurydice,* sung by singers in the pit and performed by dancers on the stage. At a house dedicated to "grand" opera, to revive *Orpheus* at all was almost an eccentricity: staging it *à la* Tchelitchev was asking for trouble. To ensure the cooperation of the Met, and so that the painter so admired by Balanchine, Kirstein and Warburg should have a free hand, Warburg undertook to pay for the production, which Kirstein was always to remember as a shining landmark in his life. Orpheus was danced by Lew Christensen, Eurydice by Daphne Vane and Amor by William Dollar.

"ORFEO BACK AT THE MET, BUT PROVES TRAVESTY" proclaimed the *New York World Telegram* the next day. The powerful Olin Downes found the production "absurd"; and in a summary of Balanchine's recent activities a few days later, he wrote, "Of the American Ballet as an element of operatic performance he [the critic] is obliged to speak in terms of great disappointment. In hardly a single instance have the ballets coincided with the operas of which they are a part." "The public liked it," Christensen explained, "but the critics thought it was awful. Of course, they thought everything Balanchine did was awful. . . . He had a hard time, a very hard time." The opera-ballet had only two performances.

In the winter of 1935–36, Stravinsky paid his second visit to the United States, conducting concerts and giving recitals with the violinist Samuel Dushkin. It was probably at the end of this tour, just before his return to France in April 1936, that he dined with Balanchine at his apartment. Lucia Davidova remembers the choreographer describing how he had cooked a delicious dinner and taken particular trouble to obtain two bottles of vintage claret, but Stravinsky arrived with two other bottles under his arm, saying that he had no faith in American wine and had brought his own.

Balanchine's admiration for Stravinsky was unbounded. Robert Craft wrote to me after the choreographer's death: "Igor Stravinsky was really a father figure to George, who several times took the trouble to fly to California to see Stravinsky, sometimes to weep on his shoulder." Stravinsky, for his part, appreciated Balanchine's musical understanding.

Either during the dinner or shortly afterward, Balanchine, Kirstein and Warburg decided to plan a "Stravinsky festival" at the Metropolitan, which would consist of a single program of three ballets by the master. A new work was to be commissioned, and the other two would be *Apollon* and *Le Baiser de la fée.* Balanchine asked merely for "a classical ballet," and on June 30, 1936, on his return to France from a South American tour, Stravinsky wrote to complain that he had not been given exact requirements. According to Kirstein, Malaieff, a friend of Stravinsky's son, came up with the idea of a poker game. The drama, such as it was, would depend on the Joker's ability to represent any card in the pack; but he would be defeated by a royal flush at the end.

In December 1936, the score of *The Card Party (Jeu de cartes)* was delivered to New York. Balanchine was fascinated by its rhythms as he tried out an adaptation of the score for the piano and spotted quotations from Rossini's *Barber of Seville,* as well as echoes of other composers. Stravinsky agreed to conduct the two-day, one-program "festival" in April, and Warburg decided to hire the New York Philharmonic, rather than use the Metropolitan's orchestra.

When Stravinsky arrived in New York at the end of March 1937, his busy choreographer was working on his third musical, *Babes in Arms,* again a Dwight Deere Wiman production with music and lyrics by Rodgers and Hart. "Peter's Journey," the Act II ballet in this, was a dream sequence, the first, it is said, to be included in a Broadway musical, so Balanchine had once again broken fresh ground.

Warburg had commissioned *The Card Party,* and he was beseiged by requests from friends to see the first rehearsal, at which Balanchine would set the choreography, so the rehearsal room at 637 Madison Avenue was jammed when Stravinsky came in, smiling and bowing to everyone. Warburg recalls that "he sat down at the piano and ran through a few little runs, and Balanchine came in looking like a dormouse and spoke to him in Russian. After a few exchanges, Balanchine sat down with his back to the mirrors, looked at the kids who were waiting for the great moment when all this would start, stared into space and finally said, 'You,' pointing to a tall girl. Then he pointed to the man who was usually her partner. 'You . . . arabesque.' So they both did an arabesque, and he had them facing each other—like bookends. After studying this carefully, he suddenly turned to them both and said, 'Scram.' The whole thing had been a false start."

Irene Sharaff had used the tarot pack of cards for her costume designs, but Stravinsky objected violently to them. Since his three "deals" were played as a possible real poker game, he wanted them to be easily recognizable to card players in the audience, and he insisted that the dancers resemble modern playing cards. Kirstein noticed that he also curbed Balanchine's prodigality of invention. "At the end of the first deal, where Balanchine had worked out a display of the dancers in a fan-like pattern to simulate cards held in the hand, Stravinsky decided . . . [that] instead of so much variety in the pictures he preferred a repetition of the most effective groupings. . . . On another occasion he composed some additional music to allow for a further development in the choreography."

In the days before music could be taped, the piano reductions to which dancers rehearsed and worked out their counts—which differed from the composer's counts—were often misleading. When a company rehearsed for the first time with an orchestra, usually on the day before the first performance, they were frequently baffled by unsuspected sonorities. Balanchine liked to make his own piano reductions, and as he worked on them he already had the sound of the full orchestra in his ears.

.   .   .

THERE had not been such a "Stravinsky evening" in the theater since the death of Diaghilev. Lew Christensen found that with

Balanchine's ballets "the character came out as the choreography developed, and a lot happened between the steps"—perhaps the most important things. "You don't just do a couple of pirouettes and walk off and spit on your hands. You work your way into it and work your way out of it." Although only one ballet was totally new, another had never been choreographed by Balanchine before, and, of course, his version of *Apollon* (as opposed to that of Bolm) had never been seen in America. The first American production of *Apollon Musagète*—as it was still called—was more of a landmark than either of the new ballets; and in the modest Christensen the role of Apollo had a great interpreter.

Memories of the Diaghilev production were still vivid in the minds of those who had admired Lifar's Apollo in Paris or London in 1928. Christensen was a totally different type of dancer both physically and temperamentally, and Balanchine took endless pains teaching him the role. Because the hero is onstage through-out and can rest only when he sits to watch the Muses' variations, Christensen found *Apollon* "a very difficult ballet." The coda was "so damned hard. It's like you're driving a team of horses, but you're in a plié with them dragging you back. . . . We used to get through it, but by that time your legs are tired and aching. And when finally . . . you have to climb this cliff . . . it's such a relief that it's like going to Heaven." Christensen discovered that Balanchine did not tell him much about his role. He was merely expected to learn the steps correctly; and the process of learning was a revelation.

He went through each detail with me, *over* and *over* and *over* again. That's how I learned how to do Balanchine technique. That's the reason I could do it kind of well, because he *really* worked on me. . . . I really got his style, his way of thinking. . . . Lifar didn't dance like I did. He danced more—easy. I danced hard, fast, sharp, quick. That's what Balanchine liked about it. I was wondering if he changed it for that one reason—if there was a change. I really don't know. He didn't say anything about it. There were some very fast pirouettes in it—which I'm sure Lifar didn't do . . . that was the hardest damn thing. I practiced that by the hour.

By a curious chance, Elise Reiman, who was to dance Terpsichore, had appeared, when hardly more than a child, in Adolph Bolm's version of *Apollon* at the Library of Congress in 1928. She remembered the old production as "stilted," and found Balanchine's a very different affair. She thought Christensen "stunning and beautiful" in his difficult variation.

Le Baiser de la fée, commissioned by Ida Rubinstein in 1928, was Stravinsky's homage to Tchaikovsky. Musical themes were taken from his piano pieces and songs, notably "None but the Lonely Heart," and Stravinsky read the theme of the composer and his Muse into Hans Christian Andersen's story of the Snow Maiden, whose kiss obliges the young man to leave his mortal bride on the eve of their marriage. Stravinsky, in *Expositions and Developments*, commented: "The fairy's kiss on the heel of the child is also the muse marking Tchaikovsky at his birth—though the muse did not claim Tchaikovsky at his wedding, as she did the young man in the ballet, but at the height of his powers."

Balanchine and his troupe came off better than Stravinsky with the critics, who were invited to the first performance on April 27, 1937. John Martin wrote, "The American Ballet covered itself with honor last night. . . . Balanchine has begun to depart from his previous absorption in seeking for strangeness and novelty. . . . *Apollon* . . . was produced for the Diaghileff Company in 1928, and it bears the strong impress of that period of artiness and affectation. . . . *The Card Party* has humorous episodes. . . . When it has been polished . . . it will be cute if nothing more. . . . *Le Baiser de la fée* is far and away the best work on the bill. . . . It is difficult to remember that the composer of these distinctly minor ballets is also the composer of *Petrushka* and *Les Noces*."

Samuel Chotzinoff in the *New York Evening Post* found that

"*Appolon* [*sic*] *Musagète* did not sound any better than when I heard it in Washington. Illustrating a dull scenario . . . it shows the celebrated composer in one of his numerous transition periods. . . . The choreography [of *Le Baiser de la fée*] . . . would do just as well for a drama by O'Neill or a tale by Kipling. . . . I suppose The American Ballet acquitted itself splendidly."

If the critics didn't like the music of Stravinsky, the Metropolitan Opera didn't like Balanchine; and Balanchine didn't like either the critics or the Met. It looked for a moment as if his future were to be on Broadway and Kirstein's on the road with Ballet Caravan.

Chapter 5

....

DIVERGING PATHS:

APRIL 1937 - MAY 1941

Althougн the American Ballet and the Metropolitan Opera did not part company until the end of the spring season in 1938, Balanchine and Kirstein had launched out in very different directions two months earlier.

Shortly after the Stravinsky Festival, Balanchine went to Hollywood at the invitation of Sam Goldwyn to make dances for a musical-comedy film, and he insisted that the dancers be recruited from the School of American Ballet. This led to a certain rivalry with Kirstein's Ballet Caravan. William Dollar, Gisella Caccialanza and Annabelle Lyon went with Balanchine, but Lew Christensen, Marie-Jeanne and Ruthanna Boris stayed with Kirstein. According to Christensen, who became ballet master of the touring company, "I stole some of Balanchine's leading dancers, so he refused to choreograph for us." Yet in private life Balanchine and Christensen got on very well: they both liked cowboy films and used to go off together to cheap movie houses on Forty-second Street. Years later, Christensen reflected, "Balanchine was a strange guy. A guy with his intellect, and he was in love with cowboy movies."

By mid-August 1937, Ballet Caravan had bookings into February 1938. This meant they could not fulfill commitments with the Metropolitan Opera, so they decided to divide themselves into two companies. Lincoln Kirstein also resigned from the board of the American Ballet that May, and both Balanchine and Warburg resigned from the board of the School.

Meanwhile, Balanchine was basking in the California sunshine. In May he and Kolya Kopeikine had traveled by train across the United States for the first time. When they arrived at the Los Angeles railroad station, they were met by reporters and photographers. Balanchine refused to smile because it was too early in the morning.

"But everyone smiles!"

"I am not everyone. I am myself. Only one person."

He and Kopeikine took a house together, and George Volodine, a dancer who was devoted to Balanchine, came to manage it for them.

According to Garson Kanin, who was working for Goldwyn at the time, Balanchine made an unprecedented impression on Hollywood, the press, the studio and Goldwyn himself. The producer was jealous of the fame of Flo Ziegfeld, the Broadway impresario, so he had hired George Gershwin, the scriptwriter Ben Hecht, Balanchine and his American Ballet to give the film *Goldwyn Follies* a touch of class. Kanin thought the last group "made Hollywood history." Their requirements and demands were unheard of. Kanin recalled:

Goldwyn cheerfully ordered a new building—a dance studio to be constructed on a faraway part of the lot. . . . He sensed . . . that he was somehow entertaining royalty. The American ballet had brought its own rehearsal musicians, wardrobe attendants, makeup artists. . . . No one except members of the company were allowed inside at any time, including Samuel Goldwyn.

For Balanchine, the lure of Goldwyn's film was its composer, George Gershwin, who unfortunately fell ill shortly after the choreographer arrived. Both Georges had hoped they might use the symphonic poem *An American in Paris.*

With his still somewhat limited English, Balanchine had trouble explaining his ideas to Goldwyn and the studio staff and understanding what they wanted from him. He therefore telegraphed to Natasha Nabokov, "Help me! Come!" Nicolas Nabokov was teaching at Worth University in upstate New York, and she was free. She came at once, accompanied by her small son.

During the first weeks in Hollywood, a period of discussions and experiments, Balanchine had time to make new acquaintances, and Mme. Nabokov witnessed several odd encounters. Balanchine had long been a fan of Fred Astaire and Ginger Rogers, and admired the latter's beauty. Muriel King, the Chanel of Hollywood, who dressed Ginger Rogers and Katharine Hepburn, doted on Balanchine and decided to stage a surprise meeting. She asked him to dinner. Balanchine told Natasha Nabokov, who was in on the secret, that he didn't want to go. She tried at once to persuade him. "I'm shy," he insisted. "You know I don't like parties." "But there's going to be a wonderful dessert!" At last he agreed. Before dinner Muriel King took him by the arm and led him into another room. "There's somebody who wants to meet you."

"Who, me?" he asked. (He could never imagine why anyone might want to meet him.)

Ginger Rogers sat waiting. Balanchine was speechless, but after she put him at his ease, they got on well. Later he went to visit her at the studio and found her on the set, reading a book. "What are you reading about?" he asked. "Christian Science." That was the end.

The composer George Antheil was in Hollywood and had established an intimate relationship with a young lady whom Balanchine also found attractive. "I'll introduce you," said Antheil. "But she's your friend—" "Take her," said Antheil generously. The girl came to supper, and Balanchine asked her what she would like to drink. "Vodka? Whiskey? Champagne?" "Do you have any beer?" she asked. Balanchine was startled. "Why do you like beer?" "Because it makes me belch so nicely."

Once again, it was the end.

According to Garson Kanin, for an entire month Balanchine refused to let Goldwyn know what was going on behind the closed doors of his ballet studio. Rumors spread. But Goldwyn admired Balanchine and persuaded himself that all the doubts and stories reported by the press were "free publicity." Nobody pointed out to him that the free publicity was costing about $15,000 a day.

· · ·

GOLDWYN had engaged as ballerina for his film the dancer Vera Zorina, whose real name was Brigitta Hartwig. She had been born in Berlin of a German father and a Norwegian mother, and had studied ballet in Berlin and London. When Dolin engaged her to act and dance in a play, her good looks made such an impression on Massine that he invited her to join the de Basil company. During the two years she remained with them, she danced leading roles in several ballets by Massine, with whom she had an unhappy romance. When he first made advances to her, she was sexually innocent, and she fell in love with him. Massine treated her abominably.

A London production of *On Your Toes* was scheduled, and her agent sent her to audition for Tamara Geva's role; she got it. Although both she and Jack Whiting were acclaimed in the leads, and although her personal success was such that she aroused the interest of the great British film producer Alexander Korda, the UFA studios in Berlin and a number of Hollywood scouts, *On Your Toes* was not a success in England. Her agent then arranged for her to make a screen test for Samuel Goldwyn's movie, and the movie magnate was delighted with the result. Zorina was dazzled by her prospects, but she was more interested in a stage career than in films, and she made conditions. Dwight Deere Wiman had spoken to her about a new musical, and she delayed signing with Goldwyn until she was certain that Balanchine, whose ballets she admired though she had met him only once, would be working on *Goldwyn Follies.* Then she agreed to a seven-year contract.

When he was told of Goldwyn's choice, Balanchine cabled Zorina at once, suggesting that she come to Hollywood to discuss their work even before her contract stipulated, promising that they would "have much fun."

On July 10, the day after Zorina's arrival, George Gershwin died of a brain tumor, aged thirty-eight. He had composed five songs for the movie, but no ballet music.

Production could not be held up. Balanchine suggested that Vernon Duke be hired to complete the score, and he was summoned from New York. Meanwhile, talks continued with Ira Gershwin, the composer's brother and librettist, about using *An American in Paris* for a ballet sequence. A week passed before Balanchine visited Zorina. During this time she was being scrutinized by Goldwyn's makeup department and hairdressers, who removed moles, filed and capped her teeth and tried to make her as close as possible to the Hollywood ideal. She also had driving lessons, while her mother went house-hunting in Beverly Hills. Eventually Balanchine called to ask her to dinner.

Zorina, whom nobody ever called anything but Brigitta to her face, now found herself plunged into a Russian "family," as she had been when she joined the Ballets Russes three years before. Although, as she wrote later, "Russians tend to be clannish, this group did not make me feel like an outsider but surrounded me with affection—mostly due to Balanchine, who was kind, gentle, and a marvelous host." Brigitta was soon learning from Balanchine in class as well as rehearsing the ballet he had prepared.

I could see [she wrote] how differently from Massine Balanchine approached choreography. His impulse was always music. . . . He played a piece over and over again on the piano until it was entirely in his head. He had no . . . diagrams with choreographic notes, but would begin choreographing by lightly touching a dancer's hand and telling him or her how or where to move. He was certain what he wanted but sometimes stood still as if listening to inner music. . . . There was no sign of rapid re-creation of preconceived ideas, but the unfolding of steps and patterns born at that moment. . . . For an inexperienced choreographer, it is a nightmare to have dancers standing around waiting to be told what the next step is. Or worse, trying choreographic sequences which do not work out. The dancers . . . sense very quickly whether a choreographer is in command or not. George's "silences" were always pregnant with ideas ready to emerge into action—with him it was merely a process of selection.

She was also impressed by Balanchine's instinctive understanding of how to make dance effective on the screen. Although he respected the technical expertise of the cameramen, sound men and cutters, he would quietly and "conspiratorially" point out the solution to a problem, never causing offense but rather a sense of relief. It was therefore galling that Goldwyn failed to appreciate the thought Balanchine had put into *An American in Paris.* The action was to take place in an International Exhibition. Sets representing the pavilions of different nations were erected all over a vast sound stage, and Balanchine timed every sequence with a stopwatch. When Goldwyn was shown the ballet, it annoyed him to find that he and his entourage were obliged, every few minutes, to have their chairs moved and walk to another set. He left in a huff and canceled the ballet, wasting four weeks of work.

Balanchine was disgusted and felt that drastic action was called for. Natasha Nabokov advised him to disappear for a few days; she would inform the studio that he had left for New York. He took a small apartment over a shop. The art director Richard Day came to North Fairfax Avenue to look for him. Natasha said he had gone

THE FAMILY: *1. Andrei, Georgi and Tamara Balanchivadze;*
2. Maria Nicolaievna von Almedingen, called Vassilieva after her mother; 3. Meliton
Antonovich Balanchivadze, drawn by his daughter, Tamara.

4

5

4. Andrei, Tamara and Georgi at a fair; 5. Maria Balanchivadze, Georgi and Tamara at the dacha in Finland, with a student friend and Andrei in the background.

6

6. *Georgi in Finland, aged about ten; his cropped hair suggests that he had already been accepted at the Maryinsky Ballet School.*

ApOLLO: *7. Serge Lifar and Alexandra Danilova in the original
Diaghilev production of* Apollon Musagète *(1928). 8. Edward Villella as Apollo (1950s).
9. Lew Christensen in the first American production (1937).*

10. Jacques d'Amboise and Suzanne Farrell (1960s). 11. Peter Martins and Suzanne Farrell (1970s). 12. Ib Andersen (1980s).

13

14

15

13. Balanchine and Vera Nemchinova in the pas de deux from Aurora's Wedding *(1925).*
14. Tamara Geva in Errante *(1935). 15. Tamara Toumanova in* Cotillon *(1936).*

16

17

16. *Balanchine's first American ballet,* Serenade, *shown
here in a later production.* 17. *Vera Zorina rehearsing with Balanchine
for the movie of* On Your Toes *(1939).*

George Platt Lynes

George Platt Lynes

George Platt Lynes

18

19

20

18. Concerto Barocco *(1941): Marie-Jeanne, William Dollar and Mary Jane Shea.* 19. *Todd Bolender as Phlegmatic in* The Four Temperaments *(1948).* 20. *Maria Tallchief and Francisco Moncion in* The Firebird *(1949).*

George Platt Lynes

21

George Platt Lynes

22

ORPHEUS: *21. Maria Tallchief and Edward Bigelow;*
22. Tanaquil Le Clercq and Nicholas Magallanes.

23

23. Tanaquil Le Clercq in La Valse *(1951).*

24

25

24. *Edward Villella and Karin von Aroldingen in* The Prodigal Son *(1960s).*
25. *Maria Tallchief and Jerome Robbins rehearsing for the
first revival of* The Prodigal Son *(1950).*

Martha Swope

26

Martha Swope

27

THE NUTCRACKER: *26. The Dance of the Snowflakes (1982); 27. Maria
Tallchief as the Sugar Plum Fairy (1954).*

28

29

28. *Edward Villella as Candy Cane (1960s); 29. Suzanne Farrell and
Peter Martins as the Sugar Plum Fairy and her Cavalier (1970s).*

Agon: *(1957): 30. Balanchine and Stravinsky at a rehearsal.*

31, 32, 33. *Diana Adams and Arthur Mitchell.*

Martha Swope

34

Martha Swope

35

LIEBSLIEDER WALZER (1960): 34. Jillana and Conrad Ludlow,
Violette Verdy and Nicholas Magallanes, Melissa Hayden and Jonathan Watts,
Diana Adams and William Carter; 35. Violette Verdy and Nicholas Magallanes,
with Robert Irving and Louise Sherman at the piano.

away. Day asked permission to search the house. It was given, but there was no sign of the missing choreographer.

Balanchine decided to disappear even farther from the studio; he, Brigitta, Mrs. Hartwig, Natasha, her son Ivan and Kopeikine set off in two cars for Lake Arrowhead in the San Bernardino Mountains. Brigitta's driving in the Los Angeles traffic made Balanchine nervous, and when it came to the hairpin bends of the climb he asked if he might take the wheel to try out her new car. The party arrived at dusk, and after dinner, Brigitta wrote, "George and I went for a long walk. It was a beautiful night, with the lake looking mysterious in the dark and huge pines silhouetted against the starlit sky."

Although Brigitta was spectacularly beautiful, with her wide-apart blue-gray eyes, delicate nose, wide, well-formed mouth, good complexion and golden hair, Balanchine had not fallen in love with her at first sight. It was Lake Arrowhead that cast the spell from which there would be no escape for the next decade.

In spite of the thirteen-year difference in age between them, Balanchine and Brigitta had their European backgrounds in common. He had spent part of his childhood in Finland, and she had been brought up by her Norwegian mother. Both had known the snow and darkness of northern winters; it was a bond between them in California. He told her about his training at the Imperial School; and she told him about her disastrous relationship with Massine. This experience had left her, as she confessed, "incapable of trusting and giving myself in love to another human being." Yet, she wrote "I knew George was good, and I felt safe and protected when we were together. He had something trustworthy and priestlike about him. . . . I called him my mystical Prince Myshkin and became utterly, completely, and totally devoted to him." But Brigitta could not respond to the intensity of George's love; and "he accepted that it would take time."

The quarrel with Goldwyn was patched up. The boss had learned his lesson and did not interfere again. What had been planned as the second ballet was rehearsed and filmed first. It had a *Romeo and Juliet* theme, with classical-dancing Montagues and tap-dancing Capulets in a battle of ballet versus modern. Goldwyn got a shock when he saw the laundry strung across the Italian street scene (a brilliant touch of Balanchine's), but when this was whisked away he enjoyed the "dance war" and admired the pas de deux of Zorina and William Dollar.

Balanchine's idea for the other new ballet was startling in 1937. The setting was a circular stage surrounded by columns with a pool in the middle and, at the back, the statue of a rearing white horse (suggested by Chirico's décor for *Le Bal*). As a poet stands musing, a water nymph rises slowly from the pool and dances on the water. Girls in ball gowns appear to dress her for the waltz. A storm interrupts the dancing, and the nymph is seen seated on the white horse, her draperies floating and gradually blown away by the wind. Finally she returns to the pool. As Balanchine described it to Brigitta, "Her body disappears . . . until only her head is visible, and then she puts her cheek on the water like pillow and she is gone like sun disappearing in ocean."

Brigitta was amazed. Even though she would emerge from the pool looking, as Balanchine said, *"very* sexy" with wet golden material clinging to her body, she knew she would have to hold her breath underwater; and the water would have to become glass for her to dance on it. Gregg Toland, the cameraman, was enthusiastic about Balanchine's idea of sinking the camera into a trough at floor level so as to make the dancers look taller. Many technical difficulties had to be overcome, but the ballet made film history.

In the course of the filming, Balanchine paid Goldwyn back for his rejection of *An American in Paris.* During one take, after Zorina had disappeared into the pool, Dollar, as the poet, ran to the brink to stare after her, lost his balance and fell in. When Goldwyn came to see the cut and edited ballet, Balanchine left the big splash tacked on at the end. Goldwyn loved the ballet, but "when the lights went up he remained silent, true to his promise of non-interference. . . . He could not afford to have his 'mad' choreographer walk off again in the middle of the production. He was greatly relieved when George confessed his joke and ran the real ending."

On September 1 Balanchine and Brigitta had a quarrel because he confessed to her about his girl friends. Next day he called her "as if nothing had happened" and took her to try on wigs. His work on *Goldwyn Follies* was completed on schedule, but he lingered a few days longer. Brigitta had to remain in Hollywood to film the "acting" part of her role. Some of this was shot at Lake Arrowhead, and Balanchine drove there with her. One night they cooked dinner together—"as if we were married," wrote Zorina, "and ate by candlelight." On October 10 it was "a very sad goodbye from George." Roses came with the message "I love you" in Norwegian. It was the title of Grieg's most sentimental song.

After Balanchine had gone, Brigitta did not lack admirers. Goldwyn himself had a crush on her. More important to Brigitta, however, was the question: Would Goldwyn allow her to make the Dwight Deere Wiman musical *I Married an Angel,* with music and lyrics by Rodgers and Hart?

· · ·

DURING the summer of 1937, Felix Warburg died, leaving an immense fund that his son Edward was to administer for charitable purposes. Edward, who had already resigned from the School, felt compelled to resign from the board of the American Ballet. He gave all the company's properties to Balanchine, who, since Kirstein was working with Ballet Caravan, found himself sole director of the American Ballet. Back from Hollywood with his dancers, he prepared to rehearse for the Metropolitan's 1937–38 season.

Toward the end of 1937 or early in 1938, *The New Yorker* magazine sent a reporter named Richard O. Boyer to the School to interview Lincoln Kirstein. He watched Vilzak holding a class and Balanchine conducting a rehearsal. When he settled down to write his piece, which was entitled "Americans Dance, Too," he had to decide on "an angle," and the line he took was to emphasize the utter strangeness of it all. It was extraordinary to him that a hairy man in a bathing suit could "flap his arms daintily in a gesture of flight." Balanchine was portrayed as exotic; and Kirstein, in a far from sunny mood, appeared about as optimistic as an Old Testament prophet.

"I have learned not to hope," Kirstein told him. "Transplanting ballet in this country is like trying to raise a palm tree in Dakota." He insisted that American ballet dancers were not inferior to European talent, but "the men especially are an unhappy crew, since most Americans become skittish at the mention of a male ballet dancer. . . . In short, there is something sinister about the whole business."

"Sinister" was the word of the afternoon. No need to ask against whom the following crack was directed: "Some choreographers fall in love with a ballerina and write ballets to bring out her best points. They're nothing but memorials to his private passion. It's really rather sinister." When Kirstein introduced him to Balanchine, Boyer noticed "the redness of his lips, his brown eyes, the sweep of his black hair. His voice was sleek, like a cat's purr." But, Boyer continued, "Kirstein drew me aside. 'He's Georgian,' " he whispered admiringly. 'Stalin's type. He seems as soft as silk, but he's like steel. He's really rather sinister.' "

Balanchine had another appointment, and the reporter watched Dollar rehearse *Apollon.* Then Holly Howard complained to him about the price of ballet shoes—four dollars a pair; and Christensen had a go at "goddam foreigners." "They make a couple of spins, and American audiences think they're wonderful." He alleged that foreign choreographers never explained to the dancer what their ballets were supposed to be about. This can only have been a dig at Balanchine.

· ■ ·

Brigitta arrived back in New York with her mother on Christmas Eve, and Balanchine gave her earrings from Cartier. Three days later he took her to *Tannhäuser* at the Metropolitan Opera.

In later years Brigitta grew angry at all the talk about Balanchine's unrequited love. "I loved George, and I love him to this day," she kept insisting. But there are different ways of loving, and she acknowledged in her autobiography that although Balanchine became increasingly important to her "as teacher, guide, mentor, and closest intimate friend" she could not "match" his love. Balanchine's soul was clearly no longer his own: his obsession was like that of the Scotsman for the Sylphide in the old ballet. He was almost bound to be dissatisfied. The mere fact that there are moments in such a relationship when the loved one's feelings do not coincide in perfect harmony with those of her lover gives him a sense of the impossibility of their union. He wants nothing less than everything; and his tragic intensity does not make him more attractive. Indeed, to be loved too much can be very annoying to the object of devotion. Brigitta confessed as much.

In the early days of 1938 Balanchine asked her to marry him, but she said, "Let's wait." This made him "depressed, jealous, withdrawn." They went together to see Thomas Dekker's *Shoemaker's Holiday* at the Mercury Theater, and the twenty-three-year-old Orson Welles, one of the new repertory company's founders, directors and actors, fell in love with Brigitta.

On February 18, after dining with Balanchine, Brigitta wrote in her diary, "George is *so* tragic, it is almost unbearable." On the nineteenth, *Goldwyn Follies* opened in New York to considerable acclaim. On the twentieth, the American Ballet danced *Serenade* at the Met, and Brigitta thought it was the best ballet she had ever seen. On the twenty-fifth, she wrote in her diary: "Dinner with Orson Welles. I have never enjoyed anything more. . . . How we talked and understood each other. He is wonderful and for the first time since Léonide [Massine] I felt my heart pounding and hands trembling."

Edward Johnson had decided to dispense with the services of the American Ballet, and he wrote on March 19, 1938, to inform Balanchine of the fact. On April 12, the day before *I Married an Angel* opened in New Haven, Balanchine gave his views on the subject to a journalist. "I try to adapt myself to the Metropolitan

. . . but no use. The tradition of the Metropolitan is bad ballet. I cannot do bad ballet . . . [Mr. Johnson] is an artist, and he could do fine things, but he has no wings. . . . These people [the rich box-holders] have been buying tickets . . . for many years and they have never seen the first act of any opera. If the Met wants new operas, let it take all the first acts and put them together in threes. . . ."

Happy to be back on the stage, Brigitta had enjoyed the rehearsals of *Angel* and considered her "dream part" of the angel married to a human "practically foolproof." Balanchine had thrown himself with childish enthusiasm into planning the winter "Honeymoon Ballet" for Brigitta, as if it were a fairy-tale honeymoon he himself was going to enjoy with her, or an excursion into their youth in the frozen north. The happy couple left in a sled "drawn by real huskies." Brigitta felt that George's love for her "spilled over" into this dance. Even so, there was at least one alarming stunt. Balanchine made her enter poised in arabesque on the boot of a roller skater, and the young man had difficulty in stopping dead at the footlights on cue. "George tried to reassure me. 'You see, will be okay. Looks fantastic—just like ice skating in St. Moritz.' " But when the roller-skating boy fell on top of Brigitta on the second night in New Haven, Balanchine decided to cut him out.

There was torrential rain on opening night in New York, but Brigitta received "thunderous applause." Balanchine himself had repainted her dressing room as a surprise.

During the post-opening supper party at Sardi's, Zorina's crowds of admirers made Balanchine jealous and miserable, and he talked nonsense. He was incapable of competition in a worldly milieu. Even before he came to America he had loved movies and been a fan of certain stars. Now he had created a movie star of his own, and this was the result.

Brooks Atkinson called the "Honeymoon Ballet" "the most entrancing ballet the musical comedy has staged for some time"; John Martin found that "George Balanchine has clinched his right to the title of the first choreographer of Broadway." *Angel* ran throughout the year and into 1939.

The American Ballet now existed only on paper, but Balanchine had employed some of its dancers in *Angel,* and he would use more in subsequent musicals. Still, if Zorina had not put everything else out of his mind, he might have been tempted by a gypsy life with Kirstein's touring troupe. Indeed, Ballet Caravan was getting more bookings, embarking on longer tours and enjoying greater success than ever before. In Chicago it launched the most popular of all its creations, Eugene Loring's *Billy the Kid,* with music by Aaron Copland. It was ballet's first Western.

On October 12, the Ballet Russe de Monte-Carlo opened in New York at the Metropolitan Opera House. This was not the de Basil company, but one directed by Massine and backed by Sergei Denham, which had split away from it. Its title, Ballet Russe in the singular, was a way of distinguishing it from the companies run by de Basil and Blum. Sol Hurok, who had sponsored six seasons of the de Basil Ballet and was now presenting Massine's troupe, had acquired almost a monopoly on ballet in America. The critics who had slighted Balanchine's young Americans were more favorable to the foreigners. Martin wrote of their "freshness."

Balanchine continued to work for Broadway. He arranged dances for *The Boys from Syracuse* (a musical version of Shakespeare's *Comedy of Errors*), which ran for 235 performances, and for *Great Lady,* with music by Frederick Loewe, which opened a week later and ran for only twenty. Since *I Married an Angel* was still playing, he could almost claim—not that he was given to claiming—that he had three shows running on Broadway simultaneously.

．　．　．

Mrs. Hartwig and Brigitta were living in an apartment at the Ritz Towers: thither Natasha Nabokov, Nicolas Kopeikine and George Volodine were bidden to a late Christmas Eve supper, which would take place after Brigitta had finished her second performance that day—for it was a Saturday. At midnight there was still no sign of her or of Balanchine; everyone waited, while Kopeikine played the piano. Charles Laskey, Brigitta's partner, lived on Staten Island, and he had arranged for Balanchine and Brigitta to be married there at the Borough Hall in St. George that morning. When the happy couple at last arrived at the Ritz Towers, no explanation was given. There was a distribution of Christmas presents. Balanchine's present to his beloved was an ermine coat, for which he had personally chosen every skin. Natasha was expecting Balanchine, who lived near her, to drive her home, but as the hours went by and he showed no sign of leaving the apartment, she fell back, mystified, on Kopeikine, who lived in quite a different direction. No announcement was made that night.

Balanchine's father had died in November 1937, so it was to his mother that he wrote, telling her of his marriage. The letter is undated.

11 East 77th Street
New York

Dear Mamoushka,

I want to give you the pleasure of a good piece of news. I got married a few days ago and am asking for your parental blessing. My wife is called Brigitta. She is of Norwegian origin. I enclose her photo.

She and I were making a film in Hollywood. She is a splendid dancer and actress. I talk to her in English and French, and at the moment she understands about two words of Russian. I shall gradually be sending you photographs of various theater and film productions.

The last film which I made in Hollywood with Brigitta was called "Goldwyn Follies." In it I made use of an entirely new principle of dancing on the screen. This summer I am again going to Hollywood to produce a new film. I do not think our films reach you in the Caucasus.

Mamoushka, ask Andryusha to have his ballet copied out, I shall send him whatever money is needed. And also send me Georgian herbs which are used in making *kharsho* [meat soup] and other dishes. And send me the recipe for making *satsivi* [cold chicken with walnuts]. I love cooking myself. And also I would like to have a black *boorka* [felt coat], write and tell me how much it will be and I shall send you the money.

Brigitta and I send our love to all of you and wish you health and happiness.

Your loving Georgi

Balanchine went to Florida after Christmas—Brigitta could not, of course, leave New York—and the press was not informed of their marriage until after his return in the middle of January 1939. A picture of Brigitta and Balanchine dancing at the Stork Club was captioned "Angel on Earth." Lucia Davidova had rented the Balanchines a self-contained duplex apartment with its own entrance on East Seventy-seventh Street. They left most of the furnishing to Mrs. Hartwig. Balanchine had his piano in the dining room. When a small fire broke out on February 23, the *New York Daily News* published a picture of the newly married pair, with the caption "Angel Fights Fire. Smoke got in her eyes. Vera Zorina, star of *I Married an Angel,* and husband George Balanchine examine damage. . . . The Angel helped firemen put out the blaze." To the press, Balanchine had become "Zorina's husband."

In February 1939, *I Married an Angel* closed in New York and went on a nationwide tour. It played six weeks in Chicago, and there Balanchine joined his wife for Russian Easter and spent three days cooking *pashka, kulich* and other delicacies in the small kitchen of a suite at the Ambassador Hotel. He and Brigitta also tried in vain to have their marriage ratified in a Catholic Church. There were obstacles. Brigitta, though a Catholic, was not yet an American citizen; George had been married in the Russian Orthodox Church under a Soviet régime but could produce no evidence that he was divorced. The priest waved them aside. They were too depressed ever again to attempt marriage in church. Besides, Balanchine did not want to create complications for Tamara Geva, who had married in America even before his arrival.

In May 1939, Balanchine and Brigitta set off for Hollywood to make a film of *On Your Toes* for Warner Brothers. Eddie Albert was Brigitta's partner in "Slaughter on Tenth Avenue," but since he could not tap, Balanchine "found a superb black tap dancer and cut back and forth from Eddie Albert's face and torso to the tap dancer's legs and feet [and] it worked perfectly." As soon as the film was completed, Goldwyn lent Zorina to Twentieth Century–Fox for another. *I Was an Adventuress* also needed a ballet, and in this Balanchine realized his ambition to conduct a symphony orchestra.

By the end of the year, Balanchine was working on a new musical, *Keep Off the Grass,* and Brigitta had signed up to appear in *Louisiana Purchase,* but the only new work of Balanchine's seen by the public in 1939 was the film of *On Your Toes.*

In November 1939, Massine's Ballet Russe de Monte-Carlo, which had been obliged to cancel its London summer date because of the outbreak of war, opened at the Metropolitan and broke all box-office records for ballet at the opera house.

Since 1938, plans had been afoot for the formation of a new American dance company, which was eventually to be called Ballet Theatre; during 1939 the planners were busier than ever. The organization started as an offshoot of the Mordkin Ballet, which had enjoyed an intermittent life since the 1920s. One of Mordkin's most talented pupils was Lucia Chase. Ballet Theatre came into being through the efforts of Mordkin; Rudolf Orthwine, a businessman; Richard Pleasant, an entrepreneur; and Lucia Chase. The fact that Chase had inherited a million dollars from her short-lived husband, Robert Ewing, was relevant. The temperamental Mordkin was an undistinguished choreographer, but Pleasant and Chase had grandiose ideas: they wanted the best of everything, whether it was Russian, English or American. Balanchine was asked to work for Ballet Theatre, but refused.

When "America's first Ballet Theatre," "the greatest ballets of all times, staged by Greatest Collaboration in Ballet History" opened at the Center Theater on January 11, 1940, William Dollar was in the first ballet, Fokine's *Les Sylphides,* and the second was *The Great American Goof* by Eugene Loring, who had been offered a higher salary than Ballet Caravan could afford to pay him. It cannot have been a happy moment for Kirstein. At the same time, he must have realized what such an assemblage of talent and famous names was costing someone—presumably Lucia Chase. (In fact, the three-week season, though moderately successful in such a huge theater, showed a loss of $200,000.) The *Herald Tribune* exulted: "Here at last is a solidly American organization."

Members of Ballet Caravan did manage to appear in the Ford Motor Company's five-hundred-seat theater at the New York World's Fair. "The pretext for our dancing [wrote Kirstein] was the fate of the horse in the path of the automobile. . . . We never knew whether or not it sold a dozen automobiles, but for six months it provided food and rent for forty dancers in . . . an eighteen-minute ballet entitled *A Thousand Times Neigh!* every hour on the hour, twelve times a day. . . ."

William Dollar did the choreography for this farcical ballet, and the company was divided into two groups led by Marie-Jeanne and Leda Anchutina. In September, Marie-Jeanne left to appear with the Ballet Russe. Balanchine, who had already staged his *Baiser de la fée* for that company during their March season, was going to revive three more of his old ballets in October, and he wanted Marie-Jeanne for *Serenade.*

The Tema Russo, which Balanchine now decided to add to *Serenade,* was written by Tchaikovsky as a lively finale, but the choreographer placed it third, so as to retain the Elegy as a dramatic ending. Like the much-worked plate of an etcher, Balanchine's first ballet conceived for American dancers, begun six years before, at last arrived at its more or less final "state," and "prints" could be made and sent throughout the world.

Although there are slow sculptural episodes in *Serenade*—the opening ritual, for example, where the strange band of women are aligned, as it appears, to salute the moon, and the beginning and end of the Elegy—the most novel and wonderful element of the work is the surge of Balanchine's corps de ballet. The unprecedented speed, first seen in the central allegro section of the Sonatina, with which the girls sweep across and twirl around is a quality that has been associated ever since with Balanchine and America. It necessitated a new kind of partnering—a pulling-apart or a brief "interlocking of horns." The girls rush at the boy, either to fling themselves away or to be thrown aside, or, after a series of wild twists, to collapse on the floor. Nowhere in the ballet is there a touch of sentiment, and the absence of a smile during the whole work is never noticed.

In the Ballet Russe *Serenade,* Marie-Jeanne danced all the ballerina roles, which in the past had been shared by two, three or more dancers, and in later years would be thus distributed again. Her appearance with the Ballet Russe was hailed by the press not as a defection from Kirstein's American company but as an accolade bestowed on a humble twenty-year-old native dancer by the illustrious Russians. In 1941 she was invited to judge a scholarship contest at the School of American Ballet. There were more than a hundred entrants; among the three successful ones was an eleven-year-old named Tanaquil Le Clercq.

·　·　·

HUROK booked Colonel de Basil's company, now known as the Original Ballet Russe, which had been touring Australia since the outbreak of war in Europe, to appear at the Fifty-first Street Theatre immediately after their rivals, the Ballet Russe de Monte-Carlo. Whether or not the public was confused as to which "Russian Ballet" they were seeing, they flocked in. Hurok therefore had two exotic troupes on his books. The Original Ballet Russe beat even the record run of its predecessors and did not close until January 12, 1941.

During this "bad time," Kirstein poured out articles denouncing Slav kitsch and exalting the classical tradition of which Balanchine—he hoped against hope—was the greatest exponent. And Balanchine continued to choreograph musical comedies.

In 1940, the year Balanchine became an American citizen, Balanchine built a house at Fort Salonga, near Northport, Long Island, as a surprise for Brigitta, and would not let her see it till it was finished. Someone gave it the awkward name of "Balarina," incorporating the first syllable of his surname with the last two of hers, but they never used it. Their first night there, the house was blessed in the Russian way with bread and salt. Brigitta drove herself home every night after the performance, but this did little to mitigate Balanchine's sense of the impossibility of love. He lost his self-possession and cried when he had dinner with friends. Natasha Nabokov scolded him. "You are even getting uglier," she said.

Only work could provide a temporary consolation. Stravinsky had moved to America in 1939; his first wife was dead, and he was married to Vera Sudeikina. In default of a new ballet score, there were several of his compositions not written expressly for dancing that Balanchine considered danceable. What ballerina could do justice to a new Stravinsky ballet?

Toumanova was back in New York with the de Basil company. One night, after she had danced *Swan Lake,* Balanchine brought Stravinsky and Tchelitchev to her dressing room. "We want to give you a present—a diamond necklace," he said. This was a figure of speech for a ballet to Stravinsky's Concerto in D for violin and orchestra. The dancers were to be only partly visible, like apparitions, dreams, insectlike or vegetable creatures appearing out of a dark night.

"Will people understand?" asked Balanchine.

Balustrade opened on January 22, 1941, with the composer conducting. To judge from old and rather bad photographs, the lovely designs of the genius Tchelitchev, not for the first time, ruined a ballet. Brigitta thought so. In retrospect, she wondered if it might have been while watching *Balustrade* that Balanchine first realized how much his ballets would benefit if costumes were reduced to the minimum. There were only three performances: presumably "people," including Hurok and Colonel de Basil, had *not* "understood."

John Martin wrote regretting that Russians, like Stravinsky, Tchelitchev and Balanchine, were replacing American artists. Brigitta was furious about this comment, but her husband told her never to give a critic the satisfaction of showing that he had hurt your feelings: "On the contrary, if you meet one, say, 'Ah, good evening! Nice to see you. Are you in New York?' " "People said he was indifferent," she wrote. "He was not. He simply hid his disappointment better than anyone I know."

.   .   .

BALANCHINE'S appearances at the School of American Ballet had been infrequent for several years, but the School was flourishing. Natalie Molostwoff, a beautiful Russian girl of Armenian descent, who was engaged in 1938 as assistant to Eugenie Ouroussow (and who was still with the School in 1987), witnessed the period of transition between 1938 and 1940. She found the tyranny of Dmitriev insupportable: "Everyone was happy till he arrived about midday, then the temperature dropped." In 1939, Kirstein had started negotiations to buy Dmitriev's shares; and, in 1940, the sad, unloved Russian was able to retire in comfortable circumstances and spend his winters in Florida. He was so sure that the School would collapse when he ceased to rule it that he gave Eugenie and Natalie letters of recommendation to serve as references when they looked for other jobs. Yet he continued loyal to the institution he had helped to found and of which he had been president. When Anatole Oboukhov arrived in New York with the de Basil Company in 1940, Dmitriev advised Kirstein to engage him because he was an excellent teacher. His advice was taken, and Oboukhov remained with the School until his death in 1962.

On March 30, 1941, a fire started in the upper story of the School. Balanchine, who was present, noticed the smell of burning at about six in the evening, then he, Muriel Stuart and Oboukhov saw smoke. He sent the students down into the street in their rehearsal clothes and called the Fire Department. Within an hour the blaze had been extinguished. When the scare was over, Balanchine said to Natalie Molostwoff, "I wouldn't have cared if it destroyed me."

Chapter 6

SOUTH AMERICAN ADVENTURE:

MAY - DECEMBER 1941

I N 1940, with a strong likelihood of America's being involved in a world war, the prospects of Balanchine's establishing a great American ballet company seemed more remote than ever. If he took stock after his first seven years in America, he must have admitted to himself that his achievement had not been impressive. *Serenade,* begun in 1934, had only recently achieved its final form—in a production for Massine's company. Neither *The Card Game* nor *Le Baiser de la fée* was of prime importance. *Balustrade* had not been liked. More and more young dancers were being well trained at the School he had founded, but he had no company of his own. Suddenly, in the early months of 1941, he had one.

Franklin D. Roosevelt, re-elected for a third term in November 1940, had appointed Kirstein's friend Nelson Rockefeller Coordinator of Inter-American Affairs, charged with facilitating commercial and cultural relations between the United States and other American republics. Thus it came about that Kirstein and Balanchine were given a subsidy to take a ballet company on tour in South America. The main advantage of the composite troupe, hurriedly assembled from the dancers of Ballet Caravan and former members of the American Ballet, was that, unlike the Ballet Russe de Monte-Carlo, with which Balanchine had lately been working, most of its artists—and certainly all its principals—had been students of the School on Madison Avenue. In this sense it was a "Balanchine company." The stars were Marie-Jeanne, Gisella Caccialanza, Lew Christensen and William Dollar. Spurred into action, Balanchine turned out two masterpieces to the music of Bach and Tchaikovsky—*Concerto Barocco* and *Ballet Imperial*—in no time at all.

Kirstein knew a good ballet when he saw one, and Balanchine's choreography for the Bach Double Violin Concerto in D minor and for Tchaikovsky's comparatively little-known Piano Concerto No. 2 in G major must have consoled him for the years of disappointment and separation.

The Tchaikovsky was the result of Balanchine and Kirstein's feeling that they should show a purely classical ballet in South America, if only to make clear that native North Americans were capable of dancing one. On consideration, the choreographer had decided not to revive *Giselle* or *Swan Lake,* but to invent a new display piece, using the vocabulary of Petipa. He would make a ballet without a story, thus allowing more time for dancing than in any one act of any long Petipa ballet. And although he chose a composition by Tchaikovsky, with whom Petipa worked, it was music of a kind to which Petipa never arranged dances—symphonic rather than divided into numbers. He would avoid all the "eccentricities" of his earlier works. Although only academic steps were to be employed, the corps de ballet, which in Petipa's day had merely formed a background to the soloists, would be an active participant, sharing the dances and technical demands made upon

the principals. Balanchine's choreography proved to be more challenging than any ever before devised for a corps de ballet.

Because no ballerina, with or without her partner, could dance
all the cadenzas in Tchaikovsky's concerto as well as join in the
ensembles, there would be a second ballerina, with two men to
support her, and two female demi-soloists, in addition to the corps
of sixteen girls and eight boys (including the two supporters).
Mstislav Dobouzhinsky, a former colleague of Diaghilev, designed
a grandiose setting. Columns and rich hangings in Maryinsky blue
and gold surmounted by an Imperial eagle framed a vista of the
Neva and the distant fortress of Peter and Paul.

One of the marvels of *Ballet Imperial*'s long and brilliant first
movement is the way in which the corps changes from formation
to formation; another is the impetuous dash of the two ballerinas'
entries. The second movement contains one of Balanchine's most
beautiful inventions. The boy partners ten girls, who extend behind him like two wings. As he lunges first to one side, then to the
other, the girls, who seem attached to his shoulders, swing to and
fro. Then, as he rushes first to the downstage right corner, then
downstage left, he is pulled back by all ten, who seem less like his
fellow human beings than like symptoms of some inner trouble
that assails him in waves. The third movement is festive, folk
accents echoing hints of a typical Russian dance in the music. In
its finale, all repeat the folk step ever faster, traveling from side
to side, and end suddenly kneeling.

．　■　．

WHILE Balanchine and his dancers traveled south, Brigitta set off
once more for Hollywood. It was five months before her husband
saw her again.

In the course of the South American tour, one of the dancers—
Georgia Hiden, an attractive and intelligent Virginian—struck up
a friendship with Balanchine and found him "great fun to be
with." She remembered many little details about him. For example, he had a habit of saying at the beginning of rehearsals, "Soon

as we start, soon as we finish!" A Cuban girl, Olga Suárez, corrected him: "That's not right. You should say, 'The sooner we start, the sooner we'll finish.'" Next day, however, Balanchine repeated, "Soon as we start—" and Olga exclaimed, "You'll *never* learn!"

The food in Rio was so good that after two days Balanchine issued an edict that the girls must skip a meal every now and then.

On June 25, the curtain went up on the first South American performance of the American Ballet, and *Serenade* was seen for the first time outside the United States. There stood the seventeen girls, eyes and right arms raised to the spotlights high up in the flies to stage right. Then came *Ballet Imperial,* performed for the first time in a real theater; it received eighteen curtain calls. Looking back more than forty years later, John Taras, by then a ballet master at the New York City Ballet, who had seen *Ballet Imperial* performed by many dancers in many companies, thought that no dancer in the role of the first ballerina ever possessed the explosive brilliance of Marie-Jeanne, who created it. Balanchine brought out and used all her strength, tension, elegance and authority. Subsequent dancers may have been her equals in technique, but none possessed her fiery, indomitable impatience, so that the original shock of her performances, which were acclaimed throughout South America, never recurred.

The second ballerina was Gisella Caccialanza, who had married Lew Christensen in May. During rehearsals with Balanchine, she thought, "How can he do this to me?" and she protested at all the running that was expected of her before she even started a variation. "What are you complaining about?" asked Balanchine. "Before your variation you're just resting." "Where?" "You're just running." It had been the same with *Le Baiser de la fée* at the Metropolitan, when he pushed her onstage to make her entrance with a series of pas de bourrée, which always hurt her feet. "He called them 'rest steps,'" Lew Christensen said.

The second performance, on June 27, opened with *Errante.* The first showing of *Pastorela,* choreographed by Lew Christensen and

José Fernandez, followed. Then came *Concerto Barocco.* Bach's Concerto in D Minor was one of the few masterpieces of old music that Balanchine ever trusted himself to turn into a ballet. He could never lay hands, as Massine had done, on a Beethoven symphony, or on a Mozart piano concerto or a Schubert quartet. Yet he dared the Bach—and brought it off.

The corps of eight girls was onstage throughout, and the first ballerina left the stage for only a few seconds. The single boy, William Dollar, appeared only in the second movement, from which the second ballerina, Mary Jane Shea, was omitted. The two principals, representing for the most part the two violins, responded to each other with extraordinary delicacy in the opening Vivace and wove intricate mazes with the eight other girls. In the Largo, the lifting of Marie-Jeanne, the first ballerina, in huge but diminishing arcs was wonderful in the way it complemented the music's climax of emotion without following the notes. Twice in the final Allegro there was an unpredictable but delightful jazzy element of syncopation when, to reiterated passages on the solo violins, the corps drummed out the rhythm on their pointes while their arms moved *against* the music from one classical pose to another.

For all its apparent simplicity, Marie-Jeanne thought the Bach a greater work than *Ballet Imperial*—an opinion that has found numerous adherents since—and her role, which called for so many contrasting qualities, the most demanding Balanchine ever made on her.

The final ballet was *Divertimento,* to piano music of Rossini orchestrated by Benjamin Britten, which proved to be one of the most popular ballets on the entire tour. It took place at a costume ball where a guest dressed as a rat scares the other guests, who are provoked to attack him. The rat is unmasked and revealed as an acrobat in disguise. Nicholas Magallanes played this part, and Marjorie Moore, who was in love with him, used to stand in the wings, murmuring encouragement and blowing kisses. One night in the course of the tour Balanchine decided to fool Marjorie and the company. Warning only the Christensens and, of course, Magallanes, he put on the rat costume and danced. He submitted to the kicks and blows of the other dancers, but when Marjorie Moore blew him a kiss he did a double turn in the air, and she got a shock. When Balanchine removed his headdress, the company fell apart with laughter.

For Kirstein, *Apollo,* which was performed on the third night, was an "unforeseen success."

Maybe the name of Stravinsky had something to do with it. Certainly Lew Christensen's inspired rendition of a cruelly difficult technical role had a great deal. He was very nervous the first night. He could even barely let his newly acquired wife . . . sew on his gilt leggings. But his turns exploded and his beats fairly crackled. The ovation at the end was something to live for. And the little pupils of the local dancing academy presented Balanchine with a wreath of bays, which he gave to Lew who didn't know what to do with it, while everyone took pictures.

At press conferences, Balanchine had his own way of being amusing. He could not take anything official seriously and talked nonsense about himself and ballet in general. In São Paulo, he surprised his interrogators by saying, "Tiller Girls [a troupe of precision dancers of the 1920s] are for older people like our grandparents. Nowadays we do different—more modern. I call it 'organized chaos.' "

When, as he liked to do, he watched *Ballet Imperial* from the wings, he made everyone nervous. One night, as he stood talking to Olga Suárez while she waited to make her entrance, he remarked, "Once you fall on stage you can never build up again. You have to fight hard to make audience forget you fall." He described how it had once happened to Olga Spessiva in the days of Diaghilev, and how she ruined her performance in *Swan Lake.* "Dancers must never fall," he concluded. Olga nodded in agreement, ran onstage and immediately fell flat.

Because of the war, there seemed to be no way to get the

company to Buenos Aires, but the American vice-consul moved heaven and earth and produced a boat. The whole company traveled first class on *El Cabo de Buena Esperanza,* which had been built to hold eight hundred and now had twelve hundred people on board. Balanchine, who shared a cabin with Dollar and Fred Danieli, complained that girls were always scratching on the door asking for Dollar.

In Argentina, a law had just been passed raising the age when young people attained majority from eighteen to twenty-one. No sooner had the crowded ship docked at Buenos Aires on July 16 than all the minors in the company—Magallanes as well as the girls—were taken off the boat and held in jail from six-thirty in the morning until five that evening. It was suggested that white slave traffic was involved. Marie-Jeanne became hysterical, and Balanchine tried to get himself arrested, too. The jail was freezing, for this was the Argentinean winter. Nevertheless, everyone was summoned to attend class by Balanchine at two the following afternoon.

Again, the opening was a success, with an ovation for *Concerto Barocco* and rave reviews the following day. Balanchine and Kirstein were soon planning an Argentinean ballet with the young composer Alberto Ginastera.

. . .

THE AMERICAN BALLET gave nineteen performances during their sixteen-day stay in Buenos Aires, then, on August 1, crossed the Río de la Plata to give several more in Montevideo, the Uruguayan capital. On August 5 they returned to Buenos Aires to take an evening train inland to Rosario, the first of three provincial cities they were to visit.

The company's two-day stay in Córdoba was the occasion for a historic encounter. Manuel de Falla, the greatest Spanish composer of the twentieth century, whose *Tricorne* had been commissioned by Diaghilev, was living in Alta Gracia, a little town a few miles away, and Balanchine drove out to visit him. In 1939, Falla had come from Spain to conduct four concerts of Spanish music in Buenos Aires. After the concerts, he and his niece had settled at Alta Gracia.

The company interpreter, John Graham Luhan, went in to interpret between Falla and Balanchine, while Georgia Hiden waited outside in the car. How one would like to know what they talked about, the two men of genius. Luckily, *Tricorne* was the one ballet of Massine's that Balanchine could praise wholeheartedly. Falla was currently working on his "Atlántida" (Atlantis), which he left unfinished at his death there five years later. Georgia Hiden remembers Balanchine coming away well pleased with the promise that Falla would allow him to produce "Atlántida" on the stage.

The dancers went on to Mendoza to give a performance, and were supposed to take the train from there to Santiago, Chile, which was only about a hundred and forty miles away. Unfortunately the two cities were separated by the highest peaks in the Andes, and there had been the worst winter storms in years. The railroad was broken, mountain villages had been submerged by snow and the highway was blocked. There was a period of anxious waiting before Kirstein eventually succeeded in borrowing a Boeing transport plane to ferry the fifty-one members of the company in two trips through—not over—the Andes. No one was allowed more than twenty-five pounds of luggage. Luhan had to take the rest—which consisted of hundreds of trunks and suitcases—through Bolivia to await the company in Lima, Peru. Most of the dancers had never flown before, and none had flown under such conditions; they were all scared stiff. Todd Bolender recalled his relief as the plane emerged from the mountains: "Everything began to turn green, and we saw the sea. The land came up at us. We landed on a shelf of green."

In Chile, Balanchine put together and presented *Fantasia Brasileira*, commissioned in Rio from Francisco Mignone two months before. It took him only one week to arrange the choreography. Although, as Kirstein observed, *Brasileira* was about as Brazilian as *Prince Igor* was early Russian, it was a successful closing number; but like others in the repertory, it would never be seen in North America.

Kirstein was obliged to fly back to the United States. The company understood that he was trying to get the male dancers excused from the draft "for six months or so." There were, however, other problems to be dealt with, and these he did not discuss with them. He had to account for the money the tour had cost Nelson Rockefeller's agency. Successful as it had been, box-office receipts had not, of course, covered expenses. In Washington, Kirstein dealt with his old friend Wallace Harrison, the architect, who represented Rockefeller. The tour was allowed to continue.

From Valparaiso, the company took a cattle boat up the west coast to Peru. They were the only passengers, apart from the smelly beasts in the hold, and the food was awful. Balanchine, who never complained, urged everyone to stick to pancakes with fresh lime juice and sugar. There was nothing to do on board but sunbathe, play games and act charades, but nearly every day the boat put in at a little port. One day when Georgia Hiden was going ashore with Balanchine and a few other dancers, he pointed out a high building in the town for which they were headed. It might have been the customs house, a government office or the jail, but Balanchine said, "That is hotel, and it's called Pacífico." It turned out that he was right, although none of them could figure out how he knew. Another day, at another small harbor town, he and his friends hired a taxi to take them inland to see some bleak nitrate hills devoid of vegetation, where there was no animal life, not even ants. The group became uneasy as they sensed that their driver was steering them in the wrong direction. "He wants to tell his wife something," said Balanchine. Sure enough, as they drove down a street in the poor quarter, a woman came running from a house to speak to the driver. Georgia decided that Balanchine must have second sight.

In Lima, they found that Aaron Copland was staying at the Bolívar Hotel. He agreed to conduct his own *Billy*, which seemed to galvanize the orchestra. The first performance, on September

10, was attended by the president of Peru, his wife and family, the head of the army and all the foreign ambassadors and ministers—except the German, Italian and Japanese—all wearing white tie. The company received the greatest ovation of the tour.

When the scheduled season ended, Balanchine, the *chef d'orchestre* Balaban and the Christensens went by air to Cuzco and Machu Picchu to see the ruins of the old Inca capital. In the (unpressurized) plane, flying at 14,000 feet, Lew and Gisella watched Balanchine grow whiter and whiter. Lew thought he "damn near died." But the excursion was worth it, and everyone, including Balanchine, took photographs. Because Peru was at war with Ecuador, the performances planned for Quito were canceled. To fill the gap, the United States Embassy in Lima arranged for extra performances there.

Balanchine left for the United States the day before the company's last appearance in Peru. Three days later, the company sailed for Colombia. By the time they returned, they had given more than a hundred performances in six countries over five months. On their arrival home, they were disbanded. Looking back on the tour, Lincoln Kirstein wrote:

I never failed to be amazed by Balanchine. He has always had a remarkable disposition for work, quiet, patient, undemanding, yet perfectly firm. But on this fantastic tour, the difficulties of which can never be appreciated by anybody but the dancers themselves, . . . he loved every inch of the journey and his own personal prestige became enormous. Long after we left Buenos Aires came insistent offers to return to the Colón.

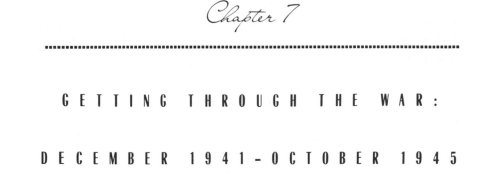

Chapter 7

GETTING THROUGH THE WAR:

DECEMBER 1941 - OCTOBER 1945

ON December 8, 1941, the United States declared war on Japan. By December 11, it was also at war with Germany and Italy. Sooner or later the draft would diminish the number of available male dancers, but because of his fragile physical condition there was no question of Balanchine's being drafted. Kirstein, however, was.

In June 1938, in an article in *Dance Magazine,* Kirstein had made certain predictions about world politics and the future of ballet in America. He took for granted—as most of the British and French did not—that war in Europe was inevitable, and he accurately dated "the closing of international frontiers" as 1939–40. The result would be that what he called "the Slavo-International company" would be restricted to appearing in the

United States with a decreasing number of foreign stars and an increasingly American—and far better—corps de ballet. Kirstein did not mention the Japanese threat, which had not loomed, but he foresaw the American entry into the war against Hitler and the alliance with Russia. Although the all-powerful Sol Hurok, fearful of being saddled with Colonel de Basil's debts, was to banish the de Basil company to South America, he would indeed present Massine's Ballet Russe and Lucia Chase's Ballet Theatre in the course of one New York season; and the Ballet Russe de Monte-Carlo, even when led by a Russian-born director other than Massine, would tour the States with an increasingly American company for twenty-two years.

Balanchine, who had to earn a living, took any work that was offered him. If Hurok had been perceptive enough to realize that Balanchine was the greatest living choreographer, and if he had supported and enlarged the American Ballet to give him the scope to create a new repertory of masterworks, how different history might have been! But it is inconceivable that the two men could have worked together steadily, for Balanchine would never have submitted for long to the tyranny of the box office. Nor could Hurok, in spite of all his influence and know-how, ever have created for Balanchine, as Kirstein was to do, a climate in which his genius could flower with the profusion it did in the postwar years.

Of all Balanchine's wartime jobs, none was odder than the *Circus Polka.* At the end of 1941, Ringling Brothers and Barnum & Bailey Circus had suggested that he do some choreography for their elephants. He agreed, on condition that Stravinsky write the music, probably realizing that the composer needed money. Balanchine telephoned Stravinsky in Hollywood on November 12; in January the composer made some notes in preparation for another talk with his choreographer: "How many minutes?" "The less the best." Balanchine went to the circus's winter quarters in Sarasota, Florida, to rehearse the elephants, and enjoyed himself tremendously. Brigitta appeared in the first performance, in New York

City's Madison Square Garden on April 9, 1942, which was a benefit for a war charity. At the end, Balanchine had both the star elephant, Modoc, and Zorina kneel in salutation to each other, touching foreheads in the sawdust.

During this period, Balanchine used to hold musical evenings in his apartment, with Kopeikine at the piano and Nathan Milstein playing the violin. He even bought a violin himself, and said to Georgia Hiden, "You must learn the piano, Dottie Littlefield can learn the viola, and then we will play very slow, very loud, everything that Mozart ever wrote!"

· · ·

THE WAR brought a wave of prosperity to the United States; and, equally ironically, ballet grew more popular than ever.

By the beginning of 1942, de Basil was in Mexico City with his company—or what remained of it—preparing to embark on a long tour of South America. It would be four years before they were seen again in the United States. Meantime, Hurok resolved to present both the other rival companies in New York. Ballet Theatre had a week at the Metropolitan Opera House, followed immediately by the Ballet Russe; then there was a week in which the two companies alternated. In spite of Ballet Theatre's ambition to be eclectic and to produce new and/or American works, both were as Russian in color and magnificence as Hurok could make them. In fact, he had shamelessly advertised Ballet Theatre as "the greatest in Russian Ballet."

· · ·

BRIGITTA had cropped her hair to be tested for the role of Maria in *For Whom the Bell Tolls,* a part she regarded as the chance of a lifetime. Believing she had got it, she sent a triumphant telegram to her husband, who was working at the Colón in Buenos Aires. After that, he wrote her regularly. He thanked her for the lock of her shorn "dark gold" hair, and wanted her to return with him to Argentina the next year; he thought Mozart would be "rather pleased" with his ballet to the Violin Concerto in A major; without her, when something funny happened, he had to "laugh alone"; he was counting the days till he saw her again. But Brigitta lost the part to Ingrid Bergman and became distraught.

Marie-Jeanne was living in Buenos Aires with her husband, the impresario Quesada, whom she had met on the tour, and Balanchine asked her to dance in the revival of *Apollon* and in *Concierto.* But she was trying to get pregnant and refused. "Balanchine didn't like that," she remembers, "and I wasn't very diplomatic. . . . I had never taken him seriously, because he had so many girlfriends. With me it was short-lived. I was one of a hundred and didn't fall madly in love with him. . . . I loved him as an artistic genius." In Balanchine's eyes, for a ballerina to have babies was a form of treachery to himself and to the Muse. Although his admiration for Marie-Jeanne's exceptional qualities never flowered into a more intimate passion, he continued to work with her and on her. She was rather self-indulgent, and he was known to give her money for steaks, to discourage her from putting on weight.

On his return from South America, Balanchine helped to direct and made dances for a version of *Die Fledermaus* called *Rosalinda,* which was presented by the recently formed New Opera Company. Lacking Marie-Jeanne, he cast a young dancer named Mary Ellen Moylan, who had been at the School only since 1940, as the ballerina.

The New Opera Company was also presenting Mussorgsky's *The Fair at Sorochinsk,* which opened six days after *Rosalinda.* Because of the failure of a short opera by Walter Damrosch, included as a curtain raiser, Balanchine's *Ballet Imperial* was hastily substituted. A company was assembled from former dancers of the American Ballet and from the School. Moylan recalls Nicholas Magallanes coming to her and saying, "Let's learn the pas de deux. You're going to be doing Marie-Jeanne's part." She nearly fainted. As she and Todd Bolender appeared only in the second act of *Rosalinda,* they were bustled into taxis after dancing *Ballet Imperial* and driven to the theater where *Rosalinda* was playing. "Can you imagine what it was like to be seventeen and doing both those shows every night?" Moylan said later. "It was awesome just being on the stage in New York City."

Among the seven men in *Rosalinda* were two, soon to be drafted, who became closely associated with Balanchine after the war. Both had started at the School the previous year and were appearing professionally for the first time. Edward Bigelow, a New Englander, was to prove the staunchest of friends. Francisco Moncion, a native of the Dominican Republic, would become one of Balanchine's most reliable dancers. When he arrived at the School, he already thought of Balanchine as *The Man.* "Although Balanchine was an odd mixture of glamour and mousiness, he had an aura about him. I really got a crush on the man, a real crush."

Balanchine tried to help old colleagues who had been drafted find congenial work in the armed services. Irving Berlin was organizing a show to entertain the troops, and Balanchine wrote to him about Zachary Solov, who had been with the American Ballet in South America: "I would be grateful if you could keep him in mind in case of a vacancy in *This Is the Army.*"

When *Rosalinda* finished its run, Mary Ellen Moylan had the option of joining Ballet Theatre or the Ballet Russe. At eighteen, she felt she was "getting on in years." Sergei Denham of the Ballet Russe came to watch her in class and offered her a job. When she asked Balanchine what he thought she should do, he "wasn't too enthusiastic." Finally he said, "Go ahead to Ballet Russe, but I will give you a piece of advice. Don't sign a two-year contract." It was excellent counsel. Within a year her salary was doubled.

In the spring of 1943, Hurok needed another ballerina for Ballet Theatre and was delighted to find that the celebrated Vera Zorina was available. Balanchine undertook to revive two of his ballets for her. His first task for Ballet Theatre, however, was the comparatively menial one of pulling together a ballet which was already in the company's repertory. *Helen of Troy* was a farce to Offenbach's music that Fokine had arranged shortly before his death the previous August. Although it had been danced in Mexico City, it was considered unsatisfactory, and David Lichine had made a new version in the fall. Now Balanchine collaborated with Lichine in devising an ending that would show his own wife off to the best possible advantage.

Three weeks later, on April 25, 1943, *Apollon*—called *Apollo* at last—was performed once more at the Metropolitan, with Stravinsky conducting. André Eglevsky danced the title role and Zorina was Terpsichore.

.   .   .

Time magazine was so pleased with a would-be learned article on Ballet Theatre's season, which was to appear on May 17, that they sent Balanchine an advance proof, asking for comment. They got more than they bargained for. The critic, in a mistaken display of expertise, had made invidious distinctions between Markova, Baronova and Zorina, calling the first a *"danseuse noble,"* whom "only the cautious conservatism of ballet's experts keeps from being hailed unreservedly as a *ballerina assoluta,"* placing the second in a lower category with the novel designation of *"mime dansante,"* and dismissing the third as a *"soubrette."* Without naming his wife, Balanchine sprang to her defense:

May 14, 1943

Gentlemen:

Thank you for sending me the article entitled "Danseuse Noble. . . ."

Most professionals of the dance have long ago given up wondering at the strange writings of the dance critics in the daily papers because they have finally realized that many of them simply don't know their subject. However, it seems a pity that when a magazine as important as *Time* devotes an entire page to the ballet, it is unable to come closer to the truth.

The author of your article juggles with magic-sounding words: *ballerina assoluta, danseuse noble, mime dansante,* without apparently realizing that the first one denotes an official rank in the theater (such as a colonel or general in the army), while the second one describes a quality and the third one a style of dancing. To say that the *danseuse noble* Markova "is well above a *mime dansante* (like Irina Baronova)" is equal to saying that Caruso was less great than Chaliapin because he was just a tenor while Chaliapin was a basso. As to the word *soubrette,* this is the first time I have heard it mentioned in connection with dancing and have associated it, until today, with the unfortunate maid in comic plays who brings in the breakfast tray and upsets it upon finding the *ingénue* in bed with the *jeune premier.*

Most professional dancers and choreographers consider Markova as one of a few great contemporary ballerinas, but they refrain from making comparisons between dancers because they know that each is outstanding in her own way and has qualities completely different from the others. It is your right to praise the ballerina you prefer, but I do not think it wise to do so by disparaging other prominent artists who may in their turn become the critic's and the public's favorite.

Sincerely yours,
George Balanchine

Neither Markova nor Baronova took part in Ballet Theatre's long cross-country tour which followed, so Hurok was at liberty to announce his "internationally famous dance stars" in "the greatest in Russian Ballet," while naming only "Zorina," "glamorous dancing star" in bold capitals three times the size of those in which the words "Ballet Theatre" were printed. During this tour, Brigitta was sometimes visited by a new admirer, Goddard Lieberson, who worked for Columbia Records. When the tour was over, she left Ballet Theatre.

In the winter of 1943, Balanchine had made dances for the musical *What's Up?,* the first collaboration of Alan Jay Lerner and Frederick Loewe, who went on to write *My Fair Lady* and *Camelot,* among others. In the spring of 1944, just about the time Private Lincoln Kirstein arrived in London, he was working on *Dream with Music,* in which Zorina starred. It was while the latter was being tried out in Boston that Georgia Hiden heard the unusual sound of Balanchine's voice raised in anger—at the stage manager. She later remarked, "That's the only time I heard you yell." Balanchine said, "It's only the second time since I came to America. I wouldn't yell at a dancer. I'd yell at Hurok."

Another musical show—operetta, rather—led to Balanchine's two-year association with the Ballet Russe de Monte-Carlo, for which he had staged four productions in 1939. Dancers were often laid off during the summer, and in 1944 Frederic Franklin asked Denham's permission to appear in an operetta based on the life of Grieg that his friends Robert Wright and George Forrest had put together in California. Denham lent the whole Ballet Russe. Danilova urged the authors to employ Balanchine as their choreographer, and they agreed. He made several dances, folk, comic and classical, using Grieg's incidental music for *Peer Gynt* and other compositions, and wrote to Brigitta, "Why don't you come out and be wife of poor choreographer?" But Brigitta was already in love with Goddard Lieberson.

Song of Norway was rehearsed in San Francisco, and Balanchine shared a hotel room with Franklin, the English *premier danseur* who was the partner of Alexandra Danilova. They had been friends since 1940, when Balanchine had produced *Serenade* and *Jeu de cartes* for the Ballet Russe, and Franklin had danced Dollar's old role of the Joker. Balanchine liked the fair-haired, cheerful young man from Liverpool and evidently saw some latent gift in him, besides his ability to dance, to partner and to please. Before he left for South America he told Denham, "When I go, this ballet has got to be rehearsed by Franklin." After Balanchine and Franklin became roommates at the Clift Hotel in San Francisco, the latter noticed that "everything was choreographed": "When we got up, the meal was ordered from downstairs, we each had so long in the bathroom, we went to rehearsals and came home on time." Then Balanchine took the opportunity to do his roommate a good turn. According to Franklin:

I was quite close to him then. One day in San Francisco I said, "There must be something else in life besides going on stage every night, dancing all the lovely ballets, having all the lovely applause. . . ." He looked at me and said, "You'd like to be doing something else?" I said yes. On the opening night of *Song of Norway* in Los Angeles, it was my birthday, 12 June. There was a cake on the stage; everyone was there; Mr. Denham made a speech. He announced, "From now on Frederic Franklin will no longer be *only* my *premier danseur,* he's going to be my *maître de ballet.* " Balanchine looked at me, wagged his finger and smiled. . . . And Danilova said, "So, young man, you are going to be my boss." I had no idea this had been arranged. . . .

Balanchine told Franklin, "You know, it's not fun being *maître de ballet,* Freddie. From now on you're going to get up every morning and stand in front of people and give and give and give. It's going to be for the rest of your life, because now you will only be giving."

One night Balanchine asked him, "Have you read *War and Peace*?" The answer was no. Another night it was, "Have you read the Sermon on the Mount?" "I suppose I must have. I really don't remember, Mr. B." "Call me George." "I can't, Mr. B." "Well, go home and read it." Franklin said later, "It was a sort of education being with him. He was very dear to me indeed."

In Hollywood, Balanchine was reunited with the Stravinskys, who were living in Beverly Hills, and it was agreed that he would make a ballet to Stravinsky's *Danses concertantes,* composed two and a half years earlier. On the morning of June 16, Stravinsky discussed with Anton Dolin the scenario of a ballet to be included in Billy Rose's revue *The Seven Lively Arts,* which was to be arranged by Dolin and danced by Markova and himself. On the same afternoon he talked to Balanchine about *Danses concertantes.* Denham, Balanchine and Eugene Berman were summoned to Stravinsky's house to decide on the costumes; then Balanchine said to Franklin, "We're all Russians. You had better come, too." When

Berman produced a piece of black velvet and a swatch of colors, an argument broke out. Finally, Balanchine told Franklin to choose. The new ballet master first picked out a vivid yellow, then some other colors, and Stravinsky's eyes lit up. During the San Francisco run of *Song of Norway*, Balanchine signed an agreement with Denham to arrange not only *Danses concertantes* but Strauss's *Le Bourgeois Gentilhomme* for "a flat amount of two thousand dollars."

Song of Norway did well at the Philharmonic Auditorium in Los Angeles, and even better when it opened in San Francisco on July 1. It was a smash hit at the Imperial in New York, so successful that a replacement cast—led by Dorothie Littlefield and Olga Suárez— had to be found to allow the principals to take part in the fall ballet season at City Center.

While Balanchine had been rehearsing *Song of Norway* in California with members of the Ballet Russe, the rival company, Ballet Theatre, happened to be there, and he undertook to make a new ballet for them, too—*Waltz Academy*, to music by Vittorio Rieti, his old collaborator on *Barabau* and *Le Bal*. Rehearsals were begun at once.

The period from summer 1944 until summer 1945, which saw the defeat of Nazi Germany and Japan, was one of frantic activity for Balanchine. His work for several different organizations necessitated constant travel around the United States. It almost seemed as if he accepted any job that would distract him from unhappy thoughts of Brigitta.

Danses concertantes was given by the Ballet Russe on the opening night of the season. There was a parade of dancers in Berman's costumes "looking as brilliant as scarabs," and when an inner curtain rose to reveal a black background, they shone more brightly still. Four pas de trois were followed by a pas de deux for Danilova and Franklin and a finale for the whole cast of fourteen. The fourth variation was danced by Mary Ellen Moylan, Nicholas Magallanes and a new dancer named Maria Tallchief.

Born in 1925, Maria was of American Indian descent on her father's side and Scottish, Irish and Dutch on her mother's. Her grandmother Tallchief had lived in a tent and carried Maria's father on her back. But since her father, like other Osage Indians, received substantial royalties from oil wells, he made his home in Hollywood, played golf and, as Maria said, "that was about it." Maria, a striking-looking girl with black hair and high cheekbones, was brought up by her mother, who was a devout Catholic. She learned music and had perfect pitch. She took ballet lessons with Bronislava Nijinska and joined the Ballet Russe in 1942. When Balanchine came to stage *Song of Norway*, Maria had seen no other work of his except *Serenade*, but the inventiveness and musical sense displayed in that had been enough to amaze her. Besides dancing in the corps in the Grieg operetta, she understudied Danilova in Anitra's dance. As she worked with Balanchine, she realized at once how much she had to learn, and she wondered at his infinite patience: "He never said, 'You're this or that, but you're not something else.' What he did say was 'If you can do a perfect battement tendu, you can do anything.' " When the second cast was being assembled so that *Song of Norway* could extend its run after Danilova, Franklin and the others had left, Maria was offered the leading role. She refused in order to continue studying with Balanchine.

■   ■   ■

THROUGHOUT the war years, John Martin did not cease to disparage Balanchine's ballets in the pages of *The New York Times*, although he was sometimes able to find words of praise for his work in Broadway musicals. When Walter Terry of the *Herald Tribune* was drafted in 1942, his place was taken by Edwin Denby, who became Balanchine's most impassioned and eloquent admirer. Denby, a Harvard graduate who had studied dancing in Germany, was a poet, better equipped than most to assess Balanchine's exceptional quality and originality. It is amusing to compare his verdicts with those of Martin.

On *Danses concertantes:*

MARTIN Mr. Balanchine has done a clever, somewhat mathematical, job of choreography, almost totally devoid of dancing.

DENBY The shift of the figures and the order of the steps is miraculously logical and light, and so even fitful changes have a grace and a sponteneous impetus. . . . The dance is like a conversation in Henry James.

On *Le Bourgeois Gentilhomme:*

MARTIN Mr. Balanchine has paid little or no attention to the style of the theater or the dancing of the seventeenth century.

DENBY After thirty years of stress on detail at the expense of flow, *Le Bourgeois* marks a complete turnabout in dance style. . . . It shows off the dancer, not the choreographer. . . .

When Claudia Cassidy, the critic of the *Chicago Tribune* and a warm adherent of Balanchine, suggested to him that "an older, more experienced troupe, say of Diaghileff vintage" might dance so sophisticated a work as *Danses concertantes* better than the Ballet Russe, the choreographer burst out with, "Why do Americans hate Americans?" He told her that the Diaghilev corps "couldn't have achieved the pinpoint brilliance of *Danses concertantes* in a million years."

Danilova was always telling Balanchine that the company should revive Petipa's *Paquita*. He invariably replied, "No, *Paquita*'s *awful* ballet, awful!" Ruthanna Boris asked him one day, "What's so bad about *Paquita*?" Balanchine replied, "Nothing. It's very very good." "Then *why* do you not want to do it?" "Because if we do *Paquita* everybody will see what I stole for *Ballet Imperial.*"

Balanchine's next production for the Ballet Russe was, in fact, a revival of *Ballet Imperial*. The great ballet was taught to the company during the autumn tour and even rehearsed after evening performances in Chicago—which was against union rules. The reason for this was that Ballet Theatre was expecting Balanchine to put the finishing touches on *Waltz Academy* in Montreal. It had to be ready for its premiere in Boston on October 5. As the Chicago premiere of *Imperial* was on the fourth, Balanchine could not stay to see it. On the afternoon of the fifth, after the dress rehearsal of *Waltz Academy,* he went for a walk with Rieti and discussed another project. Some years before, Rieti had written the scenario of a melodramatic ballet set in the Romantic 1830s that wove melodies from some of Bellini's operas into a strikingly theatrical series of numbers. He had not been able to interest either Dolin or Nijinska in the project, but Balanchine was quick to see its possibilities. Suddenly Rieti exclaimed, "What are we doing—talking about *Night Shadow*? In an hour or two we are going to see *Waltz Academy* on the stage!" "*That* old ballet!" said Balanchine.

By November, Balanchine was back with the Ballet Russe, rehearsing *Mozartiana* and *Concerto Barocco* in Houston. All the dancers hoped he would become the company's artistic director, for he had put new life into the battered troupe, but he did not like Denham, and Denham did not want to relinquish his artistic authority. Nevertheless, he wrote to a friend that *Danses concertantes* was one of the ballets most in demand: "Balanchine became a sort of adopted son and travels with us, sharing our hardships, fun, glory and drinks."

When Balanchine was on tour with the Ballet Russe, whether by train or bus, he sat alone in the front, writing in a book. Sometimes he looked out the window, as if searching for a word, then continued writing. Eventually he presented each dancer with a four-line poem, describing what he or she might be like in bed. Ruthanna Boris, he wrote, would have no room for another person because she always took her toe shoes to bed with her.

During the Ballet Russe's spring season at City Center, which opened as early as February to avoid competition with Ballet Theatre, Denham offered two "Balanchine Festivals"—programs made up entirely of Balanchine's own ballets. The pretext was that

1945 was Balanchine's twenty-fifth year as a choreographer. After the first festival, Denham came onstage to present him with a gold cigarette case. The program was *Mozartiana, Le Bourgeois Gentilhomme* and *Ballet Imperial.*

Ruthanna Boris, who had adored Balanchine since she first arrived at the School of American Ballet in 1934 wearing a pink tunic, danced in all his new productions for the Ballet Russe, as well as in the revivals of older ballets. He once told her, "I envy you because you are a Jew. You have something warm here [touching his heart] like the sun. And I have here a little dagger." She thought a lot about his character and decided that he had been deeply hurt early in life. "He was a dear, loving, anguished man," she said, but he was too proud to share his sorrow.

Ruthanna had been present when Balanchine created the first version of *Serenade;* she remembered how Heidi Vosseler had fallen down, and he had said, "Stay." Then he put Kathryn Mullowny behind Charles Laskey, who was nearsighted. And Kathryn had to propel him forward to the fallen Heidi, holding her hand over his eyes—"He can't see anyway," said Balanchine; and the adagio grew from that. *Serenade* was "a lot of little parts"; and after Ruthanna joined the Ballet Russe in 1943 she danced most of them.

One night, when they picked me up at the end to carry me off to Heaven, I thought: This is Balanchine's theory about his life. In a way it almost *is* his life, because the dancer who brings in the theme introduces it and the group picks it up—and so on. In some subconscious way, in his first American ballet, made with his children who loved him, he had poured himself out. Well, I thought, we're older now. I wonder if he would mind. And I told him, "I love dancing *Serenade,* and I find that, when I've put it all together in my mind, I know what it's about." The mask came down. [As she described this, Ruthanna made the gesture of passing her hand downward in front of her face, which in the old mime language of Russian ballet signifies darkness, secrecy, night.] "You do?" said Balanchine, with a cold stare. "That's very nice." Then he walked away.

In the first postwar period, Balanchine, who loved good food, did not forget that friends in Europe were sadly short of it.

Balanchine to The Tolstoi Foundation Inc., 289 Fourth Avenue, New York City

21 May 1945

Gentlemen,

I enclose herewith a check for $100.00 as my contribution for parcels sent to Russians in France.

I would like to put three of my friends in Paris on your list of persons entitled to receive food parcels. They are: Mr Alexandre Benois . . . Mme L. Egorova-Troubetzkaia . . . Mme Olga Preobrajenskaia . . . [He gave their addresses.]

If it is possible I would like you to use $50.00 of the amount I am sending you as a fund to assure monthly parcels for the above mentioned persons. The balance of my contribution to be used by you for any Russians in Paris that need assistance.

At the end of May 1945, shortly after the defeat of Hitler, Balanchine accepted an engagement with the Opera Nacional of Mexico to arrange ballets for operas and to stage some of his own works. His small troupe—William Dollar, Marie-Jeanne, Yvonne Patterson, Nicholas Magallanes and twelve girls, including Patricia White, who later became Patricia Wilde, and Georgia Hiden— went ahead of him by boat. As some of the others were still students at the School, Natalie Molostwoff accompanied them as chaperone. Balanchine followed by air a few days later. Georgia Hiden had stayed with him and Brigitta on Long Island, where they kept several pets—a German shepherd; Mrs. Hartwig's Pekingese, Boogie; a Yorkshire terrier called Mr. Chips; and a chicken named Joey. When Georgia asked, "How is Joey?" and Balanchine replied, "I don't know," she realized things were going badly between him and Brigitta. In fact, Brigitta had already told George, "I think we had better plan on getting a divorce."

.   .   .

BALANCHINE could almost, after all these years, have arranged the dances for *Aida, Faust* and *Samson et Dalila* in his sleep. In Mexico he also staged *Concerto Barocco, Apollo*—in which Magallanes appeared for the first time—and Fokine's *Les Sylphides.* He did not forget Stravinsky's birthday, and on July 18 he telegraphed to his revered Igor Fyodorovich:

IF APOLLO'S MOTHER WAS LETO THEN CERTAINLY HIS FATHER WAS FYODOR

It was in Mexico that Natalie Molostwoff, who had never lived at such close quarters with Balanchine before, realized that, as she put it, "there was nothing he could not do." When he discovered that the costumes provided by the theater for *Aida* were dirty and unusable, he said, "Okay. We'll make the costumes." Natalie, who was not good with her needle, nearly packed up and went home. "Why don't we buy a lot of bras and cover them with orange silk?" he suggested. This was done, and he got busy with a box of pins. Natalie observed that "the girls seemed to enjoy the fittings."

He flew back ahead of his troupe to arrange dances for *Mr. Strauss Goes to Boston,* which had its first out-of-town preview at the Shubert Theatre in Boston on August 13. The atomic bombs had been dropped a few days before.

That summer and fall, Balanchine encouraged two young choreographers. For the summer dance festival at Jacob's Pillow near Lee, Massachusetts, Todd Bolender had made a ballet to Stravinsky's *Pulcinella* suite, which he called *Musical Chairs.* Balanchine loved it, and asked, "Has Denham seen this?" He had not, and Balanchine brought him along to view it with "the whole Ballet Russe." Denham accepted the work and paid five hundred dollars for it, but insisted on changing its name to *Comedia Balletica.*

John Taras's first ballet, *Graziana,* to Mozart's Violin Concerto in G major (K.216) was given on the second night of Ballet

Theatre's season. A few days later, Todd Bolender ran into Taras outside the Russian Tea Room on Fifty-seventh Street and asked, "Have you seen George?" "No," said Taras, who never in his life called "George" anything but "Mr. Balanchine." "I haven't seen him for ages." "He has seen your ballet, and he just loves it. He wants to talk to you." Taras was incredulous, but he and Balanchine got together. Both Bolender and Taras later found out separately that when Balanchine had taken each of them to supper at Tony's, a former speak-easy, he had wept as he spoke of his troubles.

Balanchine's divorce from Zorina came through in January 1946. Todd Bolender believed he had intimate talks with Balanchine only when he was not married, that is to say, between grand passions.

Then he always turned to one. I would be upstairs at the School, having had a class, and he would say, "What are you doing? Let's have some dinner."

He was lonely, and he talked for *hours*. And it was fascinating. That was the first time I really got to know him. We went not only to Tony's but to Sammy's delicatessen on Madison, directly under the School. They had a "George Balanchine sandwich" there—smoked salmon with chopped onions.

Although he admired *Lilac Garden,* he was always using Tudor as an example of what not to do. "Don't make complicated stories in which you have aunts and uncles and mothers-in-law. The audience shouldn't have to read a program." He made fun of some of the old dancers—Pavlova, for example, people who were sacred figures. Of Isadora he said, "She's a *pig.* " He spoke *endlessly* of Spessiva. "She was so exquisitely made." He always spoke of her feet being like hands. He said, "I steal a lot from Petipa."

Though Balanchine may not have realized it at the time, he was indeed "between marriages." During Ballet Theatre's summer tour of 1945, Bolender noticed that he was interested in Maria Tallchief. The Catholic Maria had no intention of having premarital relations, however, even with Balanchine. Confessing that he was extremely attracted to her, the choreographer asked Natasha Nabokov's advice. Natasha, after talking to Maria alone, gave her opinion that matrimony was the only solution.

One day Tallchief said to Vida Brown, another dancer friend, "What would you think if I married George?" Vida asked, "George who?"

Chapter 8

....

NEW BEGINNINGS:

NOVEMBER 1945 - APRIL 1948

DURING the winter of 1945–46, the clouds began to lift for Balanchine. The war was over, there was Maria, and Kirstein would soon be getting out of the army. On January 16, 1946, the day before Balanchine's divorce from Zorina came through, he and Stravinsky dined together at Tony's. When the Ballet Russe opened its season at City Center the same day with a revival of *Le Baiser de la fée,* the role of the Fairy was taken by Maria Tallchief.

Maria was still very conscious of how much she had to learn from Balanchine. Nijinska had taught her breathing, but it was he who remodeled her body from the hips down. She had to be given correct placement and turnout; once she had laboriously acquired this, her legs, feet, strength and line would improve. Her eagerness as well as her musical gifts were a thrilling encouragement to Balanchine. In spite of her beautiful bone structure, Maria had a rather big head, and she was not tall. But she believed Balanchine had the skill to devise dances that would make her head look small. He had a gift for seeing the potential in an unskilled dancer. He *knew* what she would be capable of in his hands.

Maria created the role of the Coquette in *Night Shadow*, the ballet Balanchine and Rieti had discussed in 1944, which was first performed in February 1946; the Sleepwalker's part was danced by Danilova.

Night Shadow has as Gothic and improbable a story as *Giselle*, but in its way it is just as effective. A Poet at a masked ball is attracted first by the mistress of his Host, the Baron, then by the Host's sleepwalking wife. There is a polonaise danced by the other guests, and a fantastic divertissement performed to amuse them, but the ballet's remarkable inventions are two contrasting pas de deux. That of the Poet with the Coquette is an ingenious display of enticing, escaping and entrapping movements. The second, danced by the Poet and the Sleepwalker, is even more extraordinary.

The Poet is left alone after the other guests have gone to supper, and the Sleepwalker appears in her nightgown, with flowing hair, holding a candle. The fact that she is aware of him only in her dream gives her the unattainable quality of a *princesse lointaine*. The Poet first flattens himself against a wall to watch this tiptoeing woman cross and recross the stage, only to halt abruptly just as she seems about to step over the footlights. Not until he has knelt to interrupt her progress and bowed without evoking any response does he pass his hand over her eyes and realize her condition. Like a choreographer devising a sequence—like Balanchine himself molding a dancer at rehearsal—he grasps her lit candle to raise her on pointe, lifts one of her legs, promenades her. When he runs round to embrace her, she evades him; when he makes his arm into a barrier, she dips under it; when he interposes his whole body, she swerves and glides past him; when he extends a leg, she steps over it. He tries lying full-length on the floor, but this too fails. In a singularly touching movement, he sinks to his knees in a deep backbend and stretches both his arms to encircle her. Still she continues on her way. He catches her by the shoulders and kisses her before sending her through the arch into the castle. Looking around cautiously, he follows her. This episode unfolds to variations on what Lord Harewood called "a melody of infinite pathos and beauty," namely "*Qui la voce,*" developed and embroidered by Rieti—the aria of Elvira's mad scene in *I Puritani.*

The Coquette has spied and seen the parting kiss; she fetches the Baron and directs him to the castle door. As the guests return, she sweeps with them into a formal dance, while the Host draws a dagger and runs into the castle. A sudden halt in the music, which brings the party to a standstill, signals the Poet's death wound, and he staggers in to die. The performers of the divertissement, acknowledging their kinship with a fellow artist, raise his body aloft; but before they can carry it away, the Sleepwalker appears, takes it in her arms and walks backward with it into the castle. As we see the light of her candle shine from successive windows of the spiral staircase up the tower, we imagine her bearing him to some cold consummation of their union in an upper chamber.

This is real Romantic melodrama, but we accept it because of the beauty of Bellini's melodies, the skill with which Rieti has interwoven them and the marvelous originality of Balanchine's dance of the Poet with the Sleepwalker.

Night Shadow (later renamed *La Sonnambula*) was to become a popular work in many countries. The wonder is that Dorothea Tanning's surrealist headdresses for the ball guests in the original production did not kill it from the start. Both Martin and Terry scorned it. Denby, however, did not miss the point: "Its effect when it is over is powerful and exact. It gives you a sense—as Poe does—of losing your bearings, the feeling of an elastic sort of time and a heaving floor." In fact, Balanchine, the archclassicist, could out-Byron Byron and out-Hoffmann Gautier.

∎ ∎ ∎

IN 1946, Lincoln Kirstein returned from active service with the U.S. Army in Europe. Before the war he had succeeded in bringing Balanchine to America and founding a school—which was now better than ever—but he and Balanchine had failed to sustain their own troupe of dancers. Throughout the first postwar spring they plotted and planned. They were not yet ready to compete with the elaborate organizations of the Ballet Russe, Ballet Theatre or de Basil, but as early as March 1938, Kirstein had considered a project of staging nonprofit Sunday performances. Could a group similar to Marie Rambert's prewar Ballet Club now be formed? Plans were made, but nothing was to be announced before the fall. Kirstein asked Balanchine to discuss with Stravinsky the possibility of his composing a new ballet. Balanchine went to Hollywood for talks with the composer. On April 4 and 5 they completed the scenario of *Orpheus* and celebrated Russian Easter together.

∎ ∎ ∎

IN SPITE of the strong opposition of Mrs. Tallchief, who objected to Balanchine on the grounds that he was "foreign," divorced, not Catholic and twice the age of her twenty-one-year-old daughter, Maria and Balanchine were married at New York's City Hall on August 16, 1946. Their first home was the apartment Balanchine had been renting for several years, but they spent a weekend honeymooning at costume designer Barbara Karinska's house in Massachusetts. Maria had to go on tour with the Ballet Russe almost immediately, and for the last time Balanchine traveled with Denham's company. When Maria was dancing in St. Louis, they drove together to visit her Indian relatives in Fairfax, Oklahoma, where her brothers were cowboys. Maria's cousin Helen, who lived on the Osage reservation, gave Balanchine a turquoise bracelet that he always treasured. He felt he had married America. It was at this time that he began to wear Western plaid shirts and string ties.

▪   ▪   ▪

THE NEW Kirstein-Balanchine project was to be called Ballet Society. A handsome twelve-page announcement was sent out in October.

The most incredible and audacious decision was to sell no tickets to the general public. The only way to see a performance was to become a member. An Associate Member, in exchange for fifty dollars a year, received two seats for every performance, admission to special events, a subscription to *Dance Index* and various other publications and the chance to attend dress rehearsals. A Participating Member paid fifteen dollars a year and received one seat per performance, *Dance Index* and the Ballet Society Year Book.

Another gesture of bravado—of defiance, even—was the abolition of press tickets. If newspapers wanted to send their critics, they had to subscribe for them. This was unheard of, but newspapers toed the line. The "announcement" attracted about eight hundred subscribers.

The first program brought a regular gathering of the clans. Lew Christensen, out of the army, and Fred Danieli, out of *This Is the Army,* were together again, along with several other South American adventurers of 1941: Gisella Caccialanza, who had been dancing with her brother-in-law William Christensen's San Francisco Ballet; William Dollar, who, since Ballet International—a short-lived company under the direction of the Marquis de Cuevas—and the Mexican excursion, had worked in musicals and formed his own group; Georgia Hiden, who had been with Ballet Theatre; Beatrice Tompkins, who had been briefly with the Ballet Russe; Todd Bolender, who had danced with both Ballet Theatre and the Ballet Russe and begun to be a choreographer; John Taras, who, after four years with Ballet Theatre, had just made *Camille* on Dolin and Markova for de Basil's Original Ballet Russe. In addition to these, there were Elise Reiman, who had not worked with Balanchine since the days at the Metropolitan, and Mary Ellen Moylan, who had spent two years with the Ballet Russe and tried to sing as well as dance in a musical. There was also sixteen-year-old Tanaquil Le Clercq, whose only public appearances had been in two student performances given by the School of American Ballet.

The opening took place on November 20, 1946, at the auditorium of the Central High School of Needle Trades. Anatole Chujoy, the editor of the monthly *Dance News,* thought it was "as unlikely and unsuitable a place to present ballet as one can find in New York. A huge, barn-like hall, cold and uninviting, it is as impersonal as a railroad station. . . . It has hard, uncomfortable chairs and a stage devoid of any facilities." The instruments of the fifty-odd musicians of Leon Barzin's National Orchestra Society obstructed the public's view. For half an hour the audience sat listening to hammering and excited voices. "Then the curtain went up. The long wait, the uncomfortable seats . . . were immediately forgotten, for there was magic on the stage."

From the Hurok point of view, the first program contained all the seeds of unpopularity. But the subscribers were obviously devotees of Balanchine, old faithfuls, so that a little opera with dancing, which was new to New York, and a brand-new ballet by Hindemith were not going to put them off. The former was Ravel's *L'Enfant et les sortilèges* (translated by Kirstein and Jane Barzin, the conductor's wife, as *The Spellbound Child*), whose first performance Balanchine had staged with artists of the Diaghilev Ballet for the Opéra de Monte Carlo in 1925. The second was a new ballet, *The Four Temperaments.*

In both his productions of *The Spellbound Child,* Balanchine used two casts, with each role doubled by an offstage singer and an onstage dancer; but the Child, intended for a mezzo-soprano, was both sung and danced in the Ballet Society production by the young Joseph Connolly. The large cast was one complication—and expense. Another lay in the very nature of Colette's idea, for the Child is assailed by animals and inanimate objects—Cup, Tea Pot, Fire, Squirrel, Shepherds and Shepherdesses from the wallpaper, Princess from a book of fairy tales, Bat, Cats, Tree, *et al.,* and some of these characters converse in a mixture of English nonsense and pseudo-Oriental gibberish. No work could be more difficult to produce, especially on such a shallow stage. Todd Bolender, watching rehearsals, thought, "There's nothing you can do with it!" And most of the critics concurred.

The Four Temperaments had a long history. When Balanchine was in Hollywood in 1937, he had felt sufficiently affluent and optimistic to ask Hindemith for a ballet. Hindemith had been "willing," but he was busy. By 1940 he was a refugee, teaching composition at Yale; his financial expectations had decreased, and he made Balanchine an offer of "a danceable, nameless suite for $250." Balanchine personally paid for the score that was to become *The Four Temperaments.* But when Tchelitchev was called in, his designs and demands were so extravagant that the ballet was set aside.

When Balanchine began to make new choreography for the score, he retained Tchelitchev's idea of the four "cardinal humors" or "temperaments," the preponderance of any one of which, according to medieval lore, was said to determine a person's character. Although Tchelitchev was no longer working on the production, Balanchine accepted his recommendation of the painter Kurt Seligmann. His designs proved as disastrous as Tchelitchev's earlier ones; yet the marvels of movement were not entirely invisible beneath the dancers' cumbersome trappings.

Hindemith's scheme for *The Four Temperaments* is complicated. Three themes are stated. In Balanchine's ballet, the interpreters of the four temperaments—Melancholic, Sanguinic, Phlegmatic and Choleric—dance variations on all three. Because the pace had to be varied, Balanchine could not keep Melancholic drooping sadly throughout his scene, or Phlegmatic sagging lazily in his; each had a lively dance with partners. Inconsistencies do not matter in the light of the choreographer's blazing invention. At the premiere, Taras thought that in the final dance, "Tanaquil Le Clercq [as Choleric] appeared like a flash of lightning, searing the eyes of the audience." In this work, Balanchine crossed a new frontier and extended the possibilities of ordered movement. Chujoy wrote later that "there were requests for a repeat performance, but Kirstein and Balanchine held to their intention of performing only for subscribers. As a result there was a new spurt of subscriptions: the plan caught on." Nearly four years later, Balanchine discarded the grotesque costumes, and *The Four Temperaments* was henceforth performed in practice clothes. It is now one of Balanchine's most popular ballets all over the world.

∙　∙　∙

Soon after the end of the Japanese war, the directors of the Paris Opéra had begun writing to Balanchine. Lifar, accused of collaboration, had been "purged," and the theater needed a choreographer. In 1946, Balanchine reached an agreement with the administrator, Georges Hirsch. An attraction for him was that his old friend Roger Desormière would be conducting the Opéra's orchestra. It was understood that Toumanova would accompany Balanchine to Paris as a guest artist. On September 11, he wrote to his "*cher* Deso" about the possibility of staging *Firebird* with new choreography and getting away from the "Russian restaurant style," and about *Apollo, Symphonie concertante,* even *The Sleeping Beauty* and *Casse-Noisette.* Of these projects only *Apollo* was realized. He concluded: "I should also like to bring an American dancer . . . Maria Tallchief, who has become my wife. . . . You may be sure I should not have married a dancer who was no good. . . ."

Balanchine had not been in Paris since he had left it with Dmitriev to join Kirstein in 1933. And he had never, even in the days of Diaghilev, had so large a company as the Opéra's at his disposal. He was amazed that the Opéra dancers were so well trained, although they had been given second-rate ballets to perform in recent years, and he watched the classes of Carlotta Zambelli to discover the secret. Many of these dancers were warm adherents of Lifar, so they might well have been expected to resent Balanchine's presence, but at first he met no opposition inside the company. With all his mastery, he was so simple and natural that he inspired affection as well as respect. Only when he began to bring forward and give roles to talented girls from the school, whom the French dancers called *"les petits rats,"* and to junior members of the corps de ballet, did he provide senior dancers with a pretext for indignation. Balanchine was indeed frustrated working with *fonctionnaires* (as opposed to *employés*) who could not be dismissed; he complained bitterly to Maria that the dancers' union allowed them two hours for lunch—in the course of which they drank wine.

Mina Curtiss was in Paris working on an edition of Proust's letters, and she is our evidence that by early April the choreographer had less cause for optimism than he had had on his arrival five weeks before. In her diary for April 5 she wrote:

I had a very congenial dinner with George Balanchine last night. He is suffering the same kind of frustration I am at French laziness and inefficiency. I've got more or less used to a four-day week, a four-hour day. . . . George swears that he has at most a two-hour working day twice a week. The *corps de ballet* has only one full rehearsal a week and this week they're not having any because of the holidays. The *régisseur* [probably Hirsch, the administrator], like the director of the library, is never available without an appointment and George can't get any scores at all to plan ballets, not even some Bizet he wanted. Then Lifar has left a corps of saboteurs and he [Balanchine] doubts whether he will get even two ballets done in the six months [*sic*] he is here. However, they are making beautiful new costumes for *Sérénade.* . . .

Maria, who had had to complete the Ballet Russe tour before coming, had injured her foot in Chicago, and it was still swollen when she arrived in Paris. At twenty-one, she had never been abroad before. She was overawed by Toumanova, the inspiration of her childhood. Because George paid so much attention to his old Russian colleague and because most of the press photographs were of him with Tamara, Maria felt slightly left out of things. She had never danced on a raked stage before. When she looked down the slope of the Opéra stage toward the footlights she was scared to death.

Although Balanchine never gave class to the company, he taught Toumanova and Maria in private. He delighted in showing Paris to Maria and introducing her to people. They visited "Deso," who was to conduct Balanchine's ballets, and his wife in the country. They lunched with Matilda Kchessinskaya and her husband, the Grand Duke Andrei, and it was at "the Princess's" that Maria first met Margot Fonteyn, who was taking a holiday from the Sadler's Wells Ballet. Old friends like Nicolas Nabokov and Nathan Milstein were also in Paris.

Serenade was danced for the first time in Europe on April 30. At the suggestion of Tchelitchev, Balanchine had invited André Delfau to design the setting, which consisted mostly of white draperies. In *Apollon Musagète*, Michel Renault and Maria Tallchief were Apollo and Terpsichore. On July 2, Maria danced the Fairy in *Le Baiser de la fée*, with Alexandre Kalioujny and Toumanova as the Bridegroom and the Bride and was much praised.

Balanchine's final work for the Opéra was entirely new. Bizet's Symphony in C Major, written when the composer was seventeen, had never been performed in his lifetime; it was, in fact, not discovered and played until 1935. An exhilarating piece, with a romantic slow movement, it is ideal dance music. A complicated synopsis for a ballet, with a Ruby Priestess, a Sapphire Spirit, an Emerald Spirit and a Crystal Spirit in a Palace of Diamonds, has survived. Whoever concocted this—possibly the designer—Balanchine soon discarded it; he retained only the idea of using red costumes in the first movement, blue in the second, green in the third and white with diamonds in the fourth. He called the work *Palais de cristal.* It was the most spectacular choreography he had made since *Ballet Imperial,* and he arranged it for more dancers than he had ever before been able to muster simultaneously on a stage—forty-eight in all. Leonor Fini created a handsome grotto, and the stage was full of color and glitter.

This was to become one of the choreographer's most acclaimed and most popular ballets, yet it was created under enormous difficulties. It had been hard for Balanchine to get at the music because the archives were always shut, and hard to assemble his dancers for rehearsal. He also suffered the antipathy of Lifar's adherents. It was a real test of endurance.

Before the end of Balanchine's stay in Paris, there was a gala performance at Les Ambassadeurs restaurant in the gardens of the Champs-Elysées. Various stars were to perform, and Balanchine asked his dear Tamarochka if she would like him to arrange a number for her. *Would* she! He had found a Russian dance for solo violin by Tchaikovsky; he and Mama Toumanova discovered an old traditional costume with *kokoshnik* (beaded headdress) in the wardrobe of the Opéra. Toumanova thought that the dance was like a Fabergé jewel, but Balanchine's name did not even appear on the program. It was the last choreography he made on her.

·   ·   ·

THE DANCERS of the Opéra petitioned the directorate to give them a permanent *maître de ballet.* (Lifar would be allowed back in September, but not as a dancer, and his return caused a stage-hands' strike.) But Balanchine had never intended to stay longer than five months in Paris, because, as he told Maria, he felt that something was really starting in New York at last.

The Marquis de Cuevas had taken over the Nouveau Ballet de Monte Carlo from Lifar, and Maria's younger sister, Marjorie, had joined it. So had the tall, romantic-looking, Russian-born George Skibine; and during the Cuevas company's visit to Vichy that August he and Marjorie were married. Maria and Balanchine attended their wedding, as did Maria's former teacher, Bronislava Nijinska. Balanchine respected Mme. Nijinska, though he did not like her choreography. When she attacked him with the words, "I always thought you were such a gentleman. How could you do *Le*

Baiser de la fée when you knew I had done it?" Balanchine replied, "I *am* a gentleman. I let you do it first."

Balanchine and Maria arrived back in New York on August 14. After a weekend on Fire Island with Natalie Molostwoff, Balanchine took the train to Los Angeles. He arrived at 7:30 A.M. on August 21, spent most of every day with the Stravinskys and left on the twenty-sixth. Vera Stravinsky wrote in a letter to a friend: "Balanchine, returning from Paris, told how difficult it was for him to struggle against all the intrigues of the Opéra and the cost of living. He returned without a penny and as thin as a wick, and came here for a week [*sic*] for the sole reason of telling us in detail about his life there and how much he suffered." But surely Balanchine must also have been longing to hear how *Orpheus* was coming along, and Stravinsky must have played him some of it, even though he had not finished the orchestration.

Shortly after he got back from California, Balanchine abandoned his dancers to rehearse a new work for Ballet Theatre. He may have needed the money, but he also liked what he had been asked to do. Lucia Chase and Oliver Smith wanted a ballet to show off the technique of Igor Youskevitch, whom Balanchine had proposed taking with him to the Paris Opéra and who did not fit into Ballet Theatre's modern repertory. Charles Payne describes how Balanchine was asked if he could make a ballet to the fourth movement of Tchaikovsky's Suite No. 3 in G Major:

Balanchine took the score and returned shortly with the answer, "But of course." Four days before the company departed on tour, he auditioned and chose the female soloists and corps de ballet. In the next three days he set the first movement [*sic*] in seven hours of rehearsal. While the company was on tour, Nora Kaye conducted three one-hour rehearsals to keep the choreography fresh in the dancers' minds. Balanchine rejoined the company in Wilmington, Delaware, and continued rehearsing during the next few weeks until the opening at the New York City Center on November 11, 1947. [The premiere had in fact taken place in September in Richmond, Virginia.] In all, he had taken thirty-nine hours to create a thirty-two-minute ballet. . . . The ballet . . . was formally named *Theme and Variations* and opened on schedule. It not only provided Youskevitch with a stellar role, but it became, and has remained, one of the undimming gems in the Ballet Theatre repertory. It is safe to say that additional hours expended on its creation would not have improved this work of genius.

Before *Theme and Variations* was shown to New Yorkers, the opening performances of Ballet Society's second "season"—or, rather, second year of intermittent performances—had taken place at City Center, where future seasons were to be held. Balanchine's contribution was the Mozart *Symphonie concertante,* which was given a backcloth copied in gold monochrome from an architectural décor by one of the Bibiena family; the women dancers were dressed in the plainest white ballet costumes with the briefest of tutus; and the two *concertante* instruments, violin and viola, were represented by Tanaquil Le Clercq and Maria Tallchief—the latter appearing with Ballet Society for the first time.

Because Balanchine submitted himself completely to the subtle measures of Mozart's music, *Symphonie concertante* is probably the least theatrical ballet he ever made. It lacks even the implied man-woman relationship that classical pas de deux can hardly escape, for the single man is used for support only in the slow movement, while in the first and third movements the two women respond to each other. The music in the Andante is irresistible, but the opening Allegro maestoso and the closing Presto might seem mathematical to the inexperienced listener. The marvel of the music is the interplay between the two solo instruments and their relationship to the orchestra; and this correspondence is echoed in the choreography. Counterpoint is, after all, the most intellectual of aesthetic pleasures.

·   ·   ·

THAT AUTUMN, a handsome and intelligent girl from Buffalo named Betty Cage telephoned the Ballet Society office to ask for a secretarial job. She had been working for an avant-garde art magazine, *View,* and Tchelitchev told Kirstein she would be useful. She was hired as assistant to Frances Hawkins, the business manager, and when Hawkins left in 1948, Betty, aged thirty, was on her own. Balanchine and Kirstein came to rely on her more and more, first as a sort of personnel manager and eventually as general administrator. She held her position, which became of ever-increasing importance, for thirty-eight years.

. . .

On May 20, 1947, Kirstein wrote to Stravinsky that he wanted to have a two-week season in New York, that he hoped the composer would score *Orpheus* for a small orchestra, and that he would like to give *Apollo* on the same program. Stravinsky telephoned back that *Orpheus* required only forty-three musicians, twenty-four of whom would be strings, but *Apollo* would need thirty-six strings. On September 23, Stravinsky finished orchestrating the ballet. On October 16, when Balanchine and Kirstein received copies, Balanchine sat straight down at the piano and began to play it.

Because Stravinsky knew that Balanchine understood his music, he accepted suggestions from him. It had been agreed that at the climax of the pas de deux, when Orpheus, against the orders of Pluto, tears off his blindfold and looks at Eurydice, there should be a moment of silence in the music. "How long will it take you to die, Maria?" Stravinsky asked. It took her one measure, and this was written into the score. Balanchine then proposed that the string music in F major should return at this point, and his idea was adopted.

In December Maria was in Hollywood with her family, and Balanchine planned to join her for Christmas and spend some time with Stravinsky. He arranged to travel with Nicolas Nabokov, who had been invited by the composer. Christmas dinner was at the Stravinsky house. "There were," wrote Nabokov, "Stravinsky's daughter and her French husband, the two Bolms . . . Eugene Berman and Stravinsky's physician, Dr. Edel, . . . and, finally the two Balanchines. . . . (Balanchine and I had silver goblets for drinking vodka.) . . . Conversation, out of deference to Maria Balanchine, lingered in a kind of pigeon [*sic*] English, but after dinner and late into the night the linguistic wind blew stronger and stronger in the Russian direction. . . ."

Tchelitchev had bowed out of doing the décor for *Orpheus,* so Kirstein, who had spoken to Balanchine on the telephone, wrote to Stravinsky proposing Isamu Noguchi, an American of Japanese parentage who was famous for his fine pottery fired in Japan, for his carvings and perhaps most of all for his globular lampshades of waxed paper stretched over wire frames. His work was startling, but fortunately both the Stravinskys, who came to New York to attend rehearsals, loved the scale models they were shown.

On the evening after their visit to Noguchi's studio, the Stravinskys were to dine with the Balanchines. That afternoon George had a rehearsal, and he left a note for "dear Mashka" asking her to keep an eye on the meat in the oven and to pour two spoonfuls of wine over it; he signed himself "General Coock," with a little self-portrait wearing a chef's hat. When Stravinsky rang the bell and burst into the apartment Maria dropped the potatoes. She was upset, but he said, "Oh, Maria, they'll taste much better now."

The poet W. H. Auden, who was writing the libretto of Stravinsky's opera *The Rake's Progress,* also came—and drank a whole bottle of Cointreau after dinner. Robert Craft has recorded that Stravinsky often found it hard to make out Auden's English—and, for that matter, his French and German. Balanchine could not understand a single word he said.

Rehearsals for *Orpheus* were spread over several months. Meanwhile, two more new ballets were presented by Ballet Society. The idea for *The Triumph of Bacchus and Ariadne* came from its designer, Corrado Cagli. His fellow Italian Vittorio Rieti took a carnival song written by Lorenzo de' Medici as the starting point of a masque "celebrating Youth and Age, sacred and profane love: of a kind that might have been performed at the Florentine "court." These masques were, in fact, the predecessors of classical ballet.

Nicholas Magallanes thought that the pas de deux he danced with Tanaquil Le Clercq was a "very pretty, leaves-in-the-hair, nude-looking, drapery kind of thing." Marie-Jeanne, who had recently rejoined the company, danced a Nymph; she considered her wild solo one of the most effective of her career. Francisco Moncion played Midas, who in his greed for gold had to grovel on the ground, scratching the stage with his nails. "Make more noise," said Balanchine. "More noise! Like chalk on blackboard!"

For the next program, Balanchine staged a simplified version of the Bizet ballet he had devised for the Paris Opéra, renaming it *Symphony in C.* Since Ballet Society could provide only thirty-eight dancers, as opposed to the forty-eight he had used in Paris, every member of the corps, instead of appearing in only one movement and then the finale, had to dance in all five, so there was no question of dressing them in different colors. All the women were in white and the men in black tights with white socks and slippers.

Like the French, most New Yorkers found the ballet irresistible. "If there ever was any doubt that Balanchine was the greatest choreographer of our time," wrote Chujoy, "this doubt was dispelled when the curtain came down on his *Symphony in C.*" But John Martin was still unpersuaded: "Balanchine has once again given us that ballet of his, this time for some inscrutable reason to the Bizet symphony. Up to the middle of the third movement [when Martin left the theater to write his piece], he had used virtually all of his familiar tricks. . . . "

Nicholas Magallanes was to create the role of Orpheus, but Balanchine had begun to work out his choreography at the very beginning of 1948, before Magallanes became available, and Francisco Moncion, who would dance the Dark Angel, had not only to learn his own part but to stand in for Orpheus. Moncion found, as he had with *The Four Temperaments,* that to work on a ballet with Balanchine from the very start was intensely stimulating. "Nobody showed how to perform a movement, whether for man or woman, more wonderfully than Balanchine," Moncion explained. "His limbs expressed his mind." He took such pains that Moncion thought working with him was like a million dollars' worth of training. One day at the School, Maria came in after a class to find the two men tied together in an extraordinary knot. "Take your hands off my husband!" she exclaimed; then, after asking George if he would like chicken for dinner, she departed with a good exit line: "I'll leave you boys together."

Maria was, of course, to dance Eurydice; and the Bacchantes, who tore Orpheus to pieces after his return to a second mourning on earth, were led by Tanaquil Le Clercq, the first ballerina to be completely a product of the School of American Ballet.

Three years after she won a scholarship in 1941, she was given a fellowship. Since then, Balanchine had entrusted her with Choleric in *The Four Temperaments;* she had been singled out by the critics in Taras's *Minotaur;* she had danced with Magallanes in Merce Cunningham's *The Seasons,* with Maria Tallchief in *Symphonie concertante,* and in the second movement of Bizet's *Symphony in C.* Her father was of French origin, and her mother came from a well-to-do St. Louis family. Tanaquil, who was born in Paris, was witty, intellectual, impulsive, tall and thin, with long, Alice-in-Wonderland hair. Her mocking eyes seemed to indicate that she was cut out for comedy, but the very different roles listed above indicate how versatile she became. In 1948 she was eighteen.

None of Balanchine's dancers, who worked so hard in these months to make possible the sparse performances of Ballet Society, had any notion that he or she was in at the beginning of a great venture. None had any other employment in the theater. They rehearsed unpaid, knowing that they would receive eighteen dollars a show. They were grateful for a chance to perform, and as the date of the next program drew near, they went on diets. Maria, of course, lived with Balanchine, but he had very little money at the time, and he never took a penny from Ballet Society. Tanaquil lived with her mother. Magallanes roomed with a friend. Moncion worked as a model in an art school before going off to take class. But all of them were to look back later in wonder on these "great days" when Balanchine and Stravinsky made each one of them a star.

Kirstein thought the collaboration of composer and choreographer on *Orpheus* must have been the closest since that of Tchaikovsky and Petipa. Balanchine had told Stravinsky that the pas de deux should take "about two and a half minutes," but Stravinsky scolded him. "Don't tell me 'about.' . . . It's either two minutes and twenty, thirty or forty seconds; no more, no less."

An important part of the décor was a "translucent curtain of China silk" similar to that which had fallen from the flies to cover the heroine of *Errante.* According to Kirstein:

The silk for this curtain cost over a thousand dollars. Having it sewed and delivered to the theater cost even more, and . . . we had no cash to pay for it two days before a dress rehearsal. . . . We had spent what there was and could borrow no more. . . . Noguchi was a model of patient despair, having been refused further credit from one scenery shop because previous bills were unpaid . . . We did not notice that Balanchine had disappeared from rehearsal. Suddenly he reappeared with five hundred dollars in cash in each hand and tossed the money to Frances Hawkins. We begged to know where he'd found it; he would say nothing except that he hadn't robbed a bank.

John Taras has said of *Orpheus*:

The choreography for Magallanes was unlike anything Balanchine had done before. There were very few steps and no conventional ones. The movement was more like the miming of a song than the execution of a dance. It implied a vocal origin. The long, sustained phrases of Eurydice, as she yearned for a reaction from Orpheus, were beautifully interpreted by Tallchief. The [Dark] Angel and Apollo mimed rather than danced, as Balanchine played down the cool emotions of the score. Only the Furies and the Bacchantes really danced, and with his arrangement for the former, Balanchine was never completely satisfied. But the Bacchantes were given an extraordinary exultant choreography, in which the terrifying Le Clercq, wearing a long red wig, clawed, pounced and stamped on Orpheus, finally destroying him; and this was the passage that Balanchine most loved to rehearse at subsequent revivals.

That Stravinsky himself was to conduct the first performance of his new ballet made April 28, 1948, a doubly special occasion for the members of Ballet Society. When the ballet was over, Chujoy reported, "there was a seemingly unending ovation for the dancers, for Balanchine, for Stravinsky, for Noguchi. The audience applauded, stamped, shouted. Everyone . . . was very happy." There were four more performances by Ballet Society on the three following days, each including *Orpheus.* To these the nonsubscribing public was admitted. Yet with all its success, Ballet Society still could not count the New York City Center of Music and Drama as its home.

Shortly before the first night of *Orpheus,* Kirstein had been summoned to Nelson Rockefeller's office in Rockefeller Center to meet the latter's first cousin by marriage, George de Cuevas. The marquis offered him the Cosmopolitan Theater at Columbus Circle, which W. R. Hearst had built for Marion Davies and which de Cuevas had renovated. He announced that he and the new company he planned to found would share it with Ballet Society, and that for the latter it would be rent free. "Too good to be true," wrote Kirstein; and "too good to be true" it was. The marquis returned to Europe, and nothing more was heard of the plan. When, therefore, Kirstein was asked to pay a visit to the office of the managing director of City Center, Morton Baum, to discuss a new proposition, he was "short and irritable." Hadn't he heard it all before—from Edward Johnson at the Metropolitan, from Cuevas?

On the previous evening, Baum, lawyer, tax counsel to the city and amateur musician, had seen *Orpheus* and had fallen in love with it. By his own account:

It was the strangest meeting. Kirstein was belligerent, almost hostile to me, vituperative against the entire ballet field, its policies, managers, repertoire. He seemed not to believe in the sincerity of my call and was suspicious of everything I said. He told me that the funds of Ballet Society were exhausted and that it might have to fold, but that he would carry on his struggle to create an American ballet.

There was already a New York City drama company and a New York City Opera that held seasons at the City Center at popular prices. Baum asked Kirstein if he would like Ballet Society to participate in the opera seasons, as well as giving regular performances of its own. He emphasized that he was only one of the board of directors and that the others might not approve the idea. He explained that the drama company, with its lower costs, brought in revenue, while the opera company ran at a loss. There would be no question of diverting funds to subsidize the ballet. The ballet company would, for the time being, have to cover its own deficit, but with the amalgamation this would surely be smaller than before.

Finally he asked, "Mr. Kirstein, how would you like the idea of Ballet Society becoming the New York City Ballet?"

After a moment of stunned silence, Lincoln Kirstein exclaimed, "If you do that for us I will give you in three years the finest ballet company in America."

He ran all the way to Madison Avenue to tell Balanchine.

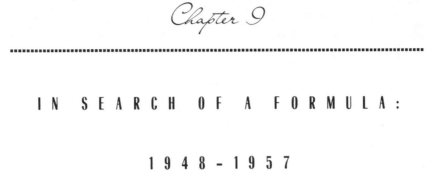

Chapter 9

IN SEARCH OF A FORMULA:

1948 - 1957

U NA KAI, a dancer in the company who later became a ballet mistress, remembers what a thrilling moment it was for the dancers of Ballet Society when Lincoln Kirstein came backstage and told them they were to become the New York City Ballet. Some of them, who had given up much to work for Balanchine, saw for the first time the prospect of financial security.

The security was, however, of a very limited kind. The final season of Ballet Society had lasted from April 28 to May 1, 1948— four days. The new company's first season would begin October 11. Until rehearsals started, the dancers would live on unemployment insurance, and Balanchine himself would be working in Europe for the Marquis de Cuevas's Grand Ballet de Monte-Carlo. During the fall, he would be back at the old grind of devising dances for operas—this time for the New York City Opera.

For the next few years, Kirstein and Balanchine were uncertain up to the last moment when their New York seasons would be—or if they would be at all. Morton Baum made money for City Center by renting it out to visiting attractions, and the new ballet company had to be fitted in when there was a gap. Once they had resigned themselves to the fact that they would never enjoy a federal subsidy—for what did Louisiana or North Dakota care about subsidizing a New York company?—and once Balanchine had firmly declined to embark on tours with Hurok, which would have meant one-night stands and a reduced orchestra, it was necessary to find other opportunities to keep the dancers dancing. At first, foreign tours were the only solution, then gradually it became possible to count on summer dates on the West Coast and in Chicago.

During all the years at City Center, Balanchine never accepted a salary. He was paid to stage ballets for other companies and occasionally to arrange dances for a musical.

When one realizes how difficult it was to hold a short New York season once, twice or three times a year; to plan tours and overcome the incessant problems that cropped up in the course of them; to meet deficits, raise money for production costs and pay dancers a meager wage, the actual making of ballets by Balanchine— several new ones every year—appears almost incidental. Yet it was for the creation of these ballets that the School and the company had come into existence; and it was to facilitate their·performance under the best possible conditions that Kirstein, Cage and production manager/stage director Edward Bigelow devoted their lives.

On October 11, the first performance of the New York City Ballet (apart from the company's participation in *Carmen* the previous day) took place. The program was *Concerto Barocco, Orpheus* and *Symphony in C*—three marvels, but chosen because there was no money for a new work.

That fall Marie-Jeanne danced in *Serenade;* and since the Cuevas company had temporarily fallen apart, André Eglevsky was free to make guest appearances in *Symphony in C.* On November 8, Balanchine surprised everyone by taking Barzin's place on the podium to conduct the Bizet. At the end the orchestra stood to applaud him.

This first season, which ended on November 23, the company played to little more than fifty percent of capacity. According to Chujoy, Kirstein, who himself had made up the $47,000 deficit, was deeply discouraged. Balanchine, however, argued that "the company simply had not had a fair chance," since the seasons of the Ballet Russe and the Paris Opéra company had emptied the purses of the ballet-going public; and Baum agreed with him. His admiration for the company had increased. He proposed that in the future the New York City Ballet be independent of the Opera, and City Center would take over from Ballet Society the financial responsibility for its running expenses, leaving the Society simply to raise money for new productions.

Jerome Robbins, whose ballet *Fancy Free* had been the basis for a successful musical, *On the Town,* and who was much in demand for devising dances on Broadway, felt irresistibly drawn to become part of the noble enterprise, and offered his services as a choreographer. He was made welcome and began work on *The Guests,* to a score by Marc Blitzstein. Balanchine also asked Antony Tudor to revive his *Time Table,* which had been performed only in South America. Its music by Copland added another American component to the repertoire.

In July 1948, Balanchine and Maria left for Monte Carlo, where Balanchine was to rehearse two ballets with the Grand Ballet de Monte-Carlo. When the company traveled to London for a season at Covent Garden, *Concerto Barocco* was given on opening night. It was the first time the work had been performed outside the Americas: but by the time *Night Shadow* was given and acclaimed at the end of August, the Balanchines had returned to the States.

In the fall, not only did all the principal dancers of the New York City Ballet—except Marie-Jeanne—return to the fold for the

November season, but little red-headed Janet Reed and dark, imposing Melissa Hayden came from Ballet Theatre to join the company. Jerome Robbins signed on as a dancer as well as a choreographer. Balanchine made him associate artistic director of the company.

. . .

AT THE end of Janaury 1949, NYCB dancers were faced with a nine-month layoff. No one could blame them if they sought employment with other companies. Balanchine was concerned that Maria, who was becoming a better dancer than ever under his guidance, keep dancing. The resuscitation of Ballet Theatre provided her with an opportunity, and she went on tour with them. Her husband rehearsed her in the "Bluebird" pas de deux from *The Sleeping Beauty*, which she danced with Youskevitch, and also in *Apollo*, *Theme and Variations* and Antony Tudor's *Jardin aux lilas*.

While Maria was with Ballet Theatre, Balanchine did his first work for television, a version of *Cinderella* to the music of Tchaikovsky, with Tanaquil Le Clercq and Herbert Bliss as Cinderella and the Prince.

One evening in the spring, when both the Balanchines were in New York together, Sol Hurok asked them to dine at the Russian Tea Room. His question to Balanchine came as a surprise: "Don't you want your wife to dance the Firebird?" Maria, with "visions of Karsavina in her mind," nearly fainted. Balanchine, who seldom showed surprise, sniffed, made his customary "mmm" noise and murmured, "Oh? Well . . . perhaps." As it turned out, this friendly suggestion from his old enemy Hurok was not entirely disinterested. Since Hurok had ceased to present Ballet Theatre, he had been paying storage fees for Chagall's *Firebird* sets and costumes. Balanchine, like the composer himself, was less fond of Stravinsky's early "Russian-export" style than of his later work, but he recognized that the Firebird would be an ideal role for Maria. A bargain was struck: New York City Ballet bought the Chagall production for $2,500, and during a summer holiday with Maria in California, Balanchine discussed with Stravinsky the form his new version, which was to be a suite from the original score, would take.

Meanwhile, the fame of *Orpheus* had crossed the Atlantic. David Webster, the general administrator of London's Royal Opera House, coveted it for the Sadler's Wells Ballet—which, incidentally, Hurok was planning to present at the Metropolitan Opera House in the fall of 1949. The company had been founded—and was directed—by Balanchine's old colleague Ninette de Valois. David Webster cabled Balanchine asking if he would produce *Orpheus* for the English company while they were in New York. Betty Cage forwarded the cable to California, asking him, "Why not tell him we'd be glad to take our company over and perform *Orpheus* for them?" This is the first known suggestion of a London season for the New York City Ballet—or of any season outside the United States. Balanchine answered that he would be busy with his own company at the time of the Sadler's Wells visit, but that he and Webster could at least discuss matters then.

The Sadler's Wells Ballet opened at the Metropolitan Opera House on October 9 with *The Sleeping Beauty;* Margot Fonteyn was Aurora and Constant Lambert conducted. New York had never seen a full-length classical ballet presented with such magnificence, and the show was a sensation. Kirstein and Balanchine, whose favorite ballet this was, witnessed the ovation, attended Mayor O'Dwyer's party for the visitors at Gracie Mansion and read the laudatory notices with mixed feelings. They could never hope for a federal subsidy such as Sadler's Wells received through the Arts Council from the British Treasury. Whatever reservations they might have about some of the British dancers and their training, there was much for them to admire—and envy.

I had written from London to ask Kirstein, whom I had never met, to write an article on the American debut of Sadler's Wells for my magazine, *Ballet.* Since Kirstein was hoping to take the New York City Ballet, sooner or later, to London, this was something he could not provide, but he wrote me his opinion very frankly, and a correspondence began which continued intermittently for over thirty years. He ended his first letter with a statement of the credo that had guided and would continue to guide his life: "Balanchine is simply the only genius of the dance since Petipa. . . . This is hard to swallow, as you know; and to dance the hard works you need a kind of heartless, soulless, angelic type of dancer, which he has invented from our school."

.   .   .

Firebird, whether choreographed by Fokine, Balanchine, Cranko or Taras, is an unusual ballet in that the ballerina's big solo comes right at the beginning and is followed by the *pas d'action* of her capture by the Prince. Maria Tallchief described how Balanchine's choreography took shape:

After the opening variation, you immediately go into the pas de deux. Breathwise and musclewise it was very demanding. [Balanchine] did the variation first and then the pas de deux; we didn't really do it all in one stretch. It was only when it was all together and I finally went through it without stopping that I realized it was practically impossible. The variation contained many low, fast jumps, near the floor, lots of quick footwork, sudden changes of direction, off-balance turns, turns from pointe to pointe, turned-in, turned-out positions, one after another. It was another way of moving. . . . There was no time.

Moncion, who danced the Prince, has said, "The ballet was made for Maria, and she went after it like a demon, with ferocity, as if possessed."

When the pas de deux, rehearsed in private, was shown for the first time to the company, they burst into applause. Even so, the ballet's overwhelming success with the public took everyone by surprise. "It was like a football stadium." Indeed, *Time* magazine wrote, "The flashing first-scene duet brought a touchdown roar from the audience." Next morning, as the Balanchines were out walking, George took Maria into Tiffany's and ordered her a gold compact with a firebird on it.

Four days afterward, Balanchine presented a new ballet, *Bourrée fantasque.* It had four movements, and Una Kai said he arranged one a day. The music was by Emmanuel Chabrier. Barbara Karinska, the celebrated theatrical dressmaker, who had worked in London and Paris before the war, arriving from triumphs in Hollywood to begin what was to be a long association with the New York City Ballet, made an extraordinarily generous gesture: she gave Balanchine the costumes for *Bourrée fantasque* for the price of the materials.

Balanchine also staged *The Prodigal Son* for the first time since the death of Diaghilev, and took endless pains rehearsing Robbins and Maria in the two main roles. Apart from his *Petrushka* for Ballet Theatre, Robbins had never been seen in a great tragic role before—and of course he had never seen Lifar in 1929. Vera Stravinsky *had,* and toward the end of her life she said there had never been a Prodigal as good as Robbins.

Balanchine left New York before the end of the season, arriving in London on March 18 to teach *Ballet Imperial* to the Sadler's Wells Ballet. Margot Fonetyn and Michael Somes, the two principals, were so used to dancing Ashton's choreography that Balanchine's demands were a shock to them. Nevertheless, Somes was thrilled by the arrangement of the piano cadenzas in *Ballet Imperial,* and always remembered how Balanchine liked "long leaps, high arabesques and little or no demi-plié, also most things done at double speed!" Later Somes became exasperated at always being congratulated on his noble manner as he walked on and off the stage in the second movement—from which Balanchine had cut all the pantomime.

Beryl Grey was happy to be chosen as the second ballerina, and was determined to learn all she could during the "wonderful classes" Balanchine gave before rehearsals. She was "amazed when he taught not to put the heel down when landing from a *grand jeté en tournant.*" Beryl became engaged to be married that spring and rushed to announce the good news to Balanchine. To her disappointment "he showed much displeasure and said a ballerina could not spare time for the luxury of being married." Still, she recognized that "he was a great man who demanded everything from his dancers and knew how to extract it."

On the evening after Balanchine's arrival, he, Kirstein, Ashton and I dined with Lydia Lopoukhova (Lady Keynes) in Gordon Square, Bloomsbury. This was very near to where Balanchine and his colleagues from Russia had taken lodgings in 1924. It was long after midnight when we started home, so the square where Vanessa Bell and Virginia Woolf had held court was silent and empty of traffic. A solitary black cat lingered near the big Victorian church at the corner; when I called "pooza-pooza!" to it in the wheedling voice I always use for addressing cats, it crossed the road to be patted. Balanchine, whose love of cats became legendary, was intrigued. Many years later, he interrupted a class he was giving in New York to inquire, when he saw me enter the room, "How are the poozas of Bloomsbury?" And during one of the last rehearsals for the Stravinsky Festival of 1972, when Kay Mazzo appeared with a very small kitten in her arms, Balanchine instantly dropped everything and went to it, crooning, "Kitty, kittteee. . . . "

. . .

KIRSTEIN was hoping to sign a contract with David Webster for a NYCB season at Covent Garden, but he found him hard to deal with; so Frances Hawkins flew over to see what she could do. She was no more successful than Kirstein and decided to leave on April 6, the day after the first night of *Ballet Imperial.*

That ballet's triumph changed everything. There were seventeen curtain calls, and the company gave its guest choreographer a wreath. Balanchine wrote to Maria that the "cold" London audience "was wild almost like New York." At a party afterward, Frances Hawkins went up to Webster to say good-bye. "Webster, all smiles, stopped her farewells; she must not leave London until he had signed our contract," wrote Kirstein. Would Miss Hawkins be at his office at eleven next morning? She would. Covent Garden agreed to pay the New York City Ballet £2,000 a week during their six-week season, and half their transportation costs. A provincial tour was also planned.

To make the London season possible, all the dancers took a cut of ten dollars a week, because living in England was said to be cheaper. The night of July 10, 1950, when the company opened their first season abroad, at Covent Garden, was as momentous an occasion for them as the opening night at the Metropolitan Opera had been for Sadler's Wells. If they failed, they might have to close for good.

Although Londoners, accustomed to spectacular classics, were slightly chilled by NYCB's sparsity of décor, they responded on the whole with enthusiasm to Balanchine's inventiveness and to the special quality of his dancers. The theater was sold to about 75 percent capacity throughout the season. Most of the critics, however, were both disappointed and disappointing. Cyril Beaumont, in the *Sunday Times,* wrote of the "cold, impersonal quality" of Balanchine's ballets, which strongly piqued Balanchine. Even a quarter of a century later, when he watched a dancer moving too carefully or "correctly" in class, he would exclaim, "Beaumont, Beaumont!" James Monahan in the *Guardian* called *Orpheus* "a mild, undramatic account of a legend which itself is far from undramatic or mild." The critics' reaction to *Firebird* was the biggest disappointment of all. The Fokine version, with its much longer score, was clearly considered sacred. But my life was changed by the revelation of Balanchine's varied genius.

The company had a week's layoff without pay, and because living in London had indeed proved cheaper than New York, some dancers, including Maria Tallchief, could afford a trip to Paris. They returned to embark with the company on an unsuccessful provincial tour of Manchester, Liverpool and Croydon.

When Balanchine and I dined alone at Venezia in Soho, I asked innumerable questions but was too scatterbrained to record most of the answers. I can remember only a few fragments. "Do you think history goes in circles, repeating itself at regular intervals?" "No, it goes in spirals." "Who is your favorite heroine in fiction?" "Natasha in *War and Peace.*" "Which is your favorite opera?" "*Don Giovanni.*" We also discussed food and cooking. Balanchine said that if he ever retired, he would like to open a restaurant— "quite a small one, just six or seven tables." He had taken a furnished flat near the Wallace Collection. It was here, at supper with Maria and Tanaquil Le Clercq, that he quoted my review of the Weber *Pas de deux romantique,* which had appeared that morning, saying I had "understood exactly" the demi-caractère, slightly tongue-in-cheek quality he had introduced into the classical pas de deux. This would hardly be worth mentioning if it were not for the fact that even admirers such as Chujoy missed the point of the duet, calling it "plain bad." It was also in Balanchine's apartment, on the Sunday night after the season finished, that Lucian Freud began a drawing of Balanchine, which he never completed. The only paper available was a sheet of foolscap ruled for the keeping of accounts.

The New York City Ballet would give only three more seasons in London before Balanchine's death thirty-three years later. In spite of this, the number of his British admirers steadily increased, and several British companies asked him to produce—or send one of his assistants to produce—some of his most popular works for them.

· · ·

To SAY that Balanchine was not cut out for matrimony—at least for matrimony American-style—is an understatement. Although in the ballet classroom it was all blood, sweat and tears for the girls he schooled and loved, "making the beautiful more beautiful" (his own expression), in the home he expected them to recline in a perfumed paradise, fanned by eunuchs. It is paradoxical that he, who liked to do his own ironing—not only

because he found the whole procedure relaxing, but because of
the unpleasant smell shirts had when they came back from the
laundry—should be irritated when Maria scrubbed the floor and
asked him to walk on newspaper. Maria had a very strong character and was not prepared to stand for any nonsense. She also
liked to play poker—which Balanchine did not—and on free
evenings Magallanes and a few other dancers were glad to have
a game with her. Friends noticed that Balanchine and Maria
were seldom alone together.

Byron once confessed, "My heart always alights on the nearest
perch." With Balanchine it was natural that the nearest perch
should be the latest young dancer he was training and creating
roles for, the up-and-coming ballerina, the rising star. In London,
he and Maria had "more or less agreed to separate." Tanaquil Le
Clercq was sharing their apartment. "I was very close to Tanny,"
Maria said later. "I had no idea there was a romance going on. I
thought she liked Lew." It was when Maria returned from her visit
to France between the end of the London season and the opening
of the tour in Manchester that she became aware of the situation.
Her response was to move out.

■   ■   ■

BALANCHINE had always loved the music of Ravel, which musicolo-
gists tended to rate as of lesser importance, because less revolutionary, than that of Debussy. Diaghilev had refused Ravel's *La
Valse,* written for him in 1920, because he found it untheatrical;
Ravel never forgave him. In 1951, Balanchine decided to make a
ballet to it, but since it was short, he decided to preface it with the
composer's earlier *Valses nobles et sentimentales.*

When Ravel composed *La Valse* in the 1920s, the theme of what
Ravel, quoting Comte de Salvandy, had called "dancing on the
edge of a volcano" was associated in his mind with 1914; to us it
may suggest 1939. It was a Romantic or Gothic theme that recalls
Poe's "Masque of the Red Death." When Balanchine decided to
link the two compositions, the first part of his ballet took on a

quality that, without having any specific period, was essentially French. By some marvel of intuition, the choreographer, who never went out in society because it tired and bored him, saw into the heart of sophisticated Paris. Here was a *beau monde* which, despite the thunder and sunsets of the Romantic movement, had never outlived the rococo period, when love was a game or an applied art, like cabinetmaking or *haute cuisine.*

The costumes for such a ballet had to attain the very height of elegance, which in France implied simplicity and understatement. Karinska had, after all, worked in Paris—and made Bérard's costumes for *Cotillon*—before she came to America. Her full-skirted ball gowns had steel-gray satin bodices, and beneath the layers of gray tulle overskirt, crimson or vermilion petticoats flashed through. These dresses, as well as the women's long white gloves, appeared at moments almost to have dictated the choreography. A characteristic gesture of the feckless girls would be a coquettish fluffing-up of their skirts. The men wore stylized evening dress, black and white.

The first of the eight waltzes in the opening section is played as an overture. The second reveals three ladies, who stand in a row facing the audience, holding up their arms affectedly in a way that appears to proclaim their charming but sinister authority. They are society's witches, who console themselves for the loss of youth by the exercise of power. As they dance, their hands make absurd, coy, mannered gestures, which seem traditional signals, like the language of an eighteenth-century fan.

The tripping third waltz, in which two lovers dance slowly, acquires an almost pastoral quality from the oboe. The fourth, for another couple, is more ecstatic. In the fifth there are plaintive clarinets. The quicker sixth is a solo for a girl. As she dips and circles, she seems to sweep the floor with her skirt. Her lover comes to rejoin her in the seventh, but is intercepted by the three affected, dangerous ladies, and the girl runs off.

A climactic phrase of music foretells the coming nightmare of *La Valse.* This may have been what gave Balanchine the idea of linking Ravel's two compositions; certainly it allows us to recognize the three ladies as harbingers of doom. The eighth waltz brings on a hesitant girl in white. (Tanaquil La Clercq later described how she enjoyed watching the earlier waltzes from the wings. When she made her entrance it was "like going to a party.") Her arms mime the music. A man comes toward her. They do backbends and at first seem not to know each other. They dance with a ceremonial and slightly depraved elegance. Dark-blue gauze curtains—which have hitherto reduced the depth of the stage—part as the music of *La Valse* begins, revealing black-draped chandeliers glimmering in the shadows; the decks are cleared for some disastrous event. Low bass rumblings are followed by eerie glissandos on the woodwinds and deceptive showers of golden rain on the harp. Lit by spotlights, dancers pursue each other in a desperate search. We have a glimpse of three ladies hiding their faces—are they the ominous trio of the preceding scene? The lights go up. The girl in white is the leader of the ball. But she is doomed. A sinister black-clad man stalks on, followed by a servant bearing gifts. At first the girl turns away in horror, then she becomes fascinated and accepts the jet necklace, the transparent black dress to be fastened on over her white one, the long black gloves. Balanchine gave Le Clercq no indications of how to act or react. The dramatic mood grew completely out of the steps. Denby paid tribute to her extraordinary interpretation when she accepted the black ornaments. "The way I remember Tanny's marvelous gesture of putting on the gloves was that when she put her hand into the glove she threw up her head at the same time, so that it was a kind of immolation, you felt, like diving to destruction." Moncion, the man in black, steers her into a frenzied dance. When at last she falls dead, she is lifted by a group of men as the crowd continues its heedless whirling.

Balanchine had found an admirable way of making a plotless, all-dancing ballet into something intensely dramatic that was also a delight to the eye. And he had done this, as always, by remaining faithful to the spirit of the music.

■ ■ ■

FROM the time of their return from England in the fall of 1950 until April 1952, when they went abroad again, the New York City Ballet came to accumulate the kind of eclectic repertory at which Lucia Chase had aimed when she founded Ballet Theatre just over ten years before. The ballets of Jerome Robbins had already added diversity to the repertory (and, God knows, Balanchine's works were diverse enough, whatever the English might think). Now Antony Tudor joined the company, bringing with him Hugh Laing, who had been his friend and the protagonist of nearly all his works, and Laing's wife, Diana Adams, from Virginia, as well as Nora Kaye, who specialized in dramatic roles. Then there was Eglevsky, who joined the company not exactly as a guest artist but as a glamorous Russian outsider. Special pas de deux were included in the programs to display his exceptional technique, which was matched by that of Tallchief. Balanchine even made a one-act version of *Swan Lake* for them, with a soaring pas de trois in which Patricia Wilde was given a chance to show her almost masculine power of beating and jumping. This *Swan Lake* shocked many of the dancers, who considered it a betrayal of the company's avant-garde tradition.

Balanchine revived *Card Party* (as it was now called) for Bolender and *Apollo* for Eglevsky. He created a comic role for Robbins in *Tyl Ulenspiegel,* and he made an American ballet, *Bayou* (about the Acadians of the Southern swamps), to please Kirstein, who wanted to use Virgil Thomson's music from the film *Louisiana Story*.

Although NYCB would always need "novelties," which, in fact, Balanchine was quite capable of turning out without help from others, there would never again be such a panicky period in the company's history. Antony Tudor did not stay for more than a year, but when he, Laing and Kaye left, Diana Adams remained behind and became a great ballerina.

In the middle of this orgy of eclecticism, Balanchine produced a ballet in his most limpid classical manner. At dinner with Lucia Davidova one evening, the music lover and balletomane Bob Sandbach drew Balanchine's attention to a Mozart divertimento (No. 15 in B-flat major, K. 287) which Toscanini had performed and recorded in 1947, and Balanchine fell in love with the music at once and forever. After he had decided to omit the second of the two Minuets and the Andante opening of the sixth and last movement, he was left with an opening Allegro, a Theme and six Variations, a Minuet and an Allegro finale. Bérard's old costumes for *Mozartiana* were used. There were five wonderful ballerinas, Adams, Hayden, Le Clercq, Tallchief and Wilde; three distinguished male dancers, Eglevsky, Magallanes and Robbins; and a corps of eight girls. "A heavenly piece," wrote Denby, "and everyone knows it immediately." It was called *Caracole*. (Balanchine's later *Divertimento No. 15* is an almost completely different ballet to the same music.)

·　·　·

NINETEEN FIFTY-TWO saw the first of the grand tours of Europe, which would be repeated with variations in 1953, 1955 and 1956. These tours were organized by the Paris agency of Léon Leonidoff, who was as fervent an admirer of Balanchine the choreographer as he was devoted to Balanchine the man. Betty Cage also traveled with the company, and soon found that there were unforeseen difficulties to contend with every day. Details of program planning and casting for the tours often had to be carried out while Balanchine was away staging ballets for European companies.

In 1952, he left for La Scala, Milan, before the end of the February–March season in New York, so Betty Cage had to plan the European tour with him while he was over three thousand miles away. She had wrung a salary of $10,000 a year for him from Morton Baum. But Balanchine wrote, "I don't want any contract with City Center. . . . I don't want any ten thousand dollars from Baum, and that's definite." Meanwhile, Antonio Ghiringhelli, Intendant of La Scala, had become a devotee of Balanchine, whose professionalism in teaching a difficult ballet to a strange troupe in the shortest possible time impressed him enormously.

Balanchine joined his company in Barcelona. Kirstein stayed at home because his mother was dying. There were fears that the more elegant Catalonians would have gone to their country houses, which was usual during Holy Week, but all turned out well, except that the box holders tended to arrive only after the first intermission. Barcelona's farewell to the company was sensational. As the final ballet, *Symphony in C,* closed, rose petals and laurel leaves fell from the upper tier of the Liceo, attendants brought on so many baskets of flowers that the stage became a garden, and a flock of doves was released.

In Paris, the Ballet was to open with one performance at the Opéra, then move to the Théâtre des Champs-Elysées for four more nights. But the Opéra staff hated them and dropped and broke their scenery. At the Champs-Elysées, stagehands sat in the flies and fired water pistols at one another during performances. It was a period when Europeans had begun to resent the "taking over" of Europe by rich Americans. But although people spoke of "Coca-Colonization" and wrote "Yankee go home" on walls, the company was booked to return to Paris in June.

Kirstein insisted that his tired troupe oblige the State Department by dancing in Berlin after the Edinburgh Festival. "We are really working for the Government now," he explained, "and very big stakes are involved. If we have official State Dept. support this time it is a very valuable precedent to establish. . . . It will also help us with the Ford Foundation, with whom I am talking. . . ."

This was the first mention of the great foundation that would play so vital a part in the later years of the New York City Ballet.

· · ·

BALANCHINE used to keep up the spirits of his company when he traveled with them by train or plane by devising limericks. These were invariably scandalous, though they did not always scan. Edward Bigelow remembered a few. One concerned "red-headed Michael Maule/About whom all the girls seemed to fall"; then "There was a young lady from the West/Whose control was not of the best./In the paper we read/Ballerina pee-ed/While doing a third arabesque."

The choreographer's English was becoming more vivid and expressive. At about this time he wrote to Betty of a fellow artist: "[Name suppressed] is a nice chappie, but I don't like his tail of disciples, extras, connoisseurs, snobs, parasites, idiots, megalomaniacs, carnivorous lizards, etc." Of an ill-matched dance partnership he said, "It's like a lobster screwing a steak."

The company appeared for a week in The Hague before settling down for six weeks in London, where Balanchine and Tanaquil rented a small house with a garden and shared it with Nicholas Magallanes and Roy Tobias. When Roy retired for the night, he used to see, through an open door, Balanchine in bed, wearing his spectacles to read a musical score. I lived nearby, and often went there for dinner. One morning as I was arriving to keep an appointment with Balanchine, Roy told me, "He's gone to the laundry with Nick." I was astounded: *"George Balanchine* has taken the *laundry!"* Roy confessed later, "It was the first time I saw Balanchine with different eyes. He had always been just one of the family, and now I realized that people outside might look on him as something sacred."

■ ■ ■

From London, Balanchine wrote a serious letter to Kirstein:

4 August 1952

Dear Lincoln:

I am very sorry to hear about your mother's death. I am so touched that she remembered me. She was always so nice to me. If it wouldn't be for her I don't think we would have a company now. But I believe that she's going to help us still, because I believe in that.

I don't think you should make any decisions now. And certainly don't put more money into the City Center. It is a bottomless pit. About your taking Baum's place, I am not very much in favor of it. It is not your nature to be involved in money and commercial things. You could be an official adviser or something like that. . . .

It would be better to think about my idea of free performances for children. Not only ballet, but drama (maybe Midsummers Nights Dream) and opera. It's the only thing for the future and the only reason for keeping a theatre in New York. I would say that if we eventually get people to help us financially it will be through this idea. There could be a committee of rich people to raise money for free performances for children. There is no progress in just inventing new small ballets every season just to exist. Until now, somehow we have created new ideas and we were progressive and now the company is established and can perform as well as the other famous companies. But that is not enough. If we continue in the same way we will become standardized, just like the others. We shouldn't do millions of little hors d'oeuvres. It is no longer progressive. And it is impossible to do new things so fast. It must be a process of evolution. But if we create a purpose for the company and for the theatre, we can afford to fill in with little things now and then, but really have time to do something interesting. The new generation which would come to the performances will be the future citizens of the United States, some poets, some musicians. We have to do something for their souls and minds. Nobody is doing anything at all except the police department.

It's true that in the beginning there will be a loss. But we would have a loss anyway, and this idea eventually will help us. The nation that develops from this public will be the reason for asking people for money. Then people will give with pleasure. Maybe the Mayor will be interested, and all the rich people. But they are not interested in giving us money to pay [so-and-so's] salary.

We would still have one matinee a week to sell tickets for,

and it will probably bring in as much money as two would. Please, Lincoln, think about this. It's not as stupid as it sounds at first. . . .

Don't worry about anything, Lincoln. Everything is all right.

Love
George

"We shouldn't do millions of little hors d'oeuvres." Balanchine had come to the conclusion that, in a desperate attempt to please, Kirstein was in danger of turning his repertory into a hodgepodge like that of Ballet Theatre.

Kirstein went to see the mayor about the free matinees and wrote to Betty Cage, "He is very agreeable and will help us. . . . He is calling a meeting." The first free matinee would be in 1960.

Meanwhile Balanchine came up with a delightful new idea for a ballet, as a result, surprisingly, of attending the Edinburgh Festival's Searchlight Tattoo, performed on the Castle Esplanade almost nightly during the three-week festival, and perennially popular. It was organized by the army and carried out with military magnificence and precision. Watching the marching and counter-marching of massed bands of pipers and drummers in their swinging tartan kilts, and the dancing of reels, Balanchine, seated in the front row with Tallchief, Le Clercq and other principals of his company, felt the fascination of Scotland's music and history. Through Walter Scott, the country had become one of the chief sources of inspiration for the Romantic movement. James Macpherson's forged poems of Ossian, the legendary Gaelic bard, were translated into several European languages. In 1829, Mendelssohn had been irresistibly drawn to visit Scotland, and his journey inspired him to compose the "Scotch" Symphony (No. 3 in A minor, Op. 56, dedicated to Queen Victoria). How delightful that the Russian-born choreographer, one hundred and twenty-three years later, should feel the same Romantic impulse and decide to make a ballet to the music of this composition!

. . .

Two Silver City cargo planes were provided for the transportation of the New York City Ballet from Edinburgh to Berlin. One was much more primitive than the other. There was a muddle at the airport, and the corps de ballet traveled on the better plane; Balanchine, the principal dancers and staff on the worse. Tallchief found that when she went to the toilet she could see the ground below through the cracks in the floor. Returning to her seat, she noticed Balanchine sitting impassively as rain fell on his head. He was, in fact, exhausted by the tour.

Yet Europe's reaction to the New York City Ballet left no doubt that the tour was a triumphal progress. The acclamations in Barcelona were unprecedented. There were twenty-nine calls at the Paris Opéra. The 4,500 seats of the Teatro Comunale in Florence were sold out. A Milan editor, whose critic saw the company there, announced "The revolutionaries of the dance have arrived from New York." The 2,100-seat theater in The Hague was sold out for a week. During the six weeks in London, as Chujoy recorded, choreographers and dancers from "at least a dozen" European countries came to see them. Their appearance at the Edinburgh Festival was well received. They were warmly applauded in Berlin. The Florentines invited the company to make their city its permanent base. Betty Cage, exasperated with the difficulties at City Center, had considered this seriously. What is more, so had Balanchine. New York City actually ran the risk, in 1952, of losing its ballet company to Europe—over Lincoln Kirstein's dead body!

. . .

BALANCHINE's dislike of communism made him vote Republican. Like many Russian émigrés, he could not help admiring what he considered the boundless political cunning of the Soviet leaders, and he believed Americans were naïve by comparison. Doubtless he thought Roosevelt had been sold down the river at Yalta. During the election campaign of 1952 it was, therefore, to General Eisenhower that he wrote, pledging his support in return for encouragement to the arts.

1 October, 1952

My Dear General:

May I first take the liberty of introducing myself: I am Artistic Director of the New York City Ballet, my name is George Balanchine. I left Russia, my country of birth, as a boy of nineteen [*sic*] because I wanted artistic freedom more than anything else, and I have found it here. I have been an American citizen for fourteen years and I am convinced that you are the man to lead this country in its fight against communism.

This letter is written in the hope that the suggestion it humbly submits may bring more votes to our future President. There is a vital section of this country's population which, so far as I know, is never mentioned in campaign speeches. —They are the artists of America: writers, poets, painters, sculptors, composers, musicians, actors, dancers. The artists and their creative efforts are an integral part of American life and an increasingly important one, with a vital influence on public opinion at home and abroad. In fact as an instrument of the "propaganda of truth" which you advocate it is unsurpassable. I am sure that you are aware of the success in this respect of American theatrical, dance, and music productions, and art exhibits abroad since World War II. I have just returned with the New York City Ballet from an extensive tour of Europe, ending in Berlin where we went at the request of the State Department. In every country people came to me to express their surprise that a native American company should achieve such a standard of excellence, for Europe is only beginning to realize that America can produce great art.

This is hardly surprising for art and artists are never mentioned by our statesmen. . . . The materialistic part of life is the only one that is talked about. But there is another part which is the spiritual life of the nation, its culture. I know that you are deeply concerned with that life as you have proved during your presidency of Columbia University. It would be wonderful if you would reaffirm that interest now. . . .

I ask you to recognize the American artists in one of your speeches and to appeal to them and you will get a million votes! I cannot presume to ask you to promise them government support, although in many respects this is sorely needed, but the assurance of your moral support would already be invaluable.

With all my good wishes and hope for the success of your campaign,

Respectfully yours,
George Balanchine
Artistic Director
New York City Ballet

Eisenhower's answer—if, indeed, he did answer—has not survived.

Having got that off his chest, Balanchine was free to rehearse two new ballets, which were ready for the winter season at City Center. This season, opening on November 5, continued for nearly three months and was the longest the company had ever had.

•　　•　　•

AT ABOUT this time, Balanchine's marriage to Maria Tallchief was annulled on the ground that Balanchine refused to let her have a child. It was stated in the newspapers that she had asked for no alimony as she was a dancer and could earn her own living. This was honorable, but her mother was "not too pleased." Balanchine had helped her move into a new apartment, which she was to share with Vida Brown. He made suggestions about the decoration and hung mirrors. She had a sudden pang and said, "I won't leave you if you'd rather I didn't." "No, no," said Balanchine, "go ahead. It's O.K." Balanchine never completely severed contact with his ex-wives. When Brigitta gave birth to her first son, he telephoned the next morning, proposing to visit her in the hospital and see the baby. Goddard Lieberson, however, thought it would be better "to wait a little." Maria remained in the company, working side by side with Tanaquil Le Clercq. In November 1952, Balanchine made *Scotch Symphony* for her and Hindemith's *Metamorphoses* for Tanaquil.

Balanchine cut Mendelssohn's somewhat portentous first movement, so that *Scotch Symphony* begins with some spirited Scottish steps by a girl and eight boys, all dressed in kilts. The Andante brings on the lovelorn, questing man in search of an evasive sylph, with whom, nevertheless, he performs a long and dreamlike pas de deux. Tallchief was associated with dazzle rather than romance, but critics acclaimed her "newfound gentle radiance" in this duet. *Scotch Symphony* is one of those Balanchine ballets—the Weber *Pas de deux romantique* is another—that hover between romance and comedy or pastiche. Like Mozart, Balanchine had an infinitely subtle way of striking a balance, and he was sometimes too subtle for his critics.

Metamorphoses, to Hindemith's *Symphonic Metamorphoses on Themes of Carl Maria von Weber* enabled Tanaquil Le Clercq to show her rare qualities of fantasy and style—but, actually, there has never been anyone like her in *any* of her roles. The economical but ingenious décor was formed by cascades of metal coat hangers, which glittered as they caught Jean Rosenthal's golden light. Karinska's costumes were weird. In the Allegro first movement, the dancers were acrobats in form-fitting leotards of a new elastic material. For the second movement, based on a Chinese theme Weber had discovered and Hindemith had transformed into what he called a "Turandot Scherzo," Le Clercq wore a "Balinese" bra, a minimal tutu, wings, a mask and a headdress with quivering antennae, thus becoming the most elegant Oriental dragonfly. She was supported by Todd Bolender, dressed as a beetle or turtle, who never rose from his knees. Balanchine deliberately set himself a new and almost impossible task—who had ever heard of a pas de deux in which the ballerina was partnered by a kneeling cavalier? Yet the passage was reminiscent of his favorite theme—his basic theme, Bolender thought—of unlucky love. Todd was told to be "very passionate." "I was the rejected lover, the ugly little man who was always just missing her, yearning but repulsed." It turned out to be a wonderful dance. For the final March everyone acquired huge wings, Magallanes "flapped on . . . to chase the beetle" and the corps made Busby Berkeley-ish patterns.

Rehearsals at City Center were held either in a sixth-floor room at the back, or on the stage when it was free. Betty Cage knew that when Balanchine was working out a new ballet he lost all sense of everything else, and as there was no money to pay overtime, whenever she thought he had reached the limit she used to leave her office on the eighth floor, go down and simply stare at him.

■ ■ ■

BALANCHINE and Tanaquil Le Clercq were married on the last day of 1952. "At midnight we all foregathered," Kirstein wrote me. "As the Russians and Russians continued to troop in, Tanny said to me: 'Oh, my God, what Have I Let Myself IN FOR?' "

At this time Kirstein was producing Shakespeare plays for City Center, and Balanchine was directing Stravinsky's opera *The Rake's Progress* at the Metropolitan Opera House. It had already been given in Venice, Zurich and Milan. Balanchine thought the Met was far too big for it. He was obliged to have crowd scenes, which were not called for in the libretto or the score; the production was too naturalistic; the harpsichord continuo was inaudible; and he disliked the conductor, Fritz Reiner, who kept pointing out "errors" in the orchestration. He loved the opera and hated the whole business.

In February 1953, after its long season at City Center, NYCB danced for the first time in Baltimore and Washington. In March, Balanchine and Tanaquil were in Milan. In July, when Betty Cage, on tour with the company, heard from Kirstein that the New York winter season might be canceled, she reported from Los Angeles that Balanchine was threatening to resign. But there was no season at City Center that fall; the company set off on another European tour instead. In October she wrote from Naples that she, too, was thinking of resigning. She complained that the State Department was paying all expenses in Germany for Ballet Theatre, and that Lucia Chase's troupe opened every program with Balanchine's *Theme and Variations* and Robbins's *Fancy Free,* giving the impression that they were the *only* American company. It was time Baum realized that the New York City Ballet was *not* a touring company. They should be sure of four New York seasons a year.

Because Sadler's Wells Ballet had broken its own record at the Metropolitan Opera House with a repertory including not only the ever-popular *Sleeping Beauty* but a new full-length *Swan Lake* and Ashton's new version of Delibes's *Sylvia* in three acts, both Baum and Kirstein were convinced that the New York City Ballet should put on a ballet lasting all evening. Balanchine suggested *Casse-Noisette (The Nutcracker).* Kirstein liked the idea. He thought it would cost $50,000, of which he allotted $20,000 to the scene builders and prop makers and $30,000 to Karinska for costumes. "Please let me hear from you about *Nutcracker,*" he wrote to Betty and Balanchine. "I am very nervous that you will want to junk it. . . ."

But Balanchine was pleased to be staging the old ballet in which he had danced as a child. From the start, his aim was to create magic: the kind that holds children spellbound and makes older people feel hopeful and young again. In *Nutcracker* he relived the Christmases of his childhood.

One of the "miracles" in the ballet is the growing of the Christmas tree. Beginning no bigger than a real tree, during Marie's dream it grows and grows, until she herself, like Alice in Wonderland, is reduced to the scale of the mice and toy soldiers who battle around her. There was no trapdoor in the City Center stage, and Balanchine insisted on a three-dimensional—as opposed to a painted—tree. Jean Rosenthal, the lighting wizard, devised a model of "umbrella-like spokes" which lay flat in a heap, hidden by piles of presents, until they were pulled upward. The estimate for making this was between five and ten thousand dollars, and Kirstein was afraid to tell Baum. When expense was discussed, Balanchine always said, "Tell Baum it will only be half as much. The production will get back the money, and he will be happy."

Given the limitations of City Center, it was extremely difficult to accommodate and control the number of children from the School who were needed for the Christmas party scene in Act I: and the ingenuity of Edward Bigelow, the stage manager, was taxed to the limit. Numbers of children playing mice or soldiers had to be crowded along stairways and in the wings, and controlled by signals. There was also a choir of forty boys from St. Thomas's Episcopal Church, who had to hum during the Snowflakes scene.

Jerome Robbins arranged the battle between the Toy Soldiers and the Mice. Balanchine stuck, when it suited him, to what he remembered of the Ivanov version, but sometimes he elaborated. He also invented a brand-new character, Dewdrop, to lead the Waltz of the Flowers in the second act. This virtuoso role—with continual entrances and exits, dazzling aerial ronds de jambes and arabesques voyagées along the line of girls, and, at one exit, a breathtaking balance—was danced to perfection in the first performance by Tanaquil Le Clercq.

The Ivanov-Balanchine pas de deux of the Sugar Plum Fairy and her Cavalier, danced at the opening on February 2, 1954, by Maria Tallchief and Nicholas Magallanes, is one of the most dazzling and at the same time moving in the history of ballet. Alexandre Benois, who attended the very first night of the ballet in 1892, felt that Tchaikovsky had invested the music for this dance, written a year before the Sixth *(Pathétique)* Symphony, with a tragic character. Indeed, each time the cymbals clash and a descending motive is repeated, there is a splendor of desperate passion about the way the ballerina hurls herself at her partner, as if risking life itself.

A week before the premiere of *The Nutcracker, Time* magazine put Balanchine on its cover. The accompanying article gave an outline of his career and quoted a few of his typical remarks: " 'When you get older,' says George Balanchine, who is 50 this week, 'you eliminate things, you want to see things pure and clear' "; and " 'Central theme of *Nutcracker:* food.' "

John Martin, who had for so long resisted the appeal of Balanchine's talent but had recently been converted, wrote in his un-appreciation of *Nutcracker* for *The New York Times:* "It denies the very basis of the 'Balanchine revolution,' which has changed the entire art of the ballet by showing it to be an art of dancing—not of miming, spectacle or story-telling." He might have been sur-prised to be told that *The Nutcracker*—which has enjoyed an uninterrupted season at NYCB every Christmas for about a month from the winter of 1954 on—would become as regular an Ameri-can habit as turkey at Thanksgiving.

. . .

IN 1954, when I was arranging an exhibition for the Edinburgh Festival to mark the twenty-fifth anniversary of Diaghilev's death, I wrote to Balanchine asking if he had any designs for ballets or portraits of himself dating from the Diaghilev period. Balanchine replied that unlike certain people—a snide reference to one or two acquisitive friends—he had no relics of his time with Diaghilev except "some pornographic drawings I made for him." I re-sponded, "I quite understand that you are not clever like Massine and Lifar . . . but I think it is extraordinarily lazy of you never to have sat to a good artist, whose portrait of you we could include in our Exhibition. After all, anyone can keep making up ballets, but it is the people who have their portraits painted by Tchelitchev who are remembered by posterity. . . . I have just got your *Complete Book of Great Ballets* [*sic*] from Francis Mason. My word, you have been busy. . . ."

He responded:

March 9, 1954

Dear Dicky,

I did sit for Tchelitchev when he asked me, but I was extremely difficult, and he didn't have the inspiration to finish it. Nobody wants to paint me. I admit I'm not very pretty. . . .

George

The reference to drawings was not entirely, as I had thought, a joke. Years later Boris Kochno showed me several drawings, somewhat surrealist and not unskilled, that Balanchine had made when the two young men were on holiday with Diaghilev in Venice. And a strange pencil sketch of Lifar in *The Prodigal Son,* pregnant, and crawling with truncated legs, was sold in the Lifar sale at Sotheby's in 1984 for £3,000. Then I discovered that Balanchine had given caricatures of himself to several American friends.

■ ■ ■

DURING the second of the three 1954 New York seasons, Balanchine produced a piece of Americana that surprised even Lincoln Kirstein. It was said that the idea came to him during a stay in Wyoming. The composer Hershy Kay recalled that Balanchine turned down his early sketches for what became *Western Symphony*—the first because it was "too much like Copland," the second because it was "too complicated." The third time he was lucky: "simple tunes with skeletal, guitarlike accompaniments" were combined in the form of a classical four-movement symphony. These tunes were mainly cowboy songs, with "Red River Valley" as the unifying theme.

Although there was no money for costumes until a year after its first performance, Balanchine contrived to give his strictly classical choreography a Western slant: there were suggestions of "the intertwinings of square-dance figures," one man strummed an imaginary guitar and another fanned himself with a hat. In the opening Allegro there were many lifts for Diana Adams and Herbert Bliss. Magallanes partnered Janet Reed in the sentimental

Adagio, and she had to hurl herself halfway across the stage into his arms. It was in the final Rondo, however, that Tanaquil Le Clercq, supported by the bouncing, grinning Jacques d'Amboise, set the house on fire with her chic, her fouettés and her provocative smiles. *Western Symphony* is one of Balanchine's "closing ballets" that has given the most joy—and has lasted.

Although in 1955 Betty Cage had sworn never to go on another European tour, she dutifully embarked on a fourth odyssey in 1956. Preoccupied as she was by moving the company from city to city in eight different countries, she still wrote to Kirstein about plans for the next two years. Should the company go to Japan under the aegis of the State Department? Should they go to South America? The State Department was beginning to regard ballet as a means of making friends and influencing people. Should they go to Russia?

Balanchine did not want to go to Russia. Could the company go without him? Ballet Theatre was longing to get there first (and in the end succeeded in doing so). City Center was in a deplorable situation, thousands of dollars in debt.

Nevertheless, there was stirring news from home. Kirstein reported, "Mayor Wagner has pushed the Lincoln Square plan [for a new complex of buildings for concerts, opera and ballet] through the Board of Estimates. . . . The City turned over the land, and the Rockefeller Foundation is close behind, and I think it is only a question of WHEN, no longer IF."

On tour, Balanchine rarely had cause to complain of an unresponsive audience. In Vienna, it is true, the public showed little enthusiasm for *La Valse*, which Ravel had intended partly as a kind of apotheosis of the Viennese waltz, and the choreographer was bitterly disappointed. "Here in Vienna at least I thought they'd understand," he said to Roy Tobias. On the whole, though, reactions in Salzburg, Berlin, Brussels and Copenhagen were enthusiastic. But it was in Copenhagen that tragedy struck.

Tanaquil Le Clercq was taken ill and did not dance on the last night. At first the doctors were uncertain of their diagnosis, but by the time the company traveled on to Stockholm—which was luckily the last stop on the tour—leaving behind Balanchine and Tanaquil's mother, Edith, who had gone along with the company for fun, it was known that Tanaquil had polio. The train from Malmö was met by Swedish health authorities in case other dancers had succumbed to the disease. Tanaquil was racked by a high fever, and Balanchine, too, grew feverish. When the news reached New York, consternation was widespread. Lincoln Kirstein wrote to Betty Cage:

Everyone has rallied around with the most extraordinary rush. John [Rockefeller] III asked if he could do anything through the Institute here. . . . Jerry Robbins, in tears, called from Boston twice and will do anything we ask him. . . . Jacques [d'Amboise] was absolutely destroyed; Carolyn [his wife] cried all day long . . . and Minnie Astor and John Martin and everyone you can think of. . . .

The programs for the New York season, opening on December 18, still had to be discussed with Kirstein, and Betty suggested that "it might be better not to do *La Valse* because George thinks of it as Tanny's and it might be painful for him."

·   ·   ·

WHEN the company returned to America, Balanchine remained behind in Copenhagen. Edith Le Clercq sent regular bulletins of her daughter's ups and downs, of her own and George's hopes and fears. Nursing Tanaquil kept her so busy that she had little time to dwell on the tragedy. Balanchine had moved into a cheap room at the top of the Hôtel d'Angleterre. During the day, he cooked special meals for Tanaquil at Vera Volkova's apartment.

It was at the suggestion of Volkova that Balanchine agreed to work once more with the Royal Danish Ballet. She thought it would distract him. Henning Kronstam, who was to dance Apollo, found the choreographer "very precise at rehearsals, absent-minded at other times. To us he was kind, very firm about what he wanted. We didn't get too many corrections. He said, 'Can you do this?' " Yet Balanchine could not concentrate long on these rehearsals, or spare much time from his cooking and his encouragement of Tanaquil. When he showed Kronstam Apollo's first variation, he did it very quickly, then said, "Here's the pianist. Here's the score. You have three hours. See what you can do." Then he went off.

Kirstein, who had presented the young Gian Carlo Menotti's immensely successful operas *The Telephone* and *The Medium* in the early days of Ballet Society, had recently agreed to put on his ballet *The Unicorn, the Gorgon, and the Manticore*, with choreography by John Butler; Butler wanted to use one of his own dancers in it. This was reported in detail to Balanchine on November 30. He wrote to Betty Cage:

[*Dictated to Edith Le Clercq, in whose hand it is*]

                                  Hôtel d'Angleterre
                                  Copenhagen
                            Tuesday? 2 or 9 December

Dear Betty,

First I want to thank you very much for your kind words of encouragement and for the cigarettes that makes us feel back home. . . .

Now about Butler: he should be very grateful to do this choreography for us without dictating his terms. If he is not satisfied with our dancers then we don't want him either. (Who the Hell he thinks he is?)

Please no "Sebastian." It is the most dreadful ballet, lousy music, stinking story—better nothing than that. I don't like Cranko idea either. Don't spend money on that junk. Let Todd do his Poulenc ballet. . . .

Tanny is getting along slowly. God will help us I believe. . . .

                                      Love
                                      George

Diana Adams wrote daily to Tanaquil, and Balanchine read her letters aloud. He later told her, "You're very *funny*!" He talked to his wife by the hour to keep her from brooding on her condition. (Both legs were paralyzed.) It was a huge effort of will. Every night he played solitaire, sitting with his mother-in-law in the hotel bedroom. Kirstein arranged that Natalie Molostwoff should fly over to spend Christmas with the stranded family.

Balanchine in Copenhagen to Kirstein in New York
[Dictated to Edith Le Clercq, in whose hand it is]

> Hôtel d'Angleterre
> Copenhagen
> Tuesday [*probably December 18*]

Dear Lincoln,

Thanks very much for your letter and clippings. Please send all clippings to me at hotel. . . . Could you write [Tanny] a cute letter?

I have already written Betty about Butler. Our company is good enough for me—should be good enough for him. . . .

Tanny is very grateful to you for the Christmas present you are giving her—Natasha [Natalie].

Edith and I are trying to be cheerful. We are hoping and hoping and hoping and waiting.

> George

Natalie Molostwoff's calm, good sense and humor brightened their Christmas. She helped to alleviate the strain under which all three exiles were living, giving them a better sense of perspective; and Balanchine had a friend to keep him company until he went to the hospital at four each afternoon.

At the Royal Theater, Copenhagen, Balanchine presented *Apollo* on January 9, 1957, and *Serenade* two days later. The New York City Ballet gave the Menotti-Butler work on the eighteenth. Betty Cage reported to Balanchine about it and he sent a handwritten letter back to her:

[End of January]

Dear Betty—Your letter just arrived. I hope that in spite of all this bedlam you have fun and your box office is plenty.

. . . Soon, it will be three months since Tanny became ill. She is some how happier in her room and we are trying to make her feel as if she were at home. I am cooking every day in Volkova's apartment and take food to the hospital.

I hear you have two pretenders on "poor swan lake." I highly disapprove of this two girls dancing it. Certainly I am not going to see them in swan when I return. (Not everybody should dance everything as president Lincoln said.) . . .

With my love to you.
Your
G.

Balanchine's single aim was to restore his wife's will to live: he was so exhausted that although he went to bed early he could not sleep. When Tanaquil got back her appetite, he took a day or two off to visit an old friend in Jutland.

The National Polio Foundation undertook to pay all expenses for the family's return journey to New York. At Lenox Hill Hospital, Tanaquil would be under the care of Dr. Jordan, an orthopedic surgeon Balanchine had found helpful to his dancers. The American Embassy made the arrangements. Nobody in New York— except Kirstein, Betty, Natalie and Edward Bigelow—was to know anything about the homecoming until Tanaquil was safely installed. The little party set off on March 13, 1957; their nonstop flight got in at 6:00 A.M.

Chapter 10

••

NEW BALLETS

FOR NEW DANCERS:

1957 - 1964

T HE first eight months of 1957 were an interlude in Balanchine's career. He set his work aside to look after Tanaquil.
When she left the hospital, he took her for treatment to
Warm Springs, Georgia. His devotion was extraordinary, but his
company felt bereft. During the summer he grew roses at their
house in Connecticut. In the winter, however, he made a dazzling
comeback. Between November 1957 and mid-January 1958, he
created four ballets so fantastically different from one another, and
each so successful in its own way, that there is no word for his New
York winter season but miraculous.

Who but Balanchine would have related, as he did in *Square
Dance,* ancient formal dances and classical steps to the American
square dances surviving from the nineteenth century, or dared to

combine the music of Vivaldi and Corelli, played onstage by a string band, with the patter of a professional "caller," standing in a corner and tossing his rhymes to individual dancers: "Down the center, lonesome gal/Now she's waiting for her pal/All alone, swing and whirl/Down the center in a butterfly twirl"? Kirstein later wanted to eliminate the caller, but Balanchine said, "Remove the caller, and it's just an inferior *Barocco.*" Eventually, however, the caller was dropped, and the ballet continued to be popular.

Who but Balanchine would have hit upon Gounod's little-known Symphony No. 1 in D major and made for two principal dancers and a corps of twenty girls and ten boys a ballet *(Gounod Symphony)* so gentle, so sweet, so unspectacular and so essentially French that one sees it as exactly the kind of work the Paris Opéra should have presented in the 1880s—but probably never did?

Who but Balanchine could have conceived the semicomic, totally flamboyant *Stars and Stripes*? After the strutting, high-stepping Rockette drum majorettes, the cabrioling soldiers saluting in midair, the pas de deux that has been called a "delightfully witty soldier's-sweetheart duet"—but which nevertheless contains difficult classical steps—the whole company swarms on for a blazing finale, and, at the very end, the music is reined in to a steady slow march (to the tune that gives the ballet its name), and the largest Old Glory ever seen in comparative closeup is unfurled to form a background. "Calculated vulgarity is a useful ingredient," Balanchine once observed, and confessed to being an old hand at working what he called "the applause machine."

The fourth major ballet of winter 1957–58, actually the second chronologically and the most memorable of all, was *Agon.* In 1954, a Rockefeller Foundation grant had enabled Kirstein and Balanchine to commission the longed-for Stravinsky ballet that would form a trilogy with *Apollo* and *Orpheus.* Its title, *Agon,* means contest or struggle.

Stravinsky interrupted his work on the score to write two other compositions, and *Agon* was not completed until April 27, 1957. Its point of departure was a French Baroque dance manual, the

1623 *Apologie de la danse* by de Lauze, with accompanying musical examples by Mersenne. Traces of this influence are evident in the names of certain old dances—saraband, galliard and bransle (although Stravinsky's versions bear little metrical resemblance to their models)—and in the tone color, reminiscent of Baroque sonority. But, encouraged by Robert Craft, Stravinsky had been employing serial techniques in his works since 1952, and they are the basis of approximately half the composition.

A document survives from Balanchine and Stravinsky's consultations over this mathematically organized ballet—a scheme of *Agon* in the composer's hand. It is written on sheets of ruled paper taped and stapled together to form one long page. For each number, Stravinsky indicated the projected timing in minutes and seconds and—by drawing stick figures, some with skirts—how many male and/or female dancers were to perform it. In its final form, *Agon* has twelve movements that are grouped into four parts punctuated by the recurring prelude (the prelude's two subsequent repetitions are called "interludes," but these three passages are essentially the same); and at the very end the twelve dancers regroup from four trios to three quartets for a coda "in imitation."

Stravinsky made a few choreographic suggestions. Balanchine said the plan of using twelve dancers was his own, but that their division into eight girls and four boys was Stravinsky's.

Diana Adams remembered the first day that a call for *Agon* was posted on the board at City Center. "I had something terribly important to do that day. . . . I had to nerve myself up to ask him, 'Could you start with someone else?' But he said, 'No, pas de deux is where I start. I have to do first.' Of course I was there."

In Arthur Mitchell, a student of the School who had danced for Balanchine in the musical *House of Flowers* in 1954 and joined the company two years later, the choreographer had found, after all these years, his first black *danseur noble*. Mitchell, with his good looks, heroic bearing and radiant personality, was chosen to dance the climactic pas de deux in *Agon* with Adams. He was not yet even a soloist, let alone a principal.

"Nothing stopped [Balanchine] when he was ready to go," Adams recalled about the rehearsals for the pas de deux. "I told him that my [left] foot was not really healed. He said, 'That's all right. I'll do everything on right foot.' "

Balanchine's choreography has next to nothing to do with the court dances after which some of the numbers were named—*next to nothing* because the roots of ballet are imbedded in the French Baroque, and the choreography naturally has a balletic basis, although in *Agon* Balanchine extended the idiom with movements that had never been seen before. Near the beginning of the pas de deux, Adams revolved into a pose in which she abruptly wrapped a leg around Mitchell's neck. Later, with one arm round her waist, he took the foot of her bent leg raised behind her in attitude; as she arched backward, he touched it to her head. Another feat called for her to balance in arabesque while he first supported her at arm's length, then stretched himself suddenly flat on the floor without having relinquished contact with her forward hand; she was to retain her pose as if unconscious of his reversal.

The time came when Balanchine wanted to show Stravinsky what he had worked out. Lucia Davidova was asked to bring him to a rehearsal. When they arrived at the School—which had moved from Madison Avenue to the Upper West Side in the previous year—Martha Swope was there to take photographs (it was her first professional assignment), along with Bernard Taper, Balanchine's future biographer. Roy Tobias remembered the scene:

Balanchine was so happy when Stravinsky came downstairs. Everyone was "at attention." Stravinsky went to the piano, took off his coat and scarf and said, "George, to work! To work!" Hitherto, in the opening pas de quatre the four boys had faced the audience. The composer suggested that they should turn their backs. This was agreed. In Melissa's variation [the Bransle gay, central section of the second pas de trois] Balanchine made me beat on the stair rail with a stick to represent the castanets. While we were working on the Bransle double [which follows], Balanchine was called to the telephone. On his return he made the boys enter together rather than in canon. During the pas de deux, Kopeikine, at the piano, said, "I'm terribly sorry. There are parts of this music I don't understand." Stravinsky said, "It's perfectly all right. I don't understand them either!"

At the end of the Bransle double, according to Taper (when Tobias threw Hayden to be caught in mid-air by Watts, while he himself sank neatly to one knee), Stravinsky exclaimed, *"Horosha!"* [Good!]. After the pas de deux, he clapped and cried, "Wonderful!"

Agon had its premiere on December 1, 1957, and from the start was recognized as a masterpiece. Programs were arranged to include six extra performances. It has since been acclaimed in many countries. After nearly thirty years, we are still rediscovering, each time we see it performed, some breathtaking wonder that we had forgotten. Although the ballet ends as it begins, we are not left with a sense of QED—nothing has been proved—but of "Here we are again, back where we started and none the wiser." It has been "pure entertainment." A contest? Yes—a kind of tournament of dance introduced and terminated by fanfares, though not for a stadium packed with applauding crowds. It is as if the dancers' infinite skills and throwaway insouciance are to be taken for granted by a small audience of their peers: they are to be appraised less for the difficulty of the feats they perform than for the cool manner and sure timing with which they ignore difficulty. This is the way bullfighters are judged.

. . .

WITHIN two months of the end of the 1957–58 winter season, the company was in Japan with Kirstein. Balanchine, who had moved with Tanaquil into an apartment on West End Avenue, stayed home, but he thought deeply about the future and came to some surprising conclusions. When Kirstein returned, leaving Betty Cage to take the dancers on to Australia, Balanchine confronted him with his ideas, and Kirstein wrote to Betty:

Balanchine wants to get through the winter as well as possible, and in the summer start from scratch with a small company and six new ballets, à la Ballet Caravan, which we feel we can book, and then enlarge the group to a company like 1947 at the Center, but there will be the difference of a repertory and ten years of work.

Betty responded with great restraint: "I am sorry Balanchine feels as he does about the company. . . . I hope he changes his mind after we get home." After some argument and persuasion, he did.

Later that year, Leon Barzin, who had conducted for NYCB since its foundation, decided to retire. He had for some years shared his labors with the former violinist Hugo Fiorato, but Balanchine and Kirstein considered it necessary to employ another *chef d'orchestre*. Balanchine's choice fell on an Englishman, the Sadler's Wells conductor Robert Irving, and their partnership led to the creation of the world's most distinguished ballet orchestra.

Another musician who joined Balanchine's team shortly afterward was the Californian Gordon Boelzner. While he was studying at the Manhattan School of Music, he learned from a girl friend that the New York City Ballet needed a pianist. Boelzner was not interested in ballet, but he applied and was engaged. It was his first job—and he was still with the company in 1987. Balanchine, who began by handing him his own piano reduction of *Orpheus*, appreciated his quickness in reading an unfamiliar score. Boelzner for his part was soon hooked by Balanchine's personality. He became the company's pianist in performance as well as at rehearsal, and finally assistant conductor.

Soon after the company's return from the Far East, Balanchine began work on a new production of *The Seven Deadly Sins*. W. H. Auden and Chester Kallman made a translation from the original German, and Lotte Lenya came from Germany to stalk the stage and harangue in her rasping voice her dancing "double," the ethereal young Allegra Kent.

In March 1959, Balanchine received the news from Tbilisi that his mother was dead. The extent to which he had been cut off from his family may be measured by the fact that his brother Andrei's cable was addressed to the Metropolitan Opera House. Lucia Davidova, on the point of leaving for Europe, was aware of Balanchine's reluctance to put pen to paper, so she begged him, "Be sure to write a nice letter to your brother." When she returned to New York some weeks later, she asked, "Did you write to your brother?" Balanchine said, "No. I just could not bring myself to write." The kind of letter in which there is "so much to say" was even harder for him than the ordinary kind.

· · ·

EXCEPT for Robert Craft, Stravinsky had no more ardent devotee than Balanchine, who was cool toward most other great contemporary composers, notably Bartók. He turned to Anton Webern in the 1950s because of Stravinsky's interest in the Austrian composer. Like his teacher Schoenberg, Webern wrote twelve-tone music, but his personal style is characterized by modesty of scale and a sense of fragmentation derived from the breakup of musical lines into tiny pieces by means of frequent silences and shifts from intrument to instrument, with consequent changes of tone color. Balanchine once told Francis Mason that as soon as he heard Webern's music he knew it could be danced to, like that of Mozart and Stravinsky.

He had made at least two plans for Webern ballets before the idea came to him, in 1959, of staging all seven of his orchestral works, which would come to less than an hour of music. Kirstein made a most unexpected suggestion: that Martha Graham contribute some of the choreography. Graham consented, and agreed to do a dance-drama about the death of Mary, Queen of Scots, to Webern's *Passacaglia.* The notion that Graham should work entirely with New York City Ballet dancers was soon discarded. Balanchine would use his own artists and make a solo for one of Graham's. Later, when Graham found she needed more music, Balanchine, who had already begun to work on the *Six Pieces* with

Adams and d'Amboise, cheerfully relinquished the music to her. Graham's part was to be called *Episodes I*; Balanchine's, *Episodes II*.

In Martha Graham's condensed mini-drama, the Scottish queen, about to die on the scaffold, relives episodes of her past life. The Graham dancers, a powerful group, interpreted Mary's ladies-in-waiting, husbands and lovers, but perhaps as a gesture of solidarity, Sallie Wilson, an NYCB dancer, represented Elizabeth of England, with whom Mary dueled in a symbolic game of tennis. The tragic presence of Graham, the way she stepped out of the monumental dress she had devised, as if escaping from a cage, and the simple device of turning a red light on this abandoned structure to mark the moment of decapitation, have remained in the spectators' memories.

In choreographing *Episodes II*, Balanchine later told an interviewer he "had to try to paint or design time with bodies in order to create a resemblance between the dance and what was going on in sound." Academic steps could have looked ludicrous accompanied by Webern's music; that Balanchine was able to find movements based on these that did not appear incongruous is proof of his unlimited invention. There were five numbers. *Symphony* (Op. 21) was for two principals and three couples. Toward the end, Balanchine, tongue in cheek, made the men invert the women to coincide with an inversion of Webern's tone row; thus upended, the women beat their legs in upside-down entrechats. *Five Pieces* (Op. 10), a pas de deux, ends with a magic trick: the girl flops over the man's right arm, head down, both hands on the floor, her right pointe resting on the stage, her left leg, bent, raised behind her; the man, who appears to be "supporting" her in this unclassical pose, looks not *at* her, but away from her, his left arm extended. His "support" proves illusory, for when he withdraws his right arm and walks away, she remains in position. Balanchine was rather annoyed that some people found this funny. *Concerto* (Op. 24) was for two principals and five women. Balanchine quoted Robert Craft's comment on the music: "At first the listener might be reminded of a switchboard sporadically lighting up, but the plot of wires between the lights is what must be illuminated"; and he confirmed that this was what he tried to do.

The *Variations* (Op. 30) were arranged as a solo for Paul Taylor of Martha Graham's company, who later became a highly inventive choreographer with a troupe of his own. The white-clad dancer was called upon to clutch himself, wrap himself up and tie himself into such perverse knots that his number seemed almost a defiant demonstration by Balanchine that he could be as crazy as any "modern" choreographer or dancer in existence. Finally, after all these perilous explorations, came the *Ricercata* (in six voices, from Bach's *Musical Offering*), danced by two principals and a corps of thirteen girls, so that the breathless spectator felt he had reached a more familiar paradise, perhaps even "come home."

· · ·

AFTER a long spell in Europe as ballet master to the Cuevas company, John Taras was back in New York. He was sitting in the hallway of the School when Balanchine walked in and asked him, "What are you doing these days?" "Nothing." "Then why don't you come and starve with the rest of us?" So Taras rejoined NYCB. Balanchine valued Taras's good memory of certain ballets that he himself recalled only imperfectly. Taras would also make new ones of his own. His return to the fold was especially timely because in 1958 Jerome Robbins had withdrawn to found a group called Ballets U.S.A., which appeared at the Spoleto Festival in Italy and toured Europe with outstanding success.

Robbins's highly involving work on two musicals, *West Side Story* and *Fiddler on the Roof,* both of which became famous, plus other work on and off Broadway, prevented him from devising any new ballets for Balanchine's company until 1968. Taras was soon rehearsing *Apollo* and restaging *Night Shadow,* now called *La Sonnambula,* which its creator had completely forgotten.

In the Bellini/Rieti ballet, the Poet was Erik Bruhn, a world-

renowned Danish dancer who was engaged as a guest artist for the
1959–60 season, and again in 1963–64. He was not only a first-
rate *danseur noble* but strikingly handsome; and perhaps Balanchine revived his "Romantic" ballet because he considered it a
work in which Bruhn and the wistful, fey Allegra Kent, whom he
cast as the Sleepwalker, were bound to make a strong impression.
This they did. The ballet that had been scorned by all the American critics except Denby when it was first given in 1946, and which
had then been admired throughout Europe, was at last accepted in
New York.

One reason Bruhn had joined the company was that he hoped
to dance *Apollo,* which had been revived for Jacques d'Amboise—danced in practice costume, without scenery—in 1957.
He never did. Choreographically speaking, Balanchine's Apollo
had a coltish side, and Bruhn may have struck Balanchine as too
beautiful.

When Balanchine decided to revive *The Prodigal Son* for Edward Villella, a highly talented dancer who had studied at the
School as a child, left to go to college and later returned, Villella
had the impression that it rather bored him to restage his thirty-
three-year-old ballet. "He did the opening and closing scenes in
twenty minutes each. He did the pas de deux for Diana [Adams]
and me in half an hour. I didn't have any in-depth coaching. In
addition, the ballet had been forgotten, and they had to bring in
Vida Brown, who had retired. I was literally learning the ballet as
I was dancing it."

Nevertheless, Balanchine gave his two principals an illuminat-
ing clue to the style needed in their weird duet. Villella explained:

At the beginning of the pas de deux the Siren and the Prodigal are
standing at opposite ends of the stage; then they begin to raise their
hands, then their elbows, holding their hands out flat. Then they lean
and fall toward each other. As we began, Balanchine said, "You know,
dear, like icons." Then he walked away. That simple idea was enough.
I went and got some books. Then I could realize the role.

Balanchine made Brahms's *Liebeslieder Walzer* into a ballet in 1960 to please Morton Baum, who had been begging him to use them for several years. Artists do not often welcome such "commissions," and the choreographer probably considered the two song cycles complete in themselves. Yet things turned out better than he had expected. The ballet has pleased many people apart from the benevolent Baum.

When the curtain rises, two pianists are seated side by side at a piano, with two male and two female singers standing nearby. There are four pairs of dancers—the girls in pink satin dresses sitting demurely on chairs, their partners behind them. As waltz follows waltz, revealing different relationships between the couples, the songs and dances cast a kind of spell, and the audience loses itself in a dream. But there is a surprise in store. After the curtain falls at the end of Part I, there is a short pause. When it rises again, the ballroom has become transparent to the stars; the girls are in ballet dresses and pointe shoes—no longer women, but ideal creatures. For the final waltz, however, they become well-brought-up, satin-clad ladies once more, seated on their chairs to applaud the music and song.

■ ■ ■

WHEN, in 1960, Balanchine held the first of his American Ballet Seminars for regional teachers from all over the United States, he spent half an hour analyzing the tendu and devoted a whole two-hour class to port de bras. This may have given him the idea of voluntary classes for his own dancers in the afternoons, for they started soon afterward. Rosemary Dunleavy, who joined the company in 1961 and is now a ballet mistress, remembers that they were held mostly during layoff periods. "You could take regular class at the School from 10:30 to 12:00, then be warm enough for Balanchine's special class from 12:00 to 2:00." Rosemary felt that Balanchine wanted to "spread his ideas across the nation"; as she "really began to learn what he was talking about," she used to go home and write it all down. She was afraid the precious knowledge might be lost. For his part, as he told Natalie Molostwoff, Balanchine spotted Rosemary early on as someone with an analytical mind and a good memory who would one day be able to reproduce his ballets—which indeed she has done.

He also believed that dancers learned from teaching. He told lively little Suki Schorer, who joined the company in 1959, that she should get a notebook and write down his corrections, which she did. In 1961, Balanchine asked her to give a class for children at the School. It happened that he came in with Kirstein at a moment when she was kneeling to mold a girl's feet into a correct position, and she overheard him say, "You see, I told you she'd be down on her hands and knees."

．　．　．

In 1962, Balanchine created one of his greatest masterpieces. He had been familiar with Shakespeare's *A Midsummer Night's Dream* since his youth; he had both danced and acted in it, and he claimed to know it—or most of it—by heart in Russian. He had a particular affection for the work, and he also loved Mendelssohn's Overture and incidental music. Mendelssohn as much as Shakespeare would guide him. Yet because he intended to make a full-length ballet, and the Mendelssohn score lasted in all no more than an hour, it would have to be augmented with additional music by the composer. Balanchine claimed that it took him twenty years to put together the score. It was the nearest he ever came to composing the music for a whole ballet himself.

The curtain rises when about one-third of Mendelssohn's Overture has been played. What remains serves as a perfect exposition, in which all the elements of the play can be presented in rapid succession. Once this is done, Balanchine is free to allot what time he chooses to dancing or to storytelling.

Shakespeare begins his comedy with the court of Athens, then goes on to Bottom and his companions. Yet the wood is the dominant presence of the play; and Mendelssohn judged it proper to begin his Overture with its changing moods and lights and tripping fairies before introducing the theme of the clowns, or the court's hunting horns, or the lovesick Helena.

Balanchine makes masterly use of the score in the first episode. The creation of a fairy court of insects played by children, whose diminutive size is accentuated by a corps de ballet of butterflies played by adult girls, wins the audience's heart from the start. Puck is established as a comic—as well as nimble—figure, who takes the public into his confidence. Special marvels are the confrontation of glittering Oberon and beautiful Titania, who struggle over the little Indian boy; the slow crossing of the stage by mourning Helena, who listlessly plucks a leaf from a tree, which is in fact the (to her) invisible Puck; and the relentless attitudes of the four courtiers, who stand like medieval carvings of (family) pride behind the amiable Theseus.

After these lightning introductions, it is time to dance. In Mendelssohn's Overture to Racine's *Athalie,* Balanchine found music for strings of extraordinary sweetness to which Titania may dance with her Cavalier, alternating with more dramatic warnings and scurries during which Puck makes unsuccessful attempts to steal the Indian boy for Oberon—only to be driven away by fairies with switches. The famous Scherzo is danced by Oberon and his followers. While Oberon gets his breath back between outbursts of beating and turning steps, the bugs and butterflies disport.

To some short passages from the incidental music (written seventeen years after Mendelssohn's youthful Overture), which Balanchine and Robert Irving patched together, Oberon tells Puck about "a little western flower," and sends him girdling round the earth in an abbreviated "forty minutes."

Without a pause, the warbling clarinets of Mendelssohn's Concert overture, *Die schöne Melusine,* have stolen upon us. These alternate with agitato passages on the strings, a rising figure that signifies despair and great sighs on the cellos, till all are finally intermingled. Thus the billing and cooing of Hermia and Lysander in their "troubadour"-style costumes, the scorn of Demetrius for Helena, the sudden love of Lysander—whose eyes have by now been anointed by Puck—for Helena, and all the consequent confusions are woven by Balanchine into a tissue of movement and action. By allowing the music to dictate his scene's artistic shape, he avoids the pitfalls of storytelling, always so tedious in ballets based on novels or plays.

An imperceptible scene change to another part of the wood brings us to Titania's bower. The Fairies' march is followed by the song "You spotted snakes," for soprano and mezzo, in which the chorus joins so sweetly with the refrain "Philomel, with melody"; and in her pink scallop shell Titania is lulled to sleep. The first part of Mendelssohn's Intermezzo provides a most effective solo for the distraught and unloved Hermia; the second part allows the briefest possible rehearsal for the clowns before Puck places the ass's head on Bottom, causing his companions to disperse in terror.

The pas de deux of Titania with Bottom in his ass's head is (to me, at least) the jewel at the heart of the ballet. It is Balanchine's triumph, not just as a choreographer—for the dance steps are very traditional—but as a man of the theater—a dramatist, even—and as a commentator on human absurdity. Like Shakespeare, Balanchine knew that the infatuated of either sex discerns qualities in the loved one which do not exist; that love is blind; that we love monsters and become monsters of jealousy when loving; that anyone can get carried away by fantastic hope on a Saturday night and wake to a nasty shock on Sunday morning. If Mendelssohn might well have been surprised to find Bottom moving to the heavenly music of his Nocturne, Shakespeare would certainly have seen the point. In comic ballets, the jokes about the awkward partner who gets on the wrong side of his ballerina or misjudges distance are all too frequent and vulgar: this is matter of finer quality. Titania goes through her motions with devout seriousness: Balanchine knows that while she seems to show Bottom tenderly how to partner her—just as a woman, without giving a lecture, might initiate an awkward boy into the mysteries of lovemaking—the clown, supporting the fairy queen in an arabesque penchée, has only to turn his grotesque head a very little and look wistfully over his shoulder at an imagined thistle to prick us with laughter. Yet even as we laugh we experience a pang of sadness. The comedy is in the pity; and it is comedy of the very highest kind, such as we recognize when Congreve's Millamant reveals the heart behind her fashionable patter, and, indeed, such as Shakespeare gives us in Titania's admiring observation to Bottom, "Thou art as wise as thou art beautiful."

Roland Vazquez, who had come to the New York City Ballet from the Christensen's San Francisco Ballet, was the first Bottom. He thought of Balanchine as someone he did not want to disappoint. "The man was so great. . . . There are no words to describe it. He was perfect. In my eyes he couldn't do wrong. He demonstrated every step, every gesture. He was different with everyone. He knew exactly what you thought and felt, what you could do—a sort of clairvoyance."

After these marvels, the act has to conclude with something more down-to-earth. Balanchine decided to bring on the Amazon Hippolyta with a pack of hounds; and he found in the Overture to Mendelssohn's cantata *Die erste Walpurgisnacht* some galloping music. He also conjured up, with the aid of Ronald Bates, the new stage manager, a "drooping fog as black as Acheron," in which the two confused pairs of lovers can quarrel and get lost, in which Puck can fence with Lysander and Demetrius in turn, impersonating the one while he abuses the other, in which all four Athenians can at last be put to sleep, then dragged into appropriate pairs. Alternating with the entries of hounds, which have horses' tails, come the reconciliation of Oberon and Titania and a series of fouettés by Hippolyta. The act ends with a rousing chorus, like a national anthem, from the same cantata, to the music of which Theseus approves the marriages and names the day.

Throughout the first busy act of this Greek-English-German fantasia there have been recognizably American gestures. Puck has kicked backsides, wiped the sweat from his forehead, then flicked his hand; Demetrius has done a downward flap of the hand, signifying "Get lost!" to the rejected Helena. To the final chords, before they follow the court back to Athens, the rival lovers shake hands and trail off with their arms round their girl friends' waists, resting their rapiers on their shoulders like baseball bats.

The drama of the ballet is now pretty well over, and the much shorter second act, like the much longer last act of *The Sleeping Beauty,* will be mainly a divertissement. Some of the choreographer's warmest admirers complained about this in 1962. In 1987, it is hard to see why.

The second act begins with the Wedding March, in which Theseus and his court process grandly in and out. For his celebratory dances Balanchine unearthed a piece of Mendelssohn's juvenilia, the Symphony No. 9 for strings. The first (allegro) movement of this, with its wistful tune, is danced by two principals and eight couples; the second (slow) movement is a pas de deux. To the third movement of this symphony, Balanchine tried to "do something for the boys." This passage, soon cut, may have justified Denby in finding the effect of the divertissement—except for the pas de deux—monotonous.

The Overture Mendelssohn wrote for his *liederspiel, "Die Heimkehr aus der Fremde,"* with its sentimental melody on the strings, brings on the court once more for a formal finale. Then we are back in the wood. The chorus sings "Through the house give glimmering light," the bugs and fairies dance, Oberon and Titania celebrate their truce, and when Puck comes "to sweep the dust behind the door," he is whisked on a wire skyward. To me, an act that begins with the grand patterns of the Wedding March, continues with such pretty music—admittedly gentle and unspectacular—contains so exquisite a pas de deux, and ends with fairy song, dance and a joke is entirely satisfactory.

At first Villella did not know how to cope with the role of Oberon. It had much more mime than was usual in Balanchine ballets, and Villella was completely ignorant of mime. At rehearsals, Balanchine tended to postpone certain passages, saying, "Well, you have an entrance here. We'll do that later. Don't worry." He even arranged the brilliant Scherzo in bits and pieces, and always took the children first. Villella began to think, "He doesn't like me," and wondered if he had a role at all. Since 1960 he had been taking class with the Dane Stanley Williams, who was a guest teacher at the School. Stanley's forty-minute barre was beneficial to a young man whose training had been interrupted between the ages of sixteen and twenty. (Villella had explained to Balanchine why he took class with Williams, and Balanchine said he understood, but Eddie felt he was offended nonetheless.) When Stanley Williams asked him about his role in *A Midsummer Night's Dream,* he complained, "I've got nothing to do; and to top it all I'm dancing with a bunch of kids." Finally, when Balanchine had "knocked off the Scherzo and put it together," Villella got "a totally different idea." With its bounding jumps and rapid changes of direction, the Scherzo was revealed as one of the greatest variations ever created for a male dancer. Yet it was only three or four days until the premiere, and Balanchine had not shown Villella the mime. Kirstein went to Williams and said, "Eddie has a pivotal role, and he's going to ruin the production. What can you do?" Stanley took Eddie in hand, and for two days they worked on the mime.

Villella recalled:

Opening night came. I did the performance. I was exhilarated. The ballet had a wonderful success. I was received very well. Next morning I was onstage, warming up at ten, waiting for rehearsal, sore and tired, in the gloom of the working lights. Balanchine came walking by, in his trench-coat, with a newspaper under his arm. He walked past me, then stopped, turned around and came back. He said, "You know, you danced *excellent* last night, *excellent*." He put his arm round me, then turned and walked away. That is probably the single biggest compliment I have ever gotten in my life. But *in addition* he put his arm around me. Our major goal in life was to please this man. It was an extraordinary moment.

Diana Adams, who had been intended for Titania but who because of injury was replaced by Melissa Hayden, remembered other moments with Balanchine. She first worked with him during the war as a member of Ballet Theatre, and he had liked her appearance, her height and her "nice long legs," but he was determined to make her move faster. She had been dancing Tudor ballets, which were not technically demanding, and she was afraid of pirouettes. Balanchine arranged *Aurora's Wedding,* took the Lilac Fairy's slow variation away from her and gave her the faster "finger" variation. At first she thought he was mad, but in time she came to realize that she was "more interesting" in the latter.

When she joined the New York City Ballet, she was taught *Symphonie concertante,* which gave her blisters; but Balanchine disregarded the blood on her shoes:

There was not an instant of sympathy. Mr. B. would look and say, "Third movement!" In Ballet Theatre I never used to rehearse on pointe—and I thought I was going to die. He'd say, "I think if you are going to do this, you should do it from a real fifth." I thought I *was* in fifth. It was from that ballet I realized I was only about half trained. At the same time I was learning *Serenade.* I was the one who came running in at the end of the first movement. I didn't think I had the endurance: but the fast part was still to come. That was the first ballet I danced with the company. He came backstage afterward and clasped me by both hands and said, "That was *wonderful!*" and I was so happy. But he was sometimes implacable.

Balanchine may have been implacable, but Diana Adams could inadvertently hurt his feelings. She had danced in the first performance of *La Valse,* and Balanchine arranged the fast fifth waltz for her and Herbert Bliss. Some nights later, since *La Valse* was the only ballet she was down for and it came last on the program, she asked if another girl could stand in for her, so that she could have the evening off. "His face crumpled, and he said, 'But it's very *nice* what I did for you!' It was very callous of me. He had worked out my role with great care. He always made a dance with one person in mind, and if another person was to dance it, he would change the steps. He never tried to make you look like someone else."

Diana thought she would never be strong enough to be a "classical ballerina," and preferred modern roles. "So I was always pulling back. There was a tug-of-war. After a performance of *Swan Lake* he would say, 'Why are you so *boring*? Why don't you do something? I don't care what steps you do, but do *something.*' He used to give me a real hard time. But I found that when I let myself go it was twice as easy." In the end she decided she was acceptable in *Swan Lake*: "odd but interesting."

■　■　■

RECOGNITION of Balanchine's company and of his fame as a choreographer was increasing throughout New York State, throughout the country and, indeed, all over the world. In 1959, the New York City Ballet had danced in Albany for Governor Rockefeller's inauguration. In 1963, it would appear in Washington at the second anniversary of Kennedy's presidency. In 1960, Balanchine's dream of free matinees for children came true. Three thousand of them, chosen from all over greater New York, poured in, gasped, cheered and asked for more. When he made his ballets available, free, to regional companies in the United States, the Atlanta Civic Ballet was the first to stage one—*Serenade*—in 1961. In 1962, the New York State Council on the Arts sent the company on its first upstate tour, and Balanchine gave lecture-demonstrations in twelve cities. In 1963 they were to begin in New York schools. By 1964, the company had had seasons in Chicago, Los Angeles, Ravinia, Washington D.C., and San Francisco, besides dancing in Baltimore, Seattle, Philadelphia and a number of smaller cities. Its members had danced in nearly every European country, in Russia, Israel, Japan, Australia and the Philippines. And Balanchine's ballets were known worldwide. Ballet Theatre gave *Theme and Variations* in Russia two years before the New York City Ballet appeared there. In the same year, *Symphony in C* and *The Four*

Temperaments were danced by the Royal Swedish Ballet in China. In 1962, Balanchine would take his company to Hamburg to celebrate Stravinsky's eightieth birthday by dancing *Agon, Orpheus* and *Apollo*. In 1963, he would work for the third time with the Paris Opéra Ballet, staging *Concerto Barocco, Scotch Symphony, The Four Temperaments* and *Bourrée fantasque*. And during these last years at City Center, his choreography began to reach an even wider public than the theatergoing one, because of his experiments—which did not satisfy him—in television.

It was also in 1963, at the very end of NYCB's City Center period, that Balanchine made one of his most unpredictable works, *Bugaku*, with music commissioned from the Japanese composer Toshiro Mayuzumi, but written for a Western orchestra. The whining, feline glissandi lead the audience to a vermilion-railed platform simulating a Japanese stage, on which the rites of marriage take place between a samurai warrior and a woman treading delicately on pointe. Although in the first and third movements the hero and heroine wear diaphanous white garments and trains held by attendants, for the central pas de deux she wears a white bikini decorated with flowers, and white tights, and he, a white leotard. Their dance is the most erotic Balanchine ever invented, and almost appears to be the fulfillment of a personal fantasy. In the first performance, the highly masculine Edward Villella remained impassive and the flowerlike Allegra Kent kept her eyes downcast, both retaining perfect manners even in the throes of stylized orgasm. (Balanchine's old friend Lucia Davidova had always told him that if people could see into his mind, he would be in prison.)

■   ■   ■

THOUGH Balanchine had choreographed Stravinsky's Violin Concerto and *Danses concertantes* in the forties, Stravinsky was wary of having his concert music appropriated for the ballet stage. Balanchine, however, successfully arranged two more ballets to Stravinsky's music never intended for the theater. These short works, *Monumentum pro Gesualdo* (1960) and *Movements for Piano and Orchestra* (1963), were, from 1966 onward, always performed together.

Monumentum pro Gesualdo di Venosa ad CD Annum, to give the piece its full title, is Stravinsky's quatercentenary tribute to a forgotten Renaissance composer; he "recomposed for instruments" three of Gesualdo's madrigals. Balanchine seized upon the score, and his ballet had its premiere less than two months after the music's first performance in Venice. Without recourse to period costumes or accessories, Balanchine made a serene evocation of the High Renaissance: the dancers embody the aristocratic, effortless elegance about which Baldassare Castiglione wrote in *The Courtier.* It must be one of the very few ballets in which none of the men jumps.

Movements was arranged for a principal couple and an ensemble of six girls. The small corps, which alone moves during the terse intermediate sections connecting the five movements, and which backs up the principals in the remainder of the ballet, is often divided into two groups of three; and these assume an extraordinary variety of poses, like eccentric modern versions of the Three Graces.

Sometimes, for instance, the middle girl of each trio will stand upright, legs apart and arms hanging, while her two comrades, facing away from her, adopt a Degas pose as they adjust their shoe ribbons; or three girls, back to back in a triangle, bend forward with extended arms; or they all take a haranguing *Lysistrata* stance, one arm raised in exhortation; or they bend forward in fourth position, hands to shoulders with jutting elbows. While the corps sustains this last pose, the man crouches like a hunter, as if holding out an invisible net to catch his ballerina, watching her turn, kick and perform arabesques before she falls backward into his arms, legs and arms wide open but with one knee bent. While the couple embrace, the two trios face outward and adopt a striding pose like marching guardsmen.

The music, for piano and orchestra, is sure to baffle, if not irritate, an audience. To stage it at all was an act of conviction and courage. Hugo Fiorato once remarked candidly, "Who . . . would listen to *Movements* of Stravinsky by itself? . . . I don't think I would. But when you hear *Movements* and you see *Movements* through Balanchine's eyes and what he has added to the score, it suddenly becomes an amazingly exciting work."

Stravinsky was well aware of what Balanchine had done to popularize his music; and he wrote that watching *Movements* "was like a tour of a building for which I had drawn the plans but never explored the result."

Movements was made on Diana Adams, who had been married for several years to Ronald Bates. Shortly before opening night, her doctor told her she was pregnant. "You'll have to lie down *today*," he added. She went back to City Center, where she happened to run into Balanchine downstairs. "He knew. He walked right past me." To Balanchine, the pregnancy was a betrayal of the Stravinsky ballet. He told John Taras, "I don't want to hear anything more about *Movements.*" Taras protested, "But the ballet's all finished." "If *you* want to do it, do it," was the only reply. So John Taras rehearsed the six girls, and Jacques d'Amboise, the male lead, took a seventeen-year-old soloist in the company named Suzanne Farrell to Diana's apartment to be taught her role by the recumbent dancer. Luckily, this girl, who was destined to become the most celebrated of all Balanchine's ballerinas, was a quick learner.

Chapter 11

....

TO RUSSIA:

OCTOBER - NOVEMBER 1962

S HORTLY after the staging of *A Midsummer Night's Dream,*
Balanchine went to West Germany to direct Tchaikovsky's
Eugene Onegin for the Hamburg Opera. Betty Cage was
amazed to receive in rapid succession four handwritten letters from
him, one of which concerned the engagement of a dancer who, at
the end of his life, was to become his closest friend: "I saw KARIN
VON AROLDINGEN dance in Frankfurt, which Lotte [Lenya]
recommended. I think we could take her, not as solo but regular."
In another letter, he asked Betty to deal with a request from Walter
Terry for permission to write his biography. "I did not want to
write to him a letter of explanation. Because it would be sort of
letter for posterity, like second-rate correspondence between famous choreographer and Voltaire. . . . Please call him and say that

my personal life is not very interesting and that Taper's book is coming out soon with everything that one can possibly find out about me, which is not very much. If Terry want to bother writing about my work . . . then he can do this without my permission . . . but I don't want to participate in it. If Terry wants to know about my inspiration or who is my Muse then he will never know that. Because I won't tell him, and it is not going to be written anywhere, for anybody to know. Don't tell him this. . . ."

In the former letter he wrote, "I agree with you about not going to Russia now, there is no reason why we should rush. . . ." Yet that very fall, in October 1962, at the end of an arduous European tour that began in Hamburg and included not only German towns but engagements in Switzerland and Austria as well, the New York City Ballet paid its first visit to Russia, and Balanchine saw the land of his birth after an absence of thirty-eight years. While the Americans were in Russia, the Bolshoi Ballet appeared in New York. It was a "cultural exchange" agreed upon by the two governments.

In addition to Balanchine and Natalie Molostwoff—who took a holiday from her duties at the School to revisit the union of republics she had left even earlier than he—there were several others who spoke a little Russian. Kevin Tyler, assistant stage manager under Ronald Bates, had been born a Russian subject; his name was originally Arkady Tkatchenko. Naturally he was given the job of traveling ahead of the company to bring the scenery and costumes from Vienna to Moscow. Attempts were made to delay him at both the Czech and Polish frontiers, since the Czechs and Poles hated Americans and Russians equally. The company arrived by air before Kevin, and everyone feared that he was lost. But the stage was set in time.

One of the dancers, Robert Maiorano, reported that the New York City Ballet was met at Moscow airport by "floodlights and interviewers, cultural-affairs officials, interpreters and State Department delegates." Kirstein thought Balanchine behaved as if he only remembered Russia before the Revolution. When he was bade

"Welcome to Russia, home of the classical ballet," he replied, "Thank you, but America is now home of the classical ballet. Russia is home of the old romantic ballet."

Andrei Balanchivadze had come from Georgia to greet his brother. The next day's *New York Times* described their reunion: " 'Andryusha, it's you,' the slender 58-year-old balletmaster exclaimed as he embraced his brother. Cameramen and photographers recorded the scene in the brightness of truck-mounted floodlights." But Patricia Neary observed that the moment Balanchine produced his American passport to make clear that he was not coming *home,* the cameras disappeared.

It cannot have been easy for the two brothers, who had not seen each other since 1918. George was now world-famous; Andrei, a respected composer, was a hero in Georgia and known throughout the USSR. His elder son, Amiran, was a physicist; his daughter, a dancer at the Tbilisi Opera and Ballet Theater; his second son, Georgi, a pianist, studying under the great champion of Stravinsky's music Maria Yudina, as Andrei himself had done. She, Balanchine, Andrei and young Georgi posed for a photograph together.

NYCB's opening performance in Russia was given two days later in the famous old Bolshoi Theater. No American company had ever appeared there until Balanchine's. Ballet Theatre, on its 1960 Russian tour, had danced at the Stanislavsky Theater and the Lenin Palace of Sports.

The occupants of the packed crimson-and-gold auditorium were taken aback by *Serenade.* In his report, printed in New York the next morning, John Martin, whom Kirstein had invited to travel with the company, tried to soften the blow:

The Russian audience is an altogether honest one. It applauds furiously when it is moved to do so, and it sits in absolute silence when it is not so moved. The evening opened in the latter mood. The first ballet was . . . *Serenade,* beautifully danced. . . . But the response was a perplexed and fairly indifferent one.

The atmosphere began to warm with the Robbins-Gould *Interplay*.
. . . Then followed *Agon* . . . which is not easy for any audience to take
at first seeing. But the pas de deux by Miss [Allegra] Kent and Arthur
Mitchell brought forth the first sign of genuine enthusiasm. When the
curtain rose on . . . *Western Symphony* and revealed a painted backdrop,
there was a wave of heartfelt relief. . . . From then on, the temperature
was high. . . . At the final curtain Mr. Balanchine was the center of the
greatest ovation. . . .

Stravinsky himself was in Leningrad when Balanchine's company opened in Moscow. His return to Russia had preceded that
of his friend by two weeks. Under Hurok's auspices he had conducted concerts of his own music in Moscow and Leningrad. He
was back in the capital in time to be received by Khrushchev on
October 11, and Balanchine managed to visit him that afternoon.

After one performance at the Bolshoi, NYCB moved to the
6,000-seat Palace of Congresses within the walls of the Kremlin,
a recently completed and luxurious hall, the main use of which—as
its name suggests—was not theatrical. It was so vast that the
dancers had difficulty putting themselves across, and applause,
however warm, tended to get lost. Applause there was, but it was
confined mostly to the end of a program. The reason for this was
the excellent buffet on the top floor of the palace. After the first
and second ballets, the spectators made a dash for the fast-travel-
ing escalators in order to gorge on caviar, hot blinis and sausages,
which were unobtainable in restaurants and stores. After two repetitions of the first program shown at the Bolshoi, the second program opened on October 12; and its final ballet, *Symphony in C*,
was considered by Martin to be the turning point of the company's
reception.

The Bizet work brought forth not only applause throughout and repeated
curtain calls at the end but also rhythmic cries of "Bal-an-chine" until
the choreographer was forced to come forward and bow his acknowledg-
ment.

At a later performance of *Agon,* Arthur Mitchell was greeted by cries of "Meet-shell! Meet-shell!" and Villella had to repeat his number in *Donizetti Variations.* Webern's *Episodes* was received with "tumultuous favor," which astounded John Martin.

The members of the company were segregated from other clients of the hotel, with their own dining room and their own bus to take them to and from the theater. Balanchine usually ate in restaurants, and very shortly after his arrival he asked his brother to recommend the best. Andrei took him to a Caucasian restaurant near the Kremlin. There was an enormous bill of fare, but one thing after another that Balanchine chose was unobtainable. He ended by eating chicken with coriander sauce; it was all there was. Usually the two brothers lunched and dined alone together, but sometimes Natalie Molostwoff accompanied them. On one of the latter occasions, all three were struck by the good manners and assiduous attention of the young man who was serving them. He seemed a phenomenon in a country where service was not on a high level. Balanchine immediately said, "He's an out-of-work actor playing the part of a waiter." This turned out to be the case.

Soon after the opening of the Moscow season, there was an enormous party at the American embassy, and Kirstein had a further opportunity to observe Balanchine enacting what seemed to be a deliberately chosen role. When Khrushchev's son-in-law, the newspaper publisher Adzhubei, came up to talk to the choreographer, he appeared to be too absorbed in his conversation with some young dancers to notice him. What Kirstein did not include in his printed account was that Adzhubei was Ukrainian, and the Ukraine was at that time a disaffected republic; Adzhubei was involved in the disaffection, and Balanchine knew perfectly well that he was a hot potato.

At the beginning of the company's second week in Moscow, President Kennedy learned from aerial photographs that the Russians were building missile sites in Cuba. On October 18—the day Edward Villella's solo in *Donizetti Variations* was encored in the Kremlin—Andrei Gromyko, the Soviet foreign minister, who was on a visit to Washington, denied that there were any such sites. It was in the bus, returning from an evening performance, that Balanchine's dancers first heard there was a possibility of war. During supper in the hotel, the waitresses, noticing their downcast looks, asked Natalie Molostwoff what the matter was. When she told them, they said, "You are artists. We don't associate you with your government."

During the following days, messages from the embassy kept the company informed of the course of events. Kirstein devised Plan A and Plan B in case of an emergency, but the cultural attaché told him, "*You* don't have plans. You leave when they tell you to leave. The first thing we will know at the embassy is that the phone will be cut off."

At best, members of the company thought, they would be sent straight home. The fact that the Bolshoi Ballet was appearing in the United States gave them hope that they would not be interned even if there was war. Balanchine said, "I've never been to Siberia."

Dancers were able to get hamburgers and bottles of Scotch from the American embassy. Returning for lunch at the hotel, they saw a mob outside the embassy preparing to throw stones. Betty Cage gave the order to drive on. As it turned out, the light was bad for the television cameras, so the "spontaneous" demonstration was postponed.

The dancers were naturally worried about the kind of reception they would get from their audience that evening. As the curtains parted, Robert Maiorano observed, "Robert Irving cautiously raised his baton. Suddenly the entire audience of six thousand rose, then cheered." Nothing could have been more heartwarming to the dancers. When they returned to the Ukrainia Hotel, they found that the waitresses had put flowers on all the tables.

On October 20, President Kennedy decided to "quarantine" Cuba. Ships were deployed in the Caribbean. On the twenty-second, the president had a difficult session with leaders of Congress, some of whom were impatiently belligerent. At seven that evening he appeared on television to inform the nation that Soviet engineers had installed in Cuba sites for medium-range missiles capable of reaching Washington, D.C., the Panama Canal, Cape Canaveral, Mexico City and any city in the southeastern part of the United States. He had therefore ordered that "all ships . . . bound for Cuba . . . if found to contain cargoes of offensive weapons, be turned back." Russian ships continued to sail toward Cuba; but on Wednesday, twenty stopped or began to make for home. On Friday, Khrushchev admitted that the missiles were already in Cuba. On Saturday, Kennedy told him they must go. On Sunday, October 28, Khrushchev complied with the president's demands; and the world breathed again.

Kirstein wrote: "Through it all, Betty Cage and Balanchine cushioned the brunt of unimaginable possibilities with such tact and skill that the danger of our situation hardly percolated down to the dancers, who, night after night within the Kremlin's walls, heard six thousand voices yell for fifteen minutes after every performance: 'Bal-an-chin, Bal-an-chin!' "

Principal dancer Violette Verdy later admitted that she and most of her colleagues were too concerned with their work to think much about politics; perhaps the men worried more. Protocol was strict, and every member of the company had to produce an identity card to gain admittance to the Kremlin. One night Balanchine found he had left his at the hotel. Although interviewers were waiting for him, and although the guards knew very well who he was, he was not allowed in. He went back to the hotel, quite pleased to have missed the journalists and to have proved how foolish the regulations were.

Programs for the Russian tour had been agreed on in advance in New York. Russian objections to *The Prodigal Son* because of its biblical theme were quashed. The only attempt made by any Russian to change the planned program took place backstage at the Palace of Congresses after the first performance of *Episodes* during the third week in Moscow. Following the tremendous ovation, which astonished the whole company, Balanchine was approached by an official who told him that Russians did not really understand this type of ballet. "What do you mean?" asked the choreographer. "Didn't you hear? They loved it." The official argued that the Webern ballet was an example of decadent modernism, unsuited to a democratic audience, and he begged that they drop this dangerous and corrupting work from the repertory. Balanchine refused.

. . .

MOST mornings Balanchine taught class, and Soviet dancers and teachers came to watch. Elizaveta Gerdt—daughter of the famous Pavel Gerdt and the idol of Balanchine's student years—now seventy years old, was a teacher at the Bolshoi School. Balanchine arranged that she should give his company a class.

When the Bolshoi directors invited members of the New York City Ballet to watch one of their own classes, they put on a show. Everybody, from the principals down, went through a demonstration that lasted two hours. But Balanchine had secretly told Suki Schorer, Gloria Govrin, Patricia Neary and Suzanne Farrell to bring their practice clothes, and it needed only a few minutes of their haphazard tendus and battements at the barre to make clear that Balanchine had given them a speed the Russians had never acquired. This was not an exhibition, but it was a proof.

At one point, Andrei asked his brother the difference between the Russian style of dancing and George's new American style. Balanchine replied, "The Russians divide the dancer's body horizontally—heads, bodies and legs. I divide it vertically." He made a slicing movement down his face to his crotch.

The Russian critics, rather like the majority of English ones twelve years before, found that the Americans had no "soul." After the first night, the former ballerina Olga Lepeshinskaya had told the news agency Tass, "Of course, we cannot accept everything we saw." The composer Aram Khachaturian said, "The only shortcoming of the American ballet troupe is the absence of a story line."

On Friday, October 26, when the company returned to the Bolshoi for their last four days in Moscow—the day when Khrushchev admitted to President Kennedy that the missiles were already installed—Balanchine was, according to *The New York Times*, "mobbed at the stage door by enthusiastic balletomanes who told him emotionally and in extravagant terms that this was the greatest thing that had ever happened in the ballet here." Although many seats had been reserved for officials or given in blocks to unions or factories, there was a group of about a hundred fans who had not missed a performance and knew even members of the corps de ballet by name.

The last performance in Moscow was recorded by television cameras. "It was a gala evening in every respect," wrote Martin, "with almost continual applause . . . and cheering and countless curtain calls at the conclusion. There is no knowing how long the demonstration would have gone on if George Balanchine had not stepped forward and made a short speech in Russian in which he invited those who wished to see more to follow the company to Leningrad." The theater staff declared that the applause throughout the season had been "unprecedented." As Balanchine joined his dancers in the bus to return to the hotel, the crowds called after him, "Come back! Come back! Come back!"

∎   ∎   ∎

LENINGRAD was, of course, magnificent, and the whole company was housed at the comfortable, old-fashioned Astoria Hotel. The moment after he had checked in, Balanchine grabbed Natalie Molostwoff by the hand and rushed out to show her his old home in Bolshoya Moskovskaya, which was not far away. He was very emotional.

In Moscow, the audience had taken some winning over. In the former capital of Imperial Russia, the public was more sophisticated. As Kirstein recorded, *Serenade* had five curtain calls; *Agon* "carried the house along with it"; during *Western Symphony*, "spirits were high, and the demonstration for Balanchine himself fairly tore the house down. There were many flowers." The only pity was that after two performances the company had to move from the Kirov Theater to the shabby old Lensoviet Palace of Culture, which held twice as many spectators.

It was inevitable that the anxieties of the tour and its crescendo of acclaim, the fears aroused by the Cuban missile crisis and the need to maintain a calm front, took their toll on those in command. On the fourth day, Balanchine decided to skip his company's week in Kiev, fly back to New York, then rejoin them in Tbilisi. John Taras was not the only one to observe that he was unusually depressed and longing to get out of Russia. He told Patricia Neary that he felt he was being spied on; he was certain his room and perhaps even his clothes were bugged; and he complained that his telephone rang and woke him all night long. He had lost weight. He also had a faint suspicion that if he were to travel alone without the company he might not be allowed to leave; perhaps he wanted to discover if this was so.

Kirstein wrote: "Balanchine leaves after tomorrow for a well-earned rest. . . . His return to his early youth has been touching in the extreme and historic in Terpsichorean annals. We went to the school and were shown his class-portraits, etc. And they made him an honorary member of the Conservatory. The reception beggars description. He has to go out and send them home. . . ."

Because of the Russian way of allotting theater tickets, and because the theater was always full, Balanchine discovered that many young dancers and musicians, as well as some of his old colleagues at the School and Conservatory, had been unable to see the New York City Ballet. Before flying to America he arranged an extra matinee for artists, to which admission would be free.

At the end of this performance a deputation presented him with a silver samovar full of roses, and Konstantin Sergueyev, director of the Kirov Ballet, made a speech. Balanchine looked at the floor for what Kirstein called "a long half minute" while the audience applauded. A woman from The Hermitage, sitting with Kirstein, translated the Russian words, which were received in breathless silence. "It was rather sad," she said. "It was simply, 'Thank you. In troubling times which we may share in time to come, try to think of us as we are tonight; we'll try to think of you as you are tonight.' "

Martin thought that perhaps the most important event of the tour was a talk on the principles of his choreography that Balanchine gave to the choreographers of Leningrad and twelve student choreographers. This took place around a table in the room adjoining the little museum on the top floor of the Ballet School on Theater Street. "The response varied from something like despair to starry-eyed eagerness. The students requested a second session, which was duly held in a corner of the theater itself."

Back in New York, Balanchine went to see the Stravinskys, whose reaction to Russia had been very different from his. Balanchine had not been received by Khrushchev—which is the last thing he would have wanted—but he, too, had been made much of by the dignitaries of the Soviet Union, by the minister of culture, Mme. Furtseva, and by the leading composers, ballet masters and dancers. He had been welcomed by his brother, by Elizaveta Gerdt, by Gusev and Mungalova, who had danced some of his earliest choreography, and by other old friends. Stravinsky's reaction had been euphoria; Balanchine's, even when he was received with acclaim in his native Leningrad, was a kind of panic. The ballet master to whom all turned for assurance had followed a sudden impulse and fled.

The Leningrad visit was much shorter than the Moscow one. *Apollo* was danced twice there, but nowhere else in Russia. Balanchine rejoined the company in Georgia. He was met at Tbilisi airport by his brother, sister-in-law, elder nephew, Amiran, and niece, Tamara. A mass was sung in the cathedral for the success of the New York City Ballet and the former Georgi Melitonovich Balanchivadze. The prayers were granted. After the first performance, at the end of an incredible ovation, Balanchine took a curtain call alone in the old Moorish-style opera house, and the audience rose to its feet in homage to the man they regarded as a compatriot.

The appearance of the American dancers in the streets of Tbilisi almost brought traffic to a halt. The fair-haired girls in particular caused a sensation. Violette Verdy, noticing how Georgian men looked at women, how eager they were to make contact with them, talk to them, touch them or escort them home, thought she had found a clue to Balanchine's adoration of the female sex.

A mountaintop picnic was given for the whole company, and the daredevil Georgians, who liked to show their contempt for danger, took the hairpin bends on the way up at high speed. "Wild Caucasian dances were performed in our honor," wrote Robert Maiorano. "A bottle of wine later, I joined in, along with Arthur Mitchell. Soon everyone was drunk with happiness. Mr. B. was toasted as everyone's brother."

Taking Natalie with him, Balanchine traveled to Kutaisi, the small provincial town where his elder half-brother Apolon lived and where his father was buried. It was a night's journey away, and since he and Natalie were tired at the end of the day's work, they hoped for sleep. This proved to be out of the question; the Georgians who accompanied them were determined to drink and sing all night long. Andrei and his son Amiran were of the party. When the honored guests got off the train early in the morning, they were driven at once to a big banquet that had been prepared at Apolon's house. They were expected to sit without eating or drinking while speeches were made in their honor. Then the toasts began. There were two other banquets that day, during one of which a group sang Georgian folk songs in Balanchine's honor; then they were driven at mad speed up more hairpin bends to a castle. However, the hospitable Georgians neglected certain courtesies: never once was Natalie shown a ladies' room. She could not think how she survived, and from then on Balanchine called her "the camel."

By the time the company reached Baku, on the Caspian Sea—a city of oil wells and caviar—and the final date of their tour, the dancers were in a state of exhaustion. A huge party was given in the hotel ballroom on the night before they left, and everybody got drunk. Shaun O'Brien put on his new Russian musquash hat and removed his pants. When the party broke up, dancers began to visit one another's rooms. Shaun called on Betty and Natalie, to find the latter ready for the morning flight, fully dressed and wearing her earrings, but fast asleep on top of her bed. Then Balanchine came in and sat down. He said, "Well, I suppose now the tour is over everybody's little love affairs will be over too. All except mine—I never had any." Shaun remarked, "You could have, if you wanted to." "No," said Balanchine, "nobody loves me." Then Shaun did something he would never have dared do if he were sober; he ran to Balanchine, sat on the arm of his chair, patted him and exclaimed, "But we *all* love you!" Balanchine looked him in the eye without expression and said, "Where are your pants?"

Chapter 12

•••

PROBLEMS IN PARADISE:

1964 - 1972

W HEN Lincoln Center, a complex of buildings dedicated to
the performing arts, was built in the early sixties, the
New York State Theater, designed by Philip Johnson,
was planned as a shrine for the works of Balanchine, but only in
the nick of time did he manage to avert a potentially fatal mistake.
The orchestra pit had been constructed to accommodate only
thirty-five musicians, the usual number for a Broadway musical.
According to Kirstein:

Concrete had been poured, but early one morning Balanchine chanced
into the auditorium, crowded with forests of scaffolding, to stage one of
the most moving and effective solos of his career. After his immediate
threat to withdraw our company from further tenancy if the orchestra pit

remained straitjacketed, power drills were brought to double the space, so that it can now, with discomfort, hold some seventy men. . . . By this time it was apparent that the State Theater would be shared by the New York City Opera. . . .

Balanchine's preoccupation, apart from space for the musicians, was the need for the most perfect dance floor possible to lessen the pains and hazards of performance. For several years he had been discussing the problem with Ronald Bates, who, after war service in the navy, had done many jobs before he became associate stage manager of NYCB in 1957.

During weekends in Connecticut, Balanchine and Bates experimented. As Don McDonagh, a dance critic for *The New York Times*, described it later, "Clearing the kitchen table, the two set to work hammering together models of a floor that incorporated a 'basketweave' principle that would be firm and also have the right degree of elasticity to minimize injury." A linoleum covering—which traveled to other stages on tour—would always be rolled out over the wooden surface.

In December 1963, *The New York Times* announced that the Ford Foundation would give $7,756,000 to ballet in America, the money to be divided between schools and companies. The director of the Foundation's humanities and arts programs, W. McNeil Lowry, was a keen supporter of Balanchine. Seven companies received grants. The New York City Ballet was guaranteed $200,000 a year for ten years, and the School of American Ballet would receive $242,500 a year, which meant that almost every student would be on scholarship and the School could afford to accept only the most talented. It was just thirty years since SAB had opened.

The Ford Foundation made it a condition of its grants that Balanchine be paid a salary. He had never accepted one before as director of either the company or the School; now he was to be remunerated in both capacities. He asked Lowry, "Do you think I might spend some of the money on a secretary?"

In 1953 Betty Cage had hired a twenty-year-old assistant named Barbara Horgan, who was then a student at Columbia University with thoughts of becoming an actress. She resigned ten years later, just before her thirtieth birthday, because she felt she was getting nowhere. At the time Balanchine took her out for a drink and asked why she was leaving. When she explained, he said, "You'll be back." Now, a year later, she was working for a photographer. Balanchine walked straight to her office and hired her. He also made over to her the $10,000 a year Ford was giving him as director of the School, but she did not discover this for ten years.

· · ·

THE winter season of 1963–64 was NYCB's final one at City Center. The last new work Balanchine staged in the old theater was *Tarantella,* a high-speed pas de deux to music by Gottschalk, designed to exploit the special talents of Patricia McBride and Edward Villella. The first work he arranged for his company at New York State Theater was *Clarinade* to Morton Gould's *Derivations for Clarinet and Jazz Band,* with Benny Goodman playing the solo instrument; he also revived *Ballet Imperial,* using a larger corps to fill the bigger stage.

Productions of *A Midsummer Night's Dream* and *The Nutcracker* were also revised and expanded; Rouben Ter-Arutunian's sumptuously redesigned *Nutcracker* sets, with their snow-heavy fir trees in the forest scene and fantastic rococo confectionery architecture in the Kingdom of Sweets, were to stir the imaginations of children for years to come. Another "spectacular" was Balanchine's *Harlequinade,* based on Petipa's *Les Millions d'Arlequin* and set to the tinkling music of Drigo—a ballet Balanchine himself had danced in as a child.

The French-born Petipa's old Russian ballet had imitated the still-older Italian commedia dell'arte, so there were opportunities for mime. Villella, who knew little about the commedia dell'arte style, later recalled how Balanchine had showed him the proper way to perform his role:

I was doing it rough and gruff in a—I thought—comical manner. But he said, "No, dear, it's commedia dell'arte, but it's French, not Italian." I still didn't understand. Then he turned around and said, "Harlequin is *premier danseur,*" and walked away. There was this elegant confidence this rogue of a Harlequin has. Harlequin is very pulled-up, not crouching. It was a point of departure.

In 1964, Balanchine took time off from the ballet to collaborate with Tanaquil Le Clercq and their cat, Mourka, on a book. He had trained the huge orange-and-white cat to jump, and a photograph by Martha Swope of the choreographer crouching to observe Mourka executing a side cabriole in midair had been published in *Life* magazine. This spurred the idea of the cat's autobiography—a very funny book describing Mourka's ancestry, ballet training in the Petipaw method, fame, friendship with Purr Mesta, lecture tour, love and excursion into space to inaugurate a Cat Star. Mourka's adventures were illustrated with photographs by Martha Swope, and the book was a success.

■　■　■

THE NEW YORK CITY BALLET now entered what came to be known as "The Farrell Years." Diana Adams, from whom Suzanne Farrell took over *Movements,* had been the one to discover her, on a scouting trip to Cincinnati in 1960. At fourteen, Suzanne already showed unusual grace, flow and musical sense but had not developed much strength. Diana hesitated to suggest that the girl move to New York and was relieved to hear that Suzanne's mother was already planning to do so.

Diana told Balanchine that in addition to her other qualities, the girl had something "special," but one of her feet had "virtually no instep." Farrell herself in later years gave the critic David Daniel an account of her strange "audition" with Balanchine. He asked her what she had prepared for him to see. She replied that she didn't know she was supposed to do a number; and her heart sank. He said it didn't matter. But instead of giving her a few steps and combinations to do, he asked her to take her shoe off the weak foot and make a pointe. He cupped his hand over the lower part of the instep and down over her toes, then pressed her foot backward so hard that it hurt. This made her angry. She stiffened her foot and toes and pushed them back against his hand to loosen his grip. He said, "Thank you." Two days later she got a letter telling her she had a full scholarship.

Soon after Suzanne entered the School, she met Balanchine in the elevator, and all she could think of to say was, "How is your cat, Mourka?" This period of shyness did not last long. Balanchine's interest in her grew rapidly. During the Russian tour they became friends, and soon after the company returned, she was promoted to soloist. In April 1963 she danced *Movements*; in December, *Meditation*—a pas de deux to Tchaikovsky music—created especially for her and Jacques d'Amboise. She was seventeen years old. The next year she danced the first ballerina's role in *Ballet Imperial* and Titania in *A Midsummer Night's Dream.* In the latter she was somewhat unsure of how to behave toward Bottom in his ass's head. "I hadn't a clue," she confessed later in a magazine article. "The boss said, 'Don't you have a cat or a dog you can talk to?' So I went out and got a cat and called him Bottom and talked his head off."

With her round cheeks and huge blue eyes, Suzanne herself as a young girl looked something like a cat, but in profile she already shone with the beauty of a Nefertiti. Her long legs and long neck made her appear even taller than she was. Silently and steadily she acquired knowledge and experience. She wanted to dance everything, and Balanchine was ready to give her everything. When Diana Adams commented to him later on the extraordinary variety of Suzanne's range, he nodded and said, "Well, you see, dear, Suzanne never resisted."

Balanchine and Nicolas Nabokov had for years discussed the possibility of staging a *Don Quixote* ballet, yet it is hard to see the work that was presented at the New York State Theater in 1965 as anything but the choreographer's homage to his "alabaster princess," Suzanne Farrell, who danced Dulcinea. Cervantes's hero was obsessed by the chivalric ideal of performing impossible deeds for the love of a beautiful lady; so was Balanchine. His ballet was a quixotic endeavor. Its many sets and costumes by Esteban Francés were handsome enough, but Nabokov's music was a strange patchwork. The justification for the ballet lay in the dances he arranged for Farrell.

Balanchine had performed in the Petipa-Minkus *Don Quixote* before the Russian Revolution. In this long work, the Don does not dance and is obliged to sit on one side of the stage for most of the evening, watching a series of divertissements to flashy music. Balanchine's Don did not dance either, but he was far from a lay figure. Balanchine called him "a secular saint," and Esteban Francés recognized him as "a Christ figure."

Within a few moments of the curtain rising on the Don in his library a maidservant, Farrell, comes in to open his curtains, wash his feet and dry them with her hair. She is thus first seen as a servant, then as the Magdalen. The Don falls asleep, and in his dream she appears to him as a damsel in distress. The walls of his room disappear, and he stands, sword in hand, to face the world. A religious procession passes: the maidservant is now the statue of the Virgin Mary.

As Balanchine taught the role of Don Quixote to Richard Rapp, he explained that the Don was "an old man, but . . . young in feeling and vigorous in movement." Balanchine himself was to play the part on several occasions, and one can imagine that he took a certain pleasure not only in sharing the ballet with Farrell, but in portraying himself as a kind of misunderstood outsider and idealist.

Act III, with its mysteriously beautiful moonlit forest, was the setting for Suzanne Farrell's great moment. Dulcinea and her two friends, supported by three knights, arrive just as Sancho has left his exhausted master sleeping. "Miraculous variations follow," wrote Denby. "Like a dream, these dances remind you of something recent. . . . The man's powerful variation . . . has arm gestures from the court dance. Dulcinea's variation—marvelous in the feet, in the novel and unorthodox épaulements—carries the hidden secret to its climax. Dancing faster and faster, more and more desperate, opposed by a woman in black like the Duchess, tortured by the enchanter Merlin, Dulcinea at last appeals to the sleeping Knight." "Fearless Farrell," someone dubbed her; the discovery that she could fall off pointe at an angle when dancing at speed was to lead to new inventions in Balanchine's choreography.

Don Quixote tilts at a giant, who turns into a windmill, is stampeded by swine, caged by courtiers and carried home. As he lies in bed, he imagines the burning of his books by the Inquisition. In a return to the opening of the ballet, he sees another vision of the Virgin and like a mystic levitating in ecstasy is raised high in the air; he collapses, sobbing, and dies. Finally the maidservant makes a cross from two sticks, walks slowly to the body of her master and places it on his breast.

Balanchine played the part of Don Quixote at the gala performance that preceded the premiere. Farrell later told a critic: "It was the most wonderful night of my life. Afterward we went to a champagne party, and then the two of us slipped away to have doughnuts and coffee. . . . He's so simple. I think I was a sort of relief to him. He doesn't expect a girl to be intellectual—and I found I could make him laugh. . . ."

Another member of the cast, Suki Schorer, who has for many years demonstrated the Balanchine style to students at the School, did not agree that *Don Quixote* was (as I suggested to her) "a crazy endeavor which didn't come off." But she thought that three hours of Nabokov's score was too much for most people.

Suzanne had no understudy, Schorer explained. "People would say, 'We have to have an understudy,' but he said, 'No, I don't want anybody else. If she can't do it, we won't do it.' She never missed a performance till she left."

I first saw *Don Quixote* nearly two years after its original production, by which time a gypsy solo for Farrell had been added. I went backstage after a Saturday matinee to congratulate first her, then Balanchine. I found him with Nabokov, tossing back glasses of brandy, and he praised the composer's versatility. "The score has music of all kinds—polyphonic, in the style of Vivaldi, a Passacaglia on the Gloria." In response to a word of praise for Farrell, he declared that she was incomparable. "I have seen every dancer, and there has never been one like her. She can do everything."

At this point, two shameless mothers with children burst into the room, exclaiming, "We want a ballerina." Balanchine's politeness was exemplary. The mothers had some idea of who he was, but they were not impressed; nor had the ballet been what they expected.

MOTHER   I don't like tragic things.

G. B.   What religion are you?

MOTHER   Jewish.

G. B.   Then you understand about sacrifice. *Don Quixote* is all true.

MOTHER   How old are you?

G. B. *(lying)*   Forty-five.

MOTHER   How long did it take you to get where you are?

G. B.   I started at eight years old. [He then explained why his company was called what it was, how many seasons it had every year, etc.]

MOTHER   How do you pronounce your name?

G. B. *(thoughtfully)*   Well, in French they say *"Bal en Chine"*—that means "a dance in China." In England they say "Bal*un*shun," to rhyme with "luncheon." In American, it's "Ball and chain."

Nabokov was laughing. Balanchine kissed both mothers and sent them off in search of someone more interesting. Then he walked me to the elevator.

·   ·   ·

WHATEVER Balanchine might say, Farrell could not "do everything" equally well. She herself complained that she had "lousy bourrées": Balanchine gave her continual pas de bourrées in *Don*

Quixote to force her to work at them. She was also not an allegro dancer and had not much of a jump. Balanchine tried to strengthen her feet, but he gave a minimum of jumping in class during "The Farrell Years." Yet, though he could see Suzanne's defects very clearly, he would not admit to anyone else that she had any. She had a strong musical sense, an incredible extension in développé and the kind of inexplicable glamour that amounts to genius.

Balanchine called her "Pussycat-fish." "Not just any cat and any fish," she explained. He meant she was a mixture of a cheetah (speed) and a dolphin (intelligence).

■   ■   ■

IN 1964 Richard Leach, director of programs at Lincoln Center, had the idea of building at Saratoga Springs in upstate New York a summer theater where the New York City Ballet and one of the big orchestras could have successive seasons in July and August. Kirstein was enthusiastic, but the New York Philharmonic had made other arrangements, so Leach at once telephoned the Philadelphia Orchestra, which fell in with the plan.

Eugene Ormandy, the orchestra's celebrated conductor, was the first to be consulted about the exact site of the Saratoga Performing Arts Center. In the early spring of 1964, Dick Leach showed him where Geyser Creek had hollowed out a natural amphitheater. At this time of year the waterfall was swollen by melting snow and roared like Niagara. Looking down through the trees, about a thousand of which would have to be felled, Ormandy said, "Dick, the waterfall must go. It will interfere with the pianissimi in *L'Après-midi d'un faune.*" Three costly dams were therefore constructed upstream. When the theater was built, it became possible, by flipping a switch, to turn off the waterfall for two hours every night.

For several months Balanchine, Kirstein and Leach held weekly meetings with the appointed architect, John MacFadyen. The roofed theater, seating 5,201, was to be open at the sides, so that at least another 5,000 could watch the dancing or listen to the music from the grassy slopes beyond. The proportions of the stage and the planning of the sight lines were to be based on those of the New York State Theater.

On April 22, 1966, Edward Bigelow drove Tanaquil LeClercq to Saratoga to inspect houses that she and George might rent; she fell in love with a ramshackle guesthouse in the Leaches' garden which no one had previously considered. Kay Leach had it painted and redecorated, and it became Balanchine's July home for sixteen years.

Balanchine had his first sight of the theater on May 6. Sitting on the windowsill of the dressing room that had been built for him and Eugene Ormandy to occupy in turn—but Balanchine relinquished it to Robert Irving—he surveyed the scene for a few moments in silence, then asked, "That is the waterfall Ormandy will turn off?" When Leach nodded, Balanchine gave his considered opinion. "Dick, much better, much cheaper—turn off Ormandy."

He never expressed any enthusiasm for the site or the theater, but the Leaches knew that he loved both. (It was the same, they noticed, when he was given a present.) His chief preoccupation, as ever, was with the stage. He and Bates had further perfected their method of construction. By June 25 the floor had been laid, and Balanchine came to test it. In silence he began to dance up and down and around, while Leach held his breath. "Better than stage in State Theater—springier" was the verdict.

On July 9, 1966, the New York City Ballet opened its first season at Saratoga Springs with *A Midsummer Night's Dream.*

●　　●　　●

THE LEACHES became and remained close friends of the choreographer. In addition to the animals on their farm, they kept dogs and cats, several of whom also made friends with Balanchine. Dick related:

We had a mongrel called Moka who became inseparable from George. Every summer she would leave us and move in with him on the instant of his arrival. George brought her bones from the store, and Moka knew the sound of his car. She was so devoted she could tell when he was about to leave. Several hours before his departure she would come and lie down under one of our bushes.

Then a tiny kitten appeared from the deep woods behind George's house and went straight to him. When he brought her over to us she *seemed* to have been there before, because she went up to all our dogs—we had six—as if she knew them; then she made straight for the back laundry, where the dogs' food was kept. George said she was "a second comer" and named her *"Bis"* [French for "encore"].

In 1966 the American Dressage Institution, whose instructors were riders from Vienna's famous Spanish Riding School, came to Saratoga and gave exhibitions to the music of Handel, Haydn, Mozart and Lanner concurrently with NYCB's performances. Balanchine spent two weeks learning to ride a retired Lippizaner stallion, getting to know the dance movements of a different creature.

· · ·

THE URGE to make big ballets for the big theater at Lincoln Center doubtless prompted both the *Brahms-Schoenberg Quartet* of 1966—a ballet to Schoenberg's 1937 orchestration of Brahms's Piano Quartet No. 1 in G minor, Op. 25—and the concoction of *Jewels* the next year. The latter, alleged to be the first "abstract" ballet in three acts, used music by three very different composers, each with choreography in a different style. Actually, it was not a three-act ballet at all but three ballets called "Emeralds, "Rubies" and "Diamonds." Balanchine made vague and contradictory statements to explain it: "The whole thing was—I like jewels. I'm an Oriental—from Georgia in the Caucasus, and a Russian. I would cover myself with jewels." "The ballet has nothing to do with jewels. The dancers are just dressed like jewels."

In *Palais de cristal,* the original Paris version of Bizet's Symphony in C, Balanchine had dressed the dancers of the four movements in red, blue, green and white costumes, and the adornments of the different sets matched. For *Jewels* there was one chandelier that turned green, red and white during the different acts. It took me nearly twenty years to accept the hybrid nature of this work; then one night the critic George Dorris pointed out to me that *Jewels* was a perfect example of American "packaging": presented as a trinity, with an expensive-sounding title, the ballet's saleability was enormously increased. Once I had connived at the deception—if such it is—I found it easier to enjoy the individual merits of the parts. In any case, *Jewels* was a smash hit from its first performance.

In "Emeralds," a group of Fauré excerpts put together by Balanchine, the ballerina's waving arms conjure up a distant, medieval dreamworld; and although there are no period steps or trappings, the horn calls in Fauré's music enhance the impression that we are *"au fond du bois"* or witnessing the animation of a *"verdure"* tapestry. The ballet is in fact an incarnation of a "tipped ballroom" behind a scrim with "a projection of the sea on the scrim, which pulsates" imagined by Balanchine in 1958. The music of Fauré, which had seduced him then, had not lost its hold on him in the intervening years.

If "Emeralds" is "French," "Rubies" is "American." Set to Stravinsky's *Capriccio* for piano and orchestra (1929), it has deformed classical movements in the style of *The Four Temperaments* or *Episodes,* but because of its music, its two principals are called upon to be more deliberately witty than dancers in those earlier works. Villella, who was in the first cast, found the steps difficult to learn, though once learned, they seemed inevitable:

We had to find our way through Stravinsky, then through Balanchine's hearing of the score and the structure of his choreography. Once you got there it was obvious—so simple. He was so logical, you'd say "Oh, of course! It's just like geometry." In the last movement when these four

boys are chasing me, I got a feeling that he was looking at me as this
street kid from Queens and interpolating that into the ballet, still keeping
a certain sense of elegance and of the wit and jazz quality of the thirties.
With Balanchine there was always layer upon layer. You could go back
time and time again and see something new. That's the major difference
between a Balanchine ballet and a pedestrian ballet.

Patricia Neary, who was also in "Rubies," remembered how
excited Balanchine became while arranging it: yet when it brought
down the house, he was jealous for Farrell's success in "Diamonds," which followed, and asked Patricia, "Was that your
mother applauding?"

For "Diamonds" Balanchine used the last three movements of
Tchaikovsky's Symphony No. 3 in D major. It was a spectacular
work with which to close the evening, an essay in the grand style
of Imperial Russia. After the subtle "Emeralds" and the unpredictable "Rubies," an audience watching "Diamonds" felt safe and
happy to applaud a kind of coronation for Farrell, supported by
Jacques d'Amboise and a corps of thirty-four in noble alignments.

Farrell has said: " 'Diamonds' is hard because you're out there
in white and there's no hiding. 'Diamonds' you can't sell. It's too
dignified to sell. And you can't cover anything up." Balanchine
himself in later years said, " 'Diamonds' is so boring. Only pas de
deux is good."

. . .

IN 1967, Balanchine escorted twenty-five dancers with a repertory
of "small" ballets to dance for a week at the Edinburgh Festival.
Jacques d'Amboise had to cancel at the last moment, which caused
havoc with the casting. Villella was dancing almost the whole
repertory, but not always with the partners best suited to him.
Balanchine even tried to make him dance the *Tchaikovsky Pas de
deux* with Farrell. He protested, "Mr. B., I really don't think I'm
tall enough." "Don't worry, dear, we'll change. You know where
you have the—we'll change. Don't worry." But after a couple of

rehearsals the adaptable choreographer had to admit that even though the strong Villella could lift Farrell onto his shoulder and catch her in a fish dive, he would need a stepladder to reach above her head and support her in a finger-turn on pointe.

As for *Apollo*, Villella had danced it several times, but with Patricia McBride. Since the outing to Edinburgh was clearly to show off Farrell, Balanchine wanted her to dance Terpsichore. Where was her Apollo to come from? Balanchine tracked down Taras in his Paris apartment and asked him to go to Copenhagen and invite Henning Kronstam. Taras flew to Denmark, but Kronstam was unable to get away. However, Vera Volkova took Taras to the Royal Theater to watch a young dancer, Peter Martins, who had been taught *Apollo* by Kronstam and had danced it in Copenhagen.

On the Saturday night before the Edinburgh opening, Martins was having supper in Copenhagen with Stanley Williams, who had by now joined the staff of the School of American Ballet on a permanent basis. By coincidence, Martins was trying to find out what chance Stanley thought he had of a job in America at the very moment Volkova got through to him at the restaurant. Would he come at once for an audition? The young man, recently promoted to principal dancer, thought it was "too late in the evening" and that he was "beyond auditioning." He agreed to meet Volkova and Taras in the morning.

On Sunday morning, Taras arranged for Martins's air fare to Edinburgh and sent the young Dane off. Martins had stipulated that Stanley Williams go with him. The two men arrived in Edinburgh that afternoon and went for a walk. Balanchine, too, was out walking, showing Suzanne the extraordinary beauties of the Scottish capital, and they met the Danes. In his memoirs, Martins recalls, "Balanchine turned to Suzanne and said: 'This is your Apollo.' She tilted her head, and gave me a slow once-over. . . . 'Well, at least he's tall.' "

At rehearsal the next morning, Balanchine offered few comments on the way Martins danced *Apollo*, although he made some minor adjustments in the pas de deux. At Tuesday's rehearsal, however, he told him, "Before we begin, . . . you know, you do it all wrong." "I had been trying to make everything beautiful and grand," wrote Martins, "and he demanded shapes that looked grotesque but were packed with energy. . . . I fell in love with this man. . . . He was so wonderfully natural. . . . He radiated knowledge and authority." Still, Martins thought the New York City Ballet was unlike any company he had ever seen. "The dancers neglected or didn't bother with precision. The emphasis was on the energy and on movement itself, on timing and quickness."

Two months later Martins received a telegram inviting him to be a guest artist with the New York City Ballet during the *Nutcracker* season in December.

But if the trip to Edinburgh gained Balanchine a dancer, it also cost him one. Patricia Neary was already fed up with Balanchine's never giving jumping in class and leaving the theater after the first ballet when Suzanne was not in the second or third. Suzanne always wore white toe shoes in *Apollo* instead of pink, so the other Muses had to conform. In Edinburgh, Neary and Gloria Govrin, who were dancing Calliope and Polyhymnia, found to their consternation that Suzanne intended to wear pink shoes after all. Furious, they rushed out to Woolworth's for some dye. Patricia was devoted to Balanchine, but this was the last straw. When she returned to New York in September she told him, "I'm leaving. You've gone too far." Balanchine protested, "I have a right to love." "You should love all eighty of us," said Patricia; and she left.

·   ·   ·

IN 1965, the year in which the Race Relations Act was passed, Lincoln Kirstein joined the protest marches in Alabama. When, in 1968, Martin Luther King, Jr., was murdered, Kirstein organized the first and only performance of Stravinsky's *Requiem Canticles*, arranged and staged by Balanchine at the New York State Theater, in his memory. This was given on May 2, 1968. I happened to be present, and wrote a review:

IN the Prelude a body of angels in transparent white gowns are seen in twilight. In the Exaudi they light their candelabra one by one. In the Dies Irae they surge about, potential Lucifers. In Tuba Mirum the hero appears—and this is Arthur Mitchell, a Negro—robed in purple and gold. During the orchestral meditation called "Interlude," the angels move lights like chessmen on the floor, and, stooping, illumine the hero's path to heaven. In Rex Tremendae he is led through diagonal avenues. In Lacrimosa, arches are formed, and a weeping girl, Suzanne Farrell, passes beneath them. In Libera Me, the angels move in circles. Then, on the first chord of the Postlude, Mitchell is raised aloft, and Farrell, like a timid soul in Purgatory, threads her way through a Stonehenge of blessed beings.

That same year, Balanchine and Kirstein helped Arthur Mitchell lay the foundation for his Dance Theatre of Harlem. A school was established on Morningside Avenue (it moved later to West 152nd Street)—Tanaquil Le Clercq became one of the teachers— and within three years the company opened its first season.

Tanaquil had developed a remarkable ability to manage by herself in her wheelchair, and with this increased independence she acquired a new group of young friends. She was, after all, only in her thirties. When Balanchine came home from work, he simply wanted to watch television. Apart from Westerns, he loved the detective series *Ironside, Barnaby Jones* and *Wonder Woman,* and he considered *The Muppet Show* the greatest American invention since the refrigerator. This was rather a strain for his wife. He was also making himself conspicuous with Suzanne Farrell. Eventually Tanaquil and he agreed to separate, with a view to divorce, but some old friends believed that she never ceased to love him.

When they parted, an awful decision had to be made: Who would have Mourka? Balanchine ceded him to Tanaquil. That summer in Connecticut, Mourka disappeared. Tanaquil frantically telephoned Balanchine, who was in Saratoga. He at once drove the two hundred miles to Weston and remained there until he had found the cat.

.   .   .

THERE was a young man in the New York City Ballet named Paul Mejia, of whom Balanchine had great hopes, both as a dancer and as a choreographer. Mejia, born in Lima, Peru, was the son of a South American father and a Russian mother, who had been a student at the School. Paul won a scholarship to the School when he was ten, and his progress, both there and in the company later, was swift. During 1968, Balanchine, Farrell and Mejia were often seen dining together in restaurants. In the autumn, Balanchine flew to Mexico to get a divorce. If the idea of marrying Suzanne was in his mind—and there is good reason to believe it was—the lady had other plans. In September 1968, the *New York Post* published in its column "Secret Stuff" a note that "the ballet world is excited about ballerina Suzanne Farrell's reported romane [*sic*] with a man of her own age." Balanchine's divorce came through on February 5, 1969, but before the winter season ended on February 16, he left for Germany to stage Glinka's *Ruslan and Lyudmila* for Rolf Liebermann's Hamburg State Opera. On February 21, Paul Mejia and Suzanne Farrell were married at the Church of St. Paul the Apostle, four blocks south of the State Theater on Ninth Avenue. Lincoln Kirstein was best man, and many members of the company were present. The next night Balanchine telephoned Barbara Horgan from Germany. He was very angry. When he heard that Barbara had been at the wedding, he implied that she had betrayed him. Her feeling had been that the sooner all the "nonsense" stopped the better; she welcomed the marriage because she thought it would give Balanchine no alternative but to see reason and "come back as a human being." Instead, he asked her if she would join him in Hamburg. She said she would, without seriously expecting to be sent for.

When she arrived at her office the next Monday, her first call was from Lufthansa, which had a prepaid ticket for her to leave the following day. Balanchine met her at the airport early on Wednesday morning, and they drove to the Vierjahreszeiten Hotel.

Their breakfast together was, for her, "a horrible experience." Balanchine swore that he would never go back to America. For ten days he and Barbara followed the same routine: they went to rehearsal every morning, lunched together and got drunk. She let him reiterate his complaints, but she felt all along that he knew he would eventually have to return to America and to his company.

Kirstein flew to the opening performance of *Ruslan* on March 30, taking Edward Bigelow with him. Next day he left for London, and Balanchine went with Bigelow to Berlin, where he came to an agreement with the West Berlin Ballet Ensemble about giving them certain works and sending dancers from New York to perform in them. He did not confide his private feelings to Kirstein but presented him with a series of absurd projects: to print no dancers' names on future programs; to commission a Georgian ballet from Khachaturian; to go to Persia in October; to go to Moscow and "give them 20 ballets." These were surely symptoms of desperation.

The spring season was due to start on April 22. On April 10, Balanchine returned to New York. His sense of humor was coming back. When Paul Mejia had been a new student at the School, one of the principal male dancers in the company had found him attractive. Balanchine noticed this and thought it a pity that the boy should be steered into a homosexual groove before he knew where his natural inclinations lay. He told Natalie Molostwoff that she should speak to Paul's mother about it. Natalie did, and the attentions ceased. Remembering this in the spring of 1969, Balanchine remarked, "No good deed goes unpunished." Meanwhile, however awkward he may have felt to be working with Farrell and Mejia under the circumstances, he took no action against them.

It was announced that at the spring gala on May 8, 1969, the closing ballet would be *Symphony in C,* in which Farrell always danced the second movement. Villella, because he was now appearing in a new Jerome Robbins work, asked to be left out of the third movement. Mejia, who had danced it several times, considered himself next in line, but he was not cast. He and Suzanne told Betty

Cage that if he did not dance in *Symphony in C* at the gala, they would both resign. There were several panicky program changes at the last minute to try to save Mejia's face and keep Farrell in the company. First, *La Sonnambula* was to be substituted for the Bizet, then the Bizet was to be given without the third movement. Finally the management settled for John Clifford's new ballet *Fantasies,* Robbins's new *Dances at a Gathering* and *Stars and Stripes.* There were no roles for either Suzanne or Paul in any of these.

On Monday, May 12, the Mejias told the press that they had resigned from the New York City Ballet. The reason proffered by Suzanne was that her husband was not given enough roles. Balanchine immediately telephoned Patricia Neary, who was appearing in Kansas: "Come back at once and do *Prodigal!*" She broke her contract and returned to the fold. Nevertheless, a certain "apathy"—to use Barbara Horgan's word—descended upon the choreographer. His only new ballet for the company in 1969 was the *Valse fantaisie* of Glinka, and it was merely a single movement from the four-movement *Glinkiana* he had staged in 1967.

Yet because of many extramural activities that year, the catalogue of Balanchine's projects in 1969, as listed in the Eakins Press *Choreography,* is longer than that of any other year in his life. Since he had agreed to allow the West Berlin Ballet Ensemble to stage his ballets, he went to work with young choreographers there, encouraging exchanges between Berlin and his own company. Between the New York and Saratoga seasons, he flew with NYCB to Monte Carlo to take part in a Diaghilev festival.

Dr. Herbert Graff, director of the Grand Théâtre de Genève, had asked him to suggest a ballet master for his opera house, and Balanchine interviewed one of his former dancers, Alfonso Catá, for the post. He then recommended Patricia Neary as ballet mistress, and after dancing with NYCB in Monte Carlo she went to Geneva to start work. In September, Balanchine staged a four-act

Swan Lake at Geneva's Grand Théâtre, with Neary as Odette. In West Berlin, he rehearsed the Berlin Opera Ballet in *Episodes, Symphony in C* and *Apollo* for its first all-Balanchine evening. Another Balanchine evening was presented at Geneva's Grand Théâtre, and the choreographer was given the title of artistic advisor.

To cheer him up, Nabokov and his new wife, Dominique, took Balanchine to spend Christmas with Baron and Baronne Philippe de Rothschild in Château Mouton in southwestern France. Although the château among the vines was a nineteenth-century Gothic building, inside the luxury was dazzling. The food and wine were perfect, but Balanchine, seated beside his hostess at dinner, was speechless. He begged the Nabokovs to cut short their visit: "Let's go to Bordeaux and have a little sausage with Beaujolais." In the train to Paris, he declared the restaurant's dinner the best meal he had ever eaten.

Barbara thought that at some time during the next few months he came to terms with himself. He was sixty-five and had been ripped apart. There were certain consummations he could no longer hope for; and he was never going to allow himself to be so miserable again.

In other directions, things were looking up. The Juilliard School had moved from its old home near Columbia University to Lincoln Center. In 1969, the School of American Ballet, which had leased part of Juilliard's third floor, transferred itself there. The four studios, nine offices, locker rooms and showers had been carefully planned. There was a handsome theater for workshop performances, in which the students would dance to the Juilliard orchestra. The new arrangement was what Balanchine had always hoped for: something like the Imperial School on Theater Street, St. Petersburg, where he had received his own training. Both training and performance could now take place on the same site. Moreover, the students chosen to dance in *Nutcracker* or *A Midsummer Night's Dream* could carry their practice tights and shoes to the State

Theater without even crossing a road; there was a bridge over Sixty-fifth Street.

. . .

FOR SOME TIME after his first guest appearances with the New York City Ballet, Peter Martins had been flying back and forth between the United States and Copenhagen, where he was expected to fulfill his duties with the Royal Danish Ballet. Presented by the latter with an ultimatum—"Either stay or go"—Martins chose Balanchine. He soon regretted this, for he began to feel that his new master was irritated by the "neatness" and "cool perfection" that were the results of his Bournonville training. He also found Balanchine's classes peculiar, and he began to study instead with his friend and compatriot Stanley Williams. He had, after all, been engaged in the first place because he was tall enough to partner Suzanne Farrell; after she left the company he felt less necessary.

The news that Martins was unhappy reached Ballet Theatre, and Lucia Chase made him an offer. Erik Bruhn advised him to accept. Martins met Lucia Chase for lunch in a restaurant to sign a contract. Suddenly it struck him that if he did, he could never go back to the New York City Ballet, for which he had left Denmark and renounced the state pension due to him on retirement. "I couldn't risk the loss of working with Balanchine," he wrote later. He did not sign.

At last he "cornered Balanchine."

I told him that . . . my ambition now was to dance his ballets . . . and I would do anything to make this possible. . . . He answered me, bluntly and directly. "You see, dear, you don't seem to be interested. I never see you anywhere, not in class, maybe in O'Neal's restaurant. When people show interest, I use them. If they don't, I leave them alone.

Martins told Balanchine that although people thought him "cool, self-possessed, distant," he knew he was full of energy and passion. He might be angry or impatient—but never bored. Balanchine said that it was up to him to prove his good intentions. If he succeeded, he could have any role he wanted. Martins later considered this conversation a turning point in his career.

Three years after she joined the company, Karin von Aroldingen, the German dancer Balanchine had met through Lotte Lenya, married Morton Gewirtz, a real estate broker, and in 1966 they had a daughter. Balanchine was much struck by the way Karin kept dancing and attending classes during her pregnancy, and he thanked her for her persistence. She had told Morton, "First I'm a dancer, then a wife, then a mother," and Morton understood this. In the plane to Monte Carlo in June 1969, Balanchine and Karin had a long heart-to-heart talk, and from that time on they were close friends. Karin, who had never known her own father, looked upon Balanchine not only as a father but as almost a god. In return, she and Morton gave him a warm family feeling, and he took a grandfatherly interest in their daughter, Margo, who was his godchild.

Meanwhile, other dancers, notably Kay Mazzo, had taken over most of Suzanne Farrell's roles. Balanchine's first ballet after Suzanne left was a jazzy piece to the music of George Gershwin songs. It was called *Who Cares?*

Chapter 13

....

HOMAGE TO STRAVINSKY:

SPRING 1972

O N APRIL 6, 1971, shortly before his eighty-ninth birthday, Stravinsky died after a long illness. Balanchine was not one of those who consider that old people's sufferings should be prolonged, that any kind of half life is better than death. Nor did he believe that death could take Stravinsky away from him. Although he must have decided at once that he would commemorate his most-admired friend, he said nothing about his intentions for over two months. He was rehearsing two works: Rolf Liebermann's *Concerto for Jazz Band and Symphony Orchestra,* in which twenty-one dancers of the New York City Ballet and twenty-three of Arthur Mitchell's Dance Theatre of Harlem took part, with Mitchell sharing the choreography; and an airport fantasia called

PAMTGG ("Pan Am Makes the Going Great"), to music taken from a television commercial.

On June 17, just before the curtain rose on the first performance of *PAMTGG*, Barbara Horgan had reason to go backstage. She found Balanchine, as usual at a premiere, standing calm and collected in the downstage right wing. He turned and said to her, "Next year, a Stravinsky festival." That was all.

The ineptness of *PAMTGG* and the indifference with which certain recent ballets by the company's other choreographers had been received prompted hints in the press that Balanchine, as choreographer and as artistic director, was losing his touch. His critics would discover in good time that he was, rather, planning his greatest endeavor.

It soon transpired, to the consternation of his colleagues, that Balanchine intended the Stravinsky Festival to last a week, with a different program every night—a far cry from the two-day, one-program Stravinsky "festival" of April 1937. He at once embarked on discussions with Robert Irving and Robert Craft, who would share the conducting. In Saratoga in July, he started work on a piano reduction of Stravinsky's very early Symphony in E flat. When the dancers went on vacation, Balanchine dined with Vera Stravinsky and Robert Craft, and Craft began to make a list of possibilities for the festival. He and Balanchine agreed that it should be a retrospective exhibition of Stravinsky's metamorphoses; and from what he wrote later, he apparently took for granted the inclusion of *Petrushka, The Rite of Spring, Les Noces* and *Jeu de cartes.* None of these, however, was to be staged.

Early in September, Balanchine and Barbara Horgan went to Rome to talk to Eugene Berman, because Balanchine had decided he was the obvious choice to design *Pulcinella.* It was probably during these discussions that the choreographer worked out a new story for the ballet he had found so "long and boring" when he saw the Massine version in the 1920s. There followed talks with Léon Leonidoff in Montecatini-Terme, where the agent took the waters every September; with Rolf Liebermann at the Paris Opéra; and with Nicolas Nabokov in Berlin. The possibility of making the Stravinsky celebration a worldwide event was clearly at the back of Balanchine's mind.

In New York in October, he had to face the question of fund-raising. Everything depended on Richard Clurman, chairman of the board of the New York City Ballet. Balanchine told him that the week-long festival *must* open on the composer's ninetieth birthday, June 18, in the middle of the spring season; that to make final rehearsals possible the theater would have to be closed for the previous week, necessitating a considerable loss of income (about $130,000, in fact); and that he estimated the cost of the festival itself at a quarter of a million dollars. There seem to have been some protests against the proposal, but Balanchine would not be deflected.

Not only would NYCB's regular ballet masters, Balanchine, Robbins and Taras, participate; they would be joined by their old colleague Todd Bolender. There were also to be works by three young choreographers in the company, John Clifford, Lorca Massine (son of Léonide) and Richard Tanner. *Orpheus,* which had not been revived for seven years, was pieced together with the aid of Magallanes, Moncion and Le Clercq, members of the original cast.

Balanchine liked to turn a press conference into a party. The announcement of the Stravinsky Festival was made at one of his favorite restaurants near the theater. Mme. Stravinsky was there, and so was Goddard Lieberson, Vera Zorina's husband and chairman of Columbia Records (Stravinsky's recording company), who was to be chairman of the festival. A literal translation of Balanchine's words to the press could read as inconsequential and baffling, with their improvised expressions and unfinished sentences; but those who were present to see as well as to hear him, to note his gestures, watch his face and experience his charm, understood very well what he was getting at. It was only when they were obliged to organize for their readers the words they had taken down that they ran into difficulties.

Introduced as "artistic director" of the New York City Ballet, Balanchine said, "Don't call me artistic director—it's terrible. . . . all right in French maybe, but better I am just ballet master. That was enough for Petipa, enough for me." There followed some sweeping statements to be taken with a glass of vodka: "Stravinsky is who is responsible for anything we are using in music . . . everything we have in music he did first. . . . He was like Einstein—nobody like him. He made *musique dansante.* There have only been three who could do it. Delibes, Tchaikovsky, and Stravinsky. They made music for the body to dance to. They invented the floor for the dancer to walk on. . . . There are men who say there is no time, no space. But Stravinsky made time—not big grand time—but time that works with the small parts of how our bodies are made. According to our bodies they made our floor."

Nancy Goldner, who had been commissioned to put together a commemorative book, records Balanchine as saying:

In Russia we don't cry when a person dies. We are very happy. We throw rice with nice sweet things in it—vanilla and natural things—into the grave. Then we go home and have an enormous table of food and drink and we drink to the health of the guy who dies. The body is gone—we don't need—but we drink to his spirit. . . . [Like Shakespeare, Balanchine often harped on food.]

To show what *really* is Stravinsky you have to start with beginning, with *Sonata for Piano,* then do *Symphony Number One,* which Stravinsky did in the memory of Rimsky-Korsakov, then Opus 2, 3, 4, and for program one finish in 1910 with *Firebird.* In program two we go to 1914, and so on. Seven programs, thirty-six works, some old, some new, to show how his sound traveled through his life. So then the whole thing is interesting—a fantastic thing he went through. He was not accepted. . . . But who cares? We do. . . .

We dancers are like sailboats, not like engine boats. We go up and down with the waves, right? We don't cut through. So we know how great Stravinsky is to us. Probably dance would stop if we didn't have Stravinsky. Music is the main thing. And good food.

This time it doesn't matter how the ballets look—maybe lousy, so fast [rehearsed in such a hurry], maybe not enough money. But the music will be beautiful. We have a wonderful orchestra—will be good. We will show Stravinsky's life through sound and then you will see the whole thing in front of you.

Questions were encouraged, and to the first Balanchine replied: "Yes, it will be a retrospective. We finish with *Symphony of Psalms*—no dancers but enormous chorus. The last night we have as much as you like cold vodka, cold vodka and something else. No, not caviar, but something."

Where else might the festival be repeated? "We're already invited to do this all again in Munich and in Paris. They cannot do it there. Why? I tell you in private why."

Which choreographers will arrange which ballets? "Everybody will choreograph what they want. What they don't want, I will use."

"How did I meet Stravinsky? Lenin died. I was so depressed I left Russia. I was twenty. Diaghilev asked me to be ballet master. I accepted. The first ballet was *Chant du rossignol.* . . . Stravinsky played the music on the piano. The tempi was absolutely right. . . . Diaghilev comes—with cane, with monocle [a bit of miming]—he sits, he listens. He wants everything faster, faster, faster. I change everything for him. Then Stravinsky comes and says, 'didn't I tell you slower, slower.' That is how we met, in 1925. So you are all invited to come to see our festival, our party."

The New York Times printed the scheduled programs, in which drastic changes were later made. In fact, only the two final programs, Saturday's and the second Sunday's, would be performed as they had been announced to the press. Chronological order was obviously not going to work, because, for example, the dull Symphony in E flat of 1905–1907 would lower the temperature of the opening program, and the *Symphony of Psalms,* with which Balanchine wanted to end the festival, had been composed in 1930, before Stravinsky even settled in America. Also the box office required that there be at least one Balanchine ballet on every program.

The vacation between the end of the winter season and the rehearsal period for the spring season was cut from the usual four weeks to two. Although during March and April nine ballets by four different choreographers were rehearsed—two of them revivals—there were still ten more works to be begun in May and two in June. When the spring season opened on May 2, the dancers were rehearsing Stravinsky ballets as well as works in the current repertory, and performing in the evening.

Robert Irving began orchestra rehearsals on May 22, and for four weeks held three rehearsals, from two and a half to three hours long, every week. In the fifth and final week, when the theater was dark, there were rehearsals during the day and every night, when each ballet had a dress rehearsal.

Most of the new works, like a number of the old ones, would be given in practice clothes or plain leotards against a cyclorama. Nevertheless, there would be some new sets and costumes, and because the latter always arrived from Karinska's workshop at the last minute, Ronald Bates decided to wait until the final week to plot the lighting of all the new ballets. He had to light twenty-one that week alone, and he worked with his crew every day from eight in the morning till midnight.

No one had ever seen Balanchine in a hurry; he did not appear in a hurry now. Tamara Geva once compared him to a general. Anyone who has seen active service in the armed forces will confirm that a commander who never gets flustered in an emergency inspires the utmost confidence. Some of the organizers in the background, with whom the dancers did not concern themselves, must have had nightmares nonetheless.

Rosemary Dunleavy, who was now in charge of arranging the daily rehearsal schedule, only once saw Balanchine annoyed. She had taken the stage for two hours to rehearse the current repertory, and he arrived expecting to finish *Symphony in Three Movements*. The final fugue was not yet arranged, and it had to be done that very moment. Thirty-two dancers were rapidly assembled. Then Balanchine, who had worked out in his head exactly what he wanted, finished the ballet in forty minutes.

Balanchine even allowed journalists to watch some of the rehearsals, and took time to talk to them. Shirley Fleming of *Musical America* found him in a tight blue-denim shirt and nondescript gray trousers, wearing his celebrated turquoise bracelet. She quoted to him words that had been attributed to him in the Stravinsky number of *Dance Index,* twenty-five years before. It was a sentence about *Apollon Musagète* being "the turning point" in his life, which taught him that he too could "eliminate." "I didn't say that," he replied promptly. "I mean somebody else said I said it." Walter Monfried of the *Milwaukee Journal* asked him, after a two-hour rehearsal, "How do you relax after such hard work?" "It's not hard work and I don't relax—why should anyone want to relax?" "You should have hobbies and recreations." "Well, I do have a hobby. I'm a collector." "Of what?" "Wine bottles . . . but I'm not like a stamp collector—I use up what's inside the bottles before I add them to my collection. I have another recreation. After dealing with physical problems and solutions, I like to go beyond the physical into meta-physical speculation." "Such as Kant?" "Yes, yes, Kant is very important. . . ."

One week before the opening of the Stravinsky Festival, Balanchine told Bob Micklin, the music critic of *Newsday,* "I know what Stravinsky wanted, just as I know what Mozart and Tchaikovsky wanted. If the music is German, Russian, English, modern, I make dance that looks like it. I was born for that reason. . . . When you are choreographing . . . you have to make it interesting enough so the public will not go to sleep! . . . There is certain music that doesn't need anything added to it. I have never choreographed *Rite of Spring.* Bach's *St. Matthew Passion* doesn't need any performance beside the music. . . . You have to be very careful not to kill the music when you make dance."

Martha Swope

36

Martha Swope

37

A MIDSUMMER NIGHT'S DREAM *(1962): 36. Edward Villella as Oberon;*
37. Arthur Mitchell as Puck.

38

39

40

41

38, 39. Suzanne Farrell and Jacques d'Amboise in Movements *(1965).*
Episodes *(1959): 40. Allegra Kent and Nicholas Magallanes in "Concerto";*
41. Paul Taylor in "Variations."

42

43

RETURN TO RUSSIA *(1962): 42. Balanchine with his brother in the latter's home
in Tbilisi; 43. Balanchine acclaimed at the Tbilisi Opera House.*

44

45

46

Don Quixote (1965): 44. Suzanne Farrell in one of her variations;
45. Richard Rapp and Deni Lamont as the Don and Sancho Panza;
46. Balanchine and Farrell as Don Quixote and Dulcinea.

Martha Swope

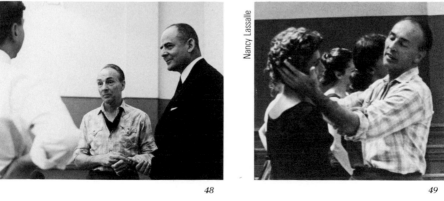

Martha Swope

Nancy Lassalle

*47. Balanchine and Farrell at a rehearsal with Anthony Blum and
Richard Rapp (1965). 48. Balanchine, Ronald Bates and Lincoln Kirstein (c. 1965).
49. Balanchine at the School of American Ballet on Upper Broadway (c. 1965).*

50

50. Balanchine's Easter supper, 1964.

JEWELS *(1967): 51. Violette Verdy in "Emeralds"; 52. Edward Villella in "Rubies"; 53. Suzanne Farrell and Peter Martins in "Diamonds."*

54

55

SYMPHONY IN THREE MOVEMENTS *(1972): 54. Sara Leland and John Clifford;*
55. The final group.

56

57

56. *Karin von Aroldingen and Jean-Pierre Bonnefous in* Violin Concerto *(1972).*
57. *Kay Mazzo and Peter Martins in* Duo Concertant *(1972).*

58

59

60

58. Helgi Tomasson in Divertissement from "Le Baiser de la fée" *(1972).*
59. Mikhail Baryshnikov in The Four Temperaments *(1978).*
60. Balanchine instructing Kay Mazzo (c. 1972).

61

62

*61. Balanchine rehearsing Merrill Ashley and Robert Weiss
in* Ballo della Regina *(1978). 62. Balanchine with Robert Irving.*

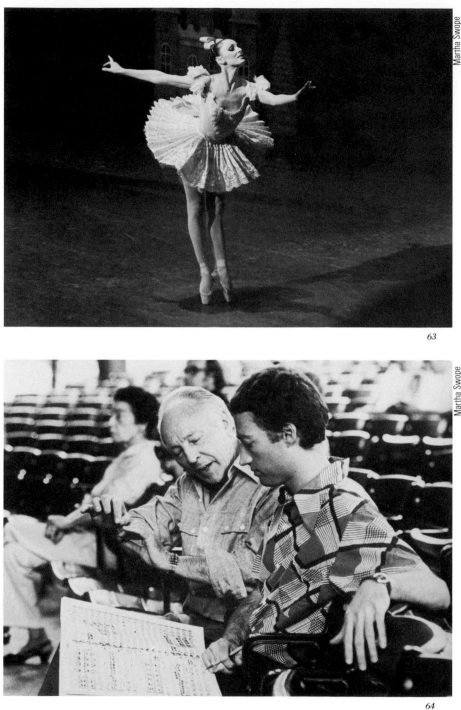

Martha Swope

63

Martha Swope

64

63. *Patricia McBride in* The Steadfast Tin Soldier *(1975).*
64. *Lucia Davidova, Balanchine and Gordon Boelzner at Saratoga (1977).*

65

65. *Suzanne Farrell in* Vienna Waltzes *(1977).*

66

67

66. Le Tombeau de Couperin *(1975). 67. Karin von Aroldingen and Adam Lüders*
in Robert Schumann's "Davidsbündlertänze" *(1980).*

68

69

68. *Darci Kistler and Sean Lavery in* Swan Lake *(1981). 69. Suzanne Farrell
and Ib Andersen in the pas de deux from* Mozartiana *(1981).*

70

70. Balanchine taking a curtain call after the premiere of
Robert Schumann's "Davidsbündlertänze," *with Suzanne Farrell and*
Karin von Aroldingen, June 19, 1980.

．　．　．

CRITICS poured in from Washington, Chicago and Toronto; from Bonn, Berlin, Cologne, Vienna, Geneva, Copenhagen and London. On June 16, two days before the opening of the festival, *The New York Times* had a headline: "The World of Balanchine Still Awhirl in Creativity." Next day, the *New York Post*'s "Woman in the News" was Vera Stravinsky.

I was at that time ballet critic for the London *Sunday Times*, which sent me to New York for the Stravinsky Festival. I attended a few rehearsals and was amazed by the atmosphere of calm.

So many things happened before the first actual ballet that I was to write:

The opening night's program couldn't stop opening. First we had Stravinsky's Fanfare [written for the opening of the State Theater and dedicated to Kirstein and Balanchine]. Then Lincoln Kirstein welcomed us. Then Balanchine explained that he was interpolating a little unannounced *pas de deux* to the scherzo of a piano sonata composed in 1902 and recently found in a Russian book by Mme. André Malraux [who had been unable to copy it, but had memorized it]. She played it while Sara Leland and John Clifford performed a springlike childish dance. Then Robert Irving's fine orchestra gave us the "Greeting Prelude" ("Happy Birthday to You"), for Stravinsky, who would have been ninety that day. Next we had flashing "Fireworks," not danced—*then* the opening ballet.

This "opening ballet" was Robbins's arrangement of the *Scherzo fantastique*. Two of Balanchine's most important creations followed. In retrospect it seems odd—even mad—to have juxtaposed *Symphony in Three Movements* and *Violin Concerto,* either of which would have been the big hit of a normal season. (These works will be considered later.) Last came *Firebird.* In this revival, Balanchine made a disastrous attempt to abolish the ballerina's rapid dances in order to have her merge with the nightmare world of Chagall's décor: the unlucky Karin von Aroldingen was laden with a train, huge wings and a bird mask on top of her head, so that she would resemble the firebird painted on the front curtain.

"City Ballet Triumphs in Stravinsky Fete" ran the headline on the front page of *The New York Times* the next morning. Each of the first five programs was of a mixed character. The sixth had more unity, being devoted to *Apollo, Orpheus* and *Agon,* the historic trilogy. The seventh had a solemn tone, as planned.

As was to be expected, the bombardment of new works, night after night, was almost too much, even for persistent balletgoers. Halfway through the week, Clive Barnes remarked to me that he was so confused he could not remember what he *had* seen. Balanchine had showered his public with gifts, flinging real jewels and false indiscriminately.

In *Divertimento from "Le Baiser de la fée,"* Balanchine used most of Stravinsky's 1950 condensation of the ballet score written for Ida Rubinstein in 1928, and created a most subtle and ingenious work. When Stravinsky shrank his ballet music to a mere divertimento, the story of the boy snatched away by a fairy had to be discarded, but the pages were indelibly stained by his original metaphor (derived partly from Hans Christian Andersen's tale "The Ice Maiden"), which equated the kiss with the blessing and the curse of genius, so the choreographer was able to shed the trivial elements of narrative without relinquishing the essence of the composer's first idea.

Pulcinella, choreographed jointly by Balanchine and Robbins, had so many ideas, so many scene changes, such a large cast and such a plethora of mime, jokes and gambols, that there was no way to get it in shape in time for its Friday-night performance. Balanchine and Robbins, befeathered beggars, appeared briefly toward the end to belabor each other with sticks. Villella mimed furiously throughout—this time (as opposed to *Harlequinade*) in what he called a "down low, gross" genuine *Italian* comedy style. Even though much of the work that had gone into *Pulcinella* was lost onstage, Violette Verdy remembered her joy at the sight of Balanchine demonstrating passages of broad mime to Villella at rehearsal: "I was there watching with Lincoln Kirstein. We turned to each other, practically with tears in our eyes because it was so touching. I said 'It's incredible—it's everything that one knows about the theater.' "

Some of the ballets that bloomed for the festival were destined to fade after one exposure, leaving no trace behind. A few survived for a season or two. In 1974, Balanchine added a new pas de deux and a new ending to *Divertimento from "Le Baiser de la fée,"* which made it more complete. It was universally agreed that, apart from this *Divertimento,* he had created for the festival three works of outstanding merit—*Violin Concerto, Symphony in Three Movements* and *Duo Concertant*—and they have not grown less wonderful with the years.

In his score for the Concerto in D for violin, Stravinsky had placed two Arias between an opening Toccata and a Capriccio finale. The first Aria was danced by Karin von Aroldingen and Jean-Pierre Bonnefous, the second by Kay Mazzo and Peter Martins.

Kay Mazzo had been in the company for ten years before stepping into most of Farrell's roles; she was promoted to principal in 1969. To have danced Terpsichore, *Agon,* Titania, *Movements* and *Episodes* had been an education for her, but in the Stravinsky Festival she helped to model new works and break into unexplored territory. She was dark and fine-boned, with the figure of an adolescent girl. By contrast, Karin von Aroldingen, who had also spent ten years in the company, was tall and fair, square-shouldered and athletic. She felt that in *Violin Concerto* "Balanchine used everything I had for the first time." Peter Martins had been a full-time member of the company only since 1970. He thought that *"Violin Concerto* was my chance to show that I could dance 'Balanchine.' . . . He would demonstrate a passage and I would dive into it with enthusiasm, . . . extending its implications, playing with its accents . . . salt-and-peppering the steps. . . . Once he saw that he had captured my intensity and interest . . . he gave still more, and the experience gave me an incredible high. . . ."

In the first Aria, although Karin excelled in steps of elevation she was not allowed any. She knew, though, that she was a "realistic dancer, not a Giselle." So she was to be "earthbound," and Balanchine told her she was a snake—"You know, a bit sneaky." The opening chord on the strings warns that the relationship between this man and woman will not be a placid one. Her dance with her partner contains strange confrontations, tangles, stalking, catching, trapping; but she somersaults away from his last embrace, and he suddenly lies flat, as if he has had enough.

The mood of the second Aria, with its singing melody, is more tender. The passages Martins and Mazzo found so difficult to learn in rehearsal passed unnoticed in performance because, as Mazzo remarked, they were not there to make people gasp but because the choreographer found them visual equivalents of the music and suited to his dancers. She had to be raised from a near split on pointe, then to end in attitude with an arm over her leg on Martins's shoulder. To match the music, which was alternately sharp and fluid, taut poses melted into collapses. She had to crumple while standing on pointe, and if he failed to catch her by the knees she would fall. ("Don't go before she goes," Balanchine told him.) For one moment Kay became a violin, lying in arabesque across Martins's body, resting her head on his left shoulder, back to the audience. Finally, as she leaned against him, he made a sweeping gesture, enfolded her neck and stretched out his hand. "Make it look like an elephant trunk," Balanchine told him, and "then move out your hand as if you're asking for money." They both bowed over his extended arm, as if to the violinist. They were supposed to be saying, Balanchine explained, "*Bonjour,* Monsieur Stravinsky."

At the end of the busy Capriccio, the twenty dancers, stationary at last, make a gesture to the audience with both hands that seems to say, "Well, that's it!"

. . .

MUSICALLY, Stravinsky's *Symphony in Three Movements* is freakish; the first movement started life as a piano concerto or concerto for orchestra, while in the second, written as part of a commission but rejected, the *concertante* instrument is a harp. Piano and harp have to be brought together somehow, and they begin the fugue in the third movement. Yet from these odd sketches what a masterpiece emerged! First published in 1946, the score contained passages of the most Dionysiac music Stravinsky had written since the 1913 *Rite of Spring.*

Imagine a world ruled by implacable women. Must they not be under the orders of one particular woman, never seen, never spoken of, even in whispers? She holds sway over all the banks, all the mineral resources, all the airlines and railroads, all the munitions factories and all the funeral parlors in the world. Through her international army of women, she controls the men who think they decide the destiny of nations. But it is Madam who gives the signal for peace or war: the first for sowing the seed, the second for gathering her harvest. In their secret rituals, her female storm troopers are drilled like a high-kicking chorus of lethal drum majorettes. To men they show a sweeter side, to obtain marriage dowries, alimony and widows' pensions. Madam transports them from one country to another according to her need for reinforcements. In the first and third movements of the symphony we hear their sealed trains passing, steam trains—for we are in the forties—which shriek when they are about to enter a tunnel.

Behind the battlefront, in no matter what war she has instigated, Madam has her girls waiting. Now, in the second movement, we are in the fifties or sixties, and Westerners are increasingly being sent to battle in Asia; Stravinsky's music for this is Oriental. It is the soldier's weekend out of battle, and he looks for solace in a woman's arms; though she may be trained in every kind of un-familiar artifice—as an Indian nautch girl, Japanese geisha or Siamese temple dancer—when he lays his head on her neck she becomes for a moment a symbol of all he loves best—mother, sister, sweetheart, the girl next door. She is expert in gilding his

moment of oblivion, a lovely interlude, well worth the money—
from which Madam will exact sixty percent.

In the third movement the trains are heard again, the women
celebrate their domination, and the surviving men are encouraged
to retain their illusions. Life of a kind must go on—for business
reasons. The sexes get together to pose for a victory photograph.
And we know what victories lead to.

That is all very well, someone who has seen the ballet may
protest, but what about the gay scudding dances of the six principals—of the man who, with jerky jumps, is the first to confront
the diagonal of threatening girls, and the man who leads the others
in the last movement? What about the jitterbugging? Even if the
diagonals and lineups of white-clad girls with ponytails, standing
with one foot advanced, stabbing the floor while they rotate their
right arms as if pitching a ball, are alarming, don't the three
principal girls smile and look charming in their conspicuous rose
pink? What about the lovers in the pas de deux? (Incidentally, the
strange nature of their movements was originally dictated by Balanchine's consideration for injuries Sara Leland and Edward Villella had sustained. One had a bad leg, the other a strained back.)
Don't they behave less as if they were in a brothel than as if they
were watching the sun rise from the window of a temple? So my
imagined scenario about the terrible women can easily be dismissed as nonsense.

And yet the impression has been shared, in part at least, by
others. In Nancy Reynolds's compendium of critical writings on
the company, *Repertory in Review,* there is, among other vivid
phrases by Paul Gellen, the following sentence: "The corps of
white-clad women suddenly leave the stage to line up from the edge
of the black sidecloths back into the wings, and you knew there
must be thousands of them stretching all around the globe." Turning to read again Stravinsky's account of how certain musical ideas
came to him, I found further evidence not incompatible with my
personal fantasy. The first movement (partly composed in 1942
with either a piano concerto or a concerto for orchestra in mind)

was inspired by "a war film . . . a documentary of scorched-earth tactics in China." "The third movement," said Stravinsky, "actually contains the genesis of a war plot. . . . The beginning . . . is partly, and in some—to me wholly inexplicable—way, a musical reaction to the newsreels and documentaries that I had seen of goose-stepping soldiers. . . . The exposition of the fugue and the end of the Symphony are associated in my plot with the rise of the Allies, and perhaps the final, albeit rather too commercial, D-flat sixth chord—instead of the expected C—tokens my extra exuberance in the Allied triumph." The slow movement in the middle was written (in 1943)—but never used—for the film version of Franz Werfel's *Song of Bernadette* and was intended to accompany the appearance of the Virgin Mary to the French peasant girl. Does it seem incongruous that the religious revelation the composer tried to convey should be transposed in my mind into so profane a context? For that matter, what would Stravinsky have thought of *Balanchine's* transformation of his goose-slepping storm troopers into women? Does not the brazen symmetry of Balanchine's final group, in which a phalanx of these women, kneeling or standing at attention, some with parallel arms upstretched in a double Hitler salute, others with arms extended sideways like flag-waggling signalers, and in which the men in the foreground are crouched like sprinters eager for the next race, bear out what Stravinsky called the "albeit rather too commercial" nature of his final chord, the celebration of a boastful "peace"?

●   ●   ●

ALTHOUGH *Duo Concertant* went into rehearsal on April 11, and according to Goldner was allotted about fourteen hours, Kay Mazzo remembers feeling that it was left very much to the last moment. Its first performance was on Thursday, June 22.

Balanchine decided to set up a reaction between his two dancers, Martins and Mazzo, comparable to Stravinsky's argument between—and marriage of—the strings of violin and piano. Throughout the initial Cantilena, however, the dancers simply stand listening to the music. Mazzo did not find it embarrassing to play this passive role, because she had been told by Balanchine, "Now we're going to have them listen," and she knew that listening to music was what the festival was about.

At the beginning of the first Eclogue, the two walk away from the musicians and stand facing the audience, a few feet apart. She raises an arm to one side, drops it; raises it again; drops it; she extends a foot, draws it in; repeats this. He takes up the challenge, plays the game. It is as simple as the opening of *Serenade*.

The two dancers experiment. He makes her try out some angular arm movements. For a moment it is as if they are conducting— rather than following—the music. They experiment with sculptural poses. They begin turning; he lifts her, and they use more of the stage. When she runs to the piano, he carries her backward in a great arc. After some beautiful port de bras, they slip into everyday slang, link arms and walk across to stare at the violin, as if seeking new ideas.

The two dancers are standing behind the piano when the second Eclogue begins. He leads her into a pas de deux, and to the singing violin she swoons in his arms. They make a révérence to the violinist, then, leaning together, face the music.

In the Gigue, they dance both alone and together. There is a bit of everything—tightrope walking, big classical movements, and as the violin plays pizzicato, ballroom dancing. They are allowed a rest on the floor, for this is a long number.

Before the final Dithyramb, there is a blackout. Balanchine had not told his dancers at rehearsals about the effect he planned, and it came as a surprise at the dress rehearsal on the morning of the performance. Mazzo had been astonished that the ballet should end with the emotional scene he had arranged: "It was quite unusual for him in his Stravinsky ballets." But she and Martins were transfigured by the lighting.

Stravinsky's short Dithyramb is not Dionysiac in character, as the dictionary says a dithyramb should be; it sings with a kind of serene ecstasy—if that is not a contradiction in terms—such as might be achieved by the success of a relationship, or the "bring-ing off" of a work of art. We may dare to guess, in passing, that Balanchine's moments of perfect fulfillment took place on a stage, for the world to witness, not in the privacy of a home. The little ballet he devised to Stravinsky's *Duo* could therefore be read as dual in significance, as well as in music and choreography.

Out of darkness, first the woman's head, then her torso, are revealed in a bright halo. She steps out, to leave her hand alone in the light. Then the hand is seen to touch her head before she vanishes again. In the pool of light both dancers' hands are seen stretching toward each other and meeting. The man appears in the light to mold her hand; then he kisses the back of it. Throughout this, her face has been invisible. He kneels in homage to the woman, ballerina, muse. She is disclosed, standing like Venus in a pose of classic simplicity. Suddenly the couple separate, and there are two pools of light. But he runs to her, and the lights merge as he kneels again. She takes first one, then the other of his hands and places them on her chest. When she runs off into the dark, he searches and then stands dejected. Her shoulders appear, then her head, looking down. She stretches out her arm and lays her hand against her cheek. His hand comes to take hers. Again he molds and kisses it and kneels, but this time sinking into the dark. Only the raised arm of Venus remains visible.

"After the premiere," wrote Peter Martins, "Balanchine em-braced Kay and me and told us the ballet was ours." Indeed, Balanchine gave it to Kay.

·   ■   ·

THE FINAL Sunday night's program began with *Choral Variations on Bach's "Vom Himmel Hoch,"* an elaborate and beautiful work that, since it required an expensive choir and a crowd of children, was never repeated. The evening—and the festival—ended, as Balanchine had always intended, with the *Symphony of Psalms.* The singers were onstage and the dancers sat around at the back or on the sides. Rosemary Dunleavy went out front to watch. She saw Balanchine standing downstage: "He had finally paid homage to somebody he loved and admired. I swear you could see him communicate with Stravinsky."

Then everyone in the audience was given a free glass of vodka with which to toast the immortal composer.

When the sums were added up, it was found that the Stravinsky Festival had cost about $348,000 (including the loss of ticket sales during the preceding week, when the theater was closed). That was nearly $100,000 more than Balanchine had estimated, and there was no money for new productions during the winter season. But it had been worth it.

"It has been a wonderful week," Vera Stravinsky told the *Washington Post*. "This audience is such a pleasure—I never saw such a good one." The reviews were without exception ecstatic. A more general comment came from Richard Poirier in the *Atlantic Monthly* for September: "In the history of ballet, Balanchine at New York's State Theater is equivalent to Shakespeare at London's Globe."

"Wasn't it extraordinary," commented Gordon Boelzner, years after, "that the energy, enthusiasm and reverence which went to create this monument to Stravinsky should have come not from a symphony orchestra in a concert hall, but from a ballet company?"

Chapter 14

⋯⋯⋯⋯⋯⋯⋯⋯⋯⋯⋯⋯⋯⋯⋯⋯⋯⋯⋯⋯⋯⋯⋯⋯⋯⋯

THE SPREADING EMPIRE:

FIRST LAST BALLETS,

1 9 7 2 - 1 9 8 1

B ALANCHINE enjoyed his Julys in Saratoga. In the morning, after he had made his tea, he took it out on the veranda. There was always a fresh croissant from Mrs. London's bakeshop and often a coffee cake of incredible richness. In summer, the usually deserted road that divided the Leaches' flower garden from their vegetable garden was busy with farm traffic, but nobody took any notice of Balanchine as he sat breakfasting in his tattered green bathrobe. Lincoln Kirstein sometimes appeared with an armful of newspapers. Balanchine's favorite newspaper reading was "Dear Abbie." He was convinced that the author wrote the letters in the column as well as the answers.

It was a matter of pride for Kay Leach to see the guesthouse kitchen was so well stocked that Balanchine had nothing to shop for. He crossed the road to pick his own herbs and vegetables and always arrived from New York with cases of wine and champagne. He gave frequent dinner parties. Karin von Aroldingen, Taras and Gordon Boelzner were often invited; from 1972 onward, Kay Mazzo, of whom Balanchine had become very fond, came too. Balanchine called Kay Leach, Kay Mazzo and Karin von Aroldingen his "Three K's."

In Saratoga or in New York, Balanchine could always produce a good meal at short notice. He often made soup or a pot roast on Mondays, when there was no performance. The refinements of his cooking were exquisite. He was an expert on herbs, and he laced his vanilla ice cream with vodka. He even made his own mustard with seeds brought from Russia, pounding them himself, mixing in herbs and sugar, adding a little tea at the end. "It was the best mustard ever," according to Kay Leach. "We use it still." He would bake the beets for borscht for almost an hour before adding the other ingredients, and his sauerkraut was prepared in Oriental style, using tiny dried mushrooms. He would then spread it over a leg of lamb. He was also very fond of potatoes. When, at the age of seventy-two, he told Dr. William Hamilton, the company's new orthopedist, that he had just bought a condominium on the end of Long Island with a thirty-year mortgage, he stressed his pleasure in the fact that it overlooked a potato field.

· · ·

In New York, Balanchine's apartment on Sixty-seventh Street, near the theater, was really two apartments made into one. He valued space and light above possessions. His white living room had two enormous windows facing north, from which he could see over the roofs of the brownstones on Sixty-eighth Street. There were smaller windows to the west and east, and Central Park was visible from the latter. The two small bedrooms on either side of the front door, one of which was used as a storeroom, looked out into a well.

Balanchine always woke when the sun rose. He made tea, read

or played solitaire; then, as Barbara Horgan was also an early riser, he called her between 7:30 and 8:00 to discuss the day's appointments. Since most of his time was spent giving class, rehearsing and attending performances, and since all these were printed on the daily call sheet, his engagement books recorded little except meetings with journalists and the directors of European theaters or the dates of his flights to Washington, Los Angeles, Paris or Geneva.

It took him no more than five minutes to walk to the theater. As he went up in the elevator he could often tell who had preceded him, for he carefully chose for each of his ballerinas a perfume he considered appropriate. On the fourth floor he passed on the left a door inscribed "Ducky," where Leslie Copeland, the English wardrobe master, got ready the men's costumes. His own corner room, with windows looking south and west, had a piano, a sofa, books and three large photographs of Mourka on the walls. He did not use it often, unless he wanted to read a score. At 11:00 it was time to teach class, but for reasons of his own (possibly to allow the dancers to warm up before he arrived, possibly because it is an old theatrical tradition) he always walked in ten minutes late.

Balanchine said that when young people joined the company their feet were clumsy, like teddy bears'. So he made them work on their tendus, repeating them again and again, starting slowly and building up gradually to an almost impossible speed. Strength in the feet was the last quality a dancer acquired and the first to go. He seriously advised his girls to do tendus at home when they were cooking. Once, after he had stood beside a boy counting, "Sixty-two, sixty-three, sixty-four," he remarked, *"Last one should be better than first."*

In jumping, a Balanchine dancer had to go up from a deep demi-plié with ferocity but land softly, through the toe, through the foot, unfolding at last with the heel barely touching the ground. He wanted a landing so soft that it wouldn't "break eggs." It did not matter how high you jumped so long as you landed "like a bird" or "like a pussycat." One day he was searching for a verb to describe the way a dancer could give the illusion of defying the force of gravity in order to land lightly. "To resist," the dancer Daniel Duell suggested; and Balanchine exclaimed, "That's it! To resist." He loved the word and from then on used it often in class.

The problem with hands, according to Balanchine, was to make them look both correctly placed and natural. They should be free at the wrists, yet solid as sculpture. "Hands must grow like leaves. . . . Not like that, it looks like dead chicken." When a dancer held her fingers together, he called it "chicken hands." He believed you should be able to see daylight between all the fingers, which were to be used as if "picking flowers or gathering in a bundle—the wash," or opening a French window onto a beautiful garden. "Then you step through to look at the garden." In arabesque you should reach farther, farther, as if stretching out for the thing you liked best—"candy, ice cream."

He told the boys that they didn't have to be sissies to have beautiful hands. He was very particular about how a boy took a girl's hand when partnering her—the fingers should be held gently over the top—and he always cited Fred Astaire as one who held his partner's fingertips delicately. So long as the ballerina was made to look right, he did not mind if her partner was not completely turned-out. The man could lounge, provided he looked strong; but he must not take the weight on both feet.

A favorite expression of despair Balanchine used with slow learners was, "I should have been a dentist. Teaching you is like pulling teeth." He once took hours to tell the story of a mule that would not move. Its rider pushed, pulled, then gave up. The man gathered sticks, piled them up underneath the mule, found two stones, rubbed them together and made a fire. Finally the mule moved two steps. One of his most repeated sayings was, "Dancers are like racehorses. They need a jockey on their backs."

If he was pleased, he said, "That's RIGHT"; and sometimes he would add, "But now, dear, make it beautiful." "Good," he remarked on one occasion. "If we go on like that, one day we'll get what we want. Not today. Because today it won't happen. Not tomorrow. Tomorrow it won't happen. Maybe next month. Maybe next year." He paused, looked round the room and concluded, "Maybe never."

During the season, Balanchine ate only a snack at lunchtime. He would say to Karin or Barbara, "Let's go to the Greek's," meaning the unpretentious diner of the Empire Hotel across the street. The Greeks in the restaurant always greeted him warmly, so that he felt at home, and after a Scotch he would order a sandwich—never the regular club sandwich on the menu but one improvised by himself, perhaps feta cheese with tomatoes. Then it was time for rehearsal.

In 1973 Melissa Hayden retired, and Balanchine made her a special ballet as a farewell present. *Cortège hongrois,* part classical, part character, was arranged to music from Glazunov's *Raymonda,* which he had used before. Melissa and Jacques d'Amboise were to lead the classical team, Karin and Jean-Pierre Bonnefous, the Hungarian character numbers. Although not one of Balanchine's masterpieces, it turned out to be a good "closing ballet."

That was the year Joseph Mazo, the dance critic of *Women's Wear Daily,* took time off to live with the company and record in detail its activities, including the staging of *Cortège;* in his book, *Dance Is a Contact Sport,* he has provided us with a good description of how the ballet was prepared. When Balanchine demonstrated the csárdás, a dance that begins with slow, dragging steps and ends in a stamping, whirling climax, he was, as Mazo pointed out, showing something he had learned at the Imperial Theater School sixty years before; the style of such a dance was second nature to him. "His knees are bent, his body seems light enough to float. His heels stamp out the rhythm, delicately but with great precision. . . ."

Another day, he rehearsed four boys in a strenuous number, which ended with tours en l'air. "That is pure Petipa," he said. "It is marvelous. So I used it. The rest of the ballet is me, but that is Petipa." Melissa Hayden had trouble with some swift backward pas de bourrée to a fast passage of music. Balanchine told her to ignore the music and do the steps to the counts. "*You* do it,"

Melissa told him. So Balanchine did it; she did it; and it proved to be just possible.

. . .

IN JANUARY 1974, Balanchine was seventy. In February, as if to show that he was still young at heart, he staged *Variations pour une porte et un soupir* (Variations for a Door and a Sigh) to *musique concrète* "sonorities" by Pierre Henry. This was an amazing twenty-minute invention for two dancers, a variation on the theme of man as victim of the cruel love goddess. For the most part, the two move alternately. The man, gray and miserable, crawls, clutches and crashes around, reduced to a subhuman state like a character in Samuel Beckett. The woman, almost a Cretan version of Berg's Lulu, with shiny black bobbed hair, has an immense train that covers the entire stage; it is later manipulated by stagehands to rise and billow in the air like a dark, poisonous cloud. Her music is that of a creaking door. The man's music resembles not so much a sigh as a bronchial wheeze. Balanchine thus compared love's anguish to a fight for breath. It was, in a way, his *Petrushka,* and it was booed at its first performance. When it was revived twelve years later, after his death, there were still scattered boos on the first night, but many people acclaimed it as a masterpiece.

No such uncertain fate awaited his next production, which was given its first performance at Saratoga that summer. With Hayden gone, Patricia McBride was NYCB's prima ballerina—not that Balanchine ever encouraged the use of such classifications. It was therefore for her—with help from the earliest of all his ballerinas, Danilova, who had an exceptional memory—that he staged *Coppélia,* in the Petipa version he had known in his youth. He had always cherished the Delibes music and once told Edwin Denby— exaggerating somewhat—that the dances in the first act to the "Variations on a Slav Theme" had been the inspiration for all his choreography.

It was another full-length ballet, good for a young audience, in which he could use children from the School and in the summer from Saratoga. He had his own ideas about how to fill the house: "If all the children in the ballet brought their brothers and sisters and parents—already we would have an audience."

In July 1974, Suzanne Farrell and Paul Mejia, who had been dancing for the past four years with Béjart's company in Brussels, but who spent the summers at their house on an island near Saratoga, came to watch performances at the Saratoga Performing Arts Center. At once, the speculation began: Would she be accepted back if she wanted to return? From New York, Suzanne wrote to Balanchine; he saw her privately, and she rejoined NYCB during the winter season of 1974–75. Mejia went to Chicago, where Maria Tallchief was director of the Chicago City Ballet, and became co-artistic director.

The company was curious to see how Balanchine would receive Suzanne. On the first day she came to class, the big hall was more crowded than it had ever been. She walked up to Balanchine and kissed him, then she took her old place at the barre. Her first, unannounced, appearance was in *Symphony in C.* When the audience recognized her, there was an ovation. McBride and Mazzo soon found that they had to give back most of the parts they had inherited.

For 1975, Balanchine decreed a Ravel Festival. This produced a bizarre crop of ballets. The choreographer staged his third version of *L'Enfant et les sortilèges,* and his other contributions ranged from the pseudo-Oriental posturings of *Schéhérazade* to the psuedo-Spanish excesses of *Rapsodie espagnole.* How different were *Sonatine,* "a stroll for two," delicately danced by Verdy and Bonnefous to a piano solo; *Tzigane,* spectacularly danced by Farrell (once more a gypsy) to a violin solo—"a new height in contemporary performance," wrote Arlene Croce in *The New Yorker*—and the *Pavane,* to more familiar music, performed by McBride alone with a scarf. Balanchine's most outrageous essay was his translation of the virtuoso suite for solo piano *Gaspard de la nuit* into dance, while his most unpredictable piece, *Le Tombeau de Couperin,* surprised by its simplicity. A beautiful invention, it outlasted the festival and is likely to remain popular, but it was almost lost before the festival took place. Balanchine worked it out in its entirety at the very beginning of the rehearsal period, which for him was unusual. Then he turned his attention to other ballets. Time passed, and Rosemary Dunleavy began to fear *Le Tombeau* would be forgotten, so she called the sixteen dancers and "got it back together again." She had difficulty persuading Balanchine to come and look at it: "Later, later," he kept saying. When at last he sat and watched the whole ballet, which he had never seen from beginning to end, Rosemary was worried by his silence. At last he spoke. "You know, dear, I like it."

It is a work without soloists. In the Prélude, Forlane, Menuet and Rigaudon, two quadrilles of eight dance separately, imitate each other, merge and part. The mood is both pastoral and elegiac. It is an amazingly varied web of pretty formations, and there had never been a ballet quite like it before. In retrospect it is tempting to regard it as the first of Balanchine's "last ballets"—something for his company to dance by his grave after he was dead.

■　■　■

ERIK BRUHN, who arrived in 1960, had been the first Danish dancer to appear, albeit briefly, with the New York City Ballet. Peter Martins, who came to stay, was the second. Then Helgi Tomasson, an Icelander but a former member of the Royal Danish Ballet, arrived. Peter Schaufuss, son of two distinguished dancers at Copenhagen's Royal Theater and already admired in England for his spectacular technique, came in 1975.

Schaufuss stayed only two years, with a gap of eight months in the middle owing to injuries. He was aware that certain dancers accused him of putting in a lot of "tricks" not called for in the choreography, but he maintained that Balanchine, whose works he admired above all others, demanded a display of virtuosity and wanted a replacement for the much-injured Villella. The real problem appears to have been that Schaufuss and Balanchine were both attracted to the same woman.

Although his tenure was brief, Schaufuss bequeathed an important legacy to the company: his Danish colleague Adam Lüders, who had also left Copenhagen to join London's Festival Ballet. Lüders came to Saratoga during his summer break and took class. Like Peter Martins, he was tall and fair, but his small head on a long neck and his long legs gave him unusual proportions. Knowing that Balanchine liked male dancers to be solid rather than willowy, Schaufuss made Lüders wear three sweaters to class. Ignoring the sweaters, Balanchine saw a special quality in Lüders that appealed to him, and he invited him to join the company as a principal dancer.

Everyone, not only Danes, wanted to dance for Balanchine. Sean Lavery, an American who had appeared with the San Francisco Ballet and danced for two years in the Frankfurt company, both headed by Balanchine students, joined NYCB in 1977. Balanchine tried him out in the Élégie of the *Tchaikovsky Suite No. 3,* with which Martins had had trouble. At the end, when the drifting girls left him alone kneeling in a spotlight, Lavery felt, as he explained later, that he ought somehow to "project," so he began to "reach for the heavens." Balanchine said, "What are you reaching for? They are all looking for you. All you have to do is just look up and think. Then it's over." Lavery found it "scary" that Balanchine stood in the wings "two feet away," but "if he just gave you a nod, it was worth a thousand words. . . . The first time he told me 'That was very good work,' I was ready to retire and open the old ballet school right then."

. . .

IF BALANCHINE's contributions to his Ravel Festival were mostly on a miniature scale, 1976 and 1977 were to bring one important work of art and two blockbusters: *Chaconne, Union Jack* and *Vienna Waltzes.*

Balanchine had staged dances for the final scene of Gluck's *Orfeo* at the Hamburg State Opera as early as 1963; in 1975 he made a version for the Chicago Lyric Opera. On January 22, 1976, he presented his own company in *Chaconne,* which took its final form the following spring when he added an opening ensemble before the first duet. A dance for twelve girls with loose hair and drifting chiffon dresses was followed by a pas de deux for Farrell, also with hair flowing, and Martins. As he lifted her swimming against the blue cyclorama, the two seemed to be moving above the clouds. Then the ballet became more formal. Among other dances were a stately pas de deux for Farrell—her hair up now—and Martins, several glittering variations for each; and at last the grand promenade for the whole cast in the Chaconne that gave the ballet its name.

Union Jack, a tribute to Great Britain in America's bicentennial year, grew from Balanchine's memories of Cockney tunes and music-hall routines, his admiration for the swing of Scottish kilts at the Edinburgh Tattoo and Kirstein's heartfelt desire to demonstrate to the United States that a corner of the American consciousness remained "forever England." In the opening scene, a kilted "cast of thousands" parades and dances to traditional tunes such as "The Keel Row" and "Dance wi' My Daddy." This is followed by a pas de deux for a costermonger Pearly King and Queen. The Royal Navy, both male and female, dance hornpipes and finally, to the sound of "Rule, Britannia," spell out the message "God Save the Queen" with waggling flag signals, while an enormous Union Jack assembles itself in the background.

Balanchine had had a clear idea of the framework for *Vienna Waltzes,* his tribute to Austria, for more than a year before he began to work on it: he had discussed the ballet with members of the company and told stage designer Rouben Ter-Arutunian from the start that "there must be five trees." Three of these "trees from the Vienna woods," where the first two waltzes and the comic "Explosions Polka" are danced to the music of Johann Strauss, are magically transformed into the glittering Art-Nouveau curlicues of a restaurant resembling Maxim's—the background for Lehár's "Gold and Silver" waltz often interpolated in *The Merry Widow.* At the ballet's close, a ballroom with chandeliers formed from the trees' roots, now risen into the air, is the setting for Richard Strauss's *Rosenkavalier* waltzes.

The newcomer Sean Lavery was amazed at the speed of Balanchine's invention. Even so, at six o'clock on the evening of the gala preview the choreographer had still not found time to finish the couples' last big circle round the stage. The dancers stood waiting while Balanchine did what was necessary; what he arranged then he never had reason to change later. He was less happy with the "Gold and Silver" waltz and kept tinkering with it.

At the premiere the enchantment began when Sean Lavery, strolling with others in the Wienerwald, took Karin von Aroldingen's hand, bowed over it and kissed it. Their waltz was followed by a sylvan interlude with Patricia McBride and Helgi Tomasson, next came the "Explosions Polka," led by Sara Leland and Bart Cook. After Ter-Arutunian's dazzling transformation scene, Kay Mazzo, all in black, wearing a Merry Widow hat, chose Peter Martins in his white-and-scarlet Austrian uniform from a group of bowing admirers. The *Rosenkavalier* waltzes had Suzanne Farrell in a white satin ball gown dancing by herself. She was joined briefly by an elusive Adam Lüders, who came and went. Then the chandeliers lit up, and the stage was suddenly filled with a crowd of swirling couples, the women in identical white gowns holding up their trains with gloved hands, the men in black evening dress; the tall mirrors seemed to duplicate their number.

•   •   •

MEANWHILE, the School was flourishing. From 1975 on, Balanchine had sent selected dancers to visit scores of cities in search of talented children: those with promise were sponsored by local corporations, often with additional funds from private sources. The New York City Ballet could, however, absorb at most eight graduates from the School a year, more often four or six. All received superb training, so those who were not accepted were much in demand elsewhere. Former dancers of the New York City Ballet were running companies or the schools attached to them in many states (as well as in Europe), and these onetime "Balanchine dancers" were beginning to feed pupils they had trained in the master's methods back into the School of American Ballet. Thus the choreographer's network spread throughout the United States. In the last years of his life, Balanchine was in the position of an emperor with many proconsuls: Maria Tallchief and Paul Mejia in Chicago; Patricia Wilde in Pittsburgh; Todd Bolender, Diana Adams and Una Kai in Kansas City; Lew Christensen in San Francisco; John Clifford in Los Angeles; Barbara Weissberger and Robert Weiss in Philadelphia; Robert Barnett in Atlanta; Kent Stowell and Francia Russell in Seattle; William Dollar in New Jersey; Frank Ohman, Carol Sumner and Edward Villella on Long Island; Mimi Paul in North Carolina; Patricia Neary in Switzerland; Roy Tobias in Japan.

The increased scale and prosperity of the company brought new problems. In the old days, Balanchine's word had been law. In the summer of 1973, when the question arose as to whether or not dancers would go to film his ballets in Berlin, a vote was actually taken.

The dancers had been told they would dance five hours a day in Berlin, but Villella warned them that in film studios you worked twelve hours. With the growing popularity of video cassettes, the producers might in the future make a fortune out of these films, and the dancers would get nothing. Many of the younger dancers wanted to see Berlin, or to go just because Balanchine wanted them to. Edward Bigelow called Berlin but failed to get a five-hours-a-day clause inserted in the contract. A ballot was taken, and the votes in favor of acceptance won, fifty-three to seventeen. Eighty-one dancers went with Balanchine to Berlin in September and danced twelve hours a day for six weeks on a bad floor.

Then the musicians threatened to strike for higher pay. Although they did not call a strike before the fall season, they would not guarantee not to strike during it. Balanchine, who was proud of his orchestra, asked associate conductor Hugo Fiorato why the musicians wanted more money. Fiorato replied that they had families to support and were entitled to a decent living. "Why," he asked, "should a garbageman get more than a musician?" Balanchine thought the answer was obvious: "Because garbage stinks." The dancers, always resentful of the musicians' higher pay and shorter hours, asked the management to ensure that they would be paid in full for the fourteen-week season, whether or not there was a musicians' strike. This guarantee was not forthcoming. The dancers voted sixty-five to eleven for a strike, seven abstaining. On November 13, 1973, the night the season did not open, there was an "opening-night party" to celebrate the publication of Lincoln Kirstein's *The New York City Ballet*. He had been telling Balanchine's dancers for twenty-five years that "there is no justice"; now democracy had raised its head. Villella said, "It's history. Dancers for years have been subsidizing their art."

Balanchine, who thought life was too short to warrant strikes, remarked that if there was no early settlement, "We'll close the theater, and everyone will go home. The girls will marry; the boys will go and drive taxicabs."

The dancers went on unemployment and took class with Balanchine. The management came to an agreement with the musicians, whose salaries were raised; and the season began a month late.

Three years later, in the middle of the *Nutcracker* season, the orchestra went on strike and no settlement was reached for several weeks. According to Kirstein, Balanchine considered leaving for Europe; and although dancing was resumed before the season ended, the loss of revenue was nearly a million dollars.

. . .

FOR SOME YEARS Balanchine had been conscious that Merrill Ashley, who had joined the company from the School in 1967, was going to be an outstanding dancer. Her legs were perfect, and her jump was big. In 1977 she became a principal, and in 1978 he made a ballet for her. This was *Ballo della Regina*, to music for dancing that Verdi had reluctantly inserted into *Don Carlos* to satisfy the requirements of the Paris Opéra. In her account of how she worked with Balanchine on this virtuoso ballet, Ashley described his adaptability, his tactful way of urging her partner Robert Weiss to adopt a nobler carriage by telling him, "This is a Nureyev entrance," his allowing her to insert a "big jeté with a backbend" which she had seen Plisetskaya do in the Bolshoi production of *Don Quixote,* and the pride he took in demonstrating all the partnering himself. *Ballo,* choreographed in a week, was shown at the gala preceding the opening of the winter season.

Balanchine had made his own piano reduction of *Ballo* for Gordon Boelzner to play at rehearsals, because none existed. Although the music was exactly suited to its purpose, he guessed that his sophisticated orchestra might scorn Verdi's tuneful numbers, so he took the trouble to tell them that he had something more interesting for them coming up; this was Hindemith's Kammermusik No. 2, for solo piano and twelve solo instruments.

It was prepared almost in secret. The musicians' strike had already prevented a production of *The Seven Deadly Sins;* Balanchine had got as far as the fifth sin when the orchestra walked out. It was on Karin von Aroldingen's return from Vienna, where she had been producing *Liebeslieder Walzer,* that Balanchine spoke to her about the Hindemith, which he perhaps intended as a consolation prize. In it he employed two couples, with—an unusual feature—a corps of eight boys. It was referred to as an inverted or neo-*Concerto Barocco* and was extremely difficult to dance. Karin called it *"Kammer-*computer." "It's so speedy," she explained, "that even a pianist can't play the notes. It took us forever to learn it. The movement is very angular, very fast. If you lose concentration for one second, you ruin it all." Sean Lavery felt that Balanchine "knew exactly what the corps were doing when the principals were doing something else. He was so fast, so in tune with the music, so ahead of himself, that we couldn't keep up with him. . . . He wanted it a bit spooky at times." Indeed, it is amazing that such inventions, such ominous images, should have sprung from the mind of a man in his seventies. Kirstein, who had not watched rehearsals, thought it one of Balanchine's greatest works.

．　．　．

THE GREAT holiday of the Russian Church is Easter, and Balanchine always served a traditional Easter feast. Days in advance he prepared pashka, kulitch, piroshki and sturgeon in aspic. In his later years the guests, apart from the hard core of Russians—Lucia Davidova, Natalie Molostwoff, John Taras, Rouben Ter-Arutunian and Eugenia Doll (one of Massine's widows)—included Edward Bigelow, Gordon Boelzner, Karin and her husband, Morton, Barbara Horgan, Kay Mazzo, the company orthopedist William Hamilton, and Balanchine's other doctor, Edith Langner.

On March 15, 1978, less than a month before Russian Easter, Balanchine had a heart attack. It was not a bad one, but he stayed away from work for a few weeks to rest—and cook. During this time Jerome Robbins, who had made a short ballet to Chopin for the celebrated Russian defector Mikhail Baryshnikov, came to see Balanchine to tell him that the young star, who was currently dancing with American Ballet Theatre, might be interested in joining the New York City Ballet. After thinking about it overnight—NYCB had never operated on the star system, and Balanchine was not certain how Baryshnikov would fit into the company—he called him at eight the next morning and asked him to come around.

The two men had met in Leningrad in 1972 during NYCB's second Russian tour. Baryshnikov had at first been taken aback by the idea of a company in which the choreographer was the star, but shortly afterward he danced in the third movement of *Symphony in C,* when Taras produced it at a benefit performance in honor of Natalia Dudinskaya. In the West he rapidly came to appreciate the range of Balanchine's invention. Although Ballet Theatre paid him well because he always filled the house, and he could command large fees for guest appearances, he aspired to dance for Balanchine. Baryshnikov and Balanchine liked each other, and Baryshnikov agreed to work for the usual NYCB rate. He made the most inconspicuous début possible the next summer, dancing, unannounced, in *Coppélia* in Saratoga. While they were rehearsing it, Balanchine constantly questioned him about Russian versions of the ballet, wanting to compare them with his own.

That July, Balanchine also taught him Villella's part in "Rubies," in which he was to make his début at the New York State Theater. In New York, he learned *Harlequinade;* the Pearly King in *Union Jack,* which he performed in traditional Russian mime style; *The Steadfast Tin Soldier; Orpheus;* the Cavalier in *Nutcracker;* the Poet in *La Sonnambula* and more than a dozen other roles. While he was learning *The Prodigal Son,* he felt that although Balanchine gave him the most meticulous instructions, especially about the penitent Prodigal's return home on his knees, the choreographer did not enjoy rehearsing the ballet.

Baryshnikov thought Balanchine, like Noverre, one of the earliest choreographers, tended to divide male dancers into two distinct types. There was the staccato, bravura dancer like Villella and the tall, imposing *danseur noble* like Martins. Baryshnikov himself did not fall neatly into either category (but then, neither did Nijinsky). He adjusted to the master's requirements but always "felt comfortable on his own scale"—meaning, perhaps, that, like Nijinsky, his genius entitled him to do things his own way. When the critics were hard on his interpretations of Balanchine's work, as he thought they usually were, Balanchine would tell him, "You're doing fine. People always misinterpret." "Balanchine was shy," Baryshnikov said, "but he was like a father to me. He was always asking, 'Are you having fun?' "

For Balanchine, however, no male dancer could ever be more important than the female. Baryshnikov noticed that he used to look scornful when a male star's fan started raving about his or her idol. "What do you mean, you're going to see Nureyev in *The Sleeping Beauty*? What do you mean, you saw Bruhn in *Giselle*?"

Balanchine often woke Baryshnikov early in the morning, telephoning to talk about the past, and the latter has given an interesting account of these conversations. "He didn't want to talk about

Diaghilev, he wanted to talk about the old days in St. Petersburg. He would speak of his character-dancing teacher, Monakhov, who taught him how to act—and he liked to act. He liked the *early* Nijinska. He knew the Russian theater very well, and he not only recited Pushkin's poems, he could say by heart Pushkin's long letter to his wife beginning *'Dusha maya'* [my soul]. This took about twenty minutes. He knew The Hermitage very well—the architecture more than the paintings." Baryshnikov believes that the fact that Balanchine was a mediocre dancer is what made him a choreographer. "The *premier danseur* is always in the wings, watching to see which rival may take his place. As a choreographer, Balanchine was more in control, more the center of attention than he would have been as a dancer. It was a question of ego. And, of course, he liked to make ballets for the women he loved." This is, perhaps, a star dancer's explanation.

■ ■ ■

In 1978, Balanchine traveled to Copenhagen with the company, but he suffered increasingly from fatigue, and in the autumn he began to have attacks of angina. In December, he went to Washington to receive an award from President Carter and had a seizure while waiting for the train back to New York. He gave class infrequently. Yet when the company set off on a tour of upstate New York in March 1979, he went to Switzerland to work with Patricia Neary, who had moved from Geneva to Zurich. Karin von Aroldingen was now teaching *Liebeslieder* to the Royal Ballet in London, and he subsequently joined her there.

Although he made *Le Bourgeois Gentilhomme* for Nureyev at the New York City Opera in April, since his heart attack he was working at half strength. Robbins, Martins and Susan Hendl had to help out with certain passages of choreography; both Anna Kisselgoff of *The New York Times* and Arlene Croce of *The New Yorker* found the result disappointing.

During NYCB's Chicago season later in April, Balanchine re-

hearsed Baryshnikov in the role of Apollo, and Taras thought he
had never seen him take such pains in teaching the role before.
He even changed the ballet. Just as Stravinsky had made condensed versions of some of his early successes, so Balanchine felt
himself entitled to cut the dead wood out of his own works—even
if it meant losing a little Stravinsky too. The first scene in *Apollo*,
in which Leto gives birth to the god, was scrapped, along with the
attendant goddesses, Apollo's first solo (which was restored in
1980 for Peter Martins and subsequent Apollos) and the staircase
that had long ago replaced the mountain of Diaghilev's day.

Since there was no longer a staircase up which Apollo and the
Muses could climb in solemn procession, Balanchine had to make
a new ending; he repeated the famous "sunburst" group and had
the three Muses, in arabesque, clinging to Apollo upstage center.
Unfortunately, the effect—with the spotlight making a kind of
setting sun behind them—looked to me like an advertisement for
orange juice.

When Baryshnikov made his first appearance in the role on May
1, his stay with NYCB was already drawing to a close. Lucia Chase
had decided to retire from the artistic directorship of Ballet
Theatre, which she had founded, and Baryshnikov was invited to
take her place. He asked Balanchine's advice, and Balanchine told
him to accept, which he did. Baryshnikov's last performance as a
member of the company was in *La Sonnambula* in Washington. He
remained friends with Balanchine, however, and was at his Easter
supper the following year.

On June 17, after a long postponement, Balanchine had a heart
bypass operation. The night before, reflecting on the possibility of
his not surviving the surgery, he remarked to Dr. Hamilton, "You
know, I wasn't meant to marry Suzanne. It was God's decision."
He had always told Lucia Davidova that he could not envisage God
as "an essence": God to him was an old man with a white beard,
as portrayed by Michelangelo, a father with whom he discussed
matters face-to-face.

. . .

DR. HAMILTON, who also lived on West Sixty-seventh Street, had a habit of dropping in on Balanchine every morning on his way to work, to make sure he was all right. He usually found him at his favorite occupation of ironing, dressed only in his jockey shorts. One day early in 1980 Hamilton sensed a different atmosphere; he felt he was intruding. Sheet music was spread over the tables and chairs. It was Robert Schumann's *Davidsbündlertänze.*

When Schumann edited the *Neue Zeitschrift für Musik,* he invented an imaginary society of young enthusiasts, sworn to fight for their ideals against the forces of reaction and philistinism. This he called the *Davidsbund,* a band of Davids challenging Goliath. Two of its members were Florestan and Eusebius, who represented contrasting aspects of Schumann's own character—the active, optimistic side and the reflective, melancholy one. In his series of piano pieces entitled *Davidsbündlertänze* (literally, the David's Club Dances), the two friends are supposed to be reliving various love affairs, happy or sad, at a ball. Balanchine identified the Eusebius music with Robert Schumann himself and his partner with Schumann's wife, the pianist and composer Clara Wieck, but the other three couples remained unidentified—unless, as some believe, the role danced by Suzanne Farrell stands for the evasive beloved who always moves out of reach. Balanchine made the "Philistines," whom Fokine (and Bakst) had brought on rather absurdly at the end of *Carnaval,* with umbrellas and old-fashioned bonnets, into more sinister characters, as if seen in the light of Schumann's unbalanced imaginings. And he insisted on the cumbersome title *Robert Schumann's "Davidsbündlertänze."*

Adam Lüders, known for his arched instep and fine partnering, who danced Schumann, had a sensitive, visionary side rare among dancers of any nationality, which must have attracted Balanchine to him from the beginning. Karin, who danced Clara, thought his engagement of Lüders was an outstanding example of his insight, but Taras had often noticed that Balanchine was drawn to the unusual.

Although Balanchine told Lüders, "You are Schumann," when Karin first read about Schumann and Clara, she could not see that she in any way resembled the latter, and yet eventually she came to recognize something of herself in the role Balanchine made for her.

Both Kirstein and Karin had given Balanchine reproductions of the work of Kaspar David Friedrich, with which, it turned out, he was already familiar, and he told Ter-Arutunian, who was to design the ballet, that he would like something of that painter's quality in the set. The painted backcloth is of a cold, still lake—or else it is the Rhine, in which Schumann once tried to drown himself. From its waters rises the ghost of a cathedral. This distant view is framed by bare trees with branches like antlers, and by lengths of gauze that billow as the dancers come and go.

At the first performance, Gordon Boelzner was seated onstage at the piano, which became part of the décor, and it could be said that he, like Lüders, represented Robert Schumann. The four pairs of dancers appeared in turn, led by the elusive Farrell, with the older Jacques d'Amboise in pursuit. Then came the melancholy Lüders, with von Aroldingen as his tender muse, followed by Heather Watts and Peter Martins, tripping and charging. Last of all, Kay Mazzo and Ib Andersen, a brilliant new recruit from Denmark, entered with an impetuous surge. Throughout the ballet, the first, third and fourth couples seemed to form a frame around the dialogues of the second in their moments of intimacy. In the latter half, all combined in what might be called "social" scenes— hunting, toasting, praying—or in a formal dance passage. Later, madness threatened the hero; black, Goyaesque enemies (the Philistine critics) appeared briefly. His wife attempted to guide, soothe and heal him, but, with outstretched valedictory arm and tragic eyes, he backed away from her toward the Rhine.

Most critics admired the Schumann ballet while expressing surprise at its quite untypical emotional character. Most also recognized something autobiographical about the work, as well as in its casting. Balanchine had remarked to an interviewer in 1972, "Mozart never put his miserable life into his beautiful, gay music." Perhaps this was as near as the objective choreographer could come—except in *Don Quixote*—to exposing his private feelings. Martha Duffy of *Time* wrote:

Balanchine may have been putting a distance between himself and this outpouring of emotion by including Schumann's name in the full title. But on opening night he seemed positively merry, pleased enough with the ballet to take four curtain calls (in the past fans have clapped blisters onto their hands trying to get him to appear once). If the old master, now 76, is thinking about death, he is thinking about it creatively and at the highest level.

At Saratoga that summer, Karin came daily to help Balanchine cook and drive him wherever he wanted to go. In the fall, he traveled with the company to Copenhagen, Berlin and Paris. In the last two cities there were celebrations of the hundredth anniversary of Stravinsky's birth.

Back at home he discovered the girl who was to be the last of his ballerinas. During rehearsals for *Le Bourgeois Gentilhomme* in 1979, a fourteen-year-old student who was "marking" as an understudy fell on her behind with such a crash that Balanchine, Nureyev, Bonnefous and Martins stared at her in amazement. Covered with embarrassment, Darci Kistler nearly went straight home to California, where Taras had found her. But the next time Balanchine saw her, she made quite a different impression. Chosen to dance the lead in *Swan Lake* in the 1980 School Workshop, she turned in a performance that became the talk of the company—and of the audiences who attended. It was an extraordinary feat for a girl of any age, and almost unbelievable in a fifteen-year-old. Darci was taken into the company in the fall of 1980, became a soloist in 1981 and was made a principal (the youngest in the company's history) in 1982. By then she had already danced the second movement in *Symphony in C* and been singled out by Balanchine for special attention. There is a revealing picture of the two of them in the dancer Toni Bentley's journal of the 1980–81 winter season:

Balanchine is working on Darci. She is blond, thin, tiny and so young. He is old, gray; he squints and arches his head upward to make her analyze herself. He rises and jumps around, showing her where to go, how to do it. "Where did you learn that? Did you go somewhere?"

He is already fearful and suspicious that she will desert him and go to another for help. She assures him that no one taught her, she just did it alone. . . . He will change it.

All eyes focus on the two, moving from Darci to Balanchine, from Balanchine to Darci. Everyone wants to know what he thinks of her every step. The eyes flit back and forth, back and forth, trying to correlate and imagine their two minds. It is romantic, Darci at [not quite] sixteen, Balanchine at seventy-six, coaching. It is beautiful to see.

Darci did not at first realize that Balanchine's interest in her work was anything out of the ordinary, and when, in class, he slapped her on the rear "like your dad would do," she thought it was "a liberty." She remembers: "He once asked me: 'Where did you learn to do an awful second position like that?' and I said, 'At your School.' " But more and more she began to see that he was offering her invaluable help and advice: "One day I'm not going to be here," he said, "so you've got to remember. Be yourself. Don't act, don't emote, trust yourself." She realized that "if you did remember all you were taught, you'd had a whole lifetime."

■   ■   ■

DURING the run of *Nutcracker* that winter, the dancers of NYCB threatened to strike unless they were given a raise. Balanchine announced that he would speak to the whole company after class. As a result, the class was so crowded that it was difficult to squeeze into a place at the barre. When it was over, Balanchine came in very calmly and called the company around him. Most of them sat

on the floor. He said the management's offer was final. If seventy
out of one hundred and five voted for a strike—"Fine, okay, I will
be happy. We will go elsewhere and make a new company in a day.
This is the fifth company, and we will make the sixth. . . . I want
a vote for myself, and I don't give a damn if it's illegal. Yes or no
from a hundred and five!"

If he had asked them to raise their hands, Toni Bentley thought,
no one would have dared not to. But he did not. After telling them
how, when he was their age and working for Diaghilev, he had sold
his pants at the flea market, he said there would be a box in which
to drop their votes. A week later the company accepted the management's latest offer.

·   ■   ·

BALANCHINE was having trouble with his left eye. He had never
liked to be seen wearing glasses, but now, when he watched a ballet
from the wings, he was obliged to wear them; a dark lens covered
the bad eye. Darci Kistler thought that even with a patch over one
eye, Balanchine saw more than most people:

A lot Mr. B. told me was about myself. Sometimes he talked to me in
a corner of the stage; once in a while he'd call me into his room. He
talked to me about music. (I used to go to concerts alone; I'd rather have
been an opera singer.) He said, "Dance should not exceed music. Never
'interpret' music. You can't choreograph Beethoven."

At the Théâtre des Champs-Elysées during the 1980 European
tour, she was about to watch from the wings a ballet she had never
seen before. Balanchine took her to a dark corner of the stage and
said, "Just listen to the music."

Balanchine was at this time complaining more and more that the
lighting was too dim; Ronald Bates was reluctantly forced to
strengthen it until the stage became, as Dominique Nabokov put
it, "like a gymnasium." The choreographer was also suffering from
a bad back and tired easily. Despite these ailments, a two-week

Tchaikovsky Festival was scheduled for June 1981 and announced to the press at the Russian Tea Room on February 9.

Five days later, outside a butcher shop on Broadway, Balanchine was accosted by Solomon Volkov, the musicologist who had smuggled Shostakovich's autobiography out of Russia. Volkov knew Balanchine by sight only, but he had read of the forthcoming festival, and he spoke about Tchaikovsky. The choreographer invited him to write a piece for the festival program, and the two men began to meet and discuss Tchaikovsky and St. Petersburg. The valuable reminiscences that emerged from their conversations, which Volkov later published, have been quoted frequently in these pages.

· · ·

BOTH KIRSTEIN (who never owned a television set) and Balanchine (who did) had been dissatisfied with attempts to film ballets in the 1960s, but in the 1970s Merrill Brockway and Emile Ardolino of the Public Broadcasting System won the choreographer over. Once converted, he took endless trouble exploring the possibilities of television technique and willingly altered his ballets to make them look better on the small screen. Several programs were filmed for the *Dance in America* and *Live from Lincoln Center* series. Ardolino found that Balanchine understood very well that "television succeeds best in closeup" and that a wide shot of a big group reduced the dancers to ants, or, as Balanchine put it, "[on television] dancers don't go away and come back, they just get smaller or bigger."

He began by disliking panning shots, but later changed his mind. "It's so boring to stay on that long, wide shot—go to the panning one," he would say. He took an interest in every detail of lighting and makeup. In 1981 he persuaded Ardolino that television would be the perfect medium for Ravel's *The Spellbound Child,* which he had always staged with difficulty. The film was rehearsed in New York, shot in eleven days in Nashville, Tennessee, edited in New York and shown on May 25, 1981. This time,

Ardolino thought, the choreographer was moderately satisfied with the result.

. . .

WHEN BALANCHINE decided to make a new version of Tchaikovsky's *Mozartiana,* which he had first arranged in 1933, then for the American Ballet in 1935 and for the Ballet Russe in 1945, he explained to Suzanne Farrell and Ib Andersen at their first rehearsal, "It is Mozart. Nobody in Russia knew much of Mozart, so Tchaikovsky, who adored him, wanted his countrymen to hear his music. This suite was like an introduction for them."

Mozartiana was Balanchine's last great ballet. Former company member Robert Maiorano, who had abandoned dancing for writing, obtained permission from the choreographer to record the shaping of *Mozartiana* day by day, from its beginning in May to its first performance on June 4. His descriptions of how Balanchine devised the most taxing steps constitute an invaluable document. One does not have to be a specialist to enjoy Maiorano's detailed account of Balanchine's patience, endurance of physical handicaps and kindness to the four little girls who formed a frame for Farrell in her Preghiera (Prayer) solo.

Farrell had nearly always been dressed in white for Balanchine ballets, but in *Mozartiana* all eleven dancers wore black. The endless trouble Balanchine took to ensure the exact line, weight and trimmings of Farrell's black *point d'esprit* skirt, worn over lighter underskirts, was a small epic in itself. In Balanchine's earlier versions of *Mozartiana,* the Gigue had been performed first, as Tchaikovsky wrote it; but to make it possible for Farrell to dance the Preghiera as well as the Theme and ten Variations—the ninth of which was her pas de deux with Andersen—the order was changed to Preghiera, Gigue, Menuet, Theme and Variations, Finale.

The season was running its course throughout the rehearsals of *Mozartiana;* the three other ballet masters were rehearsing new ballets for the festival. Balanchine himself was planning to stage part of the Sixth Symphony and, because he wanted to show something of Tchaikovsky's lighter side, "Hungarian Gypsy Airs." "Why does all music have to be the best?" he exclaimed to Robert Irving. "Let's have some cheap restaurant music." But this music seemed to get on his nerves, and he lost his temper with a photographer who was present at a rehearsal.

Everyone was relieved when *Mozartiana* was "finished," even though it had not yet been rehearsed on the stage. But Balanchine's mind had already turned to a new project. "You know, maybe . . . I think I will do a waltz for Tchaikovsky." "When?" "Tomorrow." The program of the festival (due to open in two weeks) was therefore enlarged by the inclusion of the Garland Dance from Act I of *The Sleeping Beauty,* for twenty-five women, sixteen men and sixteen little girls from the School. It was one of the loveliest dances he ever made.

Victor Castelli, who was to dance the Gigue in *Mozartiana,* injured himself during one of the last rehearsals and had to be replaced by Christopher d'Amboise, son of Jacques, who had recently been taken into the company after years at the School. Suzanne Farrell dislocated a bone in her foot during the first performance, which she still managed to finish and which was an enormous success—though *Mozartiana* was not repeated during the festival. Ib Andersen partnered her for the first time, and Balanchine thought him so subtle and so musical a dancer that he exclaimed, "Ib *is* Mozart!" In later seasons, *Mozartiana* became one of Farrell's most popular roles, and a ballet constantly reevaluated by the critics.

The Tchaikovsky Festival served to remind Balanchine's audience that he had made ballets to Tchaikovsky's music throughout the five decades he had been in America. The last work of his last Tchaikovsky program was the Sixth *(Pathétique)* Symphony. The first movement was omitted; Robbins arranged a ballet to the second; the curtain was lowered while the orchestra played the third; and the fourth was staged by Balanchine in a ceremonial manner. It took its name from the musical direction for the movement: *Adagio Lamentoso.* Karin von Aroldingen had developed tendinitis after dancing in the only performance of *Hungarian Gypsy Airs,* but Balanchine asked her if she would take part in the *Pathétique.* "It's not much dancing—it's walking, barefoot." She and other dancers were "mourners"; there were twelve angels with immense wings, hooded figures in purple and monks who prostrated themselves in the shape of a cross. A child entered with a candle and, on the final chord of the symphony, blew it out, plunging the theater into darkness. The audience, stunned and moved, did not applaud. Many people interpreted the ballet as a valedictory gesture from the aging choreographer, especially since at the end of a Russian Orthodox funeral the candles held by the congregation are blown out. Karin found it "macabre, chilling," and was shaken when Balanchine told her, "You were wonderful. You know how to mourn."

That July, Karin stayed with the Leaches in order to be nearer to Balanchine and keep an eye on him. When her husband came for weekends, he shared Eddie Bigelow's apartment at the guesthouse. Karin produced *Liebeslieder,* for the third time, for Patricia Neary's company in Zurich that August. Balanchine and Barbara Horgan flew over for the premiere and went on to Monte Carlo with Karin. Every summer Princess Grace of Monaco, who was fond of Balanchine and persistently wanted him to form a ballet company in her husband's principality, held a *"bal de la rose."* This year it was the turn of the Yellow Rose of Texas. When the band played a waltz, Balanchine led Karin onto the floor. A spotlight was turned on them; no one else danced. "He barely got through the waltz," said Karin, "but it was unforgettable."

· · ·

WHEN he was not on one of his European trips, or filming in Nashville, Balanchine's life was passed in a very small area of the West Side of New York between his apartment on Sixty-seventh Street, the School and the theater. Many of his dancers lived in the same neighborhood; if they asked him to supper he had not far to go. For the most part he dined at one of the many restaurants that had sprung up in the now quite fashionable quarter.

Did it ever occur to him, as he sat dining and gossiping with Karin and Morton—or with Suzanne, for their friendship had been resumed—that his fame was greater than that of any choreographer who had ever lived? At any given moment of the day, the chances were that one of his ballets was being rehearsed or danced or written about somewhere in the world. Between 1978 and 1982 there had been productions of twenty-four of his ballets in seventeen countries on four continents. That is, of course, without reckoning performances by the New York City Ballet. Between 1960 and 1982 there had been twenty-eight different productions of *Apollo* in countries as far apart as Norway and Uruguay, Hungary and the United States. There had been thirty-nine productions of *Serenade* over the same period, as far north as Toronto, as far south as Australia, as far west as Seattle, as far east as Iran.

Balanchine was not interested in fame, nor did he covet honors. He refused many doctorates. A few may have been accepted for idiosyncratic reasons: from Brandeis University because the first School Workshop performances had taken place there; from the University of Cincinnati to please Suzanne. These and the doctorate of Fine Arts from Northwestern University date from 1967. In 1973 he received one from Columbia University. In 1970, Mayor John Lindsay gave him New York City's highest cultural award, the Handel Medallion; it was presented to him onstage after the premiere of *Who Cares?* In 1972, at the Whitney Museum, he received the New York State Award from Governor Rockefeller; and in 1975 the National Society of Arts and Letters presented him with its Distinguished Service Award. During his final illness, the Presidential Medal of Freedom, the highest American honor for civilians, was accepted on his behalf by Suzanne Farrell. The citation read: "The genius of George Balanchine has enriched the lives of all Americans who love the dance." In 1975 he became an Officer of the French Legion of Honor; in 1978 the king of Denmark made him a Knight of the Order of Dannebrog, First

Class; in 1980 the president of Austria awarded him the Austrian Medal for Learning and Art.

But Balanchine's real reward lay in the knowledge that he had improved the quality of dancing not only in America but in Europe and other parts of the world. In an interview with a Swiss reporter taped by Patricia Neary in Zurich in 1980, he humorously summed up one aspect of his achievement:

They say classical ballet is rejuvenated. It's not rejuvenated. It's new. I was brought up in old ballet: small men, small women with big heads, short necks, little mouths like Pola Negri in silent movie. Corps de ballet never danced. They were graded—nearer the public were better. . . . Classical ballet is not rejuvenated. It's new. Now the sound is better, technique is better. Like football, swimmers, boxing are better. We taught people. I have a lot of young people. Technique won't die.

Most of the new race of slim, swift, beautiful girls had, of course, learned their craft at Balanchine's own School of American Ballet.

One day in the seventies Suki Schorer's father, the writer Mark Schorer, remarked on a fine performance of *Symphony in C,* and Balanchine said, "Yes, it's the best that's ever been." Relating this to me, Suki added, "Of course, it got better afterwards." I asked her, "Do you think it made him happy to have achieved all that he set out to do?" "Oh, yes, I think so," she answered. "I remember once he came to the School a year before he was sick. I was teaching this variation from the *Minkus Pas de Trois.* He said, 'It's amazing. When I made this variation, only *one* person could do that turning step, and now the *whole class* is doing it.' "

Interviewed by McNeil Lowry in 1979, Balanchine had boasted, "The dancing is good now; I don't have to tell them anything. . . . I tell Rosemary when she says, 'Shall I put this girl there? What would you like to do?' 'No,' I say, 'just put anybody, because they're so good—anybody.' "

Chapter 15

• •

BALLET MASTER EMERITUS:

DECEMBER 1981-

APRIL 30, 1983

ONCE, when Balanchine was teaching *Apollo* to Suki Schorer, he explained to her, "It's like Greek frieze. Go and look at the vases in the Metropolitan." (Years later, she reminded him of this: "You used to tell me to go and look at the Greek vases. What good did it do me?" Balanchine answered, "But you married a Greek, dear"—which was true, if irrelevant.)

It would be fascinating to know more about Balanchine's reactions to painting and sculpture. A choreographer is a kind of sculptor and draftsman—even, because of his complex floor patterns, an architect—but he carves in perishable human bodies and draws on air. Nancy Lassalle remembers Balanchine taking her and Maria Tallchief to the Louvre in 1947, and John Taras is sure that a famous pose in *Serenade* was borrowed from Canova's *Cupid and Psyche.*

On the other hand, Boris Kochno, who was with Balanchine on his sightseeing excursions in Italy in the twenties, believed that, unlike Massine, Balanchine never derived ideas from the visual arts. Indeed, music was all he needed to start up the engine of his imagination. But at least one supreme work of art made its mark on him. Talking to me in 1977, he spoke of and mimed "the pointing fingers" of Michelangelo's Jehovah and Adam, "as big as this room—so great!"; and this symbol of God-given life is certainly echoed in *Apollo.* In later life, however, whenever Karin von Aroldingen asked him to go with her to a museum, he said, "I've seen all that."

■   ■   ■

WHEN, in December 1981, Britain's Royal Society of Arts awarded Lincoln Kirstein the Benjamin Franklin Gold Medal for his services to the arts, Balanchine insisted on accompanying him to the ceremony. The presentation took place at a dinner at the Royal Society's house, a block away from the Savoy Theatre where Kirstein had first made Balanchine's acquaintance in 1933. After this—as it turned out, last—visit to London, Balanchine flew to Zurich to see Patricia Neary's company, then spent Christmas with Karin and her family.

He was back in New York for New Year's Eve, and gave a little supper party at home. Barbara Horgan, who knew how his state of health could vary—he would be gray and almost speechless one day and sprightly the next—thought he looked extremely well. Yet as the days went on he was always tired and kept blaming it on jet lag. When the winter season ended on February 12, Barbara left for a week's vacation in Florida. Balanchine called her on the fifth day, and she was suddenly convinced that he was dying. He said, "When you get back, we are really going to find out what is the matter with me." Dr. Langner lined up ear and eye specialists, and on March 23, tests were made.

But there was still to be one more grand endeavor: the Stravinsky Centennial Celebration of 1982. Of the fifty-five works performed during the week of June 10–18, eleven were new; however, Balanchine needed help with his two big productions.

Noah and the Flood had been commissioned for television in 1962 and telecast by CBS with Balanchine's choreography and sets by Ter-Arutunian. It was possible to reconstruct the dances from the existing film. Even so, Balanchine was obliged to call in Jacques d'Amboise to help work on the choreography. Robert Craft, who had selected and arranged the text, conducted *Noah* on the second night of the festival.

Kermit Love designed *Perséphone,* and Balanchine conferred with him regularly during the first half of 1982. The Greek myth used by André Gide as a scenario for Stravinsky's melodrama, with its narrator, singers and dancers, was a parable of winter and spring. Balanchine told Love that he considered it a ceremony, which should be performed in a church. "I'd like to do it Russian, but we can't." The singers would be ranged on either side of the stage. Vera Zorina was not only to work with Balanchine on the production but to speak the words of Perséphone, while Karin von Aroldingen danced the role.

Alas, when it came to rehearsals, the choreographer was no longer in a condition to handle the complex task. It was known that his eyesight and balance were bad, but he now appeared to lack concentration, energy and even enthusiasm. As Zorina later pointed out, few people realized how ill he was. He could not hear the tenor, and the music hurt his ears. He was unable to finish the job, and Taras did his best to pull the ballet together. For Zorina, who had been so happy to work with Balanchine again, *Perséphone* was "a searing experience."

Balanchine had also devised a *Tango,* which was danced by Karin and Christopher d'Amboise at the gala first night of the festival. A new version of the last movement of *Variations for Orchestra*, danced solo, as before, by Suzanne Farrell, was not ready until two weeks after the festival ended, and it was clear to some members of the company that Farrell, who knew so well the workings of Balanchine's mind, was responsible for certain passages of dancing. Nevertheless, *Variations* was to be officially recorded as Balanchine's last ballet.

In Saratoga in July, Balanchine's giddiness was so bad that he could not go to the theater. Karin was again staying with the Leaches, so she and Kay Leach between them managed to look after him. Kay had her ankle in a cast, but when Karin went to the Performing Arts Center to rehearse or teach, Kay used to hobble over to the guesthouse and sit enchanted while Balanchine spoke of Russian history, Peter the Great, his own early life, and his wives. "I never left them," he invariably insisted. "They always left me."

Earlier in the year he had written the music for a popular song, "The World Is Turning Fast," with lyrics by Arthur Schwartz, and sold it to the music publisher Schirmer for $1,000. (It was dedicated to Karin.) That summer he sat for hours under the trees, writing more music and lyrics, then trying them out on the Leaches' piano. He told Kay, "I'm having such trouble with my balance and can't see well, so I think I'm going to change my career." Dick Leach guessed that Balanchine composed about forty minutes of music. He did not want to be useless. When he left Saratoga for the last time on July 25, he gave Kay the manuscript of one of his songs, written in pencil.

On August 16 he went into the hospital for three nights. A cataract was removed from his left eye and a soft lens inserted. He rested at home for a few weeks but soon grew bored. Throughout September he was seeing doctors. When he went with the company to Washington for their season at the Kennedy Center in October, he was taken ill and spent ten days in the hospital, where neurological tests were made. Back in New York he had an appointment with his dentist on October 25. After that day Barbara Horgan ceased to write in his engagement book.

With a nurse living in, it was hard to achieve any privacy in the Sixty-seventh Street apartment, and Balanchine resented this. Although Barbara, Eddie Bigelow, Karin and her husband were constantly in and out, cooking for him and taking care of him, there were days when he tried to do without the nurse and was left alone. This was dangerous, because he kept falling. Once he fell as he was going to answer the telephone; another time he blacked out and called Barbara, saying he did not know where he was. As she lived on West Fifty-sixth Street, she was at the apartment with Dr. Hamilton in a few minutes.

He had Karin and Morton to dinner one night and was proud to have cooked it himself. Suddenly Morton noticed a smell of burning coming from the bedroom. A candle on the altar in front of the icons had set fire to its plastic holder, and there was a blaze. Balanchine got up, fell and struck his head against a table. Karin and Morton put out the fire.

In Zurich Patricia Neary had a premonition and flew over to see him. Balanchine cooked roast beef for her and Barbara. At 7:30 he said, "I'm so tired. I think I'll go to bed." While the two women were cleaning up, Barbara told Patricia that this was usual. Next day, when Barbara and the nurse were both present, Balanchine fell again and cracked his ribs. Patricia found him terribly changed. He asked, "Was I like this yesterday?" She told him no. "Then," said Barbara, "he was very sweet. He said, 'You've done all you can and tried everything, but I shouldn't be here. My home is not a hospital.' I was very relieved." Dr. Hamilton admitted Balanchine to Roosevelt Hospital on November 4.

·   ·   ·

UNTIL his first heart attack, Balanchine had not made a will—perhaps, Barbara Horgan thought, because he suffered from the primitive superstition that to do so would hasten his death. Then, in 1978, he asked Barbara to find him a lawyer. She first consulted her own. She wanted someone who "would not scare George to death," yet she also knew his respect for men in authority such as priests or policemen; a bright young man would not do. She was introduced to Theodore Sysol, a quiet, pleasant, elderly gentleman who knew nothing about ballet, and brought him to see the convalescent Balanchine.

"What would happen if I died without making a will?" he asked.

"Have you any relations?"

"Yes, my brother Andrei, in Georgia."

"Then all you have would go to him."

Balanchine was fond of his brother but immediately had a vision of the Russian state seizing everything. He became—to use Barbara's expression—"apoplectic" and settled down to take the whole business seriously. He said, "I don't really have anything."

"You own this apartment?"

"Yes."

"You have a car?"

"Yes, a Mercedes." This with a touch of pride.

"A house in the country?"

"Yes."

Barbara made a list: two insurance policies; money in the bank; his share in Francis Mason's book. Then there were the ballets.

Balanchine pondered for a few weeks, telephoned Sysol and saw him alone. He bequeathed his apartment on Sixty-seventh Street to Karin, his Southampton condominium to Barbara and the money in the bank to Tanaquil Le Clercq. He left his brother two gold watches Kirstein had given him.

After he had struck a great many ballets off the list because he considered them uninteresting or impossible to revive, there were about a hundred left.

He had already made presents of a few works. He had given all rights of *Symphony in C* to Betty Cage, *A Midsummer Night's Dream* to Diana Adams, *Meditation* to Suzanne Farrell and *Duo Concertant* to Kay Mazzo. Now he bequeathed to Tanaquil Le Clercq the American rights of approximately eighty ballets, the remaining rights, media and foreign, to be divided between Karin and Barbara. All American and media rights to *Concerto Barocco* were to go to Lincoln Kirstein, for whose South American tour it had been made, as well as those of *Orpheus,* which Kirstein had asked Stravinsky to write. To Edward Bigelow he left the American and media rights of *The Four Temperaments* and *Ivesiana.*

Patricia McBride was to receive world rights to *Tarantella,* the Ravel *Pavane* and the Scriabin *Etude for Piano;* Suzanne Farrell to *Don Quixote* and *Tzigane;* Rosemary Dunleavy to *Le Tombeau de Couperin,* which she had remembered so well; Merrill Ashley to *Ballo della Regina;* Barbara Horgan to *Brahms-Schoenberg Quartet;* Karin von Aroldingen to *Serenade, Liebeslieder Walzer, Stravinsky Violin Concerto, Une Porte et un soupir, Vienna Waltzes* and *Kammermusik No. 2.*

．　．　．

ALTHOUGH Balanchine's malady was not diagnosed until after his death, when an autopsy revealed that he had suffered from the rare Creutzfeldt-Jakob Disease, it was clear that he was becoming increasingly feeble, and that his mind was deteriorating. During his first weeks in the hospital he sometimes telephoned the theater, even getting through to Kevin Tyler at his habitual post, downstage right, during a performance. Then, as his grip on the concerns of everyday life weakened, he asked only for Karin. Naturally, his friends in the company came often to see him. "What wonderful flowers!" Bill Hamilton exclaimed one day. "Yes," said Balanchine, "but flowers don't make you laugh." Hamilton thought he might be missing music and bought him a Sony Walkman. "What tapes shall I get you?" "Debussy perhaps, Poulenc . . ." "Would you like some Chopin?" "No, no, *no!*" Because of Balanchine's distorted hearing, music through earphones pained him, and the experiment was a disaster. One day Hamilton found him asleep. Then he opened his eyes and appeared to be looking into the distance. He said, "You know, I still hear pretty music, and I see people doing things. But you can't tell them, you have to show them."

Since the death of Felia Doubrovska in 1980, Balanchine had made friends with Father Adrian of the Cathedral of Our Lady of the Sign, who had conducted her funeral service. This Canadian-born priest had learned Russian and been converted to the Orthodox Church. He began to visit Balanchine in the hospital.

Russian-speaking visitors were, of course, particularly welcome, as Balanchine was always most at ease speaking his original tongue. Solomon Volkov came with his tape recorder to continue his talks about Tchaikovsky and St. Petersburg. Barbara Horgan wondered if these might not be troublesome to Balanchine, as he had known Volkov for so short a time; but when she put her head around the door one day while Volkov was in the room, she saw such an expression of happiness on Balanchine's face that she withdrew silently. Balanchine did not like the music of Shostakovich, whose pupil and friend Volkov had been, so he never referred to him at all. Volkov thought this showed tact and good manners.

For four years Leslie George Katz, Nancy Lassalle and Harvey Simmonds had been working to produce their monumental book, *Choreography by George Balanchine: A Catalogue of Works,* which many researchers had labored to perfect, and which was not only a hoard of information—some of it provided by Balanchine himself and his earliest collaborators—but also one of the most beautiful books of our day. On December 24, when Nancy brought Balanchine the first copy, which he was hardly able to read, he pointed to the lyre, based on Tchelitchev's design for *Orpheus and Eurydice,* which had been used as a decoration, and which was later carved on his tombstone.

.   .   .

I WAS in New York during January 1983. I had never considered myself a close friend of Balanchine's, and I could not make up my mind whether to visit him in the hospital or not. On January 15 I finally did go with John Taras, who told Balanchine, "I've brought Dicky Buckle to see you." I wondered if I would have been recognized without this cue. As it was, Balanchine opened his arms and exclaimed, "Dicky!" Never having embraced Balanchine in my life, I was taken aback, shook hands and regretted it later. I had with me a clipping from the sports page of a London newspaper about a horse named Balanchine winning a race. The choreographer pronounced his own name, perhaps reading the headline, folded the slip of paper and stuck it into the strap of his wristwatch. That afternoon at the State Theater I watched the Mozart *Divertimento No. 15* and thought no ballet could be more exquisite or better danced. (I had said the same of *Caracole,* arranged to the same music, in 1952.)

Indeed, Balanchine appeared to have worked with Mozart, as with other dead composers, like a twin who could read his brother's thoughts. I was particularly struck by one small instance of the close "collaboration." Although I could see there were more marvelous passages of choreography in the six Variations—and I thought how delightful it was that they succeeded one another so swiftly, almost overlapping—and in the Minuet, the moment that thrilled me most came with the appearance of a singularly beautiful melody in the finale. Here Balanchine's handling of Mozart was an illustration of "the marriage of true minds." In this Allegro Molto, Mozart flirts with his audience like a brilliant woman holding her lover in suspense. When the impatient jigging begins, we think, "This is it!" but we are wrong. Yet the moment of bliss is being heralded, for the horns respond to chords on the first violins like sentinels scanning the horizon and calling from tower to tower. Then, against a pulsating accompaniment, the A-flat major theme takes off for the stratosphere, and ecstasy is upon us. How does Balanchine convey the entry of this theme in visual terms? In the most elementary way. Three dancers—a boy between two girls, their crossed hands clasped—appear suddenly upstage. With a swinging step, they advance in a diagonal, smiling. It is like a rainbow.

That night, Rudolf Nureyev, recently appointed *maître de ballet* of the Paris Opéra, was seated beside me, and he, too, admired *Divertimento.* He asked after Balanchine. The next day or soon after, Dr. Hamilton opened the door of Balanchine's room to find Nureyev kneeling beside the bed, tears pouring down his face.

Baryshnikov thought Balanchine still retained his sense of smell, and he guessed that spicy Georgian cooking might tempt him. He knew of a Georgian restaurant in Brooklyn and more than once ordered a special meal from it—even including Georgian wine and an imported Georgian mineral water. He sent his limousine for it, then served it in the hospital room himself and shared it with Balanchine.

From all over the United States old friends and colleagues came to spend a few minutes with the master of all ballet masters. Ruthanna Boris called him: "I hear you're not very well." "I can't see properly, I can't work. There's nothing . . ." "Aren't there any pretty nurses?" "Oh that, maybe yes . . ." "I think I'll have to make a little journey."

She was in Seattle. When she arrived at the hospital, Balanchine had Karin with him. Ruthanna was wearing a gold Star of David on a chain around her neck, and he fingered it. She explained its significance, then, as he would not let it alone, she took it off and, with Karin, hung it round his neck. Karin left them together, and Balanchine went to sleep holding Ruthanna's hand.

Dr. Hamilton later admitted that his idea for a seventy-ninth birthday party for Balanchine on January 22 was a mistake. Anyway, as Karin pointed out, Balanchine had always cared less about his birthday than his name day. There were only twenty or so friends in the room, but for the sick man this was a crowd. Tables, plates and glasses were brought in. Karin had made seventy-nine *kotletki,* the way Balanchine had taught her, with a sauce of mushrooms and cream. Barbara Horgan, Edward Bigelow, Suzanne Farrell, Kay Mazzo, John Taras, Jacques d'Amboise and Lucia Davidova all came, bringing gifts, but the levity was strained, and the party did not last very long. Karin and Morton remained behind to clear up.

． ． ．

BECAUSE the New York City Ballet had become so huge an operation, the members of its board decided it must be given a new director. The pretense that Balanchine was "convalescing" could not be kept up indefinitely, and few believed that he would ever return to work. Orville Schell, the chairman, had visited him in Saratoga during July in the hope of asking him to appoint an heir, but Balanchine evaded the question, and Schell had been too shy to press the point. Peter Martins had also hoped, when he went to see Balanchine, that a successor might be named, but he, too, was disappointed. While the board probably considered that it would be better to have one man in charge, it was hard to pass over sixty-four-year-old Jerome Robbins, whose fame was widespread and whose ballets were needed by the company, in favor of thirty-six-year-old Peter Martins. But Robbins was unwilling to undertake administration. At a meeting on Tuesday, March 15, it was decided to appoint Martins and Robbins jointly as ballet masters in chief. Gillian Attfield, president of the board of directors, read a statement to the company, adding that Balanchine had been voted the new title of Ballet Master Emeritus, "to leave no doubt as to our love and respect."

"His place at the head of the greatest dance company in the world . . . has been taken over . . ." wrote Clive Barnes in the *Post*. "It is all but unthinkable," wrote *The New Yorker*'s "Talk of the Town," "that there will be no new Balanchine ballets." "End of the Balanchine Era" announced *Newsweek:* "It seems inconceivable."

Balanchine, however, was beyond knowing or caring. He listened for Karin's footsteps, which he could distinguish from those of all others. She sat with him, holding his hand, day after day. But his memory was so bad that he often called her soon after she left to ask, "When are you coming to see me?"

The last words Karin and Balanchine exchanged were on Sunday, April 24. She had brought her daughter Margo to visit him. As she left, Karin said, "I'll come and see you tomorrow. May I?" "Any time." Margo lingered behind and came out crying. The nurse ran after them to say that Balanchine had spoken Margo's name.

Darci Kistler was another of Balanchine's last visitors. "No one was allowed in," she told me. "And I threw such a fit. I said, 'It's unfair that the nurses should be allowed in and I'm not.' I threw such a fit that I did get in. And Mr. B. recognized me, and he listened to me." I was sure that this girl would have known exactly what to say to the dying choreographer, and I asked no further questions.

Balanchine died at about 4:00 A.M. on Saturday, April 30, 1983. Roosevelt Hospital informed Barbara Horgan, who telephoned Lincoln Kirstein, Karin, Peter Martins, John Taras, Rosemary Dunleavy and others. Peter called Karin to ask her if she could still dance in *Kammermusik* that afternoon, saying he was sure Balanchine would have wished her to. She agreed, but she was in such a state of shock that she later could remember nothing about the performance. The funeral was to be on Tuesday, May 3, at the Cathedral of Our Lady of the Sign, where Balanchine had attended Easter services, but according to the custom of the Russian Orthodox Church a *panikhida* (memorial service) was held daily until then.

Not only was the New York City Ballet performing at the State Theater, Ballet Theatre's season at the Metropolitan was to open on Sunday and Taras was rehearsing Balanchine's *Symphonie concertante* for them. Members of Nancy Lassalle's Advisory Council had also assembled from all over the United States for the annual Workshop performances of the School of American Ballet, the first of which was held on the day of Balanchine's death. Before the curtain rose on the matinee at the State Theater, before the School's performance at the Juilliard Theater in the evening, and again before the company's evening performance, Lincoln Kirstein, Peter Martins, Jerome Robbins and John Taras came out in front of the curtain, and Kirstein spoke a few words: "I don't have to tell you that Mr. B. is with Mozart and Tchaikovsky and Stravinsky. . . ." The first ballet at the evening performance was Mozart's *Divertimento No. 15*. The last was Bizet's *Symphony in C*, in which Peter Martins replaced Sean Lavery to dance the second movement with Suzanne Farrell.

Sunday's memorial service was to be at eight in the evening. Balanchine's body lay in an open coffin in the cathedral, with a ribbon across his forehead. Taras wrote:

I went at four and pinned the President's medal on his lapel and inserted the Legion of Honor rosette. Bigelow and Barbara had decided that the coffin should be as simple as possible. The one they chose was an Orthodox Jewish one, no metal. I ran out to get flowers for the top of the coffin. On a Sunday it was difficult, but I did find a florist and brought a spray of flowers before the evening service . . .

On the second [Monday] I arranged to have the body photographed. I had brought an antique cross to put in Balanchine's hands, and a crucifix that Doubrovska wanted to be buried with, but that was found only after her funeral. I put that in Balanchine's breast pocket and hoped he would pass it on. The service that day was at two and better attended, with television cameras and the press as well. . . . To the School performance at seven, where again we appeared before the curtain. Then I ran over to the opening night of Ballet Theatre at the Met. Misha came in front of the curtain in his Harlequin make-up to say a few words, and the orchestra played a short bit of *Symphonie concertante*. The moment they started, I stood up and was followed by the entire audience. On the third I was at the church at eight to rearrange the flowers. At last a blanket of white flowers [gardenias] arrived. . . . The service at eleven was very crowded and emotional.

When the mortal remains of Balanchine were borne down into the crowded courtyard of the cathedral, the actor Tom Lacy was standing near Lincoln Kirstein, whom he had never met, and he noticed:

As the coffin was carried out of the front door at the top of the high flight of stairs, it was jostled by the pallbearers. Suddenly that Mount Rushmore figure of Kirstein's began to quake. He sobbed mightily. It was moving to be near him, not knowing him, but aware of the fifty years that tied him and Balanchine together.

It was decided to bury Balanchine in Sag Harbor, a town he had admired, which was near his Southampton condominium. Tamara Geva, Alexandra Danilova, Maria Tallchief, Tanaquil Le Clercq, Allegra Kent, Suzanne Farrell, Karin von Aroldingen and Natalie Molostwoff were present to throw white roses into the grave.

Dr. Hamilton arrived late, and earth was already being shoveled. He found Suzanne Farrell alone beside the grave and saw her throw in a rose.

The duo-pianists Robert Fizdale and Arthur Gold, close friends of Balanchine who lived nearby, had, in true Balanchine tradition, prepared lunch for the mourners. "The food was delicious," wrote Taras. "Caviar, vodka, roast ham . . ."

Balanchine's death was announced in Sunday's *New York Times,* with a long summary of his career; in the *Washington Post,* London *Observer* and London *Sunday Times.* On Monday, May 2, the tributes began to appear throughout the United States and Europe. Edward I. Koch, mayor of New York, issued a statement: "New York City mourns the passing of George Balanchine, one of the greatest artists who has ever chosen to work and live in our city. Mr. Balanchine is the acknowledged master of ballet of the 20th century; his ballets are more widely performed throughout the world than those of any other choreographer. Mr. Balanchine loved our city. He lived in New York for 50 years and gave his company the city's name. In 1980, he devoted the proceeds of the New York City Ballet's opening night to the city to purchase bulletproof vests for police officers." There was more, and Kirstein was given due credit; but in five sentences the mayor had stated seven indisputable facts.

The headlines were international: "An Immortal Legacy"; "Mentor and Master: Dance World Mourns Balanchine"; "The Joy of Pure Movement"; *"La mort de 'Mister B' ";* *"Avec Balanchine disparait le chorégraphe du siècle";* *"Balanchine: le plus grand."* In *Newsweek,* Hubert Saal began his "Farewell to Ballet's Mr. B." on a light note: "George Balanchine deplored inflated reputations. 'Why must everyone be great?' he used to ask. 'Isn't "good" good enough? Everyone's overrated. Picasso's overrated. I'm overrated, even Jack Benny's overrated.' " But Saal ended his appreciation with a just summing-up of what the ballet master had achieved:

Balanchine's ballets can be seen as a paradigm of 20th century art. . . . Their speed and economy reflect the style and pace of the century. . . . By liberating dance from story, by restlessly experimenting, by combining old and new, Balanchine stands beside Picasso and Stravinsky. But while they worked in accepted and respected mediums, Balanchine practiced what was still a second-class art. His most awesome achievement was that he elevated ballet almost single-handedly from a place below the salt to a seat at the head of the table.

In *Commonweal,* Don McDonagh celebrated the freeing of ballet from drama. He too repeated a typical self-deprecatory saying of the master who liked to "move people to music": "He compared himself to a cook or a carpenter and eschewed the word 'create' in relation to his ballets. 'Only God creates, I assemble.' "

To another interviewer, Balanchine had said:

People say, "Oh, my God, what will happen when you go?" But everybody goes. . . . It wouldn't be any good fifty years from now to do what we do now. . . . Maybe we won't even need the technique. People will look different, they will move differently. You will ask how to preserve for posterity. I say, "Preserve what?" . . . Look at the old movies. Look at Pavlova . . . it's ridiculous.

And to yet another:

I don't want my ballets preserved as museum pieces for people to go and laugh at what used to be. *Absolutely not.* I'm staging ballets for today's bodies. Ballet is NOW.

Balanchine was to the dance in the twentieth century what Michelangelo had been to sculpture in the sixteenth, and it could be argued that in one short ballet by the greatest of choreographers there were more ingenious "sculptures" than the Florentine master carved in the course of his long life. Balanchine enriched the lives of many million Americans by showing them, in a way that not even baseball could show them, the divine possibilities of the human body. He raised their standard of living.

BIBLIOGRAPHY

ALLEN, W. E. D. *A History of the Georgian People.* London: Routledge & Kegan Paul, 1932.

D'AMBOISE, CHRISTOPHER. *Leap Year: A Year in the Life of a Dancer.* Garden City, New York: Doubleday, 1982.

ANDERSON, JACK. *The One and Only: The Ballet Russe de Monte Carlo.* Brooklyn, New York: Dance Horizons, 1981.

ASHLEY, MERRILL. *Dancing for Balanchine.* New York: Dutton, 1984.

BALANCHINE, GEORGE. *Balanchine's New Complete Stories of the Great Ballets.* Edited by Francis Mason. Garden City, New York: Doubleday, 1968.

BENTLEY, TONI. *Winter Season: A Dancer's Journal.* New York: Random House, 1982.

BUCKLE, RICHARD. *Diaghilev.* New York: Atheneum, 1979.

Choreography by Balanchine: A Catalogue of Works. New York: Eakins Press/Viking. Revised edition, 1984.

CHUJOY, ANATOLE. *The Dance Encyclopedia.* New York: Barnes, 1949.

———. *The New York City Ballet.* New York: Knopf, 1953.

CRAFT, ROBERT, ed. *Dearest Bubushkin: Selected Letters and Diaries of Vera and Igor Stravinsky.* (The correspondence of Vera and Igor Stravinsky, 1921–1954, with excerpts from Vera Stravinsky's diaries, 1922–1971. Translated by Lucia Davidova.) London: Thames & Hudson, 1985.

CROCE, ARLENE. *Going to the Dance.* New York: Knopf, 1982.

CRICHTON, RONALD. *Manuel de Falla: Descriptive Catalogue of His Works.* London: Chester/Wilhelm Hansen, 1976.

DANILOVA, ALEXANDRA. *Choura.* New York: Knopf, 1986.

DENBY, EDWIN. *Dancers, Buildings and People in the Streets.* New York: Horizon Press, 1965.

———. *Looking at the Dance.* New York: Horizon Press, 1949.

———. *Dance Writings.* Edited by Robert Cornfield and William Mackay. New York: Knopf, 1987.

DE VALOIS, NINETTE. *Invitation to the Ballet.* London: Bodley Head, 1937.

————. *Come Dance with Me: A Memoir, 1898–1956.* London: H. Hamilton, 1957.

DOLIN, ANTON. *Autobiography.* London: Oldbourne, 1960.

————. *Divertissement.* London: S. Low, Marston, 1931.

DUNNING, JENNIFER. *"But First a School": The First Fifty Years of the School of American Ballet.* New York: Elisabeth Sifton Books/Viking, 1985.

FOKINE, M. *Memoirs of a Ballet Master.* Edited by Anatole Chujoy, translated by Vitale Fokine. Boston: Little, Brown, 1960.

GEVA, TAMARA. *Split Seconds.* New York: Harper & Row, 1972.

GOLDNER, NANCY. *The Stravinsky Festival of the New York City Ballet.* New York: Eakins Press/Viking, 1973.

GRIGORIEV, S. L. *The Diaghilev Ballet, 1909–1929.* Translated and edited by Vera Bowen. London: Constable, 1973.

HASTINGS, BAIRD. *Choreographer and Composer.* Boston: Twayne, 1983.

HUCKENPAHLER, VICTORIA. *Ballerina: A Biography of Violette Verdy.* New York: Marcel Dekker, 1978.

JAMES, EDWARD. *Swans Reflecting Elephants: My Early Years.* Edited by George Melly. London: Weidenfeld, 1982.

KANIN, GARSON. *Hollywood.* New York: Viking, 1974.

KIRSTEIN, LINCOLN. *The New York City Ballet.* New York: Knopf, 1973.

————. *Thirty Years: Lincoln Kirstein's The New York City Ballet.* New York: Knopf, 1978.

————. *Ballet: Bias and Belief.* Brooklyn, New York: Dance Horizons, 1983.

Kobbé's Complete Opera Book. Revised and edited by the Earl of Harewood. London: Putnam, 1976.

KOCHNO, BORIS. *Diaghilev and the Ballets Russes.* Translated by Adrienne Foulke. New York: Harper & Row, 1970.

LE CLERCQ, TANAQUIL. *Mourka: The Autobiography of a Cat.* With photographs by Martha Swope. New York: Stein & Day, 1964.

LIFAR, SERGE. *Serge Diaghilev: His Life, His Work, His Legend. An Intimate Biography.* New York: Putnam, 1940.

————. *Ma Vie: From Kiev to Kiev.* Translated by James Holman Mason. London: Hutchinson, 1970. (The original French edition of *Ma Vie* was published in Paris in 1965.)

MCDONAGH, DON. *George Balanchine.* Boston: Twayne, 1983.

MAIORANO, ROBERT. *Worlds Apart.* New York: Coward, McCann & Geoghegan, 1980.

————, and VALERIE BROOKS. *Balanchine's* Mozartiana: *The Making of a Masterpiece.* New York: Freundlich Books, 1985.

MARKOVA, ALICIA. *Markova Remembers.* London: H. Hamilton, 1986.

MARSHALL, DAVID. *A Modern History of Georgia.* London: Weidenfeld, 1962.

MARTIN, RALPH G. *Lincoln Center for the Performing Arts.* Englewood Cliffs, New Jersey: Prentice-Hall, 1971.

MARTINS, PETER, with ROBERT CORNFIELD. *Far from Denmark.* Boston: Little, Brown, 1982.

MAZO, JOSEPH H. *Dance Is a Contact Sport: A Season with the New York City Ballet.* New York: Saturday Review Press/Dutton, 1974.

MOORE, LILLIAN. *Echoes of American Ballet.* Edited and with an introduction by Ivor Guest. Brooklyn, New York: Dance Horizons, 1976.

NABOKOV, NICOLAS. *Old Friends and New Music.* Boston: Little, Brown, 1951.

———. *Bagazh: Memoirs of a Cosmopolitan.* New York: Atheneum, 1975.

NEWMAN, BARBARA. *Striking a Balance: Dancers Talk about Dancing.* Boston: Houghton Mifflin, 1982.

NIKITINA, ALICE. *Nikitina by Herself.* Translated by Baroness Budberg. London: Allen Wingate, 1959.

PAYNE, CHARLES. *American Ballet Theatre.* New York: Knopf, 1978.

Portrait of Mr. B. Photographs of George Balanchine, with an Essay by Lincoln Kirstein. New York: Ballet Society/Viking, 1984.

REYNOLDS, NANCY. *Repertory in Review: Forty Years of the New York City Ballet.* New York: Dial, 1977.

ROSLAVLEVA, NATALIA. *Era of the Russian Ballet, 1770–1965.* New York: Dutton, 1966.

SEROV, VICTOR. *Serge Prokofiev.* New York: Reader's Digest, 1968.

SIMMONDS, HARVEY, and LOUIS H. SILVERSTEIN, compilers; NANCY LASSALLE, ed. *Lincoln Kirstein: The Published Writings, 1922–1977.* New Haven: Yale University Library, 1978.

SLONIMSKY, YURI. "Balanchine: The Early Years," translated by John Andrews, edited by Francis Mason. *Ballet Review,* Vol. 5, No. 3 (Winter 1975–76).

SOKOLOVA, LYDIA. *Dancing for Diaghilev.* Edited by Richard Buckle. New York: Macmillan, 1961.

STRAVINSKY, IGOR. *Selected Correspondence, Volume I.* Edited and with commentaries by Robert Craft. New York: Knopf, 1982.

———. *Selected Correspondence, Volume II.* Edited and with commentaries by Robert Craft. New York: Knopf, 1984.

———, and ROBERT CRAFT. *Conversations with Igor Stravinsky.* Garden City, New York: Doubleday, 1959.

———. *Memories and Commentaries.* Garden City, New York: Doubleday, 1960.

———. *Expositions and Developments.* Garden City, New York: Doubelday, 1962.

———. *Dialogues and a Diary.* Garden City, New York: Doubleday, 1963.

STRAVINSKY, VERA, and ROBERT CRAFT. *Stravinsky in Pictures and Documents.* New York: Simon and Schuster, 1978.

TANSMAN, ALEXANDRE. *Igor Stravinsky.* Paris: Amiot-Dumont, 1948.

TAPER, BERNARD. *Balanchine.* New York: Times Books. Revised edition, 1984.

TRACY, ROBERT, with SHARON DELANO. *Balanchine's Ballerinas: Conversations with the Muses*. New York: Linden Press/Simon and Schuster, 1983.

TWYSDEN, A. E. *Alexandra Danilova*. London: Beaumont, 1945.

VOLKOV, SOLOMON. *Balanchine's Tchaikovsky*. Translated by Antonina W. Bouis. New York: Simon and Schuster, 1985.

WALKER, KATHRINE SORLEY. *De Basil's Ballets Russes*. London: Hutchinson, 1982.

WARBURG, EDWARD M. M. *As I Recall*. Clifton, New Jersey: Cameo Printing Co., n.d. (Privately printed edition limited to two hundred copies.)

WHITE, ERIC WALTER. *Stravinsky: The Composer and His Works*. Berkeley and Los Angeles: University of California Press. Second edition, 1979.

WILSON, G. B. L. *A Dictionary of Ballet*. London: Black. Third edition, 1974.

ZORINA, VERA. *Zorina*. New York: Farrar, Straus & Giroux, 1986.

SOURCE NOTES

A distinction has been made between interviews, which were taped, and conversations, which were not. The date or approximate date of each is included in the list below. Unless otherwise stated, it took place in New York City.

ADAMS, DIANA. Interview with J. Taras, July 17 (Saratoga, N.Y.), 1984.

AROLDINGEN, KARIN VON. Interviews with R. B., June 2 and December 9, 1985.

ASHLEY, MERRILL. Interview with R. B., November 29, 1985.

BALANCHIVADZE, ANDREI M. Interviews with Kyril Fitzlyon and R. B., October 19 and 20 (Tbilisi), 1986.

BARYSHNIKOV, MIKHAIL. Conversation with R. B., December 27 (London), 1986.

BIGELOW, EDWARD. Conversation with R. B., December 7, 1983.

BOELZNER, GORDON. Interview with J. Taras and R. B., June 11, 1984; conversations with R. B., December 4, 1984; May 15 and December 2, 1985.

BOLENDER, TODD. Interview with J. Taras and R. B., June 14, 1984; conversation with R. B., May 31, 1985.

BORIS, RUTHANNA. Interview with R. B., December 3, 1985.

BROWN, VIDA. Interview with J. Taras, March 5 (Washington, D. C.), 1984.

CACCIALANZA, GISELLA. *See* CHRISTENSEN.

CAGE, BETTY. Many conversations with J. Taras and R. B., and with R. B. alone, 1983–1987.

CHRISTENSEN, LEW, and GISELLA CACCIALANZA. Interviews with J. Taras, August 6 (San Francisco), 1984.

DANILOVA, ALEXANDRA. Many conversations with J. Taras and R. B., and with R. B. alone, 1977 and 1983–1987.

DAVIDOVA, LUCIA. Interview with J. Taras and R. B., December 9, 1983; several conversations with J. Taras and R. B., and with R. B. alone, 1984–1986.

DONALDSON, VIRGINIA. Conversation with R. B., November 26, 1985.

DUELL, DANIEL. Interview with W. Lawson, July 17 (Saratoga, N. Y.), 1985.

DUNLEAVY, ROSEMARY. Interviews with R. B., June 1 and 8 and November 30, 1985.

FARRELL, SUZANNE. Conversation with R. B., August 29 (London), 1983.

FRANKLIN, FREDERIC. Interview with R. B., May 31, 1985.

GEVA, TAMARA. Many conversations with R. B., 1977 and 1983–1985.

GOLDNER, NANCY. Conversation with R. B., November 27, 1985.

HAMILTON, DR. WILLIAM. Conversation with R. B., December 12, 1985.

HIDEN, GEORGIA. Conversations with J. Taras and R. B., May 31 and June 6, 1984.

HORGAN, BARBARA. Conversations with R. B., August 26 (London), 1983, and New York, May 16, 1985. Interviews with R. B., December 2 and 12, 1985.

IRVING, ROBERT. Conversations with R. B., 1983–1986. Interview with William Lawson, July 16 (Saratoga, N.Y.), 1986.

JASINSKY, ROMAN. Interview with J. Taras and R. B., May 15, 1984.

KAI, UNA. Interview with J. Taras, June 24, 1984.

KISTLER, DARCI. Interview with R. B., November 24, 1986.

KOCHNO, BORIS. Interviews with J. Taras and R. B., September 29 and 30 (Paris), 1983. Conversations with R. B., October 16 and 18 (Paris), 1984.

KRONSTAM, HENNING. Interview with J. Taras, April 13 (Copenhagen), 1984.

LASSALLE, NANCY. Interview with R. B., December 4, 1985. Many conversations with R. B., 1983–1987.

LAVERY, SEAN. Interview with W. Lawson, July 16 (Saratoga, N.Y.), 1985. Interview with R. B., December 1, 1985. Interview with T. Lacy, April 17, 1986.

LEACH, RICHARD and KAY. Interview with R. B., December 8, 1985.

LOVE, KERMIT. Conversation with R. B., December 12, 1985.

LÜDERS, ADAM. Interview with R. B., December 11, 1985.

MCBRIDE, PAT. Interview and conversation with R. B., November 23, 1986.

MCBRIDE, PATRICIA. Interview with R. B., June 9, 1985.

MARKOVA, ALICIA. Interview with J. Taras, September 3 (London), 1983. Telephone conversation with R. B., October 9, 1983.

MAZZO, KAY. Interviews with R. B., June 6 and December 6, 1985.

MOLOSTWOFF, NATALIE. Interview with J. Taras and R. B., October 12, 1983; interview with R. B., June 3, 1985. Many conversations with J. Taras and R. B., 1983–1987.

MONCION, FRANCISCO. Interview with J. Taras, July 11 (Saratoga, N.Y.), 1984.

NABOKOFF, NATALIE (*i.e.*, NATALIE NABOKOV). Interview with J. Taras and R. B., June 13, 1984.

NABOKOV, DOMINIQUE. Conversation with J. Taras and R. B., June 5, 1984.

NEARY, PATRICIA. Interview with Balanchine and a Swiss journalist, April 14 (Zurich), 1980. Telephone conversations with R. B., February 19 (England), 1986; April 15 (Milan–England), 1986.

NUREYEV, RUDOLF. Conversations with R. B., January 15 (New York) and September 30 (Paris), 1983.

O'BRIEN, SHAUN. Interview with W. Lawson, July 17 (Saratoga), 1985.

REED, JANET. Interview with J. Taras, October 10, 1983.

REIMAN, ELISE. Interview with J. Taras and R. B., December 19, 1983. Many conversations with R. B., 1983–1987.

RIETI, VITTORIO. Interviews with J. Taras and R. B., November 26, 1983.

SANDBACH, ROBERT. Conversation with J. Taras and R. B., December 9, 1983.

SCHAUFUSS, PETER. Conversation with R. B., November 15 (London), 1986.

SCHORER, SUKI. Interview with R. B., December 10, 1985.

SOTO, JOCK. Interview with W. Lawson, July 17 (Saratoga, N.Y.), 1985.

STRAVINSKY, VERA. Conversation with R. B., May 11, 1977.

TALLCHIEF, MARIA. Interviews with J. Taras and R. B., June 7 and 8 (Chicago), 1984.

TER-ARUTUNIAN, ROUBEN. Interview with R. B., November 30, 1985; many conversations with R. B., 1983–1986.

TOBIAS, ROY. Interview with J. Taras, November (Tokyo), 1984.

TOUMANOVA, TAMARA. Interviews with J. Taras, August 1, 2, 3 (Hollywood), 1983.

TYLER, KEVIN. Interview with R. B., June 9, 1985.

VAZQUEZ, ROLAND. Interview with W. Lawson, July 15 (Saratoga, N.Y.), 1985.

VERDY, VIOLETTE. Interview with W. Lawson, July 29, 1985.

VILLELLA, EDWARD. Interview with R. B., November 30, 1985.

VOLKOV, SOLOMON. Conversation with R. B., December 3, 1986.

ZORINA, VERA. Conversation with J. Taras and R. B., May 22, 1984; conversations with R. B., November 30 and December 6, 1984.

1. A GEORGIAN IN ST. PETERSBURG: 1904–1924

p. 5: *bishop of Kutaisi.:* A. M. Balanchivadze interview.

p. 5: *in 1897.:* New Grove Encyclopedia of Music, p. 57; Great Soviet Encyclopedia, p. 577.

p. 5: *one quarter German.:* A. M. Balanchivadze interview.

p. 5: *Kirochnaya Street: Ibid.*

p. 6: *Glinka's letters.:* The edition was published to celebrate the fiftieth anniversary of Glinka's death. The editor, Nicolai Findeizen, wrote in his preface that the book was due to "the initiative of the well-known Georgian musical figure, M. A. Balanchivadze . . ."; and added that "the esteemed M. A. Balanchivadze made publication possible." (Information kindly provided by Dr. David Brown, University of Southampton [England].)

p. 6: *allowed to keep his house . . . :* A. M. Balanchivadze interview.

p. 6: *angel-like delicacy.:* Solomon Volkov, *Balanchine's Tchaikovsky*, p. 46.

p. 6: *wonderful cook . . . :* S. Volkov, p. 91.

p. 7: *tears to his eyes.:* Bernard Taper, *Balanchine,* p. 31. I repeated this story to A. M. Balanchivadze, who said, "It's possible."

p. 7: *would see him crying.:* A. M. Balanchivadze interview.

p. 7: *Andrei a composer.: Ibid.*

p. 7: *on the piano.: Ibid.*

p. 8: *sister and brother were accepted . . . :* B. Taper, p. 37.

p. 8: *he was discovered.:* A. M. Balanchivadze interview.

p. 9: *". . . play the piano.":* S. Volkov, p. 42.

p. 9: *. . . and Pinkerton.: Ibid.,* pp. 42, 43.

p. 10: *Hop o' My Thumb.:* A. Danilova, letter to R. B., February 24, 1985. She wrote that the boys from the school appeared "in the entourage of Carabos [*sic*]" and also in "the seven brothers."

p. 10: *was determined.:* B. Taper, pp. 38, 39.

p. 10: *Marius followed him.:* Lillian Moore, *Echoes of American Ballet.*

p. 11: *of consumption.:* S. Volkov, p. 64.

p. 11: *". . . in* The Nutcracker.": *Ibid.,* p. 56.

p. 11: *". . . the Maryinsky.": Ibid.,* p. 64.

p. 11: *". . . miss a thing.":* B. Taper, p. 40.

p. 11: *Alexandra Danilova:* A. Danilova, *Choura,* p. 43.

p. 12: *"Liszt's* Préludes.": S. Volkov, p. 162.

p. 12: *occupied by the army.:* B. Taper, p. 47.

p. 12: *in Petrograd:* A. M. Balanchivadze interview.

p. 13: *loving Georgi and Andrei:* Letter in the possession of A. M. Balanchivadze, translated by Kyril Fitzlyon.

p. 13: *finally a priest.:* A. M. Balanchivadze interview.

p. 13: *on the Neva.:* B. Taper, p. 47.

p. 13: *skinned them, . . . :* A. M. Balanchivadze interview.

p. 14: *". . . one after the other.":* S. Volkov, p. 68.

p. 14: *boys' quarters. . . . :* B. Taper, p. 50. He quotes the letter Vera Kostrovitskaya wrote him.

p. 14: *". . . serious for his years.":* A. Danilova, p. 42.

p. 15: *lent him books.: Ibid.,* p. 43.

p. 15: *at the Conservatory.: Ibid.*

p. 15: *something else. . . . : Ibid.,* p. 44.

p. 16: *". . . take it seriously.": Ibid.,* p. 49.

p. 16: *". . . for ballet rehearsal.":* S. Volkov, p. 57.

p. 16: *Saint-Saëns.:* Mikhail Mikhailov, "My Classmate: George Balanchivadze." Extracts from *Life in Ballet,* ed. D. I. Zolotinsky: Leningrad & Moscow: Iskusstvo, 1966, published in *Dance News,* March and April 1967.

p. 16: *spit blood:* A. M. Balanchivadze interview.

p. 17: *pas de deux from* Swan Lake.: M. Mikhailov, *op. cit.*

p. 17: *Danilova, among others:* A. Danilova, letter to R. B.

p. 17: *demi-caractère performer.:* A. Danilova, letter to R. B., February 24, 1985.

p. 18: *his horizons.:* A. Danilova, p. 58.

p. 18: *State Theater disapproved . . . :* T. Geva's comment written to R. B. on an early draft of this chapter.

p. 18: *velvet gowns and earrings.:* Told to Lincoln Kirstein by Kyra Blanc, who had a school in Moscow. From Kirstein's unpublished diary, July 8, 1934.

p. 18: *"plastic.":* G. B. conversations with R. B.

p. 18: *180 degrees.:* The information about Goleizovsky's influence on Balanchine is from J. Taras.

p. 18: *in 1922:* Yuri Slonimsky, "Balanchine: The Early Years," p. 42.

p. 18: *kneeling or recumbent.:* Illustration reproduced in N. Roslavleva, facing p. 192.

p. 19: *"hissing and applause":* Ibid., p. 202.

p. 19: *never repeated.: Ibid.*

p. 19: *hair long.:* Photograph in B. Taper, p. 63. Balanchivadze is clearly wearing black eye make-up.

p. 19: *black shirt.:* Aileen Elizabeth Twysden, *Alexandra Danilova,* pp. 46, 47. Also Danilova conversation with J. Taras and R. B.

p. 19: *Diaghilev Ballet.:* A. Danilova, letter to R. B., March 25, 1985.

p. 20: *". . . poet and general.":* Tamara Geva, *Split Seconds,* p. 272.

p. 20: *became friends.: Ibid.,* pp. 270, 272, 277–79.

p. 20: *he was ill.:* T. Geva's comment, written on an early draft of this chapter.

p. 20: *never stood up for her.:* T. Geva, p. 285.

p. 20: *never saw her again.:* A. M. Balanchivadze interview.

p. 20: Marche funèbre.: *Choreography* quotes Balanchine's recollection.

p. 21: *". . . arms extended . . .":* Kostrovitskaya quoted in Y. Slonimsky, p. 50.

p. 21: *Vsevolod Meyerhold.:* Y. Slonimsky, p. 52.

p. 21: *played by Meyerhold.:* M. Fokine, *Memoirs of a Ballet Master,* p. 136 and fn.

p. 21: *music alone:* S. Volkov, p. 163.

p. 22: *friend of Georgi's father . . . :* T. Geva, p. 247.

p. 22: *from Kutaisi.:* A. M. Balanchivadze interview.

p. 22: *held out his arms.:* T. Geva, pp. 287–89.

p. 22: *". . . on our own.":* S. Volkov, p. 59.

p. 22: *black eyeshadow.:* T. Geva, pp. 295–96.

p. 22: *"I was.":* A. Danilova, letter to R. B., March 25, 1985.

p. 23: *"completely impassive.":* T. Geva, pp. 295–96.

p. 23: *". . . much about it.": Ibid.,* p. 305.

p. 23: *last act . . . :* First performed September 15, 1923. The Mikhailovsky Theater was later called the Maly Opera Theater, and the Eakins Press *Choreography* refers to it by that name.

p. 24: *to the audience.:* Y. Slonimsky, p. 59.

p. 24: *at the Theater School.:* A. Danilova, p. 63.

p. 24: *in Western Europe.:* S. Volkov, pp. 214, 215.

p. 24: *in 1922 . . . :* A. Danilova, conversation with R. B., 1983. She said that she and G. B. had known Dmitriev a year or two before they left Russia.

p. 25: *"sawn-off fingers. ":* N. Molostwoff conversations.

p. 25: *nature of the agreement.:* A copy of the contract was preserved by G. B. Translation by Nathalie Gleboff.

p. 26: *fake an accident.:* S. Volkov, pp. 146, 147.

p. 26: *rammed her.:* T. Geva, pp. 310–19.

p. 26: *". . . as Tamara described. ":* A. Danilova letter, to R.B.

p. 26: *commissar of the State Theater.:* A. Danilova, p. 61.

2. IN WESTERN EUROPE: SUMMER 1924–WINTER 1932

p. 27: *a recital.:* Information supplied by Tamara Geva after reading an early draft of this chapter.

p. 28: *November 1.:* A copy of this document was preserved by Balanchine.

p. 28: *"Lousy music. ":* A. Danilova, pp. 64, 65.

p. 28: *four weeks:* Programs in the Theatre Museum, London.

p. 28: *Fyodor Lopoukhov.:* A.E. Twysden, p. 53.

p. 28: *April 3, 1925.:* A copy was preserved by Balanchine.

p. 28: *rue du Pont-Neuf:* G.B. conversations with R.B.

p. 29: *taught her:* A.E. Twysden, p. 55.

p. 29: *of the group or none.:* G.B. conversations with R.B.

p. 29: *funds for all of them.:* A. Danilova, p. 67.

p. 30: *' Letter follows . . . ':* Telegram in Stravinsky-Diaghilev Foundation, New York.

p. 30: *to leave Russia.:* G.B. conversations with R.B.

p. 31: Children's Tales: Programs in the Theatre Museum, London.

p. 32: *less than indifferent . . .:* Ninette de Valois, *Come Dance with Me*, p. 68. (In "A Conversation with Alexandra Danilova," *Ballet Review*, Vol. 4, No. 4, p. 40, Danilova said, "He was excellent dancer, very able. I was always amused that Ninette de Valois never want to give him credit.")

p. 32: *new choreographer . . .:* Ibid., p. 68.

p. 32: *George Balanchin.:* Program in the Theatre Museum, London.

p. 33: *"imaginative facility. . . .":* De Valois, p. 68.

p. 33: *for the rehearsals.:* Although the Addenda to the Eakins Press *Choreography* states that *L'Enfant* was not choreographed by Balanchine, both Danilova and Markova distinctly remember working on it and being rehearsed by him.

p. 33: *watch his rehearsals.:* G.B. conversations with R.B.

p. 33: *by trifles.:* B. Kochno interview.

p. 34: *". . . sure of yourself!":* G.B. conversations with R.B.

p. 34: *from Marks to Markova.:* A. Markova interview with John Taras and subsequent telephone conversations with R.B.

p. 34: *soprano voice.:* G.B. conversations with R.B.

p. 34: *a rabbit: Ibid.*

p. 34: *come out right.:* A. Markova interview.

p. 35: *nothing to do with him.:* B. Kochno, "Balanchine: "L'Apesanteur et la grâce," interview in *Le Nouvel Observateur,* September 23–29, 1983.

p. 35: *leggings in class.:* A. Danilova, p. 73.

p. 35: *back again.:* G.B. conversations with R.B.

p. 35: *first night of* Rossignol: The first performance of Balanchine's version of *Le Chant du rossignol* is always recorded by historians as taking place in Paris on June 17, 1925, but see B. Kochno, pp. 141–144.

p. 36: *". . . understood orchestration.":* Ibid.

p. 36: *a Spanish marquis.:* T. Geva, pp. 344 *et seq.* Tamara Geva confuses the story slightly by having the Diaghilev Ballet go to Barcelona in 1926 instead of 1925.

p. 36: *her address . . .:* G. B., letter from Paris to Diaghilev in Italy, September 15, 1925. Dance Collection, Library and Museum of the Performing Arts, Lincoln Center, New York.

p. 37: *". . . aloud and throughout.":* Remark by T. Geva during a symposium on June 11, 1983. Transcript in *Ballet Review,* Vol. 11, No. 4.

p. 38: *likely backer.:* Richard Buckle, *Diaghilev,* p. 463.

p. 38: *support her properly.:* Lydia Sokolova, ed. R.B., *Dancing for Diaghilev,* p. 244.

p. 38: *". . . were everything.":* G.B. conversations with R.B.

p. 38: *"messy" libretto: Ibid.*

p. 38: *until 1929.:* Beecham's opinion is given in a letter of Lady Cunard's to Diaghilev, now in the Dance Collection, Library and Museum of the Performing Arts, Lincoln Center, New York. Newman's review was in the *Sunday Times* (London), September 4, 1926.

p. 39: *". . . throw it away.":* G.B. conversations with R.B.

p. 39: *". . . great and complete.":* Ibid.

p. 39: *Italian art?:* B. Kochno interview.

p. 39: *on September 14 . . . :* Telegram in Stravinsky-Diaghilev Foundation, New York.

p. 40: *". . . blustering confidence.":* Cyril Beaumont, *Bookseller at the Ballet* (London: C. W. Beaumont, 1975), pp. 351, 352.

p. 40: *". . . white dress . . .":* A. Danilova, p. 82.

p. 40: *would not tell her.:* Ibid.

p. 41: *"It suits you.":* Ibid., pp. 84, 85.

p. 41: *passage of dancing . . . :* G.B. conversations with R.B.

p. 41: *several companies.:* J. Taras's comment.

p. 42: *". . . time to rest.":* Dale Harris, "Balanchine on Stravinsky," *Keynote,* June 1982, p. 19.

p. 42: *a new work.:* B. Kochno conversations with R.B.

p. 42: *"Congratulations!":* G.B. conversations with R.B.

p. 42: *". . . turn very well.":* Ibid.

p. 42: *". . . don't think.":* Ibid.

p. 42: *including herself.:* A. Danilova conversation with R.B.

p. 43: *"clap her hands.":* G.B. letter to Diaghilev, September 28, 1927. Dance Collection, Library and Museum of the Performing Arts, Lincoln Center, New York.

p. 43: *". . . easy at first.":* G.B. letter to Diaghilev, undated. Dance Collection.

p. 43: *first time:* Stravinsky, telegram to Diaghilev, January 22, 1928. Stravinsky-Diaghilev Foundation, New York.

p. 43: *on Danilova.:* A. Danilova conversation with R.B.

p. 44: *"almost a joke.":* G. B. conversations with R.B.

p. 44: *"undanceable.":* Ibid.

p. 44: *discuss projects:* A. Danilova, p. 83.

p. 45: *classical ballet step.:* The account of *Apollon* is an extract from a much longer one by John Taras. Gordon Boelzner also contributed.

p. 45: *Piccadilly Circus.:* Told by Balanchine to J. Taras.

p. 46: *". . . father calling.":* G. Boelzner's recollection.

p. 46: *immediately after it):* The Mask, Vol. XV, No. 2, reprinted *Rood, Dance Horizons,* 1977.

p. 47: *"not much with him.":* The *Times* (London), June 26, 1928.

p. 47: *to cut it.:* A. Danilova, p. 98.

p. 47: *" '. . . no good.' ":* G.B. conversations with R.B.

p. 47: *turned out for the best.:* A. Danilova, p. 98.

p. 47: *to Monte Carlo.:* Beecham telegraphed from London to Diaghilev in Monte Carlo, April 30, 1928: "Handel music dispatched today." Stravinsky-Diaghilev Foundation, New York.

p. 47: *". . . pastoral allegories.":* B. Kochno, *Serge Diaghilev,* p. 268.

p. 47: *". . . bread and butter.":* A. Danilova conversation with R.B.

p. 48: *divorced Kniaseff.:* Kochno archives. This and other letters to Boris Kochno were translated from Russian into French by M. Kochno on October 15, 1984, and later from French into English by R.B.

p. 48: *"4,000 [francs].":* Telegram from Diaghilev in Berlin to Grigoriev in Paris, October 10, 1928. Stravinsky-Diaghilev Foundation, New York.

p. 48: *was unsuccessful.:* A. Danilova, p. 85.

p. 48: *". . . names on poster.":* Telegram, dated October 12, 1928, in Stravinsky-Diaghilev Foundation, New York.

p. 48: *Le Bal.:* B. Kochno conversations with R.B.

p. 49: *". . . such a fool.":* G.B. conversations with R.B.

p. 49: *". . . last few years."*: *Morning Post* (London), July 9, 1929.

p. 49: *dramatize it.*: S. Lifar, *Diaghilev*, p. 498.

p. 50: *". . . a thing about ballet . . ."*: S. Volkov, p. 210.

p. 50: *was his.*: G.B. interview with Nancy Reynolds, reported by her in *Repertory in Review*, p. 106 fn.

p. 51: *"hang onto that."*: A. Danilova, p. 89.

p. 51: *". . . were crying."*: S. Lifar, *Serge Diaghilev*, p. 582.

p. 52: *generous Balanchine.*: G.B. conversations with R.B.

p. 52: *went away.*: John Gruen, "An Olympian Apollo," *Dance Magazine*, April 1981, p. 86.

p. 52: Aurora's Wedding . . .: The *Times* (London), July 13, 1929.

p. 52: *London season:* A. Danilova, p. 106, places Diaghilev's farewell in Vichy, but this is surely wrong. See R. Buckle, *Diaghilev,* pp. 533–35.

p. 52: *in his life.*: G.B. conversations with R.B.

p. 53: *Dolin and himself.*: *Dark Red Roses* was thought to be lost, but in 1984, during research for *Balanchine,* the two-part WNET/"Dance in America" program, Merrill Brockway, Judy Kinberg and Holly Brubach heard that a nitrate print of the old movie had been found in a farmhouse in Ireland. See Holly Brubach, "In Search of Balanchine," *Ballet News,* June 1984, p. 45.

p. 53: *front page.*: Anton Dolin, *Divertissement*, p. 214.

p. 53: *". . . took me to Florence . . ."*: G.B. interview with W. McNeil Lowry, 1979, published after G.B.'s death in *The New Yorker,* September 12, 1983, p. 53.

p. 53: *"Ummm."*: *Ibid.*, p. 52.

p. 54: *returned to Paris.*: A. Danilova conversation with R.B.

p. 55: *never forget it.*: A. Danilova conversation with R.B.

p. 56: *Duke of Kent).*: G.B. conversations with R.B.

p. 56: *visa extended.*: *Ibid.*

p. 57: *wishes to Bébé [Bérard].*: B. Kochno archives. "Bébé" was Christian Bérard, the stage designer.

p. 57: *". . . doesn't love me."*: A. Danilova, p. 110.

p. 58: *Yours, G.B.*: B. Kochno archives. The Alhambra was not, in fact, to close down as soon as Balanchine believed.

p. 60: *G. Balanchivadze:* B. Kochno archives.

3. HOW KIRSTEIN BROUGHT BALANCHINE TO AMERICA: JUNE–DECEMBER 1933

p. 61: *his troubled republic.*: When no source is given for the notes in this chapter, it can be assumed that information or reported conversations are taken from Lincoln Kirstein's unpublished diary for 1933, which he offered to R. B.

p. 62: *the Civil War.:* Facts supplied to R. B. by Lincoln Kirstein in a letter of July 30, 1983.

p. 62: *undertakings were begun.:* Information given by E. M. M. Warburg.

p. 62: *"audience for dancers":* Hound & Horn, Vol. IV, No. 4, 1931.

p. 63: *be its director.:* E. M. M. Warburg information.

p. 63: *and ungrateful.:* L. Kirstein, *Thirty Years,* p. 14.

p. 66: *". . . Igor Schwezoff":* (1904–82). Dancer, choreographer, teacher. Author of the autobiography *Borzoi* (published in England in 1935, issued in the U.S. [Harper, 1936] under the title *Russian Somersault*).

p. 66: *landed like a cat.:* R. Jasinsky interview.

p. 66: *Kirk Askew:* A partner in the firm of Durlacher. Askew was Tchelitchev's dealer in America.

p. 68: *he was homosexual.:* E. James, pp. 145, 154.

p. 69: *". . . 3 years time. . . .":* Letter in the Wadsworth Atheneum Museum archives, Hartford, Connecticut.

p. 70: *there were none.:* B. Kochno conversation.

p. 71: *back and forth:* These cables were preserved in the School of American Ballet.

p. 74: NOVEMBER FIFTEENTH.: In fact, they opened in New York on December 21.

p. 75: *. . . "a stone in my heart.":* T. Toumanova interview.

p. 75: *two months later.):* R. Jasinsky interview.

p. 79: *". . . ruins here already!":* E. M. M. Warburg letter, August 11, 1987.

4. THE SCHOOL ESTABLISHED—FIRST SKETCH FOR A COMPANY:
JANUARY 1934–APRIL 1937

p. 84: *School of American Ballet.:* Unless otherwise stated, material in this chapter comes from Lincoln Kirstein's diary for 1934.

p. 85: *properly conducted.:* N. Molostwoff interview.

p. 85: *tall dancers.:* E. Reiman interview.

p. 86: *"Isn't it perfect?":* E. M. M. Warburg conversation.

p. 86: *School of American Ballet.:* E. Reiman interview.

p. 87: *". . . bite your knees.":* R. Boris interview.

p. 87: *Serenade took shape:* See L. Kirstein, *Thirty Years,* pp. 38, 39.

p. 87: *to apologize.:* R. Boris interview.

p. 88: *". . . our family place.":* E. M. M. Warburg, p. 54.

p. 88: *". . . from the shock.":* Ibid.

p. 89: *understanding of the material.:* E. M. M. Warburg letter.

p. 90: *". . . same reason as you. ":* R. Boris interview.

p. 90: *until his death.:* L. Davidova interview.

p. 90: *". . . of him as a man. ":* N. Nabokoff interview.

p. 91: *her whole placement.:* E. Reiman interview.

p. 91: *lesson in choreography.:* R. Boris interview.

p. 91: Serenade.: Told to J. Taras by G. Hiden.

p. 92: *". . . put them together. ":* L. Christensen and G. Caccialanza interview.

p. 92: *Salvador Dali: The Hartford Daily Times,* December 7, 1934.

p. 93: Mozartiana *was classical.: Mozartiana,* though announced, was not performed during the season.

p. 94: *". . . hit of the evening. ":* The New York Times, March 2 and 10, 1935.

p. 94: *". . . understand anything. ":* New York Post, March 4, 1935.

p. 94: *" '. . . join the company?' ":* L. Christensen and G. Caccialanza interview.

p. 95: *". . . looking at his girls. ":* Paul Magriel and Don McDouagh, "A Conversation with Marie-Jeanne," *Ballet Review,* Vol. 12, No. 4, p. 80.

p. 95: *the better teacher.: Ibid.,* p. 60.

p. 95: *". . . an American Ballet* [sic]. *":* The New York Times, August 18, 1935.

p. 95: *in Philadelphia.:* A. Chujoy, *The New York City Ballet,* pp. 21, 52.

p. 96: *". . . what to do. ":* R. Boris interview.

p. 96: *"He never got mad. ":* R. Tracy, *Balanchine's Ballerinas,* p. 72.

p. 96: *Elise Reiman recalled.:* E. Reiman interview.

p. 97: *" '. . . into this place.' ":* E. M. M. Warburg letter, August 11, 1987.

p. 97: *and spit.:* E. Reiman interview.

p. 97: *explaining to do.:* L. Christensen and G. Caccialanza interview.

p. 97: *erotic vein.:* A. Chujoy, p. 64.

p. 97: *attention to itself.: Ibid.*

p. 98: *" '. . . God and everybody.' ":* L. Kirstein, *Thirty Years,* pp. 67–68.

p. 98: *". . . like prima donnas. ":* New York Evening Journal, interview with Dorothy Kilgallen, August 1935.

p. 98: *extend their powers.:* E. Reiman interview.

p. 99: *appeared as beggars.:* Information supplied by Eugene R. Gaddis.

p. 99: *kiss him, too.:* K. Love conversation.

p. 99: *". . . artist on holiday. ":* The New York Times, April 12, 1936.

p. 99: *". . . before the orchestra . . . ":* T. Geva in a taped interview with Nancy Reynolds, Library and Museum of the Performing Arts, Lincoln Center, New York, October 19, 1972.

p. 100: *". . . things like this . . . ": Ibid.*

p. 100: *". . . it was very nice. ":* V. Zorina, *Zorina,* p. 119.

p. 101: *". . . PROVES TRAVESTY":* The New York World Telegram, May 23, 1936.

p. 101: *". . . are a part. ":* The New York Times, May 31, 1936.

p. 101: *". . . very hard time. ":* Barbara Newman, *Striking a Balance,* p. 32.

p. 101: *brought his own.:* L. Davidova interview.

p. 102: *". . . on his shoulder. ":* R. Craft letter.

p. 102: *a poker game.:* V. Stravinsky and R. Craft, *Stravinsky in Pictures and Documents,* pp. 331–33.

p. 102: *Rossini*'s Barber of Seville: L. Kirstein, *Thirty Years,* p. 58.

p. 102: *the Metropolitan's orchestra.:* Ibid., p. 62.

p. 102: *Broadway musical: Choreography,* p. 136.

p. 103: *". . . false start.":* E. M. M. Warburg letter, August 11, 1987.

p. 103: *". . . in the choreography.":* L. Kirstein, "Working with Stravinsky," *Modern Music,* Vol. 14, No. 3, reprinted in *Bias and Belief,* p. 34.

p. 103: *in his ears.: Ibid.,* p. 69.

p. 104: *". . . your way out of it.":* B. Newman, pp. 36, 37.

p. 104: *". . . going to Heaven.": Ibid.,* pp. 34, 35.

p. 105: *by the hour.:* L. Christensen and G. Caccialanza interview.

p. 105: *difficult variation.:* E. Reiman conversation.

p. 105: *". . . height of his powers.":* I. Stravinsky, *Expositions and Developments,* p. 73.

p. 105: *". . . Les Noces.": The New York Times,* April 28, 1937.

p. 106: *". . . itself splendidly.": New York Evening Post,* April 28, 1937.

5. DIVERGING PATHS: APRIL 1937–MAY 1941

p. 108: *". . . refused to choreograph for us.":* Allen Ulrich with L. Christensen, *San Francisco Sunday Examiner,* May 6, 1984.

p. 108: *". . . cowboy movies.":* L. Christensen and G. Caccialanza interview.

p. 108: *". . . Only one person.":* B. Taper, p. 185.

p. 108: *manage it for them.:* N. Nabokoff interview.

p. 109: *including Samuel Goldwyn.:* G. Kanin, *Hollywood,* pp. 90, 91.

p. 109: *her small son.:* N. Nabokoff interview.

p. 110: *"belch so nicely.": Ibid.*

p. 110: *treated her abominably.:* V. Zorina, pp. 97, 98.

p. 111: *working on* Goldwyn Follies.: V. Zorina conversation; see also V. Zorina, pp. 158, 159.

p. 111: *"have much fun.": Ibid.;* see also V. Zorina, p. 159.

p. 111: *on July 10:* V. Zorina, pp. 162–64.

p. 111: *ask her to dinner.: Ibid.,* pp. 164–66.

p. 111: *". . . marvelous host.": Ibid.,* pp. 166, 167.

p. 112: *process of selection.: Ibid.,* pp. 170–71.

p. 112: *four weeks of work.: Ibid.,* pp. 172, 173.

p. 113: *of the missing choreographer.:* N. Nabokoff interview.

p. 113: *". . . starlit sky.":* V. Zorina, p. 173.

p. 113: *California.:* V. Zorina conversation.

p. 113: *". . . would take time."*: V. Zorina, pp. 176, 177.

p. 114: *touch of Balanchine's):* Ibid., pp. 177, 178.

p. 114: *". . . disappearing in ocean."*: Ibid., p. 178.

p. 114: *"very sexy"*: Ibid.

p. 114: *dancers look taller.*: Ibid., pp. 188, 189.

p. 115: *". . . the real ending."*: Ibid., p. 191.

p. 115: *a few days longer.*: Ibid., p. 185.

p. 115: *"I love you" in Norwegian.*: *"Jeg elsker Dig."* Ibid., pp. 191–93.

p. 115: *by Rodgers and Hart?*: Ibid., pp. 187, 188, 194, 195.

p. 116: *dig at Balanchine.*: The New Yorker, June 11, 1938, pp. 27–30.

p. 117: *". . . love him to this day."*: V. Zorina interview with Nancy Reynolds, October 19, 1972. Transcript in the Library and Museum of the Performing Arts, Lincoln Center, New York.

p. 117: *"match" his love.*: V. Zorina, pp. 193, 201, 202.

p. 117: *she had ever seen.*: Ibid., p. 200.

p. 117: *". . . hands trembling."*: Ibid., p. 206.

p. 117: *of the fact.*: A. Chujoy, The New York City Ballet, p. 104.

p. 118: *". . . together in threes . . ."*: Article by H. Howard Taubman in unidentified newspaper, April 13, 1938.

p. 118: *into this dance:* V. Zorina conversation.

p. 118: *"'. . . in St. Moritz.' "*: V. Zorina, pp. 211, 212.

p. 118: *cut him out.*: Ibid., p. 214.

p. 118: *as a surprise.*: Ibid., pp. 219, 220, 221.

p. 118: *talked nonsense.*: N. Nabokoff interview.

p. 118: *". . . for some time"*: The New York Times, May 12, 1938.

p. 119: *". . . first choreographer of Broadway."*: Ibid.

p. 119: *"freshness."*: John Martin, The New York Times, September 8, 1940.

p. 119: *Christmas Eve supper:* N. Nabokoff interview. It was, however, Zorina who pointed out that Volodine was present.

p. 120: *no explanation was given.*: N. Nabokoff interview.

p. 120: *every skin.*: V. Zorina told R. B. that she still has the ermine coat.

p. 120: *different direction.*: N. Nabokoff interview.

p. 121: *your loving Georgi:* Undated letter in the possession of Andrei Balanchivadze, copied by Kyril Fitzlyon in Tbilisi on October 20, 1986, and later translated by him.

p. 121: *January 1939.*: The New York Times, January 16, 1939.

p. 121: *"Angel on Earth."*: New York Daily News, February 20, 1939.

p. 121: *to Mrs. Hartwig.*: V. Zorina, p. 227.

p. 121: *". . . put out the blaze."*: New York Daily News, February 24, 1939.

p. 122: *before his arrival.*: V. Zorina, pp. 230, 231.

p. 122: *". . . worked perfectly."*: Ibid., p. 233.

p. 122: *at the opera house.*: J. Anderson, The One and Only, p. 39.

p. 122: *but refused.*: Charles Payne, American Ballet Theatre, pp. 33, 36, 37.

p. 123: *". . . in Ballet History"*: Poster of American Ballet Theatre's first season, reproduced in C. Payne, p. 46.

p. 123: *$200,000.)*: C. Payne, p. 102.

p. 123: *". . . American organization . . ."*: *New York Herald Tribune*, January 30, 1940.

p. 123: *". . . twelve times a day. . . ."*: L. Kirstein, *Thirty Years*, p. 80.

p. 124: *never noticed.*: This is an extract from a detailed account by John Taras.

p. 124: *illustrious Russians.*: Numerous newspapers throughout the U.S. told the same story and used the same pictures.

p. 125: *Long Island:* Sunken Meadow Park occupies the site today. V. Zorina conversation.

p. 125: *never used it.*: V. Zorina, p. 246.

p. 125: *after the performance:* *Ibid.*

p. 125: *". . . uglier," she said.*: N. Nabokoff interview.

p. 125: *". . . a diamond necklace."*: T. Toumanova interview.

p. 125: *"Will people understand?"*: *Ibid.*

p. 125: *old and rather bad photographs:* Such as those reproduced in *Dance Index*, Vol. 6, Nos. 10, 11, 12, p. 251.

p. 126: *reduced to the minimum.*: V. Zorina, pp. 249, 250.

p. 126: *American artists.*: V. Zorina, p. 249.

p. 126: *" '. . . in New York?' "*: *Ibid.*

p. 126: *until his death:* N. Molostwoff interview.

p. 126: *upper story of the School.*: *New York Herald Tribune*, April 1, 1941.

p. 127: *". . . destroyed me."*: N. Molostwoff interview.

6. SOUTH AMERICAN ADVENTURE: MAY–DECEMBER 1941

p. 129: *vocabulary of Petipa.*: J. Taras's comment.

p. 130: *for a corps de ballet.*: *Ibid.*

p. 130: *Peter and Paul.*: This account of *Ballet Imperial* is taken from a much longer description written by J. Taras.

p. 131: *"You'll never learn!"*: G. Hiden conversation.

p. 131: *skip a meal:* John Taras diary.

p. 131: *never recurred.*: Quoted from J. Taras's specially written account, but see also Paul Magriel and Don McDonagh, "A Conversation with Marie-Jeanne," *Ballet Review*, Vol. 12, No. 4, pp. 40–42.

p. 131: *hurt her feet.*: L. Christensen and G. Caccialanza interview.

p. 131: *Lew Christensen said.*: *Ibid.*

p. 132: *pose to another.*: J. Taras's indication.

p. 132: *ever made on her.*: P. Magriel and D. McDonagh, *op. cit.*, p. 63.

p. 133: *fell apart with laughter.*: L. Christensen and G. Caccialanza interview.

p. 133: *took pictures.:* L. Kirstein, *Bias and Belief,* p. 83.

p. 133: *". . . 'organized chaos.' ":* G. Hiden conversation.

p. 133: *fell flat.: Ibid.*

p. 134: *asking for Dollar.:* J. Taras's recollection.

p. 134: *Argentinean winter.:* T. Bolender interview.

p. 135: *in the car.:* G. Hiden conversation.

p. 135: *on the stage.: Ibid.*

p. 135: *". . . shelf of green. ":* T. Bolender interview.

p. 136: *in North America.:* L. Kirstein, *Bias and Belief,* p. 90.

p. 136: *represented Rockefeller.:* L. Kirstein, *Thirty Years,* pp. 86, 87.

p. 136: *and sugar.:* J. Taras diary.

p. 136: *speak to the driver.:* G. Hiden conversation.

p. 137: *". . . damn near died. ":* L. Christensen and G. Caccialanza interview.

p. 137: *took photographs.:* L. Kirstein, *Bias and Belief,* p. 93.

p. 137: *return to the Colón.: Ibid.,* p. 90.

7. GETTING THROUGH THE WAR: DECEMBER 1941–OCTOBER 1945

p. 139: *for twenty-two years.:* L. Kirstein, "Stardom: Slav and Native," *Dance Magazine,* Vol. 4, No. 3, pp. 14–15. Reprinted in Kirstein, *Bias and Belief,* p. 44.

p. 140: *war charity.:* V. Zorina, pp. 258–61.

p. 140: *in the sawdust: Ibid.,* p. 260.

p. 140: *". . . Mozart ever wrote!":* G. Hiden conversation.

p. 141: *saw her again.:* V. Zorina, pp. 264–70.

p. 141: *". . . artistic genius. ":* R. Tracy, p. 81.

p. 141: *putting on weight.:* N. Molostwoff conversation.

p. 142: *". . . in New York City. ":* R. Tracy, pp. 86, 87.

p. 142: *". . . a real crush. ":* F. Moncion interview.

p. 142: *". . . in* This Is the Army." A copy was kept among Balanchine's papers at the School.

p. 142: *salary was doubled.:* R. Tracy, p. 87.

p. 143: *a "soubrette.":* *Time,* May 17, 1943.

p. 144: *Sincerely yours, George Balanchine:* A copy of the letter is preserved among Balanchine's papers at the School.

p. 144: *were printed.:* Poster reproduced in C. Payne, p. 129.

p. 145: *". . . I'd yell at Hurok. ":* G. Hiden conversation.

p. 145: *the whole Ballet Russe.:* J. Anderson, p. 90.

p. 145: *and they agreed.: Ibid.*

p. 145: *Goddard Lieberson.:* V. Zorina conversation.

p. 146: *". . . dear to me indeed. ":* F. Franklin interview.

p. 147: *eyes lit up.: Ibid.*

p. 147: *at City Center.:* J. Anderson, p. 91.

p. 147: *more brightly still.:* Edwin Denby, *New York Herald Tribune*, September 17, 1944.

p. 148: *studying with Balanchine.:* M. Tallchief interview.

p. 149: *devoid of dancing.: The New York Times*, September 11, 1944.

p. 149: *Henry James: New York Herald Tribune*, September 17, 1944.

p. 149: *seventeenth century.: The New York Times*, February 22, 1945.

p. 149: *not the choreographer. . . .: The New York Times*, September 15, 1944.

p. 149: *". . . a million years.":* Claudia Cassidy, *Chicago Tribune*, October 8, 1944.

p. 149: *". . . for* Ballet Imperial.": R. Boris interview.

p. 150: "That *old ballet!":* V. Rieti interview.

p. 150: *in Houston.:* J. Anderson, p. 100.

p. 150: *". . . fun, glory and drinks.": Ibid.,* p. 99. Letter from S. J. Denham to "Dear Marion" (unidentified), dated December 21, 1944.

p. 150: *to bed with her.:* R. Boris interview.

p. 151: *gold cigarette case.: The New York Times*, March 18, 1945.

p. 151: *share his sorrow.:* R. Boris interview.

p. 151: *Then he walked away.: Ibid.*

p. 152: *need assistance.:* The wording of this letter, as well as its typing, was undoubtedly the work of Natalie Molostwoff. A copy of the letter is preserved among Balanchine's papers.

p. 152: *him and Brigitta:* G. Hiden conversation.

p. 152: *". . . getting a divorce.":* V. Zorina conversation.

p. 153: WAS FYODOR.: V. Stravinsky and R. Craft, p. 467. Retrospective caption to illustration of Stravinsky with G. B. on the composer's eightieth birthday.

p. 153: Comedia Balletica.: T. Bolender interview.

p. 154: *". . . he just loves it . . .": Ibid.*

p. 154: *got together:* J. Taras's recollection.

p. 154: *of his troubles.: Ibid.* Also T. Bolender interview.

p. 154: *". . . a lot from Petipa.": Ibid.* T. Bolender interview.

p. 155: *only solution.:* N. Nabokoff interview.

p. 155: *"George who?":* Conversation reported to J. Taras by Vida Brown.

8. NEW BEGINNINGS: NOVEMBER 1945–APRIL 1948

p. 156: *line would improve.:* M. Tallchief interview.

p. 157: *in his hands.: Ibid.*

p. 158: *he follows her.:* This account of the pas de deux is by J. Taras.

p. 158: *". . . pathos and beauty"*: Kobbé's *Complete Opera Book*, p. 505.

p. 158: *". . . a heaving floor."*: *Dance Magazine*, November 1946.

p. 159: *with the composer.*: *Dearest Bubushkin*, p. 136. Entry in Mrs. Stravinsky's diary for April 4, 1946.

p. 159: *scenario of* Orpheus: *Ibid.*

p. 159: *string ties.*: M. Tallchief interview.

p. 160: *unheard of:* A. Chujoy, *The New York City Ballet*, p. 158.

p. 161: *". . . magic on the stage."*: *Ibid.*, p. 159.

p. 161: *new to New York: L'Enfant et les sortilèges* had, however, been performed in San Francisco in 1930.

p. 162: *". . . you can do with it!"*: T. Bolender interview.

p. 162: *". . . for $250."*: Letter from Ernest Voigt, representing Hindemith, September 27, 1940.

p. 162: *was set aside.*: L. Kirstein, *Thirty Years*, p. 92.

p. 163: *". . . plan caught on."*: A. Chujoy, *The New York City Ballet*, p. 162.

p. 163: *". . . dancer who was no good. . . ."*: A copy of the typed letter was kept by Balanchine, September 11, 1946.

p. 163: *the secret.*: M. Tallchief interview.

p. 164: *drank wine.*: *Ibid.*

p. 164: *for* Sérénade. . . .: Mina Curtiss, *Other People's Letters*, pp. 74, 75.

p. 165: *scared to death.*: M. Tallchief interview.

p. 165: *much praised.*: A. Chujoy, *The New York City Ballet*, p. 176.

p. 165: *Palace of Diamonds:* Typescript in the Dance Collection of the Library and Museum of the Performing Arts, Lincoln Center, New York.

p. 166: *made on her.*: M. Tallchief interview.

p. 166: *New York at last.*: *Ibid.*

p. 167: *". . . do it first."*: *Ibid.*

p. 167: *"how much he suffered."*: *Dearest Bubushkin*, p. 142.

p. 167: *November 11, 1947.*: A. Chujoy, *The New York City Ballet*, p. 177.

p. 168: *work of genius.*: C. Payne, p. 154.

p. 169: *She was hired:* B. Cage conversations.

p. 169: *same program.*: I. Stravinsky, *Selected Correspondence, Vol. 1*, p. 265.

p. 169: *thirty-six strings.*: *Ibid.*, p. 266.

p. 169: *orchestrating the ballet.*: Eric Walter White, *Stravinsky*, p. 440.

p. 169: *received copies:* I. Stravinsky, *Selected Correspondence, Vol. I*, p. 268.

p. 169: *to play it.*: M. I. Tallchief interview.

p. 169: *into the score.*: *Ibid.*

p. 169: *was adopted.*: I. Stravinsky and R. Craft, *Dialogues and a Diary*, p. 78 fn.

p. 170: *". . . Russian direction . . ."*: Nicholas Nabokov, *Old Friends and New Music*, pp. 221–222.

p. 170: *they were shown.*: *Dearest Bubushkin*, p. 144.

p. 170: *a chef's hat.*: Note from G.B. to M. Tallchief.

p. 170: *word he said.:* M. Tallchief interview.

p. 171: *". . . kind of thing.":* N. Reynolds, p. 83.

p. 171: *of her career.: Ibid.*

p. 171: *". . . chalk on blackboard!":* F. Moncion interview.

p. 171: *". . . his* Symphony in C.": A. Chujoy, *Dance News,* April 1948. Quoted in Reynolds, p. 86.

p. 171: *". . . familiar tricks . . .":* *The New York Times,* March 23, 1948, quoted in *ibid.*

p. 172: *". . . you boys together.":* F. Moncion interview.

p. 172: *a great venture.: Ibid.*

p. 172: *went on diets.: Ibid.*

p. 173: *to take class.: Ibid.*

p. 173: *"great days": Ibid.*

p. 173: *". . . no less.":* L. Kirstein, *Thirty Years,* p. 99.

p. 173: *robbed a bank.: Ibid.,* pp. 100, 101.

p. 174: *subsequent revivals.:* J. Taras's account, written November 25, 1984.

p. 174: *". . . very happy.":* A. Chujoy, *The New York City Ballet,* p. 201.

p. 174: *"Too good to be true":* L. Kirstein, *Thirty Years,* p. 102.

p. 174: *"short and irritable.": Ibid.*

p. 175: *an American ballet.:* A. Chujoy, *The New York City Ballet,* pp. 202–3.

p. 175: *than before.: Ibid.,* pp. 204, 205.

p. 175: *to tell Balanchine.: Ibid.,* p. 203.

9. IN SEARCH OF A FORMULA: 1948–1957

p. 176: *New York City Ballet.:* U. Kai interview.

p. 178: *to applaud him.:* *The New York Times,* November 9, 1948, quoted in A. Chujoy, *The New York City Ballet,* p. 209.

p. 178: *company had increased.: Ibid.,* p. 211.

p. 178: *as a choreographer.:* N. Reynolds, p. 86.

p. 179: *". . . Well . . . perhaps.":* M. Tallchief interview.

p. 179: *for $2,500,:* B. Cage conversation. Hurok later tried to maintain that this sum was only for the rental of the properties.

p. 180: *new version . . . would take.:* M. Tallchief interview.

p. 180: *in New York.:* Copy of cable from David Webster, June 10, 1949, retained in the archives of the Royal Opera House, Covent Garden.

p. 180: *". . . Orpheus for them?":* B. Cage, letter to G.B., June 13, 1949.

p. 180: *discuss matters then.:* Copy of cable sent by B. Cage, June 20, 1949, on behalf of G.B.

p. 180: *debut of Sadler's Wells:* Copy of letter to L. Kirstein, August 29, 1949.

p. 181: *". . . from our school.":* L. Kirstein letter to R.B., September 10, 1949.

p. 181: *There was no time.:* N. Reynolds, p. 98.

p. 181: *". . . a football stadium. ":* Ibid.

p. 182: *". . . from the audience. ":* Time, December 12, 1949, quoted in *ibid.*, p. 96.

p. 182: *a firebird on it.:* M. Tallchief interview.

p. 182: *price of the materials.:* A. Chujoy, *The New York City Ballet*, p. 223.

p. 182: *good as Robbins.:* V. Stravinsky conversation.

p. 182: *". . . at double speed!":* M. Somes letter to R.B., May 21, 1984.

p. 182: *second movement:* M. Somes conversation during the 1960s.

p. 182: *all the pantomime.:* J. Taras's observation.

p. 183: *". . . to extract it. ":* B. Grey, letter to R.B., May 20, 1984.

p. 183: *"Kitty, kittteee . . .":* Washington Star, June 19, 1972.

p. 183: *Ballet Imperial.:* L. Kirstein, *Thirty Years*, p. 112.

p. 183: *". . . almost like New York. ":* G.B. letter to M. Tallchief, handwritten; undated, but clearly April 7, 1950.

p. 184: *tour was also planned.:* B. Cage conversation.

p. 184: *"Beaumont, Beaumont!":* P. Schaufuss conversation.

p. 184: *". . . undramatic or mild. ":* Manchester Guardian, July 10, 1950.

p. 184: *and Croydon.:* B. Cage conversation.

p. 185: *"plain bad. ":* A. Chujoy, *The New York City Ballet*, pp. 242, 243.

p. 185: *thirty-three years later.:* In 1952, 1964 and 1979.

p. 185: *for them:* For the Royal Ballet: *Serenade*, 1950; *Apollo*, 1964; *The Four Temperaments, Prodigal Son, Agon, Allegro Brillante*, 1973; *Concerto Barocco, Liebeslieder Walzer*, 1977. For Festival Ballet: *Bourrée fantasque*, 1960; *Night Shadow*, 1967; *Tchaikovsky Pas de deux*, 1972; *Symphony in C*, 1986.

p. 185: *fanned by eunuchs.:* This phrase is the author's, but it summarizes opinions expressed to him by L. Davidova.

p. 186: *walk on newspaper.:* L. Davidova conversation.

p. 186: *a game with her.:* E. Reiman conversation.

p. 186: *". . . liked Lew. ":* M. Tallchief interview.

p. 186: *never forgave him.:* Ravel refused even to shake hands with Diaghilev, and turned away without speaking when they ran into each other in Monte Carlo at the time of the rehearsals of *L'Enfant* in 1924. Boris Kochno, who was present, told R.B. this.

p. 188: *"like going to a party. ":* N. Reynolds, pp. 118, 119.

p. 188: *out of the steps.:* Ibid., p. 119.

p. 188: *". . . to destruction. ":* Ibid.

p. 188: *heedless whirling.:* Doris Hering in *Dance Magazine*, April 1951, quoted in N. Reynolds, p.118.

p. 189: *avant-garde tradition.:* U. Kai interview.

p. 190: *recorded in 1947,:* R. Sandbach conversation.

p. 190: *". . . knows it immediately. ":* Ballet, Vol. 12, No. 9, September 1952.

p. 190: *the man.:* B. Cage conversation.

p. 190: *every day.: Ibid.*

p. 190: *from Morton Baum.:* B. Cage letter from New York to G.B. in Milan, March 10, 1952.

p. 190: *". . . that's definite.:":* G.B. handwritten letter from Milan to B. Cage in New York, undated, but about March 13, 1952.

p. 191: *impressed him enormously.:* B. Cage conversation.

p. 191: *first intermission.:* J. Taras's recollection.

p. 191: *doves was released.:* A. Chujoy, *The New York Ballet,* pp. 340, 341.

p. 191: *during performances.:* B. Cage conversation.

p. 191: *Edinburgh Festival.:* L. Kirstein letter from New York to B. Cage in Paris, May 9, 1952.

p. 191: *". . . I am talking . . .":* L. Kirstein letter from New York to B. Cage in Florence, May 14, 1952.

p. 192: *". . . a third arabesque.":* E. Bigelow conversation.

p. 192: *". . . carnivorous lizards, etc.":* G.B. letter to B. Cage.

p. 192: *". . . screwing a steak.":* K. Tyler's recollection.

p. 192: *". . . something sacred.":* R. Tobias interview.

p. 194: *love George.:* G.B. in London to L. Kirstein in New York, letter dated August 4, 1952, undoubtedly typed by B. Cage.

p. 194: *". . . calling a meeting.":* L. Kirstein in New York to B. Cage in London, August 7, 1952.

p. 194: *tartan kilts:* U. Kai interview.

p. 194: *principals of his company:* M. Tallchief interview.

p. 195: *on the worse.:* B. Cage conversation.

p. 195: *fell on his head.:* M. Tallchief interview.

p. 195: *exhausted by the tour.:* A. Chujoy, *The New York Ballet,* p. 357.

p. 195: *Paris Opéra.: Ibid.,* p. 344.

p. 195: *sold out.: Ibid.,* p. 350.

p. 195: *". . . from New York.": Ibid.,* p. 351.

p. 195: *for a week.: Ibid.,* p. 355.

p. 195: *to see them.: Ibid.,* pp. 361, 362.

p. 195: *in Berlin.: Ibid.,* p. 362.

p. 195: *permanent base.: Ibid.,* p. 351.

p. 195: *so had Balanchine.:* B. Cage letter to L. Kirstein in New York; date indecipherable, but sometime in June 1952.

p. 196: *by comparison.:* E. Bigelow conversation

p. 197: *"not too pleased.":* M. Tallchief interview.

p. 197: *hung mirrors.:* V. Brown interview.

p. 197: *"It's O.K.":* M. Tallchief interview.

p. 198: *"to wait a little.":* V. Zorina conversation.

p. 198: *". . . gentle radiance":* P. W. Manchester in *Dance News,* December 1952.

p. 198: *impossible task:* He told Tanaquil Le Clercq: "I'd like to pose myself a puzzle." N. Reynolds, p. 143.

p. 199: *". . . but repulsed.":* T. Bolender conversation.

p. 199: *" '. . . Myself IN FOR?' ":* L. Kirstein letter to R.B., January 2, 1953.

p. 199: *whole business.:* G. Boelzner conversation.

p. 199: *to resign.:* B. Cage letter to L. Kirstein, October 3, 1953.

p. 200: *four New York seasons a year.: Ibid.,* October 3, 1953.

p. 200: *Karinska for costumes.:* L. Kirstein letter to B. Cage, October 9, 1953.

p. 200: *". . . to junk it. . . .":* L. Kirstein letter to B. Cage, October 26, 1953.

p. 201: *afraid to tell Baum.:* L. Kirstein, *Thirty Years,* p. 132.

p. 201: *". . . and he will be happy.":* B. Cage conversation.

p. 201: *tragic character.:* Alexandre Benois, *Reminiscences of the Russian Ballet,* (London: Putnam, 1941), pp. 138, 139.

p. 202: *" '. . . Nutcracker: food.' ": Time,* January 25, 1954, pp. 30–34.

p. 202: *". . . or story-telling.": The New York Times,* March 28, 1954.

p. 202: *". . . drawings I made for him.":* G.B. letter to R.B., February 1954.

p. 202: *". . . from Francis Mason. . . ." George Balanchine's Complete Stories of the Great Ballets* contains much valuable evidence from Balanchine himself, as well as notes by Mason on ballets by other choreographers that Balanchine could not possibly have considered great. It has gone into many editions, been continually revised and sold more copies than any ballet book ever published. Francis Mason, who had contributed to *Ballet* magazine, became cultural attaché at the American Embassy in London and later curator of the Morgan Library and editor of *Ballet Review.*

p. 203: *George:* G.B. letter to R.B., typewritten, March 9, 1954.

p. 203: *Diaghilev in Venice.:* These drawings are in Boris Kochno's collection.

p. 203: *for £3,000.:* Illustrated in Sotheby's catalogue *Ballet Material and Manuscripts from the Serge Lifar Collection,* No. 64.

p. 203: *four-movement symphony.:* N. Reynolds, p. 161.

p. 204: *to Russia?:* L. Kirstein to B. Cage, September 14, 1956.

p. 204: *dollars in debt.:* L. Kirstein to B. Cage, September 28, 1956.

p. 204: *". . . no longer IF.":* L. Kirstein letter to B. Cage, October 2, 1956.

p. 204: *". . . they'd understand":* R. Tobias interview.

p. 205: *grew feverish.:* B. Cage letter to L. Kirstein, October 31, 1956.

p. 205: *you can think of. . . .:* L. Kirstein letter to B. Cage, November 3, 1956.

p. 205: *". . . painful for him.":* B. Cage letter to L. Kirstein, November 6, 1956.

p. 206: *Then he went off.:* H. Kronstam interview.

p. 207: *"You're very funny!":* D. Adams interview.

p. 207: *hotel bedroom.:* N. Molostwoff conversation.

p. 207: *about it:* B. Cage letter to G. B., January 18, 1957.

p. 208: *to his dancers.:* B. Cage conversation.

10. NEW BALLETS FOR NEW DANCERS: 1957–1964

p. 210: *". . . an inferior* Barocco.".: L. Kirstein letter to B. Cage, May 14, 1958.

p. 210: *"the applause machine. ".:* "A Word from George Balanchine," introduction to NYCB's 1957 winter season in a *Playbill* program, November
19, 1957.

p. 211: *composer's hand.:* Reproduced in the souvenir program of NYCB's
Stravinsky centennial celebration, June 1982.

p. 211: *was Stravinsky's.:* G.B. interview with Dale Harris, *Keynote,* Vol. VI,
No. 4, June 1982.

p. 211: *". . . I was there.".:* D. Adams interview.

p. 212: *" '. . . on right foot.' ":* *Ibid.*

p. 212: *to a rehearsal.:* L. Davidova interview.

p. 212: *Balanchine's future biographer.:* B. Taper's comments on the rehearsal
are given in his captions to Martha Swope's photographs, pp. 264–70.

p. 213: *". . . understand them either!".:* R. Tobias interview.

p. 213: *"Wonderful!".:* B. Taper, p. 269.

p. 213: *extra performances.:* I. Stravinsky, *Selected Correspondence, Vol. 1,* p.
291.

p. 214: *ten years of work.:* L. Kirstein letter to B. Cage, July 11, 1958.

p. 214: *". . . after we get home.".:* B. Cage letter to L. Kirstein, July 16, 1958.

p. 214: *Robert Irving:* L. Kirstein letter to B. Cage, August 6, 1958.

p. 214: *first job:* G. Boelzner conversation.

p. 215: *". . . myself to write.".:* L. Davidova interview.

p. 215: *notably Bartók.:* G.B. interview with Dale Harris, *Keynote,* Vol. VI, No.
4, June 1982.

p. 215: *in the Austrian composer.:* Craft wrote: "In the years between 1952 and
1955 no composer can have lived in closer contact with the music of
Webern." Robert Craft, "A Personal Preface," *The Score,* June 1957.

p. 215: *soon discarded.:* Don McDonagh, *Martha Graham* (New York: Praeger,
1973), p. 257.

p. 216: *the music to her.:* *Ibid.*

p. 216: *". . . in sound.".:* G.B. interview with Jonathan Cott, reprinted in
L. Kirstein, et al., *Portrait of Mr. B.,* p. 133.

p. 216: *found this funny.:* In G. Balanchine, p. 205, Balanchine is recorded as
saying, "I sometimes think Americans feel obliged to laugh too much
when there is not any reason to."

p. 217: *tried to do.:* *Ibid.,* p. 206.

p. 217: *". . . starve with the rest of us?".:* J. Taras's recollection. He returned
to New York in December 1959, and was appointed ballet master in
1960.

p. 218: *accepted in New York.:* Various degrees of admiration are registered in
quotations from the press, given in Reynolds, pp. 199, 200.

p. 218: *. . . realize the role.:* E. Villella interview.

p. 220: *might be lost.:* R. Dunleavy interview.

p. 220: *reproduce his ballets:* N. Molostwoff told this to R.B. in 1985.

p. 220 *". . . on her hands and knees.":* S. Schorer interview.

p. 220: *put together the score:* G. Boelzner described how this was done in a letter to R.B. dated April 4, 1985.

p. 223: *". . . of clairvoyance.":* R. Vazquez interview with W. Lawson.

p. 224: *"do something for the boys.":* V. Verdy interview with W. Lawson.

p. 225: *on the mime.:* E. Villella interview.

p. 225: *extraordinary moment.: Ibid.*

p. 226: *"more interesting":* D. Adams interview.

p. 226: *sometimes implacable.: Ibid.*

p. 227: *". . . like someone else.": Ibid.*

p. 227: *"odd but interesting.": Ibid.*

p. 227: *asked for more.:* Nancy Lassalle, then secretary of Ballet Society, raised $5,000 to pay for this.

p. 229: *performed together.:* In 1963, *Monumentum* was coupled in performance with *Movements,* and this pairing stuck. The principal couple are always the same in both works, but the other women in *Monumentum* arc always taller than the six in *Movements.*

p. 229: *Gesualdo's madrigals.:* In 1954, Stravinsky had concluded that Gesualdo's music was "uniquely vocal in character," but in 1960 he found three pieces he "could at least conceive of in instrumental form." I. Stravinsky and R. Craft, *Expositions and Developments,* p. 118. The three madrigals were Nos. 14 and 18 of Book V and No. 2 of Book VI.

p. 230: *". . . exciting work.":* Hugo Fiorato in "A Symposium on the Balanchine Style," chaired by Francis Mason, held at the Milford Plaza Hotel, June 11, 1983, and reprinted in *Ballet Review,* Winter 1984, p. 12.

p. 230: *". . . explored the result.":* I. Stravinsky and R. Craft, *Themes and Episodes,* p. 24.

p. 230: *". . . past me.":* D. Adams interview.

p. 230: *the only reply.:* J. Taras's recollection.

p. 230: *recumbent dancer.:* David Daniel, "Diana Adams on Suzanne Farrell," *Ballet Review,* Winter 1982, p. 16.

11. TO RUSSIA: OCTOBER—NOVEMBER 1962

p. 231: *". . . solo but regular.":* Letter from G.B. to B. Cage, dated Sunday 11 [February 1962].

p. 232: *"Don't tell him . . .":* Letter from G.B. to B. Cage, undated but evidently mid-February 1962.

p. 232: *set in time.:* K. Tyler interview.

p. 232: *". . . State Department delegates."*: R. Maiorano, p. 163.

p. 232: *before the Revolution.*: L. Kirstein, *Thirty Years*, p. 170.

p. 233: *". . . romantic ballet."*: R. Maiorano, p. 163.

p. 233: *". . . floodlights."*: *The New York Times*, October 7, 1962.

p. 233: *cameras disappeared.*: P. Neary conversation.

p. 233: *Maria Yudina:* A. M. Balanchivadze interview.

p. 234: *greatest ovation. . . .*: *The New York Times*, October 10, 1962.

p. 234: *on October 11:* I. Stravinsky and R. Craft, *Dialogues and a Diary*, pp. 273–85.

p. 234: *restaurants and stores.*: J. Taras's recollection.

p. 235: *". . . Meet-shell!"*: R. Dunleavy interview.

p. 235: *John Martin.*: *The New York Times*, October 31, 1962.

p. 235: *all there was.*: B. Cage conversation.

p. 235: *to be the case.*: N. Molostwoff interview.

p. 235: *a hot potato.*: B. Cage conversation.

p. 236: *possibility of war.*: *Ibid.*

p. 236: *". . . your government."*: N. Molostwoff interview.

p. 236: *". . . be cut off."*: B. Cage conversation.

p. 236: *even if there was war.*: B. Cage conversation with W. Lawson.

p. 236: *to drive on.*: B. Cage conversation.

p. 236: *was postponed.*: L. Kirstein, *Thirty Years*, p. 176.

p. 236: *". . . then cheered."*: R. Maiorano, p. 176.

p. 236: *all the tables:* N. Molostwoff interview.

p. 237: *president's demands:* Details of the Cuban crisis were derived from Robert F. Kennedy, *13 Days*, and David L. Larson, ed., *The "Cuban Crisis" of 1962: Selected Documents and Chronology.*

p. 237: *" 'Bal-an-chin!' "*: L. Kirstein, *Thirty Years*, p. 175.

p. 237: *worried more.*: V. Verdy interview with W. Lawson.

p. 237: *regulations were.*: N. Molostwoff interview.

p. 238: *Balanchine refused.*: B. Cage interview.

p. 238: *company a class.*: V. Verdy interview with W. Lawson.

p. 238: *had never acquired.*: P. Neary conversation.

p. 238: *to his crotch.*: A. M. Balanchivadze interview.

p. 238: *". . . a story line."*: Quoted in *The New York Times*, October 31, 1962.

p. 239: *". . . Come back!"*: *Ibid.*

p. 239: *very emotional.*: N. Molostwoff interview.

p. 240: *". . . many flowers."*: *The New York Times*, November 1, 1962.

p. 240: *". . . send them home . . ."*: L. Kirstein postcard from Leningrad to R.B. in London, November 4, 1962.

p. 241: *" '. . . you are tonight.' "*: L. Kirstein, *Thirty Years*, pp. 177, 178.

p. 241: *". . . theater itself."*: *The New York Times*, November 9, 1962.

p. 242: *the female sex.:* V. Verdy interview with W. Lawson.
p. 242: *"the camel":* N. Molostwoff interview.
p. 243: *"Where are your pants?":* S. O'Brien interview with W. Lawson.

12. PROBLEMS IN PARADISE: 1964–1972

p. 245: *New York City Opera. . . . :* L. Kirstein, *Thirty Years.*
p. 245: *"to minimize injury.":* Facts derived from Don McDonagh article in NYCB winter season, 1982–83, *Playbill.*
p. 245: *ballet in America: The New York Times,* December 15, 1963.
p. 246: *"You'll be back.":* B. Horgan interview.
p. 246: *for ten years.: Ibid.*
p. 247: *point of departure.:* E. Villella interview.
p. 247: *on a book.:* Tanaquil Le Clercq, *Mourka: The Autobiography of a Cat,* with photographs by Martha Swope.
p. 247: *". . . no instep.":* David Daniel, "Diana Adams on Suzanne Farrell," *Ballet Review,* Winter 1982, p. 11.
p. 248: *full scholarship.: Ibid.*
p. 248: *". . . your cat, Mourka?":* Suzanne Farrell interview with Hubert Saal, *Newsweek,* January 13, 1969.
p. 248: *". . . and talked his head off.": Ibid.* The white cat Bottom, with his black mask, was one of the characters photographed by Martha Swope for *Mourka.*
p. 248: *". . . Suzanne never resisted.":* D. Daniel, *op. cit.,* p. 16.
p. 249: *"alabaster princess.":* The phrase is used in N. Reynolds, p. 238.
p. 249: *"a secular saint.": Ibid.,* p. 236.
p. 249: *"a Christ figure.": Ibid.,* p. 238.
p. 249: *". . . vigorous in movement.": Ibid.,* Richard Rapp quoted.
p. 250: *". . . the sleeping Knight.":* Edwin Denby, *Dance Magazine,* July 1965.
p. 250: *"Fearless Farrell":* N. Reynolds, p. 238.
p. 250: *Balanchine's choreography.:* In a public interview with Francis Mason, given at New York University on October 22, 1985, Suzanne Farrell described how Balanchine asked her to repeat a dangerous off-balance step, and then incorporated it into his choreography.
p. 250: *a mystic levitating:* A comparison of Denby's.
p. 250: *". . . make him laugh. . . .":* Suzanne Farrell interview with Hubert Saal, *Newsweek,* January 13, 1969.
p. 250: *". . . till she left.":* S. Schorer interview.
p. 251: *to the elevator.:* From notes taken by R. B., February 5, 1967.

p. 252: *to work at them.:* Suzanne Farrell in a public interview with Francis Mason, cited above.

p. 252: *dolphin (intelligence).: Ibid.*

p. 252: *at Saratoga Springs:* R. and K. Leach interview.

p. 252: *every night.: Ibid.*

p. 253: *". . . turn off Ormandy.": Ibid.*

p. 253: *was the verdict.: Ibid.*

p. 254: *[French for "encore"].: Ibid.*

p. 254: *retired Lippizaner:* L. Kirstein, *Thirty Years,* p. 191.

p. 254: *". . . dressed like jewels.":* N. Reynolds, p. 247.

p. 256: *a pedestrian ballet.:* E. Villella interview.

p. 256: *". . . your mother applauding?":* P. Neary conversation.

p. 256: *". . . cover anything up.":* N. Reynolds, p. 250.

p. 256: *"Only pas de deux is good.":* P. Neary conversation.

p. 257: *finger-turn on pointe.:* E. Villella interview.

p. 257: *show off Farrell.:* P. Neary conversation.

p. 257: *sent the young Dane off.:* J. Taras letter to R. B., February 4, 1986.

p. 257: *". . . he's tall.":* Peter Martins, p. 37.

p. 258: *". . . timing and quickness.": Ibid.,* pp. 37–38.

p. 258: *season in December.: Ibid.,* p. 39.

p. 258: *some dye.:* P. Neary conversation.

p. 258: *she left.: Ibid.*

p. 259: *blessed beings.: Sunday Times* (London), May 12, 1968.

p. 259: *with Suzanne Farrell.:* N. Molostwoff conversation.

p. 259: *found the cat.:* R. and K. Leach interview.

p. 260: *together in restaurants.:* P. Neary conversation.

p. 260: *believe it was:* See Chapter 14, second note for p. 300 *(". . . God's decision.")*

p. 260: *". . . of her own age . . .": New York Post,* September 12, 1968.

p. 260: *was best man: Ibid.,* February 27, 1969.

p. 260: *be sent for.:* B. Horgan interview.

p. 261: *to his company.: Ibid.*

p. 261: *to Kirstein:* L. Kirstein letter to B. Cage, April 1, 1969.

p. 261: *"give them 20 ballets.": Ibid.*

p. 261: *". . . goes unpunished.":* N. Molostwoff conversation.

p. 262: Stars and Stripes.: *The New York Times,* May 13, 1966.

p. 262: *returned to the fold.:* P. Neary conversation.

p. 262: *descended upon the choreographer:* B. Horgan interview.

p. 262: *and his own company.: Choreography,* p. 38.

p. 262: *Alfonso Catá:* B. Horgan interview.

p. 262: *to start work.:* P. Neary conversation.

p. 263: *ever eaten.:* D. Nabokov conversation.

p. 263: *so miserable again.:* B. Horgan interview.

p. 265: *in his career.:* P. Martins, pp. 56, 60.

p. 265: *his godchild.:* K. von Aroldingen interview.

13. HOMAGE TO STRAVINSKY: SPRING 1972

p. 267: *list of possibilities:* Nancy Goldner, *The Stravinsky Festival of The New York City Ballet,* p. 229.

p. 268: *into a party.:* V. Donaldson conversation.

p. 268: *chairman of the festival.:* *The New York Times,* March 7, 1972.

p. 269: *". . . made our floor. ":* N. Goldner, *Stravinsky,* pp. 13, 14.

p. 270: *in front of you.: Ibid.,* pp. 14–15.

p. 270: *". . . our party. ": Ibid.,* pp. 15–16.

p. 270: *to the press.:* *The New York Times,* March 7, 1972. All seven proposed programs are printed.

p. 271: *in the evening.:* N. Goldner, pp. 234, 235.

p. 271: *till midnight.: Ibid.,* p. 237.

p. 272: *in forty minutes.:* R. Dunleavy interview.

p. 272: *". . . said I said it. ": High Fidelity/Musical America,* June 1972. G. B. interviewed by Shirley Fleming. She was referring to "Stravinsky in the Theatre," in *Dance Index,* edited by Minna Lederman, Vol. VI, Nos. 10, 11, 12, 1947.

p. 272: *". . . Kant is very important . . .": Milwaukee Journal,* June 4, 1972. G. B. interviewed by Walter Monfried.

p. 272: *". . . when you make dance. ": Newsday,* June 11, 1972. G. B. interviewed by Bob Micklin.

p. 273: *Vera Stravinsky.: New York Post,* June 17, 1972.

p. 273: *the opening ballet.: Sunday Times,* (London), June 18, 1972.

p. 274: Italian *comedy style.:* E. Villella interview.

p. 275: *" '. . . about the theater.' ":* N. Reynolds, p. 304.

p. 275: *". . . everything I had . . .":* K. von Aroldingen interview.

p. 275: *". . . incredible high. . . .":* P. Martins, p. 61.

p. 276: *Balanchine told him.):* K. Mazzo interview.

p. 276: *". . . asking for money. ":* P. Martins, p. 61.

p. 276: *". . . Monsieur Stravinsky. ":* R. Dunleavy interview. See also Jonathan Cott's interview with G. B. for *Rolling Stone,* quoted in *Portrait of Mr. B.,* p. 135. G. B. states, "I made a little bow to Stravinsky."

p. 278: *a strained back.):* R. Dunleavy interview.

p. 278: *". . . around the globe. ": Ballet Review,* Vol. IV, No. 3, p. 72.

p. 278: *concerto for orchestra in mind):* Alexandre Tansman recorded his impression that Stravinsky's early version of what became the first movement was to have been a *concertante* part for the piano. Stravinsky told Craft

(*Expositions and Developments*, p. 77) that he thought of it as a "concerto for orchestra."

p. 279: "*. . . tactics in China.*": I. Stravinsky and R. Craft, *Dialogues and a Diary*, pp. 83–85.

p. 279: "*. . . Allied triumph.*": *Ibid.*, pp. 51, 52.

p. 279: *Virgin Mary:* I. Stravinsky and R. Craft, *Expositions and Developments*, pp. 65–66.

p. 279: *last moment.:* K. Mazzo interview.

p. 280: *festival was about.:* *Ibid.*

p. 280: "*. . . Stravinsky ballets.*": *Ibid.*

p. 281: "*. . . ballet was ours.*": P. Martins, p. 69.

p. 282: "*. . . communicate with Stravinsky.*": R. Dunleavy interview.

p. 282: *winter season.:* N. Goldner, p. 244.

p. 282: "*. . . such a good one.*": V. Stravinsky interview with Jean Battey Louis, *Washington Post*, June 26, 1972.

p. 282: "*. . . from a ballet company?*": G. Boelzner conversation.

14. THE SPREADING EMPIRE: FIRST LAST BALLETS, 1972–1981

p. 284: *his "Three K's.":* R. and K. Leach interview.

p. 284: *leg of lamb.:* K. von Aroldingen interview.

p. 284: *a potato field.:* Dr. W. Hamilton conversation.

p. 284: *into a well.:* B. Horgan interview.

p. 285: *day's appointments.:* *Ibid.*

p. 285: *Paris or Geneva.:* B. Horgan allowed R. B. to go through G. B.'s engagement books, held by Ballet Society.

p. 285: *considered appropriate.:* K. von Aroldingen interview.

p. 285: *ten minutes late.:* Joseph H. Mazo, *Dance Is a Contact Sport*, p. 30.

p. 285: *when they were cooking:* S. Schorer interview.

p. 285: "*. . . be better than first.*": D. Duell interview.

p. 285: *touching the ground.:* R. Dunleavy interview.

p. 285: *"break eggs.":* M. Ashley, p. 62.

p. 286: *often in class.:* K. von Aroldingen interview.

p. 286: *solid as sculpture.:* J. H. Mazo, p. 38.

p. 286: "*. . . like dead chicken.*": *Ibid.*

p. 286: "*. . . look at the garden.*": R. Dunleavy interview.

p. 286: "*. . . ice cream.*": *Ibid.*

p. 286: *beautiful hands.:* K. von Aroldingen interview.

p. 286: *both feet.:* R. Dunleavy interview.

p. 286: *moved two steps.:* Told by Suki Schorer to J. Taras, December 12, 1983.

p. 286: *". . . a jockey on their backs."*: M. Ashley, p. 188.

p. 286: *". . . make it beautiful."*: *Ibid.*, p. 233.

p. 287: *"Maybe never."*: J. H. Mazo, p. 39.

p. 287: *cheese with tomatoes.*: B. Horgan interview.

p. 287: *used before.*: He had produced *Raymonda* for the Ballet Russe in 1946; in 1955 he staged *Pas de dix*, in 1961, *Valse et variations.*

p. 287: *". . . great precision. . . ."*: J. H. Mazo, p. 120.

p. 288: *just possible.*: *Ibid.*, p. 128.

p. 288: *all his choreography:* Repeated by Edwin Denby to R.B. in the 1940s.

p. 289: *kissed him:* S. Farrell conversation.

p. 289: *"a stroll for two"*: N. Goldner, *The Nation,* June 7, 1975, quoted N. Reynolds, p. 320.

p. 290: *". . . I like it."*: R. Dunleavy interview.

p. 291: *sweaters to class.*: P. Schaufuss conversation.

p. 291: *"Then it's over."*: S. Lavery interview with W. Lawson.

p. 291: *". . . school right then."*: S. Lavery interview with Tom Lacy.

p. 292: *began to work on it:* R. Dunleavy interview.

p. 292: *Three of these:* Rouben Ter-Arutunian, lecture to the Friends of New York City Ballet, June 8, 1984.

p. 293: *tinkering with it.*: S. Lavery interview with W. Lawson.

p. 294: *School of American Ballet.*: N. Lassalle interview.

p. 294: *a bad floor.*: J. H. Mazo, p. 297.

p. 295: *". . . garbage stinks."*: B. Taper, p. 345.

p. 296: *partnering himself.*: M. Ashley, p. 158 *et seq.*

p. 296: *for them coming up:* *The New York Times,* May 6, 1984. Leon Goldstein, the author of the article in which this incident is recorded, had been a member of NYCB's orchestra for more than thirty years.

p. 296: *". . . keep up with him. . . ."*: S. Lavery interview with W. Lawson.

p. 296: *". . . spooky at times."*: S. Lavery interview with T. Lacy.

p. 296: *greatest works.*: L. Kirstein, *Thirty Years,* p. 299.

p. 297: *Natalia Dudinskaya.*: M. Baryshnikov conversation.

p. 297: *usual NYCB rate.*: L. Kirstein, *Thirty Years,* p. 315.

p. 298: *with his own.*: M. Baryshnikov conversation.

p. 299: *". . . the women he loved."*: *Ibid.*

p. 299: *result disappointing.*: Anna Kisselgoff, *The New York Times,* April 10, 1979. Arlene Croce, *The New Yorker,* May 7, 1979.

p. 300: *which he did.*: M. Baryshnikov conversation.

p. 300: *". . . God's decision."*: Dr. W. Hamilton conversation.

p. 300: *face-to-face.*: L. Davidova interview.

p. 301: *Davidsbündlertänze.*: Dr. W. Hamilton conversation.

p. 301: *his insight:* K. von Aroldingen interview.

p. 302: *Both Kirstein and Karin: Ibid.;* also Kirstein letter to R.B., July 30, 1983.

p. 303: *". . . gay music."*: G. B. interviewed by Louis Bolto, *Intellectual Digest,* June 1972.

p. 303: *highest level.: Time,* June 30, 1980.

p. 304: *beautiful to see.:* Toni Bentley, *Winter Season,* p. 124.

p. 304: *". . . a whole lifetime."*: D. Kistler interview.

p. 305: *drop their votes.:* T. Bentley, pp. 89–91.

p. 305: *". . . listen to the music."*: D. Kistler interview.

p. 305: *"like a gymnasium."*: D. Nabokov conversation.

p. 306: *for the festival program:* S. Volkov, pp. 11, 12.

p. 307: *moderately satisfied:* Emile Ardolino, "Balanchine and Television," an essay in the brochure "A Celebration of George Balanchine: The Television Work," annotating a series of screenings held at the Museum of Broadcasting, New York, September–November 1984.

p. 307: *". . . an introduction for them."*: R. Maiorano and V. Brooks, p. xix.

p. 308: *"When?" "Tomorrow."*: *Ibid.,* p. 134.

p. 308: *"Ib is Mozart!"*: E. Bigelow conversation.

p. 308: *been in America.:* *Serenade,* 1934; *Ballet Imperial,* 1941, revived as *Tchaikovsky Piano Concerto No. 2,* 1973; *Swan Lake,* 1951; *The Nutcracker,* 1954; *Allegro Brillante,* 1956; *Tchaikovsky Pas de deux,* 1960; *Meditation,* 1963; "Diamonds" from *Jewels,* 1967; *Tchaikovsky Suite No. 3,* 1970.

p. 309: *". . . how to mourn."*: K. von Aroldingen interview.

p. 310: *east as Iran.:* These statistics are derived from the Eakins Press *Choreography.*

p. 311: *" '. . . the whole class is doing it.' "*: S. Schorer interview.

p. 311: *" '. . . anybody.' "*: G. B. interview with W. McNeil Lowry, *The New Yorker,* September 12, 1983, p. 53.

15. BALLET MASTER EMERITUS: DECEMBER 1981–APRIL 30, 1983

p. 312: *". . . a Greek, dear"*: S. Schorer interview.

p. 312: *in 1947:* N. Lassalle conversation.

p. 313: *visual arts.:* B. Kochno interview.

p. 314: *". . . but we can't."* K. Love conversation.

p. 314: *"a searing experience."*: V. Zorina conversation.

p. 315: *passages of dancing.:* M. Ashley interview.

p. 315: *"They always left me."*: K. Leach letter to R. B., January 1, 1986.

p. 315: *for $1,000.:* G.B. interview with John Corry, *The New York Times,* May 16, 1982.

p. 318: Kammermusik No. 2: B. Horgan conversation.

p. 318: *during a performance.:* K. Love conversation.

p. 319: *withdrew silently.:* B. Horgan interview.

p. 319: *good manners.:* S. Volkov conversation.

p. 319: *as a decoration:* N. Lassalle conversation.

p. 321: *down his face.:* Dr. W. Hamilton conversation.

p. 321: *Ruthanna's hand.:* R. Boris interview.

p. 321: *a mistake.:* Dr. W. Hamilton conversation.

p. 322: *press the point.:* B. Taper, pp. 385, 386.

p. 322: *was disappointed.: Ibid.,* pp. 391, 392.

p. 322: *". . . Balanchine ballets.":* The New Yorker, March 28, 1983.

p. 322: *"It seems inconceivable.":* Abigail Kuflik, *Newsweek,* March 28, 1983.

p. 322: *those of all others.:* Dr. W. Hamilton conversation.

p. 322: *". . . coming to see me?":* J. Taras's recollection.

p. 323: *Margo's name.:* K. von Aroldingen interview.

p. 323: *no further questions.:* D. Kistler interview.

p. 323: *about the performance.:* K. von Aroldingen interview.

p. 324: *". . . and Stravinsky . . .":* Jennifer Dunning, *The New York Times,* May 1, 1983.

p. 324: *Suzanne Farrell.:* Mindy Aloff, *Nation,* June 4, 1983.

p. 325: *him and Balanchine together . . .:* T. Lacy letter, February 24, 1986.

p. 325: *a rose.:* Dr. W. Hamilton conversation.

p. 325: *indisputable facts.:* Statement by Mayor Edward I. Koch, for release Monday, May 2, 1983.

p. 326: *". . . Immortal Legacy":* Sheryl Platow, *Washington Post,* May 2, 1983.

p. 326: *". . . Mourns Balanchine":* Amy Pagnozzi, *New York Post,* May 2, 1983.

p. 326: *". . . Pure Movement":* Michael Walsh, *Time,* May 9, 1983.

p. 326: *". . . 'Mister B.' ":* Le Matin, May 2, 1983. Article signed R. S. (René Servin).

p. 326: *". . . le plus grand.":* Les Nouvelles Littéraires, April 5–May 1, 1983.

p. 326: *head of the table.:* Hubert Saal, *Newsweek,* May 9, 1983.

p. 326: *"'. . . I assemble.' ":* Don McDonagh, *Commonweal,* June 3, 1983.

p. 326: *. . . it's ridiculous.:* G. B. interview with W. McNeil Lowry, *The New Yorker,* September 12, 1983.

p. 327: *Ballet is NOW.:* G. B. interview with Louis Bolto, *Intellectual Digest,* June 1972.

INDEX

RICHARD BUCKLE founded the magazine *Ballet* in England in 1939, and edited it, with a six-year gap during World War II, until 1953. From 1948 to 1955 he was ballet critic of the *Observer* and from 1959 to 1975 of the London *Sunday Times.* He has written many books, including the biographies of Diaghilev and Nijinsky and two volumes of autobiography. He designed The Diaghilev Exhibition (Edinburgh Festival and London, 1954–1955), and as his methods of display were considered novel, he was asked to design twenty others. In the late 1960s he conceived the idea of a theater museum for London; this was officially opened in the former flower market in Covent Garden on Shakespeare's birthday, 1987. Buckle admired Balanchine in the 1930s, met him in 1948, praised him on the first visit of the New York City Ballet to London in 1950, when most of the English critics were apathetic, and never doubted that he had raised the art of ballet to new heights.

JOHN TARAS, dancer and choreographer, was on the South American tour with Balanchine in 1941. He has been a ballet master of the Markova-Dolin Ballet, the de Basil, the Grand Ballet du Marquis de Cuevas, the New York City Ballet, the Paris Opéra and the Berlin Deutsche Oper. In 1970 he re-joined Balanchine, with whom he remained until 1983, and whose ballets he mounted throughout the world. In 1984 he became associate director of American Ballet Theatre.